O9-BRZ-901

JONATHAN LASH
KATHERINE GILLMAN & DAVID SHERIDAN

A
SEASON
OF
SPOILS

A SEASON OF SPOILS

THE REAGAN ADMINISTRATION'S ATTACK ON THE ENVIRONMENT

90-123

PANTHEON BOOKS NEW YORK

All rights reserved under International and Pan-American Copyright Conventions.
Published in the United States by Pantheon Books, a division of Random House,
Inc., New York, and simultaneously in Canada by Random House of Canada
Limited, Toronto.

Library of Congress Cataloging in Publication Data

Lash, Jonathan, 1945–
A season of spoils.

Includes bibliographical references.
1. Environmental policy—United States. 2. United States—Politics and government
—1981– . I. Gillman, Katherine. II. Sheridan, David. III. Title. HC110.E5L34 1984
363.7'00973 83–43142 ISBN 0–394–53333–X
0–394–72146–2 (pbk.)

Manufactured in the United States of America

First Edition

DEDICATION

This book is dedicated to the federal civil servants who persevered in their efforts to turn the promise of America's environmental laws into reality. They have had a hard struggle with little glory, but they have served their country well.

This book has been supported by six national environmental groups:

Environmental Policy Center
Friends of the Earth
National Audubon Society
National Parks and Conservation Association
Natural Resources Defense Council
Wilderness Society

They have done a great deal to disclose and contest the unfortunate policies described in this book. Without them, the story would have been even more terrible than it is.

CONTENTS

CONTENTS

ACKNOWLEDGMENTS

The intelligence, inquisitiveness, and integrity of Tom Keenan, our researcher, colleague, iconoclast, and friend, have done much to make this book possible. His zippy prose appears at many places in the book. The wit, good sense, and nimble fingers of Barbara Pratt made a special imprint on what we wrote. To both Tom and Barbara we offer warm and affectionate thanks.

Destry Jarvis of the National Parks and Conservation Association provided enormous help to us in writing about the National Parks. Bob Cahn helped with that portion of the book and much else, encouraging, goading, and always demanding more.

Many others gave us gracious and invaluable assistance. Over four hundred people gave us their time and thoughts in interviews. Most of their names appear in the book or the reference notes; some, by choice, do not. We thank all whom we interviewed.

Some whom we interviewed went far out of their way to be helpful, giving us meals, shelter, tours of parks or wilderness, and helping us find information. A few whom we want to thank specially are: Cyndy Chapman, a woman who loves birds and people; Donna Robbins, whose story was one of many we did not have space to use; Jim Cubie; Caroline Isber; Phil Clapp; Dan Buck; Jane Saginaw, who fought to protect children in Dallas from lead; Elsa Bruton for her research and sage counsel; the Blue Mountain Center and Harriet Barlow; Jim Montieth;

Andy Stahl; Earl Sandvig; Randal O'Toole; Brant Calkin; Bob Burnett; Michael Sherwood; David Crow for his swift and careful completion of important research; Elsa Leviseur, a champion of the Santa Monica Mountain National Recreation Area; Scott Reed; William Meiners; and Guntram F. A. Werther, a courageous ex-civil servant.

In addition, we were helped by the able professionals on the staffs of the Energy Conservation Coalition, the Environmental Policy Center, the Environmental Defense Fund, Friends of the Earth, the National Audubon Society, the National Parks and Conservation Association, the National Wildlife Federation, the Natural Resources Defense Council, the Union of Concerned Scientists, and the Wilderness Society.

Richard Frandsen and Patrick McLain of the Oversight and Investigations Subcommittee of the House Committee on Energy and Commerce not only did much of the investigation that disclosed the stories in our book, but they took the time as well to read portions to help us to assure their accuracy. We are grateful for all they did.

Joseph Lash, Ellie Lash, Jane Dustan, Robert Caro, and John Sims, a wonderful lawyer who can also edit, all read the manuscript and provided helpful and encouraging comments.

Finally, we thank Pantheon Books and our editor Wendy Goldwyn for suggesting that we write this book, bearing with us as we did so, and working hard to make it a success.

Jonathan Lash
Katherine Gillman
David Sheridan

INTRODUCTION: HOW COULD THIS HAPPEN?

Lead. Since antiquity, man has known it as a poison. It is pervasive in our land, accumulating in our bones and vital organs and those of our children. Especially children, causing loss of intelligence, learning disabilities, erratic behavior, sometimes seizures and death. Four percent of all children, 18 percent of inner city black children, are affected by lead in their bodies. On the top of the list of regulatory changes sought by the new White House in 1981 was quick relief for gasoline refiners from requirements to reduce the amount of lead in gasoline, the most important source of lead pollution. How could this happen?

Wilderness. By conquest, treaty, and purchase, the government of the United States acquired nearly two billion acres of land. Sixty percent of it is gone now, in private hands. After a century and a half of abuse, we have begun to try to protect some of the remainder and in particular to preserve a little of the wilderness that once blanketed our nation. Yet in 1982 a trespasser went onto our wilderness land and began to drill a gas well. The stewards of our land, the new Administration, did next to nothing about it. Indeed, they encouraged the trespass. How could this happen?

Ronald Reagan was President. The hated liberals were vanquished. He sought sharp changes in the tone and objectives of the federal government. He believed simply that government should spend less, do less, and interfere less with private enterprise. For 25 years since he began to make his living and his reputation as a conservative lecturer, Ronald Reagan had spent his time among those who argued there was too much government. He believed government was in the hands of people who "think control is better than freedom." He believed the bureaucrats had shackled American industry through regulation. "There are," Reagan said, "tens of thousands of . . . regulations I'd like to see eliminated."

Environmental regulations were a particular target of his disapproval. His premise was simple: Industrial production results in wealth and progress. Wealth and progress keep us strong. Regulation does nothing to contribute to production; on the contrary, it is a hindrance. Governmental action that interferes with the strength and progress of America makes no sense and must be stopped. As one industry advocate warned, there had been a "massive regulatory binge" that must be undone because "our society is built on stuff that comes from a hole in the ground, and if we don't unplug the red tape stuffing the hole this country is going to be in a hell of a mess."

Reagan did not see or understand the problems that made regulation necessary. He knew nothing of children afflicted by lead pollution. He believed air pollution had been "substantially controlled." He never saw the clearcut mountainsides in the Northwest sliding into once-bright rivers. He had no concept of the dangers of 15,000 hazardous waste sites sprinkled across the country. He could not believe that industry would pollute if it were wrong. Industry to him was a group of men he knew and respected, not an institution driven by the pressures of profit and competition. In his eyes, regulations were not necessary protection, but absurd restrictions on the enterprise of reasonable men. Environmental problems were, for the most part, a flimsy pretext for federal control of private activity.

Reagan and his advisers questioned the motives of those who advocated and those who implemented regulatory requirements. In a speech that he repeated often, James Watt asked, "What is the real nature of the extreme environmentalists, who appear to be determined to accomplish their objectives at whatever cost to society? Is it to delay and deny energy development? Is it to weaken America?" Reagan and Watt spoke of "restoring balance" to environmental policy, but seemed unable to distinguish between the public interest and private economic self-interest.

Years before, in his autobiography, *Where's the Rest of Me?*, Reagan had said his mission was "to make people aware of the danger to freedom in a vast permanent governmental structure so big and complex it virtually entraps Presidents." When he became President, he was determined not to be entrapped. He would avoid the snares laid out by federal bureaucrats for those who endeavored to reform the government and diminish the power of the bureaucracy. That meant not listening overmuch to what "they" said should not or could not be done. He would stick to what he believed, to what he thought he knew, and he would choose people to serve him who saw the world as he did, people tough enough to resist capture by the bureaucracies he appointed them to run. They must know whom to trust and whom to scorn. In this crusade they would rely on the counsel of the regulated industries. What was not necessary, however, was knowledge of the environmental problems their agencies were charged by law to address, or experience in dealing with those problems. Few had either. They were chosen for their zeal, not their wisdom.

This book is the story of the people Reagan chose to turn his rhetoric into reality. It is the story of James Watt, Anne Gorsuch, and a few dozen others and what they did and did not do. It is the story of the chaos and controversy that arose as they tried to wrench the laws and the institutions of government to suit their purposes. It is the story of their ineptitude, malfeasance, and occasional viciousness. Ultimately, it is a story of the collision of ideology with reality.

The problems that Congress, over a decade, had passed laws to address are real. Those laws have real support among the public. The mandate Reagan gave to those he put in charge of the agencies responsible for carrying out those laws was to deal with the problem of overregulation, not underprotection. They did so, and that caused a ruckus. Their policies were not popular. They were not wise. Often they were not legal.

We have written this book to answer three questions: What happened? How could it happen? What does it mean? We offer our answers in the form of a story, not a lesson or a lecture. We talked to the people who were part of the story and endeavored to let them and the events they took part in speak for themselves.

We have not tried to tell the whole story. There is much of importance we have left out because we had neither the time nor the space to look at everything. For example, we do not tell the story of the failure to enforce the strip-mining law. Between two and three thousand mines are operating in violation of the law. Federal inspectors were threatened with dismissal if they cited violations as they were required to do by law when state officials failed to act. A federal court has, thus far without success, sought to compel the Interior Department to collect $40 million in penalties owed by violators. It is a scandal that affects real people, but, like many other similar stories, we have had to put it aside.

Is the story important? We of course believe it is. What the federal government does or does not do determines whether there are poisons in our air and water, whether what little wilderness we still have survives, whether our lakes are killed by acid rain or our forests are squandered, whether we get a fair return for public resources we sell, whether those who pollute illegally are punished, or whether the victims of hazardous waste are helped or ignored. Dozens of political appointees have been driven from this Administration by scandal, but the only one actively prosecuted was former EPA Hazardous Waste chief Rita Lavelle. She was convicted of perjury and obstructing the congressional investigation of her program.

What has been done, and the way it has been done, to environmental policy exposes a philosophy of government. After a year and a half of investigating malfeasance and incompetence at EPA, Congressman John Dingell said: "The problems we found were really symptoms of something pervasive in the way these people run the government. They have no respect for the law. It is basically government by royal edict instead of according to the Constitutional processes they are sworn to uphold."

Most important, the story is not over. Ronald Reagan brought Anne Gorsuch and James Watt to Washington in 1981. In 1983, he reluctantly let them depart. They were loyal to him from start to finish, and he has stuck to the beliefs that he and they shared.

A
SEASON
OF
SPOILS

1

THE EDUCATION OF ANNE GORSUCH

"I'M GOING TO WASHINGTON"

On November 4, 1980, Ronald Reagan won the Presidency, leading his party to gains in the House of Representatives and to control of the Senate for the first time since 1952. The nation repudiated Jimmy Carter. He won only 41 percent of the vote and ran behind other Democratic candidates all across the country.

Reagan's victory and Carter's defeat were especially pronounced in Colorado. Widely viewed as a weak and ineffectual president, Carter had become a symbol of inept and pervasive federal meddling in local affairs. He won only 31 percent of the vote in Colorado, running 220,000 votes behind Democratic Senator Gary Hart, who won reelection.

President Reagan appointed two Coloradans, Anne Gorsuch* and James Watt, to head the two federal agencies with the greatest responsibilities for the environment—the Environmental Protection Agency and the Department of the Interior. They brought with them the contentious politics of their state, and the hard resentment Colorado

---

*Anne Gorsuch married Robert Burford in February 1983. For most of the period described in this book she was Anne Gorsuch, and for the sake of clarity we will use that name, since Robert Burford appears as a character in his own right in this story.

conservatives felt toward the federal government. To understand what happened to environmental policy when Ronald Reagan became President one must consider Colorado.

Where the high dry plains meet the "Front Range" of the Rockies, in Denver, Boulder, Greely, Colorado Springs and a string of other towns and suburbs, Colorado has been gathering people. The state's population has grown by almost 70 percent since 1960. The immigrants came largely from the South and the Midwest, drawn by the beauty of the mountains, the skiing, hiking, fishing, and hunting, and by the state's growing wealth. Energy and minerals production, recreation, timber, and agriculture fueled a boom in Colorado. Downtown Denver sprouted glass-and-steel office towers. Residents jokingly called the city "Houston North," as more and more energy companies located offices there.

The conflict that resulted was inevitable—no different than the conflict between development and protection in other states, except that it was more bitter. People in Colorado wanted wealth and development, but many also wanted to protect the jagged beauty of the Rockies. In 1979 the 264,000-acre Rocky Mountain National Park attracted three million visitors. The State had 32 of its own parks encompassing 174,000 acres. Coloradans and their guests spent 21 million dollars on hunting and fishing licenses.

At the same time, industries that depended on exploiting the Rockies grew swiftly. Colorado produced coal, oil, gas, lead, silver, zinc, and other metals. The value of energy and minerals extracted in Colorado grew 275 percent between 1970 and 1980. Expenditures for recreation tripled.

The conflict between development and protection first came to a head in 1972. Young activists organized a referendum on state funding for the 1976 Winter Olympics that were to be held in Colorado. They argued that the games would be expensive and would cause lasting damage to the state's environment, while benefiting only developers and a few businessmen. Their motto was "Don't Californicate Colorado." The referendum passed and the games were moved to Austria. Two years later Dick Lamm, one of the leaders of the referendum effort, was elected Governor and Democrats took control of the state legislature.

In Washington Congress passed strong new laws to control air and water pollution. President Nixon had already established the Environmental Protection Agency, and for the first time industry faced direct

4

federal requirements to control pollution, and the need to obtain federal permits for industrial projects. Industries in the West reacted with particular bitterness. The obligation to negotiate with federal bureaucrats over the form and fitness of private industrial projects offended western notions of freedom and individual liberty. Many Westerners already resented the federal government, believing it to be a creature of the East that collected taxes in the West to invest in decaying eastern cities while retaining ownership of nearly a third of the land in the West. In the mid-1970's resentment grew to antipathy. And in Colorado the antipathy became a visible element in local politics.

Joseph Coors, the conservative Colorado brewer with extensive western energy and mineral interests, established the Mountain States Legal Foundation in Denver in July 1977. The purpose of MSLF was to "fight in the courts those bureaucrats and no-growth advocates who create a challenge to individual liberty and economic freedoms." The Board of Directors of the Foundation included officials from AMAX, a huge coal and minerals company, Amoco, and Conoco. The contributors were oil, gas, coal, and utility companies with major holdings in the West and leases on federal resources; among them: Exxon, Consolidated Coal, Gulf, Utah Power and Light, Chevron, Amoco, Occidental Oil Shale, Pacific Power and Light, and, of course, Adolph Coors Co. The first head of the Foundation was James Watt.

At the same time a new faction formed in the Colorado legislature. After the Olympics Referendum and the 1974 election, according to Colorado Congressman Timothy Wirth, "the Right felt they had to respond and started pouring money into Colorado politics. A lot of Coors money. A lot of energy industry money. They didn't succeed in knocking me or Dick Lamm or Gary Hart off, but they had a tremendous impact on the legislature, and helped to legitimize right-wing ideology in the state." Republicans recaptured control of the legislature in 1976. A small group of aggressive and ideological conservatives began to dominate the Republican caucus. They fought programs designed to assist Colorado's large Hispanic community, eliminated the Colorado Commission on Women, slashed the state's budget, and killed an effort to initiate rudimentary planning for the explosive growth taking place along the "Front Range" of the Rockies. They were extreme, but effective.

They dubbed themselves "the crazies" and opponents took up the name with satisfaction. "They were a very tight little social group, almost like a high school clique. You had to be conservative and agree with them on everything," says Betty Neal, a fellow Republican legislator. One of them told her, " 'Betty, you're a closet crazy.' He meant it as a compliment, but I didn't take it that way. If you didn't agree with them on just one bill," Neal adds, "then you were branded as impure —not a true conservative."

One recurrent theme in the "crazies' " legislative battles was opposition to federal regulation and to environmental regulation in particular. The regional headquarters of the EPA were in Denver and the "crazies" regarded the idealistic young lawyers and scientists at EPA with suspicion and contempt.

Freda Poundstone, a conservative activist and lobbyist for the construction industry who raised campaign funds for many of the "crazies," says of the EPA, "the environmentalists were just in control down there. They put out all these harassing regulations and spent billions of dollars and they didn't accomplish a damn thing. You could see the awful waste. They just wanted to control everything."

The "crazies" battled with EPA over how to control Denver's air pollution problem, the "brown cloud" that hovered in the thin air over the city half of the days of the year. When the legislature refused to approve the stringent pollution control measures, EPA imposed "sanctions" on the state. In December 1977, conservative legislators, represented by James Watt, sued EPA to block the sanctions but lost. The battle left the conservatives in the legislature with what Anne Gorsuch later called a "well-founded resentment at the heavy-handedness" of the federal bureaucrats in EPA. It was, she said, an example of the federal government taking "very inappropriate" action in an area that it had no business regulating. EPA officials note simply that their action was explicitly required by the Clean Air Act. The question was whether Colorado would obey a federal law enacted to protect public health.

The "crazies" sought repeatedly to weaken Colorado's water quality rules to ease the restrictions on industries and resorts located on pristine streams. For four years they blocked passage of state hazardous waste legislation. "They see no value in the environment for itself. A mountain, a stream, a forest have value only for human use, and the importance of that use can always be expressed in dollar terms," says Myrna Poticha, a member of the Colorado Water Quality Control Commission. "That means, of course, that only uses need to be protected, and use for development has the highest value of all."

The "crazies" were led by two very bright and very conservative young legislators: Anne Gorsuch and Steve Durham. Virtually everyone who has dealt with Anne Gorsuch describes her as quick-witted and articulate. Freda Poundstone, a friend and ardent admirer, says "she is the smartest woman I ever knew." Paula Herzmark, a former member of Governor Lamm's cabinet and frequent opponent of Anne Gorsuch in legislative battles, describes her as "sharp, poised, and super-controlled." She is a striking looking woman with piercing green eyes, thick dark hair, and a taste for elegant clothes.

The daughter of a conservative physician, she had a strict Catholic upbringing. Associates describe her as a "real sackcloth-and-ashes type." She graduated from the University of Colorado Law School at age 20, and married Denver lawyer David Gorsuch. She won a Fulbright Fellowship to India where she taught English and studied Indian criminal law.

Gorsuch was elected to the legislature in 1976, while working as a lawyer for the local phone company. She represented the suburban Denver district in which she had grown up. After her first session, reporters and other legislators selected her as "outstanding freshman legislator." Reelected in 1978, she was among the leaders of a successful effort to depose Ron Strahle, the moderate Republican Speaker of the Colorado House, and to elect Robert Burford in his place. Burford's one-vote victory in the Republican caucus was achieved when Anne Gorsuch called a fellow legislator vacationing in Hawaii, a woman she had known in college, and persuaded her to switch her proxy from Strahle to Burford. A popular conservative rancher, not regarded as one of the "crazies," Burford rewarded Gorsuch with the chairmanship of a powerful House committee, and subsequent referral to her of a series of important bills.

Her fellow legislators saw her as smart, very hard-working, and rigidly ideological. She fought hard for what she believed and never forgave those who opposed her. One long-time member of the legislature observed "she was like one of the Bourbons; you know, they say the Bourbons hadn't learned anything or forgotten anything for 100 years." "She judged people by their beliefs," says lobbyist C. L. Harmon. "She was quick to reject them if they didn't agree with her and rarely changed her mind." Her relations with other legislators, except her group of "crazies," were strained. Many of the women in the legislature felt she could not work with other women, a problem that was exacerbated when

7

she led the bitter and successful campaign to abolish the Colorado Commission on Women.

She thought of herself as cool and tough. She was willing to advocate conservative positions others deemed extreme and to face the resulting attacks on her without flinching. She told a reporter, "Whether you contact my friends or my enemies, they'll tell you two things: I'm intelligent and I'm capable of making hard decisions."

Anne Gorsuch was "the sparkplug of the 'crazies,' " says Myrna Poticha, but "Steve Durham was their strategist and enforcer." Described as "crafty," "cunning," "tenacious and ruthless," Durham rarely sponsored bills, but knew, better than any other legislator, how to force —or prevent—action by the legislature.

Durham was elected to the legislature in 1974 at age 26. He was the manager of a small amusement park, "a crummy little tourist trap," says Harmon. He soon became a masterful political manipulator. One lobbyist describes him as "very effective—a risk taker, not concerned with being popular, but he was impatient. If he thought something was right he was not at all concerned how he got there."

Durham was feared and, by some, mistrusted. He was viewed by opponents as a vindictive bully. He sometimes seemed to play the role of a cowboy from an earlier age, taking unpopular positions in order to prove he was tough enough to resist criticism and popular pressure. He bragged to EPA employees—after Anne Gorsuch put him in charge of the Denver regional office in 1981—that he carried a gun and had done so while a member of the legislature.

One environmental issue that provoked a harsh confrontation in the legislature was hazardous waste, and Anne Gorsuch was at the center of it. The federal hazardous waste law passed in 1976 not only required EPA to establish and enforce rules for the safe handling and disposal of hazardous wastes, it authorized states with effective laws of their own to take over implementation of portions of the federal program.

Colorado did not have a state hazardous waste law and Anne Gorsuch and the "crazies" opposed every effort to enact one. "She wanted to leave control of siting waste dumps with the counties who would be more responsive to industry, and to keep us out of it," says Dr. Frank Traylor, Colorado Commissioner of Health and a former Republican legislator. "She preferred to have the federal government take responsibility for any regulations, rather than have them setting standards for the states to meet. It was a pretty strange position for a believer in returning authority to the states. She wouldn't listen to arguments on the other side, and she wouldn't even discuss compromise bills."

In the spring of 1980 Traylor finally called House Speaker Burford. He warned Burford that the issue would eventually heat up in Colorado, and that Republicans in the legislature would look bad if they had simply blocked all action on hazardous waste. Burford appointed Gorsuch to chair an "interim" committee on hazardous waste, while the legislature was out of session. Gorsuch and Burford stacked the committee, which included representatives of industry and local government, as well as members of the legislature.

"When she took on that committee she had the goal all set out. She was going to hold a lot of hearings and then send a message to Washington: 'Screw you, we won't do anything, you can take the heat for this dumb law,' " says one person who worked closely with Gorsuch on the committee. "That's just what she did, too. She held day after day of hearings and peppered the EPA and the Health Department with questions. Then she would give them more questions to answer by the next hearing." Martha King, a staff member, says that after the hearings "she would have me write letters for her to sign with more questions. To get the right tone I'd think to myself 'Dear Jerks.' " "We answered so many questions for her," said Traylor, "that when the hazardous waste bill finally did come up there wasn't anything we couldn't answer. Not that it mattered what we answered, she had her mind made up."

"When we finally wrote up the report of the committee," recalls one person who worked on the report, "she tried to edit it so every argument in favor of regulation sounded dumb. . . . Anne just didn't believe the problems were real. She thought it was all an excuse for government control."

When Ronald Reagan won, having campaigned with conservative rhetoric, having blamed government for the nation's ills, and having, when he referred to it at all, deprecated the importance of the environment and the effects of pollution, it was a vindication for the "crazies." They had fought visible and bitter battles. They had been attacked in the press. Their opponents called them extremists. But Colorado gave Reagan a landslide. As one opponent observed, "They had waited it out and now their time had come. They had power in the nation and they would really show people what they could do."

Anne Gorsuch did not run for reelection. She was in the midst of a divorce, and her hard line, especially on women's issues, had not played well in her district. But shortly after the election she got a call from Freda Poundstone. The President-elect had asked Poundstone, a long-time Reagan supporter and political operative for Reagan's close friend Joseph Coors, to head the Colorado delegation on the presidential transition team. Poundstone immediately asked Anne Gorsuch to join her.

In early December 1980, Gorsuch strode into the office of Maria Garcia, a lobbyist with whom she had formed a friendship.

"You ought to congratulate me."

"What for?" asked Garcia.

"I'm going to Washington."

"What are you going to do?"

"I want to work on the environmental stuff. I want to be Deputy Administrator of EPA."

Gorsuch and Garcia went to celebrate at an elegant bar near the state capitol. Gorsuch was jubilant. She felt she had run out of room in the legislature. "I was a success," she said, "but look at the competition." Now, she told Garcia, she would have a chance to carry out the conservative reform agenda at the national level. "She could've had a lot of other jobs," according to Freda Poundstone, "but she wanted EPA. It's such a mess."

The Environmental Protection Agency was not high among the priorities of the new White House, however. The White House personnel office struggled to produce job candidates whose political background and philosophy were sufficiently conservative and who were also qualified. One staffer at the personnel office says, "It was chaos. We'd move from one crisis to the next. We had no connection with the people setting policy."

The EPA transition team prepared a list of candidates for all the top EPA jobs. "We were looking for conservative Republicans with an environmental background," recalls one member of the EPA transition team. "The brutal truth is, there weren't very many. I believe our choice for Administrator was John Quarles."

Quarles, a former EPA general counsel and a lawyer representing the interests of a variety of industries, was rejected early on as too moderate. So was Henry Diamond, another industry lawyer and former regulator. So was Gordon Wood, an Olin Corporation lobbyist who was vetoed by representatives of the Chemical Manufacturers Association because he had argued that his colleagues should support and help to shape the Superfund legislation passed the year before. Lyn Nofziger, political counsel to the President, told reporters the test for each candidate was "Are you a Republican, and if you are, are you the best Republican for the job—or is there a Reagan Republican out there?"

By the end of January 1981, the White House was feeling mounting pressure from those disgruntled by the President's failure to appoint any of their candidates to top jobs. Hispanic Americans had delivered substantial support for the President, especially the Cuban community in Florida. Senators Dole, Baker, and Domenici met with the White House staff to urge them to move quickly and visibly to appoint Hispanics. Even greater pressure came from women's groups who complained that the only woman among scores of top appointments was U.N. Ambassador Jeanne Kirkpatrick.

Shortly after the inauguration, in late January 1981, John W. Hernandez, Jr., visited Washington for a conference. Dean of the College of Engineering at New Mexico State University and a moderate Republican, he had not campaigned for Ronald Reagan, but he liked what he heard as the President took office, so he stopped by to see his friend, New Mexico Senator Pete Domenici. "I said, 'What's up with the new Administration, anything? I'd be interested in either energy or the environment.' And he said, 'How would you like to be Administrator of the EPA?' There's a place on his carpet by the couch where I absolutely dug in a heel—it was a really scary thing."

Domenici called senior members of the White House staff urging Hernandez's appointment. As an engineer and occasional consultant to EPA Hernandez had a knowledge of some of the issues facing the agency. And, of course, he was Hispanic.

Domenici received a positive response. Hernandez interviewed with the Vice-President and Domenici issued a press release announcing that Hernandez would get the job. But then things went awry. The White House staff was infuriated by the press release. More important, Hernandez's interviews did not go well. He made a particularly bad impression on top aides to Office of Management and Budget Director David Stockman who asked whether Hernandez believed that the EPA could be cut in half. Hernandez said no. He said he believed that the EPA science and research capabilities should be upgraded and that a variety of statutes imposed mandatory responsibilities on EPA that it had yet

11

to fulfill. Cuts should be made, Hernandez said, but not 50 percent. As a consequence, Stockman strongly opposed Hernandez; he was not a true believer.

In early February a new candidate surfaced, raising new concerns. The Teamsters' Union had actively supported Ronald Reagan in the election—helping to deliver blue-collar votes. The Teamsters began to pressure the White House to appoint Michael Balzano, the man who had engineered that support for Reagan, to be EPA Administrator. Balzano was a high school dropout who worked his way to a high school diploma at age 25 while working as a trash collector. Later, he earned a Ph.D. and considerable publicity as the trash man who wrote a prize-winning thesis on the Peace Corps. He ended up in the Nixon White House and then as Director of Action.

The Personnel Office feared that the Teamsters were interested in EPA because of the more than $3 billion a year in water and sewer construction grants controlled by EPA, and the $1.6 billion in hazardous waste cleanup funds soon to be spent. Personnel Director Pendleton James referred to him as that "garbageman" and felt he had to be stopped. They looked at the other candidates, an aide recalls, and they concluded that "Hernandez just didn't have the political wherewithal to do it." Although Anne Gorsuch was still slated to be the Deputy, she had made very good impressions in several interviews and had strong political backing. They began to consider her as a candidate for Administrator instead of Deputy Administrator.

Gorsuch campaigned hard for the Administrator's job. Through James Watt she arranged an interview with Pendleton James. Freda Poundstone and Colorado Republican Chairman Phil Wynn lobbied on her behalf. Joseph Coors, a leading member of the President's "kitchen cabinet," said, according to one person involved in the process, that he "didn't think a woman could handle the EPA job." But with Watt, Poundstone, and his wife, Holly, supporting Gorsuch, Coors eventually backed her.

Gorsuch did well each time she interviewed. Unlike Hernandez, Gorsuch made it clear in an interview with David Stockman that she was committed to the President's program including budget cuts. Stockman regarded her answer as a firm commitment to the drastic cuts he wanted to make at EPA, and he supported her nomination.

On February 21, 1981, President Reagan announced his choice of Anne Gorsuch to be the Administrator of the Environmental Protection

Agency. She was the highest-ranking woman, and, at 38, one of the youngest of the President's top appointees.

"She went to Washington to *do* for the President, and she went for the power. She was a true believer carrying all the right-wing baggage and values and she was going to put her philosophy into action." That harsh view from one Colorado opponent was echoed in a different form by Freda Poundstone:

Anne was trying to do a job within the President's philosophy. She didn't want to just throw money at the problem, she wanted to make things work. I know Anne and the President feel the same. They don't want twenty-five years more bullshit.

Anyone can regulate everything, Anne was looking for alternatives. But people there [at EPA] are entrenched. They are threatened by fresh ideas. They are little old men thinking of retirement.

Anne could really have done something if they'd given her a chance.

She came from the ragged edge of environmental conflict in Colorado to a position of power and political visibility greater than either she or the White House understood.

She did not think of herself as "anti-environmental" any more than she labeled herself an "environmentalist." In this she and President Reagan were much alike. Both said they believed in protecting the environment, but they thought the problems of doing so and the consequences of not doing so were much exaggerated by people with selfish political or economic motives. Ronald Reagan during his campaign proclaimed that air pollution had already been "substantially controlled" and said that he would invite the steel and coal industries to help him "rewrite clean air rules." In his inaugural address he stated: "Government is not the solution to our problem; government is the problem."

Anne Gorsuch in speeches and testimony during her first year as Administrator barely mentioned pollution or its effects on human beings. When she did refer to the problems that her agency was responsible for solving, it was in brusque tones—mechanical problems subject to technical solutions.

Like the President to whom she remained loyal through good times and bad, Anne Gorsuch thought the real problem was too much government: too much government interference with industry, the great en-

13

gine of American prosperity, and too much taxation to support a wasteful and bloated bureaucracy. Government regulators had gotten out of hand, and environmental regulators were among the worst of them. When she took over management at EPA she believed it was working badly and she wanted to correct the malfunction. She did not think overmuch about what the machine produced.

NO SYMPATHY FOR THE PATIENT

EPA is the most powerful regulatory agency in the government. It was created by President Nixon in 1970 in the aftermath of Earth Day. In creating EPA, Nixon stated that only by governmental action "can we effectively ensure the protection, development and enhancement of the total environment. . . ." And in putting responsibility in the hands of a single federal agency, he recognized that "for pollution control purposes the environment must be perceived as a single interrelated system. . . ."

Soon after it was established, EPA's responsibilities began to increase. Clean air legislation was passed within months, and clean water legislation a year later. During the mid-1970's, as the nation became increasingly aware of the dangers posed by toxic chemicals, Congress delegated to EPA extensive new powers and duties to deal with chemical production and wastes.

By January 1981, EPA had some 14,500 employees; regional offices in Boston, New York, Philadelphia, Atlanta, Chicago, Dallas, Kansas City, Denver, San Francisco, and Seattle; research laboratories in twenty states; and responsibility for the implementation of nine* major environmental statutes. The agency had an operating budget of $1.35 billion and administered $3.5 billion a year in construction grant programs to

---

*EPA is responsible for implementation and enforcement of the following major statutes:

Clean Air Act
Clean Water Act
Marine Protection Research and Sanctuaries Act (ocean dumping)
Federal Insecticide, Fungicide and Rodenticide Act
Safe Drinking Water Act
Toxic Substances Control Act
Resource Conservation and Recovery Act (hazardous waste)
Noise Control Act
Comprehensive Environmental Response, Compensation and Liability Act (Superfund)

assist local communities to build water and sewage treatment facilities. The Superfund legislation, passed in 1980, had added the $1.6 billion hazardous waste cleanup fund to the Agency's responsibilities.

EPA is not big compared to the Department of Defense: 970,000 employees (not counting the armed forces) and a $280-billion budget; or the Department of Agriculture: 120,000 employees, and a $42-billion budget. But EPA is huge compared to other government agencies whose primary function is regulation. The Federal Trade Commission, for example, has 1,275 employees and a budget of $65 million. And EPA's regulatory power reaches virtually every industry and local government in the country.

The Clean Air Act requires EPA to regulate air pollution from over 150 million cars, trucks, and buses, and over 20,000 factories, power-plants, and other major stationary sources of pollution. The Clean Water Act makes EPA responsible for the control of water pollution from close to 100,000 different sources. Other laws make EPA responsible for protecting the public from harm as a result of our society's production of over 500 billion pounds a year of hazardous wastes, 1.2 billion pounds a year of pesticides, and several thousand new chemicals each year.

Federal law requires the EPA Administrator to make decisions that affect everything from the cost and performance of a new Chevrolet to the way a farm community in Oklahoma disposes of its sewage. Decisions that determine whether children in urban areas will breathe debilitating lead fumes and whether fish will survive in the water of rural streams and lakes. Few of the decisions are easy, almost none free of controversy.

After the President announced her nomination, Anne Gorsuch began to prepare for what she anticipated would be difficult confirmation hearings. She occupied an office at the Interior Department supplied by her fellow Coloradan, James Watt. Reporters and other government officials trying to reach her were surprised when they called the number supplied by the White House and the receptionist answered "Secretary Watt's office." Watt had already been confirmed despite bitter opposition by environmentalists. He was able to supply resources to assist her in preparing for her confirmation. And Watt had experience with, and strong views about, federal environmental statutes for which Mrs. Gorsuch would be responsible.

While Gorsuch was there Watt began what was widely perceived as a purge of Interior Department lawyers too dedicated to conservation.

15

He told a meeting of National Park concessionaires: "When you read the press you're going to find out that I can be cold and calculating, and indeed I can. But we are going to get ahold of this thing fast. . . . If a personality is giving you a problem, we're going to get rid of the problem or the personality, whichever is faster." He described his assertion of power at the Interior Department as forcing the bureaucrats to "yield to my blows."

Four months passed while Mrs. Gorsuch awaited confirmation and James Watt made radical changes at the Interior Department. The association with Watt fostered an impression that Anne Gorsuch never completely dispelled, that she was a mere lieutenant in his army, carrying out his central plan. It was a largely erroneous impression, unjust to a strong-willed and opinionated politician, but it shaped expectations for her nevertheless.

EPA meanwhile marked time. Top officials appointed by President Carter left, and the White House named a senior civil servant at EPA, Walter Barber, as Acting Administrator. Barber managed the agency with little guidance from the new Administration. He presented a reduced budget to the Congress as he was instructed by the Office of Management and Budget. He formed a task force of career staffers to develop proposals for reform and simplification of the Clean Air Act. They wondered about their new Administrator, and they worried. Rumors about massive firings and radical policy shifts crackled through the Agency. The staff began to hunker down.

"She was more remote than would be typical," said Barber, but she had been a "dark horse" candidate not identified by the transition team. She perceived that "she might have problems with confirmation to start with [and] that she wanted to make some major changes in the agency, that she could dictate; she basically felt that over the four- or five-month period she would be better served to stay away—and she did."

Former administrators Ruckelshaus and Costle offered to meet with Gorsuch to discuss the EPA's problems and pitfalls, but she rebuffed them. She had been chosen after all to bring change to the EPA. The Administration's perception, according to Barber, "the articulated perception was that all of the people who were in the Washington syndrome were . . . too close to Washington, they were part of the system, and we need a new look from outside the system."

So Anne Gorsuch formed her own transition team. Her closest adviser was James Sanderson. A lawyer from a Denver firm, Sanderson had been regional counsel in the Denver office of EPA in the mid-1970's. Before that he had worked for Senator Gordon Allott. His law firm represented a broad range of energy, mining, and development interests, including Coors and Chemical Waste Management, Inc., a subsidiary of the largest hazardous waste disposal firm in the country.

While at the firm Sanderson was active in Colorado Republican politics, and worked on several cases for James Watt's Mountain States Legal Foundation. Sanderson knew Gorsuch "just casually, in passing in politics." Senator Allott's daughter was one of her closest friends. Sanderson was apparently recommended to her by Joseph Coors as a reliable and intelligent conservative with an inside knowledge of EPA, and a clear understanding of what needed to be done.*

Sanderson can be smooth and personable, but at EPA he was ruthless. Walter Barber described him as "bright and aggressive. His politics are written all over his face. He comes from the hard Right. He knew the agency and felt that relative to his political views the agency was way over to the left. . . . He basically, between strength of personality and closeness to Anne and style, just knocked people down. People just didn't quite know how to deal with that. He'd sit in a meeting, and if he didn't like what you were saying, he'd say 'Well, where do you plan to be working tomorrow?' . . . People were afraid of him and still are."

The other adviser closest to Anne Gorsuch was John Daniel, and he was, in many ways, incongruous. In 1980 he had managed the congressional campaign of a friend and neighbor who was a liberal Democrat. A lawyer and engineer, Daniel had worked for state environmental agencies in Alabama and Ohio, lobbied on behalf of the American Paper Institute, and, most recently, represented Johns Manville, the Denver-based manufacturing and mining company. Daniel was recommended to Gorsuch by Watt aide Stanley Hulett.

Sanderson was virtually the only adviser who could directly and openly contradict Gorsuch. Daniel became more and more close to Gorsuch, "but because of his background," says an EPA official, "he had to be more Catholic than the Pope. He rarely contradicted her. He defended and supported her. She never learned the rule that in Wash-

*Several Administration officials assert that Sanderson's role was in part to "oversee" Mrs. Gorsuch, and that he was to be the real power of the Agency. Sanderson scoffs at this assertion. He says he was a mere spear carrier. "I had an awareness of how to be a staff assistant, how to help carry books, get meetings put together, write letters. . . ."

ington there are no permanent enemies or friends. If someone opposed her, that was it, they were against her. John Daniel reinforced those instincts. He would circle the wagons and stand by her in the ring telling her how tough she was."

The new Administrator was eager to move quickly once confirmed, and she, Sanderson, and Daniel began to plan a reorganization of the Agency while she awaited her confirmation hearings. Sanderson concluded "he needed someone who knew the federal personnel system" and contacted a Denver acquaintance, Seth Hunt. Hunt had worked with Sanderson while Sanderson was EPA regional counsel and left in late 1976. He met Anne Gorsuch and was smitten. "She was absolutely a beautiful woman . . . the most intelligent person I've ever met . . . very warm, very dedicated, she had a mission, she really considered it a calling. . . ."

Hunt, although initially reluctant, was convinced that Anne Gorsuch would make important changes and he was flattered to be asked to help. When Gorsuch looked at EPA, he said, "what she saw was a bunch of terrible federal regulations being administered by EPA and other federal agencies, that were becoming extremely cumbersome on the American public, and expensive. . . . She also had the impression that there were a lot of wasteful practices in just the way a federal agency was managed. She wanted to get in and manage an agency right."

The rumors that had flown through the Agency were not far wrong. She knew what had to be done. She planned drastic cuts and swift policy changes. To do that, she believed, she must avoid being "captured" by the EPA staff. Several months later Anne Gorsuch said privately that she isolated herself from the EPA staff on the advice of James Watt. She was going to perform radical surgery and she didn't want to develop too much sympathy with the patient. "Watt told her," says Joe Foran, her Deputy Chief of Staff, "that it's a lot easier to fire people you don't know."

REGULATORY RELIEF

It was May 1, 1981, before Anne Gorsuch emerged from her self-imposed Interior Department exile.* Beneath the bright heat of televi-

---

*Gorsuch and Hernandez took office four months after the Inauguration. Most other Presidential appointments to EPA were delayed for months after that, and the President

sion lights, she presented herself to the Senate Committee on Environment and Public Works to be confirmed as Administrator of the Environmental Protection Agency. Ronald Reagan's opening assault on the federal budget was already under way, and Gorsuch promised to be another symbol of the radical change overtaking Washington. The Senate hearing room was crowded, so crowded that the proceedings had to be moved to a larger room. The press swarmed around Gorsuch until Senator Domenici demanded that they be moved aside so that he could see the nominee.

Gorsuch was impressive. She was cool and careful. She parried hostile questions with ease. She made it clear that her mission at EPA was the "reform," which would mark her tenure at the Agency. "The President," she said, "is committed to regulatory reform, and . . . I share [that] commitment." "There is no greater opportunity to effectuate that goal," she said, "than the one ahead at EPA." Major surgery would be required. "I believe that it is important to emphasize that the reform is not limited to withdrawal of unnecessary or overly burdensome singular regulations, but envisions a much broader scope."

Her testimony only echoed a theme heard often in Washington in the spring of 1981. Ronald Reagan had promised in the campaign that "there are tens of thousands of . . . regulations I would like to see eliminated." In her first public statements, Gorsuch had confirmed her intent to follow "faithfully" Reagan's "real effort to review what's on the books" at EPA. Indeed, the efforts to eliminate regulations were well under way long before Gorsuch arrived.

David Stockman was the bright, brash, and conservative young congressman who played the role of Jimmy Carter to prepare Reagan for his television debate during the campaign. Stockman too agreed with the President's rhetoric. An astute student of institutional politics in Washington, Stockman concluded that the Office of Management and Budget was the place to put that rhetoric into practice. After the election, Stockman set out to become Director of OMB.

Both to further his chances and to influence the new Administration, Stockman wrote the President, in mid-November 1980, a widely leaked memo called "Avoiding a GOP Economic Dunkirk." Stockman

---

never appointed anyone to lead EPA's massive research program while Gorsuch was in office. The top management slots at EPA were not completely filled by Reagan until December 1983.

argued for a program of radical policy changes. His memo focused on tax cuts, spending cuts, and regulatory relief for industry, relief in particular from environmental, safety, and health regulations. As a member of a congressional committee with jurisdiction over many EPA programs, Stockman had been a vitriolic opponent of much that EPA did. Characterizing EPA's growing regulatory responsibilities in the 1980's, notably those for control of hazardous wastes and toxic substances, as a "ticking regulatory time bomb," Stockman proposed to Reagan "swift, comprehensive, and far-reaching regulatory policy corrections" to choke off the "mind-boggling outpouring" of regulations from "heavily biased" "McGovernite no-growth activists" who had taken over government regulation. He called EPA anti-pollution programs "an incredible morass of new controls and compliance procedures." Hazardous waste rules he termed "a monument to mindless excess." The requirement that chemical manufacturers submit safety data to EPA prior to the manufacture of potentially dangerous chemicals he called "[m]ulti-billion dollar overkill."

Stockman called for "regulatory ventilation," by which he meant "unilateral administrative actions to defer, revise, or rescind existing and pending regulations." He listed fourteen candidates for "ventilation," twelve of which were health or environmental regulations. He also urged the President to consider "an omnibus 'suspense bill' " to postpone upcoming regulatory deadlines and even to *ban* rulemaking by agencies for a full year.

Late in November, Stockman said, Reagan called him to say, "Dave, ever since you battered me in those mock debates I've been looking for some way to get even. Now I think I have the answer. I'm going to send you to OMB."

OMB was ready for Stockman. Already in the last years of his Administration, Jimmy Carter had increased OMB's power to keep watch over federal regulatory agencies. The most important figure in this effort was tough-talking, colorful Jim J. Tozzi, who had headed the Environment Branch (the OMB office responsible for EPA) since 1972. Years before, Tozzi had decided that there might not be much more that could be done to control federal spending, but that a great deal could be done to curtail federal requirements that made industry spend. He embarked on a campaign to give OMB the same kind of control over agency regulations that it already had over their budgets.

Tozzi's special target for all those years had been environmental regulation: "I thought, to start the process, the right horse was EPA ... not because of the budget, but 'cause of all the regs." By 1980, Tozzi was close to what he calls his "objective for twenty years," the "set-up of a management control system on regulations government-wide." Through legislation and executive orders, Carter had left OMB "the biggest grant of authority in the world." It was a perfect implement for the new Administration's attack on regulation. "You have to remember," says Tozzi, that "OMB is an institution which works with a sort of rebuttable presumption against anything." The presumption against regulation, especially environmental, was now Presidential policy.

Stockman knew Tozzi and was in touch with him within a few weeks after the election to enlist his aid in preparing the assault on regulation. While Jimmy Carter was still President, two months before Anne Gorsuch was nominated, and half a year before she took over at EPA, OMB staff and David Stockman planned the rule-by-rule deregulation of environmental protection.

Tozzi says "We had it all cranked up. I had these two big books that had all these analyses of [regulations, and they had] ... their wish to control [those regulations]. It was time to put it all together."

What they put together were regulatory hit lists. In December Stockman asked a former EPA official, Eric Stork, to survey industry and final "opportunities for regulatory changes at EPA." Stork met with two dozen business lobbyists just before Christmas, and by the turn of the year had sent their lists to Tozzi.

Tozzi was soon joined by James C. Miller III, a former economics professor and outspoken deregulator who became his boss, and C. Boyden Gray, counsel to Vice-President George Bush. "We hit the ground running," said Miller. "All the work was done in the transition period. We knew what we were doing the minute we came in. Stockman let me loose and said, 'Be tough.' " "It was really nice," says Tozzi, "because there was no one in the government, you see. I loved it! Got more done in that first four months. . . . Things just moved real nice. It just went downhill when they started appointing people."

While things moved "real nice" at OMB, there was no one at EPA. Anne Gorsuch, even after she was nominated, stayed away. In the last week of the Carter Administration, EPA had produced a last-minute explosion of regulation, seven major regulatory actions, two consent agreements, and $200,000 in fines. Then EPA went quiet. "We just sat around for four months, doing nothing," says one top official.

On January 22, 1981, Reagan announced the first official step in the new administration's "regulatory reform" campaign. This was the constitution of a Presidential Task Force on Regulatory Relief, chaired by the Vice-President and composed of four Cabinet officers and three high-level White House officials. The Task Force included Stockman. It was staffed by the new Office of Information and Regulatory Affairs in OMB, headed by Miller and Tozzi. Along with Presidential aide Rich Williamson and Vice-Presidential counsel Boyden Gray, they would direct the Task Force in its mission: to "cut away the thicket of irrational and senseless regulation" by both "review[ing] pending regulations [and] study[ing] past regulations with an eye towards revising them."

A week later, the President, following the advice in Stockman's memo, instructed agency and department heads to "postpone" for 60 days the effective dates of pending final regulations and to refrain from making proposed rules final. One hundred seventy-two final regulations and a hundred or more proposed rules were subject to the so-called "freeze" (although OMB exempted those regulations it wished to allow to go into effect). The freeze was designed to trap the regulations issued or proposed in the Carter Administration's final weeks.

Announcing the freeze, Miller explained simply that "a lot of things were pushed through that won't pass the litmus test in this Administration." There were questions about the legality of the freeze, and even about what "freeze" meant, says Tozzi, but "that's why it's good . . . to be a non-attorney in that job, because . . . if you're gonna move the government around you can't be constrained by little things. You have to take a risk."*

Having accomplished the "defer" portion of Stockman's strategy, Miller sought a further expansion of OMB's power, an Executive Order requiring agencies to give OMB advance notice of and virtual veto power over forthcoming regulations, as well as a broad retrospective mandate to "revise and rescind" both frozen and existing regulations. Stockman's influence and Tozzi's experience again enabled them to act before the agencies could resist. "This was really action," says Tozzi. "Jim Miller came in here . . . and he was really hep on an Executive Order. And I wanted one too. So that was a happy marriage; . . . we got

---

*In July 1982, the United States Court of Appeals for the Third Circuit held one part of the freeze illegal after the Natural Resources Defense Council sued to compel EPA to put a frozen set of rules into effect.

the Executive Order out in a month after the President came in. And Miller was so right. We'd never get that out now."

The President signed Executive Order 12291 on February 17. It gave OMB extraordinary power and, as Miller testified, "established the preeminence of the task force in matters involving regulatory relief." It requires an agency to write a "regulatory impact analysis" before proposing a major new rule. The analysis must quantify the costs and benefits of the rule, and the agency must adopt the least costly even if not the best approach that the law permits. As Gary Dietrich, a former EPA official says, "Executive Order 12291 gave Jim Tozzi the power to regulate the government's power to make private industry spend, and that's a big deal."

The Executive Order allowed OMB to review and hold up all regulations. As one Task Force member, conservative economist Murray Weidenbaum, observed: "OMB is the agency that sits astride proposed legislation, proposed budgets, proposed executive orders, and now also proposed regulations." Jim Tozzi, who knew his power resided largely in the simple requirement that everything be cleared by him, puts it another way: "If you roll me on the substance, that's okay. But if you roll me on the procedure, I have a very long memory. I get very attentive. Some people have tried it, and funny things have happened to them." OMB had a clear White House mandate to cut back on regulation and the agencies knew it. Free from any responsibility for substantive action —to ensure clean air or control hazardous wastes—OMB could focus on costs. That was their imperative.

Already notorious for its secretive ways, OMB deemed itself free of the legal requirements imposed on agencies to maintain reviewable records of their work, contacts, or sources of information. "I see no problem in off-the-record contacts with us," said Miller. And they left no tracks. "We will not maintain a file and a record," Miller proudly told Rep. John Dingell. If a rule is rejected or returned to an agency, "It will be communicated over the telephone." Putting things in writing would of course mean that OMB's influence on rules, and industry's influence on OMB, would be easier to trace. Tozzi says candidly, "I don't leave fingerprints."

The procedures required by law for federal agencies issuing regulations have a basis in common sense. They allow everyone to comment on proposals and also reveal who is saying what to the government and how the government responds.

Before an agency proposes a regulation, the agency staff analyzes relevant data, assesses the agency's legal authority, and prepares a decision document for the head of the agency. The agency head decides policy questions presented by his staff and a formal proposal is published in the Federal Register. Anyone who wants to may comment on the proposal, offering new data, criticizing the agency's analyses, and arguing issues of policy. When the period for comment ends, the staff reviews this entire "record." The agency is required to consider and respond to each substantial issue that commenters raise. Based on the record, the agency head makes the final decision on what the agency should do. If the agency is challenged in court, the court reviews the legality of the agency's action on the basis of the record. The safeguards built into the law—the Administrative Procedure Act—have evolved over decades of experience. They are designed to assure basic fairness, even at the cost of a little delay.

Under Executive Order 12291, the Office of Management and Budget reviews agency actions on the basis of gut instincts and industry complaints. Tozzi says he could "tell in about four minutes if a rule made sense." When industry had complaints, he did not want long legal analyses; "I needed to know why you thought it was bad, whether it was economically blah-blah, why did it impact you?" The long rulemaking record, the legal basis of the rule, the opportunity for public comment were just too cumbersome for OMB. "We should read the record," says Tozzi, "but we didn't." When OMB reviews a rule, Miller testified, "we are not evaluating a record."

Since OMB has enormous power but makes no record of what it does or why, it does not worry about procedures the law requires. No court can effectively review what OMB does. Thus, if a statute requires EPA to regulate pollution to protect the health of the most vulnerable members of the public, OMB can still insist that EPA adopt a standard that protects fewer people, and costs industry less.

The system was crafted to respond to industry complaints. As Boyden Gray told a briefing in April 1981, while the Task Force and OMB could "not operate as a conduit" to guarantee agency decisions, they could serve as "a coordinator, as a catalyst, as a prod. We can help set deadlines to get action. . . . We can eliminate conflicts." In response to a lobbyist's question about how best to get action on a problem, he provided this example:

Well, if you go to the agency first, don't be too pessimistic if they can't solve the problem there. If they don't, that is what the Task Force is for. We had an example of that not too long ago, but the people were not being completely candid with their own top people or with the Task Force. We told the lawyers representing the individual companies and trade associations involved to come back to us if they had a problem. Two weeks later they showed up and I asked if they had a problem. They said they did and we made a couple of phone calls and straightened it out. . . .

Later, explaining himself to Rep. Mike Synar, Gray insisted his office was open to all callers. "Anybody?" asked Synar. "Yes," said Gray. "My mom and dad who are upset about something?" "Absolutely." After Rep. Albert Gore read into the record a list of Miller's meetings, concluding with "the U.S. Chamber of Commerce . . . Ford Motor Company a couple of times, the Chemical Manufacturers Association, and so forth," Synar said, "It does not look like my mom and dad are getting in there."

With its authority established, and its conduct beyond effective oversight, OMB began the job of regulatory relief, taking the implicit mandate in that phrase—regulatory *relief*—seriously, and emphasizing not so much improving regulations as removing them. Chris DeMuth, who replaced James Miller in September 1981, when the President named Miller Chairman of the Federal Trade Commission, said he and Miller and Stockman believed environmental regulation should be a primary target of their regulatory relief efforts because they believed "there are scores, hundreds of regulations on the books that are imposing costs without much positive result in terms of environmental or health improvement."

For OMB, the purpose or benefits of the regulations were of little importance. Free from responsibility for substantive action—to control air pollution or protect the public from toxic wastes—OMB should focus on costs. Nobody stacked up the benefits against the costs and looked at the difference. "Let's say you had a real bad environmental reg," says Tozzi, "that didn't cost much. Maybe we should—all that good stuff—but we didn't. The cost was the alarm bell." The focus was only on the cost to industry of complying with a regulation. The cost to society of *not* regulating pollution was not part of OMB's mandate. Tozzi concedes that it is almost impossible to calculate the benefits of regulation in monetary terms. "You consider them, but to put it in numbers is crazy." "Of course," he adds, "this isn't benefit-cost . . . we're just here to represent the President."

Amid rumors that the incoming Administration would impose a long-term freeze or even a one-year moratorium on regulation, Acting Administrator Walt Barber, Acting Policy Chief Roy Gamse, and General Counsel Michele Corash went to see Jim Miller, who had asked for reform initiatives. They put together what Gamse says was a "credible list" of initiatives: they "wouldn't have been done under Carter, but they weren't illegal." The meeting was a failure. Miller did not ask for their ideas but "just unveiled his own list of withdrawals and small actions without real impact." Miller was, Gamse thought, desperate for quick results.

Corash called Boyden Gray, a former colleague at a Washington law firm, to ask whether EPA could provide solid regulatory reform initiatives for the new Administration. "Tell us what you want to accomplish and we'll try to help," she told him. Corash advised Gray to stay away from a moratorium, keep the freeze short, and allow exemptions for rules with court or statutory deadlines. She explained that many EPA actions were required by statutory or court-ordered deadlines and that some rules could be good. Some regulations, she reminded him, "relieve burdens as well as impose them," and "an absolute freeze on regulations [would] impose significant costs on industry." Her practical advice was taken, but the dialogue on substantive reform "had no impact," she says. "They wanted things the Vice-President could announce."

EPA quickly suspended some rules on noise from garbage trucks that the President could refer to in a February 18 announcement of a package of "significant" regulatory relief actions. Next, Vice-President Bush announced on March 7 that EPA would soon change the definition of a "source" under its air pollution rules so as to "ease a regulatory burden on industries."*

On March 25 another Vice-Presidential press conference announced the opening of a new phase in the regulatory relief campaign. Most of the regulations frozen two months earlier were to be released, but 36 rules were held for review with the hope, Bush said, that "there will be an awful lot of changes made in them." EPA rules on toxic water pollution and pesticides were among those held up. Another list of

---

*The Court of Appeals later overturned the change after a lawsuit by the Natural Resources Defense Council. The case is now before the United States Supreme Court.

existing regulations to be reconsidered included three more EPA rules. The number three is perhaps misleading. One of the rules to be redone was the entire system for controlling hazardous waste.

The Task Force announced a special package of "actions to help the U.S. auto industry" on April 6. Barber says, "The big push was: What can we do to provide some monetary relief to the auto industry?" The answer was still another regulatory hit list, a hodgepodge of 34 environmental, health, and safety rules. The package was largely based on a collection of complaints General Motors had circulated a year before without success. The EPA staff soon learned GM's influence had increased. An EPA group working on a set of auto industry relief measures went to OMB to brief Jim Miller. Mike Walsh, then head of EPA's mobile source office, says, "We had developed a set of proposals that provided substantial relief to the industry without gutting the program, and still keeping health protection more or less intact. Miller and his staff made it clear that the industry, especially GM, wanted much more." GM got what it wanted.

Economist George Eads said that in the auto package "the agencies are being given the signal that the results should come out a certain way before the necessary analysis has even been begun." "If you take a look at the automobile package," said Boyden Gray, "it is a pretty good overview of how we hope to proceed." The *Wall Street Journal* noted: "Access for the auto industry has improved—some would say in an almost revolutionary way."

At his March 25 press conference, Bush had announced that he was sending letters to businesses, trade associations, organized labor, and so on, inviting them to nominate their least-liked federal regulations. Four and a half months later, on August 12, Bush announced the initial results: an "overwhelming" volume of complaints, some 2,500 pieces of regulatory hate mail. That exercise resulted in a new hit list of 30 more regulations, four of them affecting EPA. Large programs were taken on in this round: the entire system for registering pesticides, the requirement that chemical manufacturers notify EPA before producing new and potentially dangerous substances, the "consolidated permit" system for new industrial facilities, and the rules lowering the amount of lead in gasoline.

Lead in gasoline became the most controversial of all. The evidence of lead's dangers to children's health, especially the health of children in the inner city where motor traffic is heavy, is unassailable. But the

Task Force wanted "quick" relief for "small refiners." The Task Force seemed ignorant of what the rules involved, however. They did not know that children were affected, or even cars: "We're talking about using lead in boats or in farm machinery in rural areas," said Gray. The Task Force also seemed unaware that the rule they were attacking had the support of virtually every health scientist with any knowledge in the matter. The Task Force announcement took the EPA staff by surprise, and provoked determined resistance.

The Task Force, by and large, listened to business and only business. On June 13, 1981, OMB reported that regulatory relief had already saved over $20 billion for American industry. They neither mentioned nor considered what it had cost the public in terms of injury to health and the environment.

Even with its expanded authority, OMB could not totally revolutionize federal regulation. They could prevent action but not compel it. Thus, Jim Miller explained, "The key to our success is really, I believe, the fact that the regulatory appointees at the agencies—the Reagan political regulatory appointees—are people who are dedicated to reform." Or, as one Commerce Department official phrased it, the Cabinet and sub-cabinet "are the most business-oriented group you've seen in Washington in a long time."

Anne Gorsuch was confirmed as EPA Administrator on May 5, 1981, and sworn into office on May 20. OMB had already wrought enormous changes in the Agency's program while EPA was leaderless (Barber, a civil servant, had little political clout). But the advocates of regulatory relief expected little change after Gorsuch's arrival. James Miller predicted: "You will see a very different set of regulators at the Agency than we had in the past." Gorsuch, he said, was "a very smart woman." "She is tough," he added. "She is dedicated to the President's principles of regulatory relief."

A few weeks later, a curious incident took place that foreshadowed future problems for Gorsuch. At Miller's invitation, Gorsuch went to the American Enterprise Institute, a business-oriented "think tank" in Washington, to be briefed by a group of conservative economists. They described a series of market-based incentive systems which they believed would work more efficiently than the traditional forms of regulation used by EPA. The session was a disaster. Mrs. Gorsuch, according to one of the economists, "seemed disinterested [sic], as if we were politically irrelevant theorists she didn't have to bother with." When they explained one proposal to allow industries to buy, sell, and save rights to pollute, "she seemed to think it was like selling indulgences." She communicated that she was not interested in better regulation so much as less regulation. Nolan Clark, for a short time a top Gorsuch aide, who counted himself a conservative economist, says, "Each side left thinking the other was nuts."

After she was sworn in, Gorsuch, for the first time, spoke to the EPA staff. Already shaken by her long isolation, the constant rumors about her plans, and by the actions of the Regulatory Relief Task Force, the staff was not reassured by what Gorsuch said:

In the future, EPA will contribute to the new federalism by constantly watching for ways to shift the decision-making process from the banks of this local, now much cleaner Potomac, to the local courthouse and state capitols.

She concluded by saying she hoped

the EPA of the Reagan Administration [would] be remembered for the money it saved taxpayers because we streamlined regulations, cut down on permit-processing time, and we together cut back on the required paperwork for EPA projects.

We should work together to keep a lid on those unnecessary regulations which have created hardships on our national industries, driving up the cost of consumer goods.

HARD TIMES AND HIT LISTS

In the fall of 1981 pollster Louis Harris testified before a House committee on public sentiment regarding the Clean Air Act. He told the committee: "not a single major segment of the public wants the environmental laws made less strict." Far from eroding, he testified, support for the Clean Air Act "has gotten stronger in 1981, partly because people have taken for granted in many areas of government certain things they believe in, and somehow they have an impression that the Clean Air Act is now threatened, and in the face of this we see out there a growing constituency aroused by this."

From the start, the Administration was on a collision course with public support for the environmental laws and few top officials in the White House or EPA comprehended the breadth of that support. On the Clean Air Act in particular, the Administration was determined to respond to the complaints of industry that compliance with the Act was expensive and inordinately complex. Weeks before Anne Gorsuch was confirmed, Kitty Adams, one of her special assistants, was working on a set of options for amending the Act. Adams, who had worked on Clean Air issues for the Business Roundtable before becoming an independent consultant, worked with Frank Blake and Nancy Maloley of Vice-President Bush's regulatory relief staff. Day after day they met at the White House with industry representatives to find out what they wanted.

The EPA staff, too, was working on Clean Air Act amendments, seeking to simplify its requirements and to make compliance cheaper without sacrificing human health or permitting areas with still clean air to become polluted. According to Dave Menotti, a senior EPA attorney, "We knew improvements could be made and we knew the political pressure on the Act would be enormous. We could feel industry anger and resistance building by the mid-1970's as we pushed for compliance."

The staff working group, directed by Acting Administrator Barber, developed a series of options for amendment of the Act. Although they were unable to get clear policy guidance from the new Administration, they tried to respond to what they thought were the Administration's priorities. "We were professionals and we wanted to be perceived that way. We tried to prepare a sensible draft but were prepared to take orders."

A small group briefed Gorsuch on the Act before her confirmation. It was a cold, disheartening meeting. The staff spoke, she listened and asked a few questions. There was no dialogue. Immediately after she was sworn in a much larger group briefed her on the working group's recommendations. Mike Walsh, the director of the mobile source program, spoke first, for nearly an hour, almost uninterrupted. When he finished Gorsuch said, "Thank you, Mike. Walt, what's next?" Again, there was no interaction.

At another meeting a week later Gorsuch made it clear they would have to start over again. Menotti says, "Our work went out the window and we began a period of intense effort. A new draft almost every week. Each time there'd be a list of huge changes to make—sometimes internally contradictory."

In one briefing Mike Walsh objected to an amendment that would make state programs for inspection and maintenance of pollution control equipment on cars optional. He recalls that Gorsuch smiled icily and said, "I don't want you preaching to me about how the states will respond. I was in the Colorado legislature. We would have done more and done it better, but for the heavy-handed interference of EPA." Walsh persisted, pointing out that EPA had tried the voluntary approach for seven years and it had been a dismal failure. "The whole room was tense. It was clear we were not supposed to 'discuss' issues with her as we had with past Administrators."

The drafting process became increasingly frenetic. The staff sensed an almost impenetrable barrier of mistrust between them and the Administrator and her top advisers. The new crowd seemed more inclined to believe what industry lobbyists told them than what the career staff at EPA said. Industry representatives saw the change too. One chemical company representative said, "Some in my industry thought now we have *our* people in there. Our views will be listened to and our data will be believed. It wasn't very smart." Barber observes:

The whole tenor of the Administration in the first six months was "industry has a better answer for environmental problems—they understand the problems better, and they can make this thing work better and their advice is to be heeded." Whose views were being solicited? Whose views were being heeded in drafts that appeared on the Clean Air Act, etc.? It was pretty clear.

On the Clean Air Act, industry wanted a great deal. One corporate executive said, "We only have a few things we really want changed. The rest doesn't bother us. But other companies and other industries have other problems. When you put it all together there's not much left of the Act." Draft after draft went out for review and came back for change. Even Anne Gorsuch became frustrated as she took drafts to the Cabinet Council on Natural Resources and the Environment and was told, according to Barber, that they "didn't go far enough." "The industry guys . . . got carried away with themselves and they just— through their inroads into the regulatory reform group and the [Cabinet Council], etc.—were just asking for everything imaginable."

Kathleen Bennett, a former lobbyist for the paper industry who had been nominated to head the air program, brought back one draft heavily marked up by someone outside the Agency, saying she had gotten it from John Daniel and she wanted the staff to incorporate the changes.

31

It came to be known as the "Zorro draft" because, say several staffers, it had been "all slashed to hell by a mysterious stranger."

Dave Menotti, who was the lawyer in the general counsel's office responsible for the air program, was outraged by the draft. He told Bennett he and his staff could not effectively advise her if she was going to accept outside suggestions without letting them review the effect of the changes on the Act. She was taken aback and assured Menotti she had not meant to insult anyone, but she had been instructed by John Daniel to make the changes. Daniel thought the proposals were excellent. "What," she asked, "is wrong with the proposals?" "That led to an incredible session that lasted most of one Tuesday night," says Menotti, "in which one member of my staff after another explained why the stuff was clumsy and unworkable. It would have left the Act full of impossible contradictions and ambiguities."

In late June 1981, someone leaked one of the drafts to Congressman Henry Waxman, Chairman of the House subcommittee dealing with the Clean Air Act. Waxman was indignant and called the proposal "nothing less than a blueprint for destruction of our clean air laws." He warned the White House that their proposal would lead to a "furious and acrimonious battle that is to no one's advantage."

Waxman was right. The leaked draft set off the first of many public tempests that buffeted Anne Gorsuch. "Everyone jumped all over us," said Vice-President Bush, "even advocates [of substantial changes in the law] felt it went too far." The Administration retreated and was never able to pull together a proposal that was acceptable to industry and to congressional leaders. Instead the Administration adopted a set of eleven general "principles" on clean air that had no effect on congressional action. "Nobody," says Walt Barber, "could have sold that thing the way they finally got it cobbled together. You can't market compromises if you're not allowed to compromise and the industry won't give up anything. . . ."

Dr. John Hernandez, the Deputy Administrator, was sworn in a few days after Mrs. Gorsuch. He was, in most ways, a very different person. Affable and gregarious, he hated the detail work that Gorsuch insisted upon. Yet, he too arrived imbued with a determination to heed the claims of those whom the Agency regulated. The states, too, he felt should be freed of EPA insistence that they meet the detailed requirements of federal law. "Instead of using words like 'shall' and 'must' " with the states, Hernandez said, "we're going to use words like 'may' and 'here's a good idea.' "

Sometimes he seemed curiously unaware of what it meant to be the second highest official in the most powerful regulatory agency in the country. On occasion, he wrote grades and professorial comments on technical papers developed by offices within the Agency. He was garrulous and sometimes unpredictable. When one staffer tried to talk to him about the problem of acid rain he become irate and shouted "never use those words to me. There is no such thing." He says that he knew a lot about the operation of the Agency's $3.5 billion construction grant program, but adds, "the only thing I didn't know was all that bureaucratic nonsense you had to go through, and the rules. I've never been strong on reading rules. . . ." He often seemed, commented one EPA staffer, "an engaging amateur."

Hernandez saw himself, and initially at least, Anne Gorsuch saw him, as the "house scientist." He believed he could improve the scientific basis of EPA decisions, yet he came across as rather crudely attempting to "cast doubt on everything" that would support regulation. Other scientists were not impressed. One who met him socially was shocked at his concept of risk assessment, and appalled when Hernandez announced that he hoped to be admitted to the National Academy of Sciences after his work at EPA.

During the first months at EPA, Hernandez seemed eager to be a part of the little group exercising power on the 12th floor, the top floor of EPA where he and Gorsuch and other top officials had offices. But Gorsuch did not like him and kept him at a distance, and he was not well suited to the 12th floor power struggles that went on constantly. Gradually, Hernandez wielded less and less authority. He wandered late into morning meetings still wearing his tennis whites. When Gorsuch was away, John Daniel ran things. As time passed, Hernandez perhaps lost his zeal, but in the early months he took actions that later returned to haunt him.

Soon after he was sworn in he stumbled into a controversy that only became public two years later, after Anne Gorsuch had resigned, while Hernandez was Acting Administrator. It led to his own resignation a few days after a congressional committee investigating EPA made the incident public, but even now he calls the incident "all bullshit."

What Hernandez did was not complex or devious, but it revealed

33

his approach to government, and it served as another strong signal to the staff of how the tides had shifted at EPA.

In mid-June 1981, representatives of the Dow Chemical Company called Hernandez to ask him for a copy of a report drafted by the EPA Region V office in Chicago, which had been leaked to two newspapers. The report assessed evidence of dioxin contamination in the Great Lakes Region. One of the report's conclusions was that the Dow manufacturing plant in Midland, Michigan, was "the major if not the only source" of dioxin contamination in the Saginaw Bay area. Hernandez gave Dow a copy and reviewed it himself.

After reviewing the report Hernandez contacted Region V Administrator Val Adamkus about it twice. On the first occasion, Adamkus later testified, Hernandez "angrily denounced the report and called the work of our people trash." He told Adamkus to expect a call from Dow to comment on the report. In another call, reflecting one of Dow's complaints, Hernandez asked Adamkus why "Dow keeps coming up" in the report. Hernandez also communicated his dissatisfaction with the report to scientists at EPA headquarters who were in charge of a task force dealing with dioxin.

The impetus for the EPA report was the discovery of dioxin in gull eggs and fish in the Great Lakes, with the highest levels found in fish taken from Saginaw Bay. Dow's Midland, Michigan, plant discharges waste water into two rivers, the Tittabawasee and the Saginaw, which flow into Saginaw Bay.

To help EPA decide how to deal with the problem, Adamkus asked a scientist on his staff to assemble all of the information available on dioxin contamination in the Great Lakes Region and the reported effects of dioxin on human health.* "I wanted to pull together everything we knew, so we in the Region would not be shooting from the hip."

Adamkus was particularly concerned because he knew from experi-

---

*Dioxin is highly toxic, but controversy about the human health effects of dioxin and the level of exposure at which it is dangerous continues, in part because there is some evidence to suggest that human beings are less sensitive than many animals, including some test animals.

Dioxin is a useless byproduct of the manufacture of certain sterilants and of 2, 4, 5-T. This herbicide, together with another one, 2, 4-D, made up the defoliant Agent Orange, used to strip Vietnamese forests and crops during the Vietnam War. The Dow Chemical Company made 2, 4, 5-T until 1979.

ence that Dow could be feisty and combative. "The record shows we have more confrontation than cooperation from Dow," he says. Dow had not allowed EPA investigators to examine the Midland plant for contamination. On another occasion when EPA used aircraft to look for hazardous waste problems on a number of plant sites, it was Dow that went indignantly to the Justice Department and got top Justice officials to agree to stay away from Dow plants. "In fact," Adamkus said in July 1983, "even now, this very moment, after all the controversy and all the public concern over dioxin, we still get no cooperation from Dow."

So Adamkus was wary and wanted a full report before he took action. The report was ready in May 1981, and the principal author sent it to a number of EPA scientists and lawyers in Washington for review. They suggested changes, but generally praised the report. Several, however, expressed political concerns. Dr. Milton Clark, an EPA toxicologist and the author of the report, noted that the chairman of EPA's dioxin working group in Washington said that " 'no one here disagrees with your conclusions.' He believed that putting in print my conclusions [about the danger of eating contaminated fish] could inflame the public. Moreover there is some concern over the new political atmosphere in Washington."

On June 13, 1981, the *Toronto Globe and Mail* published a story based on a leaked draft of the report, and Region V felt the full impact of the "new political atmosphere." After Hernandez's angry call, Dow called.

In a conference call with the EPA staff, Dow officials went through the report line by line, starting with the cover page. "They thought the title was inappropriate," said Clark. "We spent several minutes on this." The Dow people also wanted EPA to change its risk estimates, and to soften or delete references to miscarriages and Agent Orange. Most important, Dow wanted to delete the report's conclusion that Dow was "the major if not the only source" of dioxin contamination in the Saginaw Bay area.

"This was our own document, to help us decide what to do," said Adamkus, "but Dow was calling as if to give us instructions."

In the end, Adamkus did not resist. He had meantime heard from Washington. "They actually repeated the same request to us . . . that we heard from the Dow people," Adamkus said. He described conference calls between the Washington task force and the Chicago regional office. Adamkus assumed the task force members were speaking for

Hernandez; indeed they often made statements such as "John doesn't want it that way." Adamkus said it was clear that "Dow's comments carried a very heavy load with our headquarters, and if we want to get the blessing of headquarters to release the report, we definitely have to do something about this." The report came out minus the conclusion about Dow as the source of dioxin contamination, and minus a warning against eating fish from the contaminated area.

Hernandez denies issuing orders to change the report to Dow's liking, and no one in Region V ever reported receiving such an order directly. Hernandez gives several justifications for his actions, one of which was that "it was important to have Agency documents reviewed by knowledgeable scientists." He adds: "However, upon reflection, I believe that it might have been better to have circulated the draft report for comment more widely."

The incident typified Hernandez's problem at EPA, according to Walt Barber. The Administration was eager to help industry and Hernandez was part of that effort. "He's Deputy Administrator, and casual comments, referrals to third parties, etc., carry a lot of weight. And when you say to Dow 'review this and give your comments back to Region V' —that has tremendous significance. . . ." Hernandez could have gotten Dow's comments and dealt with them "judiciously," says Barber. "But to let some industry guy go into the Region and say 'I've got the Deputy's stamp of approval and you've got to make the changes I tell you to make' . . . creates a whole different kind of aura. And I'm sure those Dow guys played it for all it was worth."

Another signal that shook the Agency's staff was the discovery that the new top officials had brought in lists of Agency staff and advisers to be gotten rid of. It began during the transition period when, according to Ernie Minor, a member of the transition team, job applicants' résumés "flowed in, but so did a lot of letters on people to get rid of" from individuals who "just didn't understand what a career civil service is." Minor paid little attention to the letters, trying to focus on finding candidates for top jobs, but, he said, "then you get a guy like [Louis] Cordia who thinks he has some higher calling and begins developing a bunch of 'hit lists.' "*

---

*It later turned out Minor himself was on one list, acknowledged as a Reagan supporter, but deemed unreliable because of his ties to William Ruckelshaus, the first Administrator of EPA, later brought back to EPA after Gorsuch's resignation.

Cordia was a young staff member from the conservative Heritage Foundation.* He had edited the bitterly critical chapter on EPA in the Foundation's influential report *Mandate for Leadership*. He was a member of the EPA Transition Team, but the chairman of the team eventually threw him out. Nevertheless, Cordia ended up at EPA as a low-level political appointee—with his lists.

One long list rated EPA science advisers with such comments as "technically good, but should not be kept on the job, bad policy"; "interesting, once a protégé of a reputable individual, bright and held in high esteem, now an environmentalist, should go"; "fair scientist, competent, however bad policy"; and a positive comment: "interesting enigma, applied ecologist, excellent administrative background and experience, yet a follower, won't stand out in front, definitely keep."

Many of the scientists were university professors. A biochemistry professor at Harvard who had developed a new method to measure dioxin contamination was labeled "poison . . . a Nader on toxics." Another professor, formerly chief physicist at IBM, was denominated a "bleeding heart liberal." The entire radiation program was deemed "responsible for continued public awareness for the sole purpose to scare. They should all go."

About 90 scientists, both on independent advisory committees and on the EPA staff, were rated on the basis of comments Cordia solicited from representatives of industry and conservative groups. Another list included the names of top bureaucrats in the Agency who had somehow provoked the ire of one of the industries regulated by EPA, and consequently came to be branded as "unacceptable to this Administration."

Cordia circulated his lists to senior appointees within the Agency. He did not have authority to get rid of anyone, but others did. Jim Sanderson and his aides Seth Hunt and Chip Wood, together with Cliff Miller, a morose and taciturn personnel officer from the Denver EPA office whom they brought to Washington, put together an organization chart of the EPA with top career officials' names on magnetic strips. The names were annotated with colored dots: brown for those who must be gotten rid of, red for those to be transferred to less responsible positions, and blue for those deemed loyal to the Administration. Hunt later said the chart, kept on the wall of Cliff Miller's office, was merely a "briefing tool" to explain

---

*The Heritage Foundation, like the Mountain States Legal Foundation, was largely a creation of Joseph Coors.

to Gorsuch the intricacies of the personnel structure, but top appointees say they were called to Miller's office and shown the names of career employees working for them who were to be transferred or fired.

One senior official recalls seeing a short list of employees viewed unfavorably by industry in John Daniel's hand at a meeting of senior appointees in the Administrator's private dining room. Notes taken by Daniel at a White House meeting between Gorsuch and White House staff member Craig Fuller in 1983 (after the list became public) reveal that the White House had located the "Chamber of Commerce list" which White House Personnel Director Pendleton James sent to Gorsuch in 1981. Daniel added "(not acknowledging this)."

In late October 1981, an official of the National Association of Manufacturers told an industry meeting, "There are a number of people who have been with EPA a number of years who are doing a fine job and a few who are ready to tear you apart." Some of those latter "now are pussycats," he added, and advised his audience to let Gorsuch know "if you know of any tigers turned pussycats . . . and maybe there will be a review of their performances."

The Assistant Administrator for Air, Noise, and Radiation, Kathleen Bennett, the Associate Administrator for Policy, Nolan Clark, and Clark's successor, Joe Cannon, all resisted instructions to act against career employees whom they had found to be competent and professional, but Sanderson intervened, purporting to speak for the Administrator, and almost always prevailed.

Some of the career employees on the list against whom action was taken were:

Sandy Gardebring, Enforcement Chief in the Chicago regional office, fired when she refused a transfer to a job in Washington with "no particular responsibilities." Adamkus, the Regional Administrator, fought the move, arguing her competence, but he was told she was on the list and had to go.

David Tundermann, a lawyer and policy analyst in Washington, forced out when he refused a transfer to become a laboratory chief in Cincinnati—a job for which he had no qualifications and which he had never sought.

Sheila Prindiville, deputy regional administrator in San Francisco, fired when she refused a transfer to Washington. The transfer was justified on the grounds that her job was to be eliminated, but a new deputy was named before she left.

Paul Stolpman, Director of the Office of Air Policy, was abruptly transferred and kept away from work on acid rain, on which he was an expert.

Clark, a conservative lawyer and adamant free market economist with no instinct for bureaucratic streetfighting, lost his own job in the struggle. He had already clashed with one of Gorsuch's assistants over his refusal to rely on what he regarded as incorrect data on delays caused by the Clean Air Act, and with Gorsuch herself over his insistence on testing the factual premises for proposed reforms. He found that he liked and trusted his staff. They were able and dedicated, and not in the least ideological. When he was told he had to get rid of his deputy and another top staffer, he balked. In a few weeks, he was out. Roy Gamse, Clark's deputy and one of the "hit list" targets Clark sought to protect, says, "Nolan was fired because he spent too much time listening to staff and seeking answers to questions when Gorsuch thought it should have been obvious to him what the President wanted." Shortly afterward, Gorsuch picked Sanderson to replace Clark.

The staff knew about the "hit lists" and about colleagues who had been treated shabbily or worse. They saw what happened to Clark and the suspicion with which Gorsuch and Sanderson seemed to regard them. Their response was hostility and fear. Some resisted. Some left.

There were a few anomalies. While Agency morale collapsed, a few senior bureaucrats developed relatively comfortable relations with Mrs. Gorsuch and her top aides. They provide an illustration of how Mrs. Gorsuch's views of the Agency were shaped.

One was David Menotti, the senior lawyer in the General Counsel's office on air pollution issues. He first met Anne Gorsuch when senior members of the staff briefed her on the Clean Air Act before her confirmation hearings. She seemed "icy, reserved, aloof. I was furious at myself because she asked me a question [on procedures for approving state clean air plans] and I blew it. I thought that was it." But a few weeks later Menotti was called in on the Sunday of Memorial Day weekend and spent seven hours briefing her on the ramifications of an important clean air case. "She was cordial, challenging, very open to argument on the legal issues. It was fun. We ended up taking her out to dinner at Blimpie's." Jim Sanderson was at the briefing, and he too was "open and easy to talk with."

Menotti was not unknown to Sanderson. They had dealt with each other on legal issues while Sanderson was Region VIII counsel in Denver. Shortly after Gorsuch's nomination, while she was awaiting confirmation, Michele Corash, who had stayed on as EPA's general counsel after the election, contacted Sanderson about Menotti and another lawyer. She wanted to make Menotti, who was well respected as an able and level-headed professional, Associate General Counsel for Air, a job she knew would become extremely tough as the Congress worked to amend the Clean Air Act. But she was worried that the move would be perceived as a Democratic ploy, and would be reversed as soon as Gorsuch took office.

So she contacted Sanderson, who was frequently at EPA. "It was pretty obvious he was acting for Anne and it was possible to run decisions by him informally." Corash had made a very calculated effort to stay on good terms with both Sanderson and Seth Hunt, an effort that was facilitated by her own good contacts in industry as a former partner in a Washington firm and her personal charm. She told Sanderson that Menotti was not only smart, but that, as an attorney who had been in private practice, he clearly understood his obligation to "find out what his client wanted and try to make it happen." Sanderson "asked about Menotti's political affiliation, and I told him," says Corash, "that I didn't know. I also, as diplomatically as I could, tried to let him know he shouldn't ask that kind of question, because it was illegal."

Menotti is convinced that Sanderson recommended him to Gorsuch. "We got along comfortably when he was in Region VIII. He was easy-going and pragmatic then—hard to square with the guy who descended on the Agency like an avenging angel. I can never forgive what I heard he did to some of the staff people, but in my case I think he must have told Anne I was okay." The other lawyer whom Corash recommended to Sanderson whom Sanderson did not know was not so fortunate. He remained in an "acting" status until he finally quit.

Bill Hedeman was another anomaly. He had been in charge of the EPA Office of Federal Activities under the Carter Administration. The office doubled in size while he was there and, by criticizing environmentally harmful federal pork barrel projects, earned the wrath of conservative politicians. In the fall of 1981, Hedeman learned that Sanderson was making inquiries about him. Hedeman had been a lawyer at the Army Corps of Engineers responsible for the permit program that protects wetlands and waters throughout the country, under Section 404 of the Clean Water Act. The Corps often clashed with both environmentalists and the EPA over the program. But while Sanderson was EPA regional counsel in Denver, Hedeman had advised him on a 404 case he was handling. Their dealings had been cordial. Hedeman heard that in response to his inquiries Sanderson had gotten satisfactory answers about him from the Corps. Soon afterwards, Sanderson and John Daniel offered Hedeman the job of running the new "Superfund" program. "They didn't just offer it. They were very supportive and urged me to take it." Once in the job, he never had any difficulty dealing with Anne Gorsuch.

Isolated from her own agency by choice, by circumstances, and by style, in the early months of her administration Anne Gorsuch often saw EPA through Jim Sanderson's eyes. Sanderson and John Daniel, whom she had made her Chief of Staff, remained her closest advisers. Indeed, the White House did not allow her to choose any other top appointees at the Agency. The only exceptions were Sanderson, who was never confirmed, and Joe Cannon, whom she chose a year later for Sanderson's job, after Sanderson withdrew his name. Cannon is still at EPA, in charge of Air Programs, the only member of Gorsuch's administration to survive; he was untouched by scandal. With these exceptions, however, EPA jobs were slowly filled by candidates sent over by the White House Personnel Office.

They were not a distinguished group. Put in charge of programs involving thousands of employees and millions of dollars, affecting the health of every American and the conduct of virtually every industry in America, they were for the most part undistinguished advocates for the industries EPA regulated. Not one was from the long lists of qualified candidates prepared by the Transition Team. "Not a single one had any substance," says one top civil servant. "What struck all of us was that none of us had ever heard of them. They had no managerial experience, no regulatory experience, little Washington experience, and no knowledge of the statutes they were supposed to carry out."

In addition to Nolan Clark, who was forced out in the fall of 1981, the list included:

Robert Perry, a bland-looking, bespectacled 47-year-old lawyer who was General Counsel and later Associate Administrator for Legal and Enforcement Counsel, as well. He had been an army lawyer and remained an officer in the Reserves. He had also been a Justice Department attorney and, for a number of years, a trial counsel for Exxon. Perry proved a superb bureaucratic infighter and many EPA lawyers viewed him as a "bully," and called him "Colonel Bob" behind his back. He had his top assistants keep notebooks with derogatory information about members of his staff. When something went wrong, he could be irrational—he once demoted a supervising attorney because she had not been able, despite repeated efforts, to reach him to tell him about a recent judicial decision before the White House called to ask about it.

Perry was particularly reluctant to give "bad news" to Gorsuch and often failed to warn of the possible consequences of her actions. "My strongest recollection of Perry," says one of Gorsuch's assistants, "is of him in a staff meeting sitting with his hands clasped in his lap, rocking back and forth and saying 'it's all right, Anne, we'll handle it.' "

Rita Lavelle was Assistant Administrator for Solid Waste and Emergency Response. She became a figure of considerable notoriety after she was fired by President Reagan. The circumstances of her demise set off a month of intensive media coverage of the problems at EPA that ultimately led to Gorsuch's own resignation.

Lavelle had been a public relations flack for Cordova Chemical, a subsidiary of Aerojet General, a California company with a record of environmental violations and serious hazardous waste problems. While there, she had, she said, "developed and implemented a major community relations campaign to counter environmental pollution charges brought against the corporation." Lavelle knew White House counselor Edwin Meese from earlier work as a low-level press aide to Governor Ronald Reagan of California. She claimed that she was offered the EPA job when she complained to her friends at the White House about how the hazardous waste program was being run. Meese held the Bible at her swearing-in ceremony.

Gorsuch, after interviewing Lavelle, urged the White House to find a different job for her, but was overruled. Gorsuch and her close advisers treated Lavelle with disdain. John Todhunter, Assistant Administrator for Toxics, says he would never have discussed the issues involved in assessing the health risk caused by exposure to toxic chemicals with Lavelle. "Rita was not a person who had the background to get into that issue in my opinion." But, of course, the assessment and elimination of such risks was exactly what her job entailed.

Her staff viewed her with a combination of horror, pity, and contempt. She was not vicious or mean, but inept, not even aware of how little she knew. Notes written on a sheet with the printed inscription "I'd rather be playing tennis," defined her objectives at EPA as "1. Change perception (local and national) of Love Canal from dangerous to benign. 2. Obtain credible data that (1)50 of nation's most dangerous hazardous waste sites have been rendered benign. 3. Provide credible proof that industries operating today are not dangerous to the public health." It sounded as if she were still doing public relations for industry instead of running the EPA hazardous waste program.

Gary Dietrich, an engineer with 23 years of government service, was the top civil servant in Lavelle's office. He describes accompanying her to testify before Congress as "the most embarrassing thing I ever had to do in the federal government." He adds that she often got herself in trouble because she knew little about the field and "didn't take the time to understand the complexities. She had a proclivity to make very poorly thought out statements." Eric Eidsness, Assistant Administrator for Water, says, "She was fundamentally out of touch with reality. Her reality was changing every day."

Since leaving EPA, she has been convicted of perjury.

Dr. John Todhunter was a 31-year-old assistant professor of biology at Catholic University who was appointed Assistant Administrator for Pesticides and Toxic Substances. He had been a science adviser to the American Council on Science and Health, an industry-funded "public interest" research group primarily known for its pro-industry positions. Of the Council's 111 donors, all but 27 have a direct or indirect interest in the subjects the Council writes about. The point of view expressed by the Council's papers is generally consistent with the interests of its supporters, concluding, for example, that health hazards from pesticides (such as 2, 4, 5-T) or food additives (caffeine) or diet (fats, sugar) are overblown. Todhunter had actively supported Reagan and, with the backing of the head of the American Council on Science and Health and North Carolina Congressman James Martin, he served on the transition team for the Consumer Product Safety Commission and became a leading candidate for a variety of senior posts at EPA.

Although Todhunter had neither administrative nor regulatory experience, he was placed in charge of an office with a staff of more than a thousand people with extensive regulatory responsibilities under two major statutes. He says he prepared himself by reading the statutes. "And one thing I'm pretty good at is structural analysis of the statutes on things that pertain to chemical safety. . . . So I had a pretty good conception of how the system was supposed to work. . . ." All that remained, he said, was to "clear up the differences" between how it was supposed to work and how it did work. "It wasn't that difficult."

He is an intelligent man but somber, reclusive, and rather secretive by nature. He kept most of his staff at a distance. One of Gorsuch's special assistants says Todhunter "ran that program like the Mafia"; his staff "felt cowed" by him. He was deeply critical of the way EPA and the nation had dealt with the risks associated with chemical production and use, and he set out to impose on the Agency what he considered a better set of scientific premises.

Frederick A. Eidsness, Jr., is the son of a successful engineering consultant who contributed heavily to Republican candidates. An engineer himself, Eidsness (who, according to his staff, took to using the name Eric because he disliked being called Freddie Junior) had held a variety of consulting jobs, including a brief but unsuccessful stint with the federal government, but he had neither management nor Washington experience. He was deeply influenced by his work for two local governments in Colorado, and was suspicious of federal authority in the water area.

Kathleen Bennett is a thoughtful and rather gentle person who became Assistant Administrator for Air, Noise, and Radiation, a job in which she was, a colleague says, "terribly out of her depth." She had been a lobbyist for Crown Zellerbach and the American Paper Institute, but seemed ill-equipped to handle the high-pressure politics involved in representing the Administration in the Clean Air Act debate. Several congressional staffers finally urged her just to stay away. Bennett was and is deeply loyal to Anne Gorsuch, but she also feared her. Gorsuch, according to the staff, "treated Bennett like shit." Partly as a result, Bennett agonized over major decisions, and her office fell far behind in issuing required air pollution control regulations.

Gorsuch had not chosen her senior staff, and there was no one among them who seemed able to challenge the assumptions on which her administration foundered. Few of them understood the complexities or the potent politics of the regulatory process, or saw the necessity for even this Administration to build broad coalitions. Joe Cannon, who learned quickly and saw the dangers of Gorsuch's stubborn, ideological view of the world but still regards her as an admirable and intelligent person, concedes sadly that he never really confronted her. "She's not a person who likes to have things suggested to her." John Daniel, who must have understood, for he did have long Washington experience, seemed to "feel compelled to out-Sanderson Sanderson" and often encouraged Gorsuch toward pugnacity and defiance.

From the start, they fought among themselves. Career civil servants said they had never seen infighting to compare with that around Gorsuch. The staff was frightened and dejected, and the Agency did not work.

"EVERY CASE YOU REFER TO HEADQUARTERS WILL BE A BLACK MARK AGAINST YOU"

In early May 1981, just before Anne Gorsuch was confirmed, she attended a reception organized by the Washington Environmental Law Group for her and John Hernandez. The group includes government lawyers who work on environmental issues, private lawyers who represent industry on environmental questions, and a smattering of lawyers from environmental organizations. Mrs. Gorsuch had been scheduled to speak at the reception, but instead she and Hernandez just circulated and shook hands.

Ed Kurent, then an enforcement attorney at EPA, met Gorsuch that evening. He was talking to a lawyer from a large firm who was describing a case he was working on. Mrs. Gorsuch came over and introduced herself. "I said I was Ed Kurent and I worked in water enforcement at EPA. She just kind of went cold. There was a painful silence." The other attorney mentioned that he and Kurent had been discussing an interesting enforcement case he was handling, and began to describe the issues. "She took a step back. She looked at me with this icy stare and said, 'I'm going to eliminate both your jobs.' Then she just turned and walked away."

Three weeks after she took office, Mrs. Gorsuch announced a reorganization that eliminated the EPA enforcement office. The 2,100 lawyers, technicians, and support staff who had enforced the air, water, hazardous waste, pesticide, and toxic chemicals laws were transferred into the program offices that dealt with those statutes. Only a skeleton staff was left with Enforcement Counsel William Sullivan, a stout, agreeable man with a red face and graying hair whose previous experience had been in private practice, often representing steel companies.

The reorganization plan was designed by Seth Hunt, the low-level Denver personnel officer whom Sanderson had brought to Washington. It was planned in such haste and isolation that the actual personnel actions required months and created chaos. Long-dead staff members were transferred, and living staff members were left without offices or positions. The plan reflected Gorsuch and Sanderson's strong belief that EPA enforcement had been overzealous. In the past, they felt, there had been too little effort to cajole violators into voluntary compliance. The new approach, said Gorsuch, was "a marked contrast to the 'rush to litigation' regulatory strategy employed by the previous Administration."

According to Hunt, one of the Agency's major problems had been that it was "full of attorneys. Way more than we needed." The enforcement attorneys in particular, says Hunt, were "just hanging round waiting for something to do." It was, he argues, essential to put the enforcement attorneys under the control of the program officials who dealt regularly with industry. "[I]t's like if you're in an auto accident, you're the person who should decide if you're going to sue someone or not. You'll ask your attorneys for advice, but you don't want to be doing something and then find out all of a sudden that your attorney has filed suit on your behalf, unbeknownst to you."

The attorneys, he complains, were so oriented to enforcement that they wrote "legal kinds of permits" so strict that if "you violate any parts of this, man, we've gotcha. . . ." That, Hunt contends, reflected the wrong "mind-set" because, "Hey, what are we after?"

If the objective was a clean environment, reasoned Gorsuch, Hunt, and Sanderson, there was no reason to punish a company that violated the law if it ultimately corrected the violation. On one occasion, Chief of Staff John Daniel supported a staff recommendation that EPA seek legislation making particularly serious water pollution violations a felony. "You're just not with me today, John," she chided him angrily. "You're sounding like someone else. When are you going to understand environmental violations are not felonies; they are misdemeanors at most. I have been a DA."

The irony was that EPA's enforcement record was, in fact, mediocre. Michael Brown, William Sullivan's successor as Enforcement Counsel, says, "EPA has never been especially enforcement-minded. It has always wanted to be a nice guy and somehow stay friends with the regulated industry." But the Agency cannot be effective that way. "I was at [the Department of] Commerce, and in private practice, and I know corporations are run by normal decent human beings, but as institutions they follow simple rules of self-interest. They won't, they can't comply because it is 'nice.' They respond to pressure."

Shortly after the reorganization, Enforcement Counsel Sullivan told the administrators of EPA's ten regional offices that they should not send any case to headquarters to be reviewed for possible action until they had explored "every opportunity for settlement." "Every case you do refer," he added, will "be a black mark against you." The effect was immediate. Enforcement actions plummeted. Three hundred thirteen cases had been referred by the regions in 1980. The number fell to 59 in 1981.

Several incidents during the ensuing months confirmed the staff's belief that the "12th floor" did not want aggressive enforcement. On July 10, 1981, a fire and explosion destroyed the General Disposal Company's hazardous waste dump in Santa Fe Springs, California. Debris showered a nearby residential area, and contaminated water ran through the neighborhood and onto a beach. The spill killed fish and the beach was closed.

Santa Fe Springs became the first test of the "Superfund" law passed seven months earlier. EPA began an emergency cleanup. Then in August the bulldozers, trucks, and mechanized shovels were ordered to stop. Attorneys for one of the responsible parties, Inmont Corporation, had initiated negotiations with EPA. While EPA had authority to pay for the cleanup from the specially created "Superfund" and then to sue the responsible parties to recover the cleanup costs, Gorsuch wanted to hold expenditures from the fund to a minimum.

Inmont was willing to complete the cleanup "voluntarily" if EPA would free the company from further liability. Doug MacMillan, the Director of Hazardous Waste Enforcement, and two other EPA lawyers were negotiating with the Inmont lawyers over the extent of the required cleanup and the amount Inmont would spend to complete the job. Although Inmont had initially been flexible, suddenly the negotiations bogged down. MacMillan was perplexed. He could not figure out what had caused the change in attitude, and he knew it was important to resolve the issue quickly. Not only was the idle construction equipment on the site costing EPA $10,000 per day, there was a danger of further explosions and harm to people living nearby. Some local residents were so infuriated by the delay that they had fired rockets onto the site in an attempt to reignite it and speed the cleanup.

MacMillan called Sullivan to explain his problem. He then learned that he was not the only representative of EPA negotiating with Inmont. Thornton ("Whit") Field, the Special Assistant to the Administrator for

Hazardous Waste, had also spoken with the Inmont attorney on a number of occasions. In fact, it later turned out that Field spoke to the Inmont attorney fifteen times discussing the merits of the EPA case and disclosing the "bottom line" figure EPA attorneys had decided they could accept.

Field was a young attorney who had come to Mrs. Gorsuch from the Adolph Coors Company. He had been a nonelected member of the Interim Hazardous Waste Committee of the Colorado legislature which Mrs. Gorsuch had chaired. The EPA negotiators were outraged by his conduct, but there was little they could do. A few weeks later, they settled the case with Inmont—at their "bottom line" figure. The settlement, concluded over the objections of the Justice Department, gave Inmont a blanket exemption from future federal action related to the dump and committed the government to testify on behalf of Inmont in any suit filed by local residents for damages caused by the explosion and fire. Both the chief of environmental enforcement at the Justice Department and the General Counsel of the Commerce Department wrote to Sullivan to ask that EPA never again agree to such terms.

The problem in the Inmont case was that neither Sullivan nor Field trusted the EPA attorneys. Both had represented industry and felt that they could resolve problems quickly by dealing with the companies that were targets of EPA enforcement. They were, in fact, inclined to believe what the companies told them, either without checking with the EPA staff, or despite what the staff said. Sullivan says it was partly an institutional problem. "I negotiated around people because there was no central file I had access to with up-to-date case information. It was inevitable I would get a misimpression from time to time." Nevertheless, he acknowledges that he made mistakes and "got burned" on several occasions.

Lack of information was not the issue in the settlement negotiations over a suit in which environmental groups on one side and industry on the other challenged EPA's hazardous waste permitting regulations. Industry badly wanted lifetime permits for hazardous waste facilities instead of the ten-year permits proposed by EPA. The legal and technical staffs at EPA resisted the industry proposal because lifetime permits would essentially foreclose the possibility of tightening permit conditions in response to new information about health hazards or improved technology to control those hazards. Industry also sought a provision that would allow existing waste dumps to expand by 50 percent without meeting the more stringent rules applicable to new facilities. This, the staff argued, would create a giant loophole in the regulations.

Whit Field rejected the staff's arguments—a decision he, or at least Anne Gorsuch, in whose name he was acting, was entitled to make. Then he and Associate Administrator Frank Shepherd negotiated an agreement with the industry attorneys. They did so in a meeting from which they barred Nancy Long, the Justice Department lawyer, and Lisa Friedman, the EPA lawyer, who were attorneys "of record" (formally representing EPA before the U.S. Court of Appeals) in the case.

Khristine Hall, representing the environmental groups, refused to participate. "To hold such a meeting as this with attorneys of record excluded . . . seems to me to be in conflict with the code of ethics." Nancy Long was stunned. She resigned from the case, and, when her new boss Assistant Attorney General Carol Dinkins would not back her up, she left the Justice Department.

The June 1981 reorganization left EPA's legal affairs under the management of three men: William Sullivan, Robert Perry, and Frank Shepherd. A fresh-faced and handsome young attorney from Florida, Shepherd was in charge. He is a lifelong conservative activist. He identifies himself with the "high-minded *National Review*" strain of conservatism.* Shepherd had experience neither in Washington nor in the ramiform politics of large bureaucracies. He soon found himself buffeted by internecine quarrels. General Counsel Robert Perry and Enforcement Counsel Sullivan saw Shepherd as a naive upstart. They resented everything from the fact that his office was the largest and had a private bathroom to the warm relations he quickly developed with the staff.

The squabbling exacerbated the difficulties created by the reorganization. Sullivan, who had been left with ambiguous authority and little staff, argued strenuously for more of both. Perry, with long bureaucratic experience in both the military and Exxon, worked just as assiduously to expand his own authority. Shepherd was dismayed. "It appeared to me that there was too much infighting among the appointees. The Reagan Administration was elected to carry out a proper and positive change in government. Where I stood it looked as if people lost sight of that. When I made decisions I tried to think how the people out in Florida or in Michigan who voted for the President would want that

---

The National Review is the conservative magazine edited by William F. Buckley, Jr.

decision making to occur. What would my father or friends want? They deserve something better than infighting.

"I knew administrations are brief. We had a Constitutional duty to faithfully execute the law. The best we could do would be to leave behind a positive sense of decision making—a conservative approach to implementation of the laws."

Within weeks, Shepherd resigned. His uneasiness in his position became intense when he was stripped of his authority over a case because of his failure to take a position he thought wrong and unreasonable. In 1976 EPA had entered into a "consent decree" (a formal agreement approved by the court) with the Natural Resources Defense Council and the National Coal Association. The agreement settled a suit filed by NRDC that sought to compel EPA to regulate certain toxic pollutants under the Clean Water Act. EPA agreed to issue regulations controlling discharges of 65 categories of toxic pollutants. In 1979, EPA got an extension of the deadlines set in the agreement.

By 1981 EPA was nearly ready to issue the rules but was behind the court-ordered schedule. Industry had petitioned the Task Force on Regulatory Relief to get EPA to move to vacate the decree or at least to seek to have the decree modified to remove or weaken three major provisions. Gorsuch wanted the decree vacated. She detested the limitation on her discretion as Administrator and was particularly galled by the possibility that the environmentalists might at any time ask the court to hold her in contempt for failing to meet the deadlines. Shepherd tried to dissuade her, arguing that there was no legal basis to vacate the decree. It would be a mistake, he told her, to argue an unreasonable position to the court. "I felt we should make a credible and responsible argument to the court."

Shepherd thought he had convinced Gorsuch, and at the end of July 1981 EPA filed a motion seeking only to modify the consent decree. But he was mistaken. "After the motion was filed, she blew up because I did not seek to vacate the decree. I tried to explain the difficulties of abrogating something that has been agreed upon, but she was adamant." She transferred authority over the case to Sullivan, and Shepherd went back to Florida.

He remains distraught at what he sees as a fumbled opportunity for conservative reform. "The whole thing was a big mystery to me. It didn't work the way I thought the world works. I sometimes wondered, 'Is this the real world or some aberration?' I hope that's not the real Washington."

After Shepherd left, fighting between Sullivan and Perry intensified. A new reorganization in October 1981 required top lawyers in each regional office to report to Perry rather than Sullivan or to the now vacant office of the Associate Administrator. A few months later, however, Sullivan won the right to retrieve many of the attorneys transferred away from him in the June reorganization. This change, far from encouraging the beleaguered enforcement lawyers, panicked them. They were aware that the new budget prepared by Gorsuch did not allocate additional resources to Sullivan for lawyers or support staff. They saw the new reorganization as a step up onto the gibbet.

Their fears worsened when many were interviewed by Peter Paul Broccoletti, Sullivan's deputy, a lawyer who had worked for the Nixon campaign in 1972 and had recently been a "strength consultant" to the Denver Broncos football team. Broccoletti, who identified "his people" by having them wear American flag lapel pins, asked the returning lawyers questions that immediately put them on guard, including what outside organizations they belonged to. "If you said in the interview that you were a member of the National Audubon Society, receive the Sierra Club's magazine, and give money to NRDC, you'd be stamped as the kind of person they don't want around," said one lawyer.

"The enforcement program just descended into chaos," says Tom Gallagher, the long-time chief of the National Enforcement Investigations Center, EPA's crack investigative arm. "The reorganization was all structure. Anne, Hunt, and Sanderson just didn't think about substance and function. The program offices didn't know what the hell to do with lawyers. The lawyers couldn't work without technical support, and no one knew who had responsibility to develop strategy, work up cases, or approve anything. It was 'man the lifeboats, every man for himself.'"

As the stories about what was happening began to leak out of EPA and enforcement figures continued to drop, public and congressional criticism increased. Sullivan, realizing he had to produce something that looked like enforcement, proposed to the Administrator that EPA launch an all-out cleanup effort in the Niagara River Basin, an area that included not only Love Canal but more than 100 other hazardous waste sites. Surface waters in the area were contaminated by toxic discharges from fifteen major industrial plants and industrial waste-water discharge by the city of Niagara Falls. Gorsuch had been invited to appear on the CBS-TV show "60 Minutes" to discuss the area's problems.

Sullivan proposed coordinated action with the State of New York and the Canadians. Permitting efforts would be accelerated. EPA would push the City of Niagara Falls to quickly complete a sewage treatment plant and EPA would initiate a series of high-priority targeted enforcement actions. Gorsuch, according to Sullivan, liked the idea of announcing what he called "an agenda of coordinated short-term actions," but told him, he says, "Sullivan, you're getting too enforcement-minded." Without enforcement, the idea became moribund.

At the end of March 1982, Perry, who had assiduously courted Mrs. Gorsuch's favor, convinced her that someone had to take charge of the enforcement mess. On Friday, March 26, she appointed him to fill the Associate Administrator slot vacated by Shepherd six months earlier. The following Monday, Perry stripped Sullivan of all authority, and a week later, vanquished in the fratricidal savagery, Sullivan resigned.

While EPA spokesmen stolidly insisted that criticism of their enforcement record was irrelevant "bean counting," and Gorsuch said that EPA would no longer evaluate enforcement "merely by counting cases," Perry sent off telegrams to the Regional Administrators threatening to cut their legal staffs still further if they failed to meet case quotas he now had set. In light of what had taken place during the preceding months, the Regional Administrators found it hard to take what they contemptuously called "the Perrygrams" seriously.

Late in April 1982, Gorsuch called the ten Regional Administrators to Washington. She asked Mike Brown, the new Enforcement Counsel hired by Perry, to write a speech for her demanding more enforcement from the regional offices. That was unusual, but even more unusual was her decision to release the speech in advance to the press. Although she did not read the text, she did berate them. "It was a hot day and the air conditioning wasn't on yet," recalls Brown. "She said, 'If you think it's hot now, wait until you see what happens if I don't see some action.' " She stared coldly around the room, catching each official's eye. "It was very tense."

Then Perry jumped in, telling the Regional Administrators the problems with enforcement were all their fault. "Several of them," says Brown, "said, 'Oh yes, Anne, we know, we've always understood you wanted strong enforcement,' but when I checked they had referred almost nothing."

Valdus Adamkus, the Region V Administrator, whose office had by far the best enforcement record, was bewildered. He knew what Sullivan had said to him about "black marks." He remembered that when he had called John Daniel to try to save Sandra Gardebring, his top enforcement attorney who was on the "hit list," Daniel had said she had to go. "He told me she stepped on too many toes." Adamkus could not contain himself. A large, warm, voluble man, Adamkus grew up in Lithuania and came to the U.S. after spending much of the Second World War as a refugee. He worked his way through college and engineering school, and gained some local fame delivering Lithuanian votes for Republicans in the overwhelmingly Democratic city of Chicago. He speaks with the thick accents of Eastern Europe but with the eloquence of emotion and sincerity.

"I said, 'I would like to clear the air. I was told to negotiate until I was blue in the face and it would be a black mark against me if I referred a case. Now I hear that is not so. What do you really want?' At this point, I was brutally interrupted by Sanderson. He said, 'What the Administrator told you is very clear.' Sanderson said that to speak as I did could only be said by someone who does not understand English. I was so hurt."

The room fell absolutely silent. No one knew what to say. Finally, they broke up for coffee. "One person after another," says Adamkus, "came to me to apologize for what Sanderson had said, and to say I was right to speak as I did. Later Sanderson came to me and he smiled and told me he had not meant what he said, but he had to say it because there were too many career staff in the room and my remark might leak out."

Brown thinks Gorsuch did mean what she said. "She had learned she had to have enforcement, but she could not admit she had made a mistake, so she had to revise history; she had to say, 'I never told you not to enforce.'" Most were not convinced, and another reorganization a few days later did nothing to help. EPA's enforcement machinery was crippled. Dispirited and cynical, the attorneys had neither the resources nor a clear mandate to enforce the law. "There was," Sullivan now admits, "no direction, no positive program. Anne never did set any substantive goal. She was like a drama critic who sat down to write a play. She only knew what she didn't like."

"I HAVE BEEN ATTACKED OVER THE LAST SEVERAL WEEKS BY EVERY MAJOR NEWSPAPER AND MOST MAJOR MAGAZINES"

Cutting the federal budget for everything but defense was President Reagan's first priority. By the time Anne Gorsuch arrived at EPA, the initial budget confrontations in the Congress were nearly over. EPA was cut 12 percent. But Gorsuch was as deeply committed to reducing what she saw as waste at EPA as she was to any other single goal. She achieved considerable success in that effort, but she paid a high price for her success. The cuts contributed to the swift and increasingly visible disintegration of EPA. They helped to create a public image of Gorsuch as a cold and ruthless butcher savaging a popular program, and, ironically, the internal battle over the cuts left those in the Administration who wanted even deeper cuts bitterly angry at her. It was not what she had expected.

The President had said he believed it was "time to check and reverse the growth of government." He had made it clear that he thought that much that EPA did was unnecessary and excessive. During the campaign he had accused EPA of going beyond environmental protection. "What they believe in is a return to a society in which there wouldn't be the need for industrial concerns. . . ." Gorsuch shared that view and wanted to prove, says her friend Freda Poundstone, "that she could really accomplish something without breaking the taxpayer." She believed enormous savings could be achieved through simple improvements in management. "With each passing day, I find that to say that the agency has been mismanaged in the past is charitable. It has not been managed at all."

During the summer of 1981, she began to work on the budget for 1983. While previous Administrators had dealt only with broad policy questions presented by the budget, Gorsuch examined every detail. She sat through day after day of budget hearings during which program managers described their plans and resource needs. She questioned every aspect of the Agency's program and personally decided the fate of each subcomponent of the budget. She worked with the Agency's comptroller, Morgan Kinghorn, a conservative, serious, taut, and very bright young technician who had come to EPA from OMB a few years before. Kinghorn told her that OMB's opinion of EPA was not high and that they expected her to make cuts of 20 percent in the Agency's operating budget. She set out to meet that goal.

The EPA operating budget had been $1,355 million when Reagan took office. That paid for 14,500 scientists, lawyers, technicians, inspectors, administrators, and support staff. She proposed to cut the budget to $975 million. Those who worked on the budget with her say she "really believed she could make the cuts without harm. At that time, she didn't know much about the Agency and if you challenged her too hard she wrote you off, she'd never deal with you again. So it was a very, very expensive learning process." There was another problem, says a senior budget official: "She didn't understand the budget gaming that went on within the Administration. She thought OMB would just congratulate her for carrying out the President's program."

In mid-September 1981, Morgan Kinghorn, John Hernandez, Jim Sanderson, and Joe Cannon took the proposed budget to OMB. After a short time, Kinghorn was called out of the meeting by OMB officials and given a new set of ceilings for EPA spending. They required additional cuts half again as big as the first. Staggered by the magnitude of the OMB demands, Kinghorn did not bother to return to the meeting; he went straight back to EPA to brief Gorsuch. Meanwhile, according to Cannon, the others walked out of OMB "feeling like we were on another planet." They were aghast at OMB's attitude toward the Agency. They recommended, and Gorsuch agreed, to give OMB the revised budget figures it demanded but to treat the process as a crazy OMB "fire drill," not a serious budget exercise.

The Gorsuch proposal was leaked to the press and Congress shortly before it went to OMB. The leaked budget caused a small but increasing furor, much of it generated by a former EPA official, William Drayton. Under the previous Administration, Drayton had been EPA Assistant Administrator for Policy and Resource Management and had been in charge of the budget process.

A small, intense, ascetic man, Drayton physically resembles one of his heroes, Mahatma Gandhi. He had studied economics at Oxford and law at Yale and then spent five years at a distinguished New York management consulting firm. While at EPA, he had eagerly sought to foster the kind of decentralized participatory management at EPA that had "made companies like 3M and Hewlett-Packard such vital and successful institutions." He often infuriated other EPA officials both by his introduction of what they saw as cumbersome procedures and his insistence on lengthy technical analyses of the costs of proposed regulations. "The closest we ever came to a scandal while Doug Costle was

Administrator," says one former senior official, "was when several of us almost threw Bill Drayton out the 12th floor window."

Drayton is a stubborn man, and a compulsive collector of information—all kinds of information: numbers, anecdotes, proposals, and gossip. Once set on an idea, he pursues it with obdurate energy. The proposed EPA budget and the stories he heard from senior bureaucrats who quietly contacted him set off every alarm in his being. The whole management process he had built and all the careful workload analyses and resource plans he had crafted were being wrecked. No one outside the Agency seemed to understand how drastic the damage was. Drayton felt compelled to try to stop it.

He became an effective and infuriating gadfly to Mrs. Gorsuch in the fall of 1981. He knew and understood the details of her budget and could talk at length about its consequences. And that is exactly what he did. He talked to environmental leaders, he talked to congressmen, he talked to local activists, he talked to garden clubs—to anyone who would listen and most especially to the press. He told them the proposed budget was a "disaster," a "bomb in the basement," part of a "plan to gut the Agency." He organized a committee of former EPA officials and used them to collect and analyze new information, and then he started his calls all over again.

While Gorsuch insisted "[t]here are numerous ways that EPA can do a better job with fewer resources," more and more people outside the Agency doubted it. Her budget proposal represented a 28 percent cut from 1981. The workforce was to be cut 30 percent, research by 40 percent. Drayton pointed out that in staff and "purchasing power" (considering the impact of inflation) the proposed budget would put EPA back where it was in 1973, before the passage of the hazardous waste law, Toxic Substances Control Act, Safe Drinking Water Act, and Superfund.

Called to testify before one congressional committee after another, Gorsuch stonily refused to discuss or even acknowledge the leaked budget document, but she was adamant in her insistence that the President's program was to shrink government and EPA should and would be cut. It was time, she said, "to move away from regulation for the sake of regulation—to put aside confrontation for the sake of confrontation." She rejected the practices of her predecessors who had measured environmental progress "in terms of how much money was spent, how many scientists and administrators were hired, and how many regulations were issued. Very little thought seems to have been given to whether money was spent wisely or effectively. . . ."

On Friday the 13th of November 1981, EPA received its OMB "passback," OMB's formal counterproposal to Gorsuch's budget. They demanded cuts nearly twice as deep as those proposed by Gorsuch. The cuts would reduce EPA to a little more than half the size it had been in January 1981. David Stockman had personally approved them. They reflected the view, expressed in one OMB briefing package, that "fewer regulators will necessarily result in fewer regulations and less harassment of the regulated."

Gorsuch was furious. She had personally wielded the scalpel in making deep cuts at the Agency. She had brought EPA in line with the President's program. And now OMB was suggesting she had not done enough. Her staff urged her to appeal the OMB cuts. She agreed. They worked all weekend on a lengthy and strongly worded letter.

She wrote that she was "deeply committed to meeting the President's environmental and fiscal objectives" and believed she had done so. The OMB cuts, she wrote, threw "in disarray a number of major redirections I have proposed. . . ." The passback, she continued, "smacks of a bottom line in search of a reason." She warned of the political consequences of OMB's proposal. "The unfortunate leaks of my September 15 submission indicate the kind of uproar that will accompany additional reductions of the magnitude that your staff suggests. My political and career staff, as well as I, have been attacked over the last several weeks by every major newspaper and most major magazines." The OMB proposal would shift to the President criticism coming "in many cases from the heart of the President's own constituency."

It was a remarkable letter, echoing much of what critics had said to her, and arguing for deference to political opposition that in almost all other instances she treated with outward contempt. Her usual response to opposition was belligerent defiance. Now, that was what she offered OMB. Her letter concluded with a threat to appeal to the President.

On November 19 she was scheduled to meet with David Stockman. That morning the letter was on the front page of the *New York Times*. Sanderson and Daniel, apparently without her authorization, had leaked it. Press aide Byron Nelson personally prepared and mailed or delivered the leaks, and the resulting stories made it clear the leak was "official." Stockman had not yet received the letter. He read about it in the paper as his limousine brought him to work. Gorsuch was stunned by her staff's ploy. "I have," she said later, "been screwed by those who love me."

The meeting with Stockman did not go well. He thought she had made a commitment to accept his cuts when he interviewed her. He told her she was a political appointee and it was her job to take the heat for the President's programs, as he had been doing for months. Nothing was resolved, but the discussions revealed OMB's deep antagonism toward EPA and the belief of Stockman and his staff that long-term control of EPA regulations required much deeper cuts. They were especially hostile to EPA research, which, they believed, would only fuel demands for more regulation in the future.

On Monday, December 7, they took the dispute to the White House Budget Review Board, presided over by Presidential Counselor Edwin Meese and Chief of Staff James Baker. Gorsuch had her staff prepare briefing books for each member of the Board. She explained her budget and argued that EPA had offered cuts as deep as those at any agency. Stockman, however, would not budge. He was by then aware that the recession and the President's tax cuts were going to cause huge federal deficits, far larger than he had predicted. Those deficits, he argued, required that every agency accept deeper cuts.

Baker, according to senior EPA officials, was concerned about the political ramifications, while Meese, leafing through his briefing book, wondered what all the fuss was about. Like Stockman, says John Hernandez, Baker and Meese viewed the EPA from "a general interest in regulatory reform, and they viewed budgetary reform as one of the ways you did it."

Only one minor issue was resolved. Emerging from the meeting, Gorsuch exploded in frustration, telling her staff, "OMB just doesn't play fair." Stockman wouldn't compromise on anything. Stockman, too, say several officials who were involved, was bitter. He felt more and more strongly that Gorsuch had broken her blood oath.

Three days later, Gorsuch took her appeal to the President. For three hours in the Cabinet room, she and John Hernandez argued their case to the President and the senior White House staff. Hernandez was exhilarated. "It was surprising to me, the reception by the President was so warm and so easygoing that I had no problem talking, being fluent, debating Stockman and Murray Weidenbaum and these other guys." On each issue, the President said only, "We'll certainly take each of these under consideration; we'll consult with the Vice-President and we'll make a decision on it." A short time later, the President called to tell Gorsuch she had won, but to ask that she find some additional research cuts if possible.

The final cuts left EPA 29 percent below 1981 in total budget, 30 percent in staff, and 42 percent in research. While the battle temporarily improved her credibility with Congress, it left both Stockman and the White House staff suspicious of her ability to control the Agency and concerned at what they perceived as political ineptitude. The controversy was not over.

The drastic budget cuts that Gorsuch proposed, even though less than OMB eventually sought, meant huge cuts in the EPA staff. Late in the summer of 1981, Gorsuch asked John Horton, the Assistant Administrator for Administration, to begin planning the firing process, called, in government lingo, a Reduction in Force or "RIF." Horton was a New Jersey businessman allied politically with Labor Secretary Raymond Donovan. He viewed the Agency, says a senior official, as if it were a shoe factory—all that mattered was the bottom line. A member of his staff says, "He had absolute tunnel vision. All he saw were dollars. He simply didn't care about the consequences of the cuts." A shrewd man, Horton nevertheless wanted to prove he was a tough, effective Reaganite, and he took on the task of planning the RIFs with enthusiasm.

The EPA budget for 1982 had already been cut and cut again. Nevertheless, enough employees were quitting in 1981 that not many would have to be fired in 1982 to stay within the budget. Horton was not content to wait and see whether the 1983 budget (just submitted by Gorsuch to OMB) required RIFs. He planned to bring the EPA staff down to the proposed 1983 levels in 1982. That, after all, would save a great deal of money, reduce the administrative burden of the RIFs, and get the politically painful operation over with in one quick action.

His staff and representatives of the program offices met weekly to plan the mechanics of the RIFs. Every second or third meeting, Cliff Miller, the Administrator's personnel specialist and the keeper of the color-coded hit list, showed up. The numbers they worked with were chilling. Forty percent of the headquarters staff was to be fired, and most of the remainder would be demoted or transferred as a consequence of the firings.

"He wanted fewer people and less dollars," says a member of the planning group. "What that would do to the programs was not something he thought about." In September, when OMB demanded additional cuts, Horton embraced those numbers and planned bigger RIFs. He believed, this staff member asserts, "that if he RIFfed 10 percent more than necessary he'd get credit for the savings and then they could hire less extreme people."

By early November 1981, two new factors complicated Horton's planning. First, at EPA and even at OMB, questions had been raised about the legality of firing employees supposedly protected by the civil service laws to meet the requirements of a budget not yet even submitted to, let alone approved by, Congress. The second factor complicating the process was attrition among the EPA staff. Disgusted by policy changes, frightened by rumors of mass firings, and frustrated by mismanagement, hundreds of employees were quitting each month.* As a consequence, the need for mass firings began to disappear.

Horton was not deterred. Supported by Cliff Miller and, at least initially, by John Daniel, he focused on nascent plans to reorganize virtually every part of the Agency. Horton told Gorsuch in a memo:

We may wish to state that the workforce adjustment is a result of reorganization rather than budget cuts. As you know, we have to state the legal reason for a RIF. The reasons available to us are budget reductions, lack of work or reorganization. It was felt that, if we should undertake a RIF in the January or February timeframe, we might be in a difficult position to justify a RIF based on congressionally unapproved FY 83 figures.

There is, of course, some liability in using reorganization as a RIF basis in that the responsibility for the reorganization is yours. While if we used budget cuts as a reason for RIF's the responsibility lies elsewhere.

The reorganization would provide the administrative vehicle for elimination of large numbers of staff and would, at the same time, centralize power in the hands of the political appointees. Warned by his staff that the plan would leak to the press and cause enormous repercussions, Horton responded that that was "too bad." Cuts, he said, were "what the taxpayers voted for."

---

*Mrs. Gorsuch frequently disputed charges of high attrition, but figures supplied by EPA to the House Appropriations Committee in 1982 showed that 4,129 employees left during fiscal year 1981 and 236 were RIFfed—together, almost a third of the staff. The actual staff decline was less (1,859 between January and September 1981) because some employees were replaced.

The plan did leak, and on January 3, 1982, a story in the *New York Times* reported cuts in the headquarters staff from an already shrunken 4,700 to "about 3,500 and perhaps as low as 2,500" during 1982. Horton was quoted confirming the reorganization plan and commenting, "I come from business and my initial impression when I got here was that this agency is fat. . . . It offends my sense of efficiency as a businessman. We just don't need all the people who are here."

Joe Cannon read the story and called Morgan Kinghorn to find out what was going on. They agreed the plan was politically, administratively, and morally wrong. Cannon says, "I said it was illegal and I had only the purest ideals of the revolution in mind: if we reorganized and RIFfed, then we couldn't get anything done." The two of them wrote a careful memo arguing against RIFs but trying to avoid criticizing anyone on the 12th floor directly. Neither was confident of his standing with Gorsuch.

The memo argued there was no budgetary reason to fire anyone and that RIFs in connection with a reorganization would harm the Administrator politically, make it harder to defend her budget, and "hurt regulatory reform" by causing confusion and anguish within the Agency. The memo apparently never reached Gorsuch, but it persuaded John Daniel, who, with Cannon and Kinghorn's help, drafted an even stronger memo to Gorsuch. "The reorganization," he warned, "would not fundamentally improve operations," but would "have potential for massive disruption of FY 1982 and 1983 outputs at a critical time for the Administration." In addition, he wrote, "proceeding with the proposed reorganizations, with or without RIFs, will result in a firestorm of opposition."

Horton, Miller, and Sanderson continued to advocate the reorganization, but Gorsuch was hesitating. Then, on February 2, Russell Train, Administrator of EPA under Presidents Nixon and Ford, published an op-ed piece in the *Washington Post* harshly critical of Gorsuch's management of EPA. In it he wrote:

It is hard to imagine any business manager consciously undertaking such a personnel policy unless its purpose was to destroy the enterprise. Predictably, the result at EPA has been and will continue to be demoralization and institutional paralysis. Attrition within the agency is running at an extraordinary 2.7 percent per month or *32 percent a year.* . . .

As one who served two Republican administrations from 1969 to 1977 and who voted for President Reagan, I must record my profound concern over what is happening at EPA today. The budget and personnel cuts, unless reversed, will destroy the agency as an effective institution for many years to come.

It was the first time one of Gorsuch's three predecessors had spoken out. Two days later, Gorsuch issued an extraordinary open letter to the EPA staff saying, "For months now, we have been bombarded with countless press reports and rumors of massive personnel reductions planned for this agency. These ceaseless rumors have disturbed and distressed me greatly because of their significant negative effect on you, the employees of this fine agency." She promised no one would be fired in 1982 or, she hoped, in 1983.

The next day, at a press briefing on the 1983 budget, top political appointees (except Gorsuch, who stayed away) insisted the whole furor was based on erroneous rumors. A career staffer who expected to leave the Agency soon asked in a loud stage whisper, "Would you buy a used car from these people?"

The controversy added to White House doubts about Gorsuch's ability to control the Agency and deepened suspicion among the public and members of Congress that the Administration was indeed intent on destroying EPA. Staff morale was little improved by Gorsuch's letter. Few were convinced by her assurances. In fact, by the end of FY 1982, the EPA staff was down 19 percent, more than three times the average decline for other non-defense agencies of the federal government.

WHIFFS OF SCANDAL

To the White House and to many members of Congress, the fracas over the EPA budget and staff had a familiar sound—the groans of a bureaucracy being cut. Every federal program has its constituency, and when the Administration began its assault on non-defense spending the supporters of those programs protested. It was no surprise to hear environmentalists and their friends making a row about cuts at EPA. In early 1982, however, a new set of controversies arose at EPA that had nothing to do with the budget. They seemed more like old-fashioned scandals.

On December 29, 1981, President Reagan announced his intention to nominate Jim Sanderson to the number three post at EPA, Assistant

Administrator for Policy and Resource Management. Sanderson was Gorsuch's choice for the job, the first Presidential appointee at EPA whom she had chosen, and she had had to battle several members of the White House staff to get him nominated.

A week later Rep. Patricia Schroeder, a Denver Democrat, wrote and released to the press a letter calling upon the EPA Inspector General, Matthew Novick, to investigate allegations of conflict of interest against Sanderson. Her letter was based upon an anonymous but detailed letter from an EPA staffer in Denver who charged that on September 19, 1981, Sanderson had used his influence as an assistant to Gorsuch to reverse a decision he believed was detrimental to several of his Denver clients. Sanderson had béen at EPA as a consultant, rather than as a full-time member of the staff, and he maintained his law practice and continued to represent a number of clients with matters before EPA.*

When he first arrived in Washington, Sanderson met with Deputy General Counsel Mary Doyle, the ethics officer at EPA. "He came in," she says, "wearing elephant cufflinks as big as silver dollars and kind of flashed them in my face as if I might have forgotten who won the election." Sanderson asked about the restrictions imposed on him by the Ethics in Government law. She told him that until he had been employed for 60 days he was prohibited only from representing clients in actions against the United States, but that once he served more than 60 days during any period of 365 days he was prohibited from representing anyone on any matter "pending" in EPA, even if it was not a matter in which he personally played a role as an EPA official. Sanderson, Doyle says, "did not much like the restrictions," and she ended up writing two careful memoranda to make the rules absolutely clear. In one she warned, "Since *any* representation by you of outsiders before EPA would create the *appearance* of conflict of interest in view of your role as Special Assistant to the Administrator, I previously advised you that you should avoid any such representation even before the statutory 60-day period had passed."

The anonymous letter from Denver specifically alleged that Sanderson had called Steve Durham, Gorsuch's former colleague in the Colorado legislature, whom she had appointed the EPA Regional Administrator in Denver. Sanderson was alleged to have instructed Dur-

---

*His clients included Coors, the Denver Water Board, Snowmass, and Chemical Waste Management, the operators of the Lowry Landfill.

ham not to approve Colorado water quality rules that Sanderson, on behalf of several of his clients, had challenged in court. Durham's last-moment refusal to sign the letter approving the standards—a letter he had ordered his staff to write—was curiously at odds, the anonymous EPA attorney observed, with his frequently expressed belief that EPA should not interfere with state decisions.

Schroeder's letter to Inspector General Novick drew little attention, but as the weeks passed she and reporters for the Denver papers uncovered additional information, and the story refused to die. Senate action on Sanderson's nomination was held up while Novick investigated the growing list of allegations.

Novick briefed Gorsuch on the progress of his investigation. On April 20, 1982, he sent her his report. While the six-paragraph summary at the front of the report exonerated Sanderson, Novick's memo to Gorsuch transmitting the report warned of "numerous areas of interest in the evidence gathered that could prove troublesome or embarrassing to the Agency should someone choose to make them an issue." Among those he pointed to were:

1. Sanderson's attorney, Paul Cooper, acknowledges that it is possible that Sanderson used his EPA staff to schedule meetings with clients and may have used a government car for personal business. However, he asserts that this is a common practice that goes with Sanderson's rank.

5. There exists an unresolvable conflict in testimony between Steven Durham on one hand, and David Standley, James Thompson, and Gene Lucero on the other. All three men said Durham told them that his decision not to approve the Colorado water standards and stream classifications was out of his hands as he was following instructions from Headquarters. Durham denies having said this.*

6. Thompson said Durham's change of mind regarding approval of the Colorado water standards coincided with a telephone call Durham received from Sanderson. Both Durham and Sanderson denied the allegation that Sanderson directed Durham to withhold approval of the standards.

---

*Lucero had been Deputy Regional Administrator and later became director of hazardous waste enforcement in Washington. Thompson was Acting Regional Counsel, and Standley was Director of the regional water division.

7. Durham's change in position regarding approval of the Colorado water standards coincides with a conversation Thompson had with William Pederson, attorney, EPA Office of General Counsel. Pederson told Thompson that he received a call from Sanderson as a private attorney inquiring about the options a Regional Administrator would have in regard to the Colorado water quality standards. The options that Pederson gave Sanderson were the same options that Durham said he had after the alleged call from Sanderson.

8. In Pederson's testimony he relates how he and Perry and Thompson all agreed that they had no concern about a possible conflict of interest on the part of Sanderson because the State had withdrawn its submission of the standards. This was a faulty premise as the State had not withdrawn its submission.

9. Sanderson acted as a conduit for Colorado State Senate President, Fred Anderson, to obtain legal advice from EPA's Office of General Counsel on proposed law S.B. 10. Frank Traylor, Director of the Colorado Department of Public Health, testified that Sanderson saw him in May as a private attorney representing Coors and tried to influence him regarding S.B. 10.

10. Finally, the investigation shows that although it is legally permissable [sic], Sanderson frequently did work for clients on days he was employed at EPA. He claimed that on these days he worked 10 to 14 hours. He also claimed that he worked over 24 days of two hours or more at EPA without compensation. This claim could be viewed as an attempt to avoid the additional legal restrictions imposed after 60 days' employment. After 60 days' employment, an employee has a conflict of interest if he represents a client who had a matter pending before EPA. If he worked less than 60 days he must have been involved personally and substantially in the matter as an EPA employee in order to be in violation. Also, after 60 days a financial disclosure statement is required.

The following day, April 21, Novick delivered the report to White House Counsel Fred Fielding with a cover letter similar to that he had sent Gorsuch, but stripped of any suggestion that Sanderson had done anything improper or potentially embarrassing. Novick provided the report to Representative Schroeder, and, while Novick gave her no indication of the problems he had identified in his memo to Gorsuch, Schroeder reacted indignantly to the contrast between the bland exoneration offered in the summary and the evidence contained in the report.

Novick said there was "no evidence" that Sanderson's clients had matters "pending" before EPA or that Sanderson worked beyond the 60-day limit. Schroeder pointed out, however, that the report itself showed that Sanderson had billed his clients for what he described as EPA-related work and in fact had billed the Denver Water Department for work he described as "Water Class: Work on EPA Issues" on the day Thompson, Lucero, and Standley said he had called Durham to intercede in the decision on the Colorado standards. Schroeder also complained that Sanderson had refused to disclose most of his billing records to the investigators. Schroeder noted that the records at Sanderson's law firm showed him working many more days at EPA than did EPA records and that he clearly exceeded the 60-day limit.

No action was taken against Sanderson by Gorsuch, the White House, or the Department of Justice, but on June 3, 1982, he withdrew his name from consideration for the EPA post. Schroeder wrote a long letter to Attorney General William French Smith criticizing the report. Novick, in his own letter to the Attorney General, defended his report, saying it was not his job to draw conclusions and that the question raised by Schroeder should be answered in a Department of Justice investigation. The months passed and the Department of Justice remained silent. As congressional and press attention focused on EPA in late 1982 and early 1983, additional charges relating to Sanderson's representation of Chemical Waste Management, Inc., surfaced. Finally, Novick's letter to Gorsuch became public. Members of Congress wrote the Attorney General, the Director of the FBI, and the President calling for a complete investigation.

On August 11, 1983, sixteen months after receiving Novick's report, five months after Anne Gorsuch resigned, the Justice Department released its report on its investigations of EPA. It was a vague and inconclusive document, curiously anonymous. It provided no new information and gave little hint what evidence it was based upon.

The report, and a second report issued several months later, exonerated every EPA official except Rita Lavelle. It answered few of the questions raised by members of Congress about Sanderson's conduct, and failed to acknowledge or respond to much of the evidence collected by Novick or congressional investigators. Congressman John Dingell called it "basically a whitewash." He pointed out that it ignored numerous allegations and left most questions unanswered.

The only Reagan appointee actually prosecuted for her conduct in office was Rita Lavelle. She was convicted of perjury and obstructing a congressional investigation. Ironically, she was acquitted of charges that she manipulated hazardous waste cleanup funds to help Republican candidates and hurt Democrats. Politics, according to her staff, was the prevalent theme of Lavelle's administration of the Hazardous Waste Program. However, federal prosecutors never introduced one significant piece of evidence: Lavelle not only discussed her political strategy with her own staff; she also discussed it with members of the White House staff.

There is a lesson in Lavelle's conviction, but it is not that wrongdoers reap their just reward. The prosecution of Rita Lavelle stands in stark contrast to the Administration's treatment of other misconduct at EPA. Other officials accused of wrongdoing were given the benefit of every doubt, technicality, and loophole. Lavelle apparently was the only one who could not be saved.

While the Sanderson controversy festered, Mrs. Gorsuch found herself entangled in a new imbroglio. On December 11, 1981, at the request of Senators Schmitt and Domenici of New Mexico, she had met with representatives of Thriftway Company, a small refiner with plants in New Mexico and Texas. The Thriftway representatives claimed that EPA regulations requiring them to reduce the amount of lead in the gasoline they produced were breaking the company. They asked to be excused from the requirements. Gorsuch told them there was no procedure for such a waiver and that she did not want to have to deal with a flood of similar requests from other refineries. Then, according to contemporary memoranda and sworn affidavits, she went on to say that the EPA regulations would soon be changed and that "it did not make sense to enforce a regulation after changes had been proposed." When Thriftway's lawyer asked for confirmation of this extraordinary promise in writing, she later admitted, "I said he had my assurance."

As the meeting broke up, she asked Larry Morgan, the aide to Senator Schmitt, who had set up the meeting, to remain behind. When he emerged from her office, Morgan told the Thriftway representatives that Gorsuch had said to him she could not tell Thriftway to break the law, but she hoped they had gotten the point. They had.

At the beginning of February 1982, Congressman Toby Moffett—with the help of persistent investigative reporter Frank O'Donnell—uncovered the incident and demanded an investigation. Completed two months later, the Inspector General's investigation confirmed that Gorsuch had said she would not prosecute Thriftway if it violated the regulations, but concluded that she had done nothing wrong. That conclusion satisfied few people outside of the Administration and, as Gorsuch reported to Ed Rollins, the President's Assistant for Political Affairs, the issue "triggered significant adverse publicity."

The adverse publicity did not change the attitudes of those running EPA. On February 10, 1982, John Todhunter issued a memorandum instructing Regional Administrators not to take enforcement action for violation of the toxic substances or pesticide laws "if a violation does not evidence intentional or repeated disregard for the law and where appropriate corrective action is taken." Two weeks later, enforcement chief Sullivan instructed the Regional Administrators that they need not take enforcement action against waste dump operators violating rules "in the process of modification or change. . . ."

The turmoil caused by the allegations against Sanderson and by the Thriftway incident was made far worse by a decision Gorsuch made at the end of February 1982. On February 25, EPA suspended the three-month-old ban on the burial of drums containing liquid hazardous wastes in landfills. The suspension was intended to permit industry to continue its long-time practice of burying liquid wastes in steel drums while EPA implemented an agreement negotiated with industry in the fall of 1981 to weaken the ban. Although the earlier negotiations had not been secret, EPA gave no prior public notice of the suspension, and the public had no opportunity to object in advance. In fact, EPA did not expect much public reaction, because the ban had been in effect for only a few months.

They were wrong. The reaction was swift, angry, and intense. It had the unmistakable immediacy of spontaneous outrage. It seemed as if everything that EPA had done since the new Administration took office had been a retreat. Here was a simple and rudimentary rule that outlawed an unquestionably dangerous practice and Gorsuch was unwilling to enforce it. The explanation that the ban was only three months old and was going to be weakened anyway did not appease but inflamed public opposition. The country was generating something like a billion pounds of hazardous waste a day and the new Administration had suspended, frozen, delayed, or announced it would reconsider virtually the entire system of rules designed to protect the public from what seemed an avalanche of poisons.

Twenty-five days after it was suspended, the ban was reimposed. A week after that, EPA announced a reversal with respect to other hazardous waste regulations that had been suspended. The clamor roused the interest of the White House. White House staff members contacted Republican congressional leaders to ask whether Gorsuch should be replaced. In March, at Gorsuch's request, Craig Fuller, Secretary of the Cabinet, came to EPA for a briefing on the Agency's programs. Gorsuch knew White House staff members were beginning to question her competence, and she wanted to impress Fuller. But Fuller was more bored than impressed, according to Gorsuch's Deputy Chief of Staff Joe Foran. "His eyes glazed over and he sat there like 'gee, that's very interesting, what else do you have to tell me.' " They did agree that Gorsuch would report weekly to the White House on possible controversies brewing at EPA. Thenceforward, EPA "issue alerts" were circulated to senior White House staff members and OMB officials.

The environmental issue was perplexing to the White House. They were used to dismissing environmentalists as extremists, people not really committed to the basic goals of the nation. The White House staff knew little and cared less about environmental problems. Norman Livermore, the top environmental official in Reagan's administration while he was Governor of California, observed that after leaving the governorship Reagan "really hasn't had any environmental advisers. . . . So things are left up to [Joseph] Coors and people like that, who feel they've been strictured by environmental laws and regulations." The only environmental problem the White House cared about was overregulation, and the only people whose counsel they had sought were those who felt they were "overregulated."

Presidential Counselor Edwin Meese met with three environmental leaders—Russell Peterson, head of the National Audubon Society, Jay Hair, head of the National Wildlife Federation, and Michael McCloskey, head of the Sierra Club—in early February 1982. The three men came away appalled. Meese had insisted that Interior Secretary Watt was doing a good job and that there was "not a shred of truth" in their criticism of Anne Gorsuch. EPA, he added, "was loaded with Nader types" when Reagan came to office. Their concerns, Meese told them, stemmed from misperceptions.

Yet polls in the spring of 1982 showed that public anger over the Administration's environmental policies might hurt Republicans in congressional elections that fall. While the environment was not as important to voters as the economy, one poll found up to 13 percent of voters would vote for or against a candidate purely on the basis of his support for strong environmental laws. Another poll showed voters picking Democrats as the party best able to deal with the environment by a 51 percent to 11 percent margin.

The Congress, responding to increasingly explicit public support for strong environmental laws, dealt the Administration one defeat after another. While the President prevailed on budget cuts and arms policies, Congress rebuffed Administration attempts to weaken the clean air, clean water, pesticide, and endangered species laws. They voted against Secretary Watt's wilderness proposals, and the House passed (but the Senate did not act upon) legislation closing loopholes the Administration had opened in the hazardous waste laws.

Anne Gorsuch and James Watt were the symbols of the Administration's policy. Watt had developed a strong conservative constituency and a positive if not peaceful relationship with the governors of many of the western states. He worked with and cultivated conservatives in the Senate and in industry.

Anne Gorsuch had no such support. "She is very strong-willed," says Joe Cannon. "She has little understanding of Washington. She just didn't learn that you have to develop friendships and linkages with the White House. . . . She's all business; she doesn't understand the benefit of talking about things and getting to know people. We rarely 'just talked.' " Another aide comments, "It wasn't just environmentalists. She had frosty relations with Congress, with the press, with the governors, and with industry. She saw herself more as a judge than a politician. She thought her role was to sit aloof, listen to the facts and decide." She stiffened if she thought someone was trying to push her around.

She did not ride, manipulate, and use the political pressures on her and her agency. She sought instead to ignore them. She resented pressure and treated those who pressured her as adversaries. Yet almost everyone she dealt with wanted something from EPA, and most of them, rough or smooth, hostile or sympathetic, applied some sort of pressure. She was in a political position, and pressure is one of the primary tools of the political trade.

She felt it unfair that she was so widely criticized. She accused environmentalists of "distorting the facts and creating a certain amount of hysteria." She was concerned, she said, because "a lie told often enough becomes the truth." She often told interviewers she "resented" having to answer hostile questions and that the press was being "used"

70

by environmentalists. Her solution was public relations. She hired Donald Ferguson, a Denver public relations consultant, to help her and other top political appointees to get their side of the story out. She scheduled more time for private interviews with reporters, and finally, in October 1982, she briefed Ed Meese.

"She wanted to convince the White House," says Foran, "that no one could manage these issues without controversy. She wanted to show him what she was doing for the President." She had her staff prepare an elaborate and upbeat set of papers and charts which they dubbed "Meese's Pieces." She argued that the Agency had absorbed steep budget cuts but was still more efficient. Under her direction EPA had cleaned up backlogs in applications for pesticide registration and emergency use exemptions. Toxic effluent guidelines would be issued on time.* A backlog in approval of state clean air plan revisions had been eliminated. Gorsuch felt such achievements would vindicate her not only in the White House but with the public as well.

To outsiders, however, her claims of major improvements at EPA seemed incongruent with reality. By October 1982, 89 percent of all regulatory actions at EPA were behind schedule or had been canceled or postponed. The rate at which permit renewals under the Clean Water Act were processed fell by two-thirds, leaving most of the industrial and municipal facilities in the country operating under expired permits.

In 1977 Congress had required the EPA to establish specific air pollution rules for a wide variety of industries. When Gorsuch took office, 37 standards had been adopted, 12 had been proposed, and 49 were in preparation. By fall 1982, despite repeated promises that the standards would be promulgated promptly, EPA had adopted only one new standard. No progress had been made in the regulation of toxic air pollutants: 3 billion pounds a year of chemicals suspected to cause cancer or other chronic disease were being dumped into the air by industry. No progress had been made in reviewing hundreds of pesticides registered on the basis of inadequate safety data. Virtually no progress had been made cleaning up hundreds of dangerous abandoned waste dumps iden-

---

*The guidelines were issued, but it was curious for her to express such pride in that fact, for they were issued under the compulsion of a court order. Frank Shepherd had left the Agency after battling with Gorsuch over his failure to ask the court to free her of the obligation to issue the guidelines.

tified by EPA. Enforcement of the environmental laws had slowed almost to a standstill.

OMB exacerbated the problems caused by turmoil and dissension within EPA. By the end of 1982, over a thousand regulatory actions, some major, most minor, had been reviewed by OMB. Virtually all were delayed. Some were simply sent back to the Agency or disappeared into indefinite delay—what Congressman Albert Gore called the "regulatory black hole at OMB."

John Daniel, in sworn testimony before Gore, recalled OMB's extensive stalling of a rule governing the disposal of radioactive waste, "sent to OMB [on] Christmas Eve day of 1981" and finally "released on the last day of 1982. I remember that," he testified, "because our radiation staff had a birthday party for this particular regulation Christmas Eve to celebrate its year of residence."

When Gorsuch, under pressure of a court-imposed deadline, issued a regulation setting toxic water pollution limits without OMB concurrence, Jim Tozzi called Daniel late in the evening and said "words to this effect: that there was a price to pay for doing what we had done, and that we hadn't begun to pay." Increasingly, Gorsuch ended up in bitter confrontations with OMB as well as with Congress and environmentalists.

Stockman and the OMB staff recognized the shift, however small, and it increased their hostility toward the Agency and Gorsuch. OMB's blistering midterm assessment of the Agency in November 1982 said that EPA's "inability to work constructively with the White House on regulatory reform initiatives [has] turned a potential political asset into a political liability for the Administration." Charging EPA with resisting and circumventing its efforts to relax environmental rules, with "considerable political embarrassment" as the cost, the OMB critique pinned the blame on "EPA's political appointees, [who] appear unable to debunk the assertions of their staff."

Some members of the EPA staff felt Mrs. Gorsuch had genuinely changed by late 1982. Sanderson had gone. She was angry and disillusioned at OMB's approach to the Agency. She had learned that she needed and could rely on the career staff. She worked closely with Bill Hedeman, Director of the Superfund office, and Steven Schatzow, the Director of the water regulation office. Both men respected her and enjoyed working with her. But to the outside world, and to many on the staff, she gave no sign she had changed and made no gesture toward conciliation.

The summary of "Meese's Pieces" asserts revealingly, "The approaches which have served us in the first year and a half will continue to characterize our work in the two years to come. . . ." At least outwardly, the discord, protests, and defeats had made no dent.

COVER-UP, CONFRONTATION, AND COLLAPSE

Congressman John Dingell is a big, stubborn man whose deep belief in the integrity of governmental institutions often confuses both friends and opponents. He can be courtly and eloquent and he can be loud and intimidating. He is the Chairman of the powerful House Energy and Commerce Committee, which has jurisdiction over most of EPA's programs. During 1979 and 1980, he had been at odds with environmentalists over legislation to promote coal use and the development of synthetic fuels. In 1981 and 1982, he had sponsored amendments to the Clean Air Act that environmentalists bitterly (and successfully) opposed, and which the Administration, unable to write its own bill, supported. He is from Michigan and he believes in the U.S. automobile industry. He thinks the industry should get a break from pollution control requirements. So his opponents called him "Tailpipe Johnny" and his bill the "Dingell Dirty Air Bill."

But in the fall of 1982, Dingell's efforts to amend the Clean Air Act had been stalled by public opposition and the astute maneuvering of Congressmen Henry Waxman and Timothy Wirth. At the same time, Dingell had become increasingly concerned about EPA's failure to deal with hazardous wastes and in particular its failure to enforce the law. His Oversight and Investigations Subcommittee (of the Energy and Commerce Committee) had held numerous hearings on the implementation of the hazardous waste laws and Superfund and had become, as Dingell put it, "very tired with delay and empty promises and excuses." His staff had collected extensive data on the crippled EPA enforcement program and was receiving a steady stream of leaks from within the Agency. The information seemed to show a pattern of political manipulation interwoven with absurd incompetence.

Both Dingell and Congressman Elliott Levitas began negotiating

73

with EPA in September 1982 to obtain documents relating to hazardous waste dumps subject to potential Superfund action. For more than a month, they arranged one agreement after another under which Committee staff would review the documents, only to see the agreements crumble when Justice Department attorneys intervened. While EPA provided some documents, many were withheld. The EPA and Justice Department responses continued to waver, shift, and contradict one another. Finally, Perry told Dingell's staff that the Department of Justice had instructed EPA not to release the documents but to send the originals and all copies to Justice. That, says Dingell, "really rang a bell. That was exactly what they told William Casey when we were investigating the ITT-Geneen thing. We weren't about to put up with that kind of stuff in this case." On October 21, 1982, Dingell issued a subpoena to Gorsuch to appear before his committee and provide specific documents.

Dingell became increasingly angry and suspicious. It was obvious, he felt, that his committee faced "the obstruction of an important congressional investigation. . . ." The investigation, he pointed out, involved "specific allegations of misconduct and unethical behavior by an [EPA] official," to which the documents were highly relevant. He had, by then, received information relating to Rita Lavelle's failure to excuse herself when she learned that her former employer was involved with the Stringfellow site in California. Once on the warpath, Dingell is dogged, pugnacious, and very crafty. He was determined to get the documents.

The White House was not deeply troubled by the building confrontation with Dingell and Levitas. In the congressional elections on November 2, 1982, Republicans held onto their narrow majority in the Senate and lost fewer seats than predicted in the House. The environmental issue, White House staffers concluded, had not hurt them at all. "The conventional wisdom that jelled at the White House," says a former member of the White House staff, "was that there was no 'green vote' of significance. The environmentalists didn't amount to diddly squat and they didn't have to sweat the issue." Thus, the White House, in particular White House Counsel Fred Fielding, was amenable to the Justice Department's recommendation that they defy Dingell's subpoena (and one issued a month later by Levitas).

The Department of Justice wanted to establish the "privilege" of the Executive Branch to withhold documents from Congress. The Supreme Court had for the first time acknowledged the possibility of such a privilege in its 1974 opinion holding that Richard Nixon could *not* withhold evidence subpoenaed in connection with the Watergate trial. In late 1981, the Justice Department had prevailed on the President to assert "executive privilege" to withhold documents subpoenaed by Dingell from Interior Secretary James Watt. But on that occasion, the Administration backed down when Dingell's committee voted to ask the full House to hold Watt in contempt of Congress. Now the Department of Justice urged the White House to renew the confrontation.*

Gorsuch argued strenuously against withholding the documents. She thought the legal basis for doing so was weak, and that the political repercussions could be enormous. She was concerned, as well, that she would be left out on a political limb if the battle went badly. White House Counsel Fred Fielding assured her they would back her, and senior Justice Department officials said they would not back down this time, they would take the case all the way to the Supreme Court if necessary.

On November 30, 1982, President Reagan instructed Gorsuch "that sensitive documents found in open law enforcement files should not be made available to the Congress or to the public except in extraordinary circumstances. Because dissemination of such documents outside the Executive Branch would impair my solemn responsibility to enforce the law, I instruct you and your agency not to furnish copies of this category of documents to the Subcommittees in response to their subpoenas."

There was no claim that the documents affected national security or United States relations with foreign countries. The President did not suggest that any of the documents had been prepared for or reviewed by him or even his staff. He was implicitly asserting the right to withhold any Executive Branch documents at any time that he chose. It was a stupendous expansion of a controversial doctrine.

Members of Congress from both parties were angry. Conservative Republican Mark Marks wrote the President to protest the decision to withhold the documents, calling assertion "of executive privilege in this

---

*Several members of Dingell's committee have expressed the belief that the involvement of Justice Department lawyers in improper discussions of political deadlines for the settlement of a Superfund case contributed to their desire to have Superfund enforcement documents withheld.

case bizarre, at best." In a series of hearings, Gorsuch stiffly defended the President's decision while Committee members angrily pointed out that law clerks, consultants, and in some cases industry lawyers were getting the materials forbidden to Congress.

Dingell made public the fact that extensive material relating to the Stringfellow Acid Pits in California had been omitted in lists prepared by EPA of the documents being withheld. His staff had alerted EPA and Justice Department officials because some of the materials had already been leaked to him. Dingell warned that there was mounting evidence that cleanup funds for Stringfellow had been held up in an attempt to influence the California Senate race.

On December 10, 1982, the House Public Works Committee voted to refer to the full House a resolution holding Gorsuch in contempt of Congress for her refusal to honor Levitas's subpoena. The full House was scheduled to take up the contempt resolution on the evening of December 16. Gorsuch had a small Christmas party in her 12th floor offices that night. There was a cake with an enforcement file made of frosting on it and a betting pool on how many congressmen would support Gorsuch in the House vote.

They watched the proceedings on TV. When Congressman Levitas rose to present the contempt resolution, he explained to the House his efforts to reach a compromise with the Justice Department. Gorsuch was jolted. She had known nothing of the negotiations and felt Levitas had offered extraordinary concessions to the Administration. Just before ten in the evening, the House voted 259–105 to hold Mrs. Gorsuch in contempt. She was fatalistic about the vote. She had foreseen it and felt sure the Congress would eventually get the documents.

Moments after the vote, the Justice Department filed suit against the House asking the court to block the contempt proceedings. The suit was styled *United States of America v. The House of Representatives*, and it infuriated members of Congress. They viewed it as a gesture of extraordinary arrogance that the Administration should regard itself as "the United States" in a suit against another co-equal branch of government. The contempt statute, unlike most criminal statutes which simply describe an offense, explicitly required prosecutorial action, authorizing the House or Senate to certify the failure of a witness to comply with a subpoena "to the district attorney for the District whose duty it shall be to bring the matter before the grand jury for their action." The

Justice Department, however, instructed the district attorney to ignore the House vote and to take no action against Gorsuch.

Lawyers for the House asked the court to dismiss the Administration's suit, arguing that it was inappropriate for the courts to intervene in a conflict between Congress and the Executive. The brief for the House stated, "This case can be seen as the first instance in which the Executive Branch, or certain officers thereof, seek the aid of the federal judiciary to be excused from either the application or performance of federal statutes that the Executive Branch is sworn to obey and execute."

Meanwhile, the entire nation's attention was suddenly drawn to the problems of hazardous waste. Freak floods swept through the Midwest just before Christmas. When the Meramec River receded on Christmas Eve, the residents of Times Beach, Missouri, were warned not to go home. A decade earlier, waste oil contaminated with dioxin had been sprayed on the town's roads. The flood had uncovered and dispersed the poison. Day after day, the media showed men in "moon suits" inspecting Missouri sites for contamination. Many of the stories mentioned criticism of Anne Gorsuch and Rita Lavelle for doing too little too slowly to deal with hazardous waste.

The new Congress came to Washington in January 1983 and, contrary to White House perceptions, it was substantially more sensitive to environmental issues than the Congress that had left Washington a month before. Dingell was more determined than ever to get the documents the Administration was withholding and to question EPA employees under oath. Many of the employees were eager to be questioned.

During February, EPA unraveled. On Thursday, February 3, 1983, the district court dismissed the Justice Department suit against the House. The next day, Anne Gorsuch asked Rita Lavelle to resign after discovery of a memorandum drafted for Lavelle by Gene Ingold, one of her aides, apparently to be sent to the White House, in which she said Robert Perry "is systematically alienating the primary constituents of this Administration, the business community." When Lavelle's aides were discovered removing documents from her office, armed guards were posted in front of her door, but not until after she had removed or destroyed scores of documents. Lavelle refused to resign and on Monday, February 7, the President fired her. It was then discovered that paper shredders had just been delivered and put into use at the hazardous waste office.

The claim of executive privilege, the firing of Lavelle, Times Beach, the shredders, and the dismissal of the Justice Department suit set off a kind of "feeding frenzy" among the media. The number of reporters covering EPA jumped from a handful to a horde. They began to scrutinize the Agency with care and skepticism. Old scandals—Thriftway, the never-completed Sanderson investigation, the "hit lists," the collapse of enforcement—were reexamined. New ones were discovered: Lavelle's apparent misrepresentation to a congressional committee about her efforts to have a "whistle-blower" fired; Sanderson's representation of a hazardous waste firm while participating in EPA meetings on hazardous waste issues; Horton's use of government resources for his private business; Lavelle's frequent lunches with industry representatives. More than that, months of poor performance and bad decisions became the subject of searching examinations by the press.

While the President assured the nation in a press conference that, if there was any suggestion of wrongdoing at EPA, documents would not be withheld from Congress, Gorsuch quietly referred such evidence regarding Lavelle to the Justice Department. She was under enormous pressure. Publicly she argued that criticism of her was partisan "political harassment. The old rule of the loyal opposition is to harass, delay, destroy, and finally stop." Privately, she importuned the White House to release the documents. On February 17 she met with the President, Baker, Deaver, Meese, Fielding, and Fuller and argued that the legal issues had been overshadowed by the political consequences. Until the documents were released, she warned, they could never overcome the appearance of a cover-up. Fielding told the President the issue would soon be resolved by a compromise with the Congress.

The next day, Congressman Levitas agreed to accept limited access to the documents. Gorsuch was distraught. She was convinced that Dingell would not accept the Levitas agreement (he did not) and that nothing less than full disclosure would blunt public criticism. While she was the one subject to criminal contempt proceedings and taking the brunt of the public criticism, the White House and the Justice Department not only refused to heed her advice, they would not even let her know what was going on. She concluded, Joe Cannon says, that someone in the White House, probably Fred Fielding, was out to get her. "Actually," says Cannon, "it was probably more like *Murder on the Orient*

Express—they all killed her. She didn't have any friends at the White House."

On February 20 a tense and subdued Gorsuch married Robert Burford. A few days later the White House announced a "fresh start," appointing temporary replacements for Rita Lavelle, John Horton, and Inspector General Matthew Novick. Gorsuch objected to the temporary replacements, saying they looked like a "strike force" sent in to deal with wrongdoing. She urged again that the White House release the documents. She resisted appearing to announce the new appointees, telling White House staffer Craig Fuller, according to John Daniel's notes, "I've never lied and I don't like it. I think we ought to turn these GD [sic] documents over or we're going to bring this pres [sic] to his knees." Fuller responded, Daniel's notes show, "Personally my heart goes out to you, and I don't like asking you to lie."

Gorsuch (and John Daniel) met again with the President the next day, together with Vice-President Bush, Senator Paul Laxalt, and Craig Fuller. She argued that there was no point in insisting on executive privilege after the Levitas agreement. He should release the documents to end the public criticism. The President asked her to discuss the issue with Attorney General William French Smith. She met with Smith that evening. He, according to Daniel, was "unsympathetic to AMG's position and said that asserting executive privilege had nothing to do with her problems."

Although convinced that the executive privilege claim had a great deal to do with her problems, Gorsuch remained mystified about why the criticism was directed at her. Several top aides recall her appearance at a press conference at which reporters grilled her about the problems at the Agency. Afterwards, she asked senior officials who were there how she had done. Most of them loyally assured her she had been magnificent, but one official who dealt frequently with Congress demurred, saying she had failed. "Why?" asked Gorsuch. "I told the truth." The official told her that was not enough, and because she had been defiant rather than humble and had refused to concede she had made mistakes, the criticism would not let up.

Indeed the pressure was building. On March 1, Dingell wrote the President reminding him that he had repeatedly promised that he would "never invoke executive privilege to cover up wrongdoing." Dingell recited page after page of evidence of wrongdoing, unethical conduct, and potential criminal behavior and said it was time for the President to make good on his promise. He made it very clear that with or without the documents his investigation would proceed.

After a congressional budget hearing, Bill Hedeman recalls, he and Gorsuch were mobbed by reporters screaming questions about Lou Cordia's hit lists. When she escaped into an elevator, the reporters raced down the stairs and surrounded her as she tried to reach her car. She returned to her office bruised and despondent. She wept bitterly and told Hedeman that the Agency could not take much more of the crisis, but that she had a plan to end it.

The next day, March 3, Justice Department officials told her that, since they were now investigating EPA, they would no longer represent her in the battles with Congress over the withholding of documents. Gorsuch was incredulous, telling the Justice Department, according to Daniel's notes, "That's not what I was told when we got into this."

The following day, Richard Hauser, Deputy to Fred Fielding, wrote a memo to the Department of Justice to advise them:

Ernie Minor, a Member of the Council on Environmental Quality, has advised that on August 4, 1982, he participated in a luncheon on board the *Sequoia* in which EPA Administrator Burford [Gorsuch], Secretary Watt, (then) Under Secretary of the Interior Hodel, EPA Staff Director John Daniel, CEQ Chairman Allan Hill were attendees. (Minor states that former Secretary Edwards and Deputy Secretary Ken Davis also were present for part of this luncheon.)

Minor advises that to his best recollection Burford stated, during that luncheon, that no money would be released for a Stringfellow (California) clean-up until after the elections. Minor advises that CEQ Chairman Hill recollects Burford stating, "I'll be damned if I am going to let Brown take credit for that [Stringfellow clean-up]."

The memo also disclosed that Hauser had advised Justice Department officials of the same information by telephone the day before. The story was immediately leaked and was published in the *Los Angeles Times* the same day.

While the President continued to express confidence in Gorsuch, the White House staff wanted her out, and on March 9, 1983, she resigned. On the same day, the White House agreed to turn over the disputed documents to Dingell's committee, and they were delivered the next day. Two days later, asked about Gorsuch's resignation, the President said:

I never would have asked for her resignation. She was doing a job and we, this Administration, can be very proud of our record in environmental protection.

And believe me it tops what we found when we came here. . . . But I don't think the people who were attacking her were concerned about the environment. I don't think they were concerned about any possible wrongdoing. . . . And frankly I wonder how they manage to look at themselves in the morning.

Anne Gorsuch was brought down by her own view of the world, by her single-minded adherence to the President's own rhetoric and by the machinations of the Justice Department and the White House staff. It was a sad and tawdry spectacle that damaged the EPA and its people and had serious consequences for the American environment. It is revealing that Ronald Reagan saw none of that, explaining what happened in terms of nameless selfish and unscrupulous enemies.

2
RISKY
BUSINESS

THE DUMPS

The stories that unfolded about President Reagan's EPA in the early months of 1983 sometimes seemed as complicated and full of unfamiliar names as a Russian novel. Few people followed them in detail. But one fact stuck out. The hazardous waste dumps that had scared the nation for the past five years, ever since Love Canal, were not getting cleaned up.

Behind the headlines about sweetheart deals and lunches at French restaurants with industry lobbyists lay these revealing numbers: in two and a half years EPA completed the cleanup of just five of the 419 waste sites on the national priority list, and planned to finish only eleven more in the following year. In 1980, Congress had established a Superfund, mainly paid for by the chemicals industry, for the express purpose of speeding the cleanup. EPA used less than one-quarter of the money that Congress provided.

Some delays, it appears, were dictated by politics. According to sworn testimony before a congressional committee, Rita Lavelle, EPA's hazardous waste chief, had a frankly political motive for shutting off Superfund help to western mining waste sites. She was afraid that the mining states would resent the federal intrusion and that the 1984 election campaigns of western Republican senators might suffer. And,

Anne Gorsuch said, she had held up a $6-million grant to clean up the huge Stringfellow acid pits in Riverside, California, because Jerry Brown, then governor of California and Democratic candidate for the Senate, might get the credit.

Indeed, according to the director of the Superfund program, "there was a constant desire to tie the announcement of [Superfund] sites into election campaigns." Every Superfund cleanup proposal was "delayed," he said, "until the strategy could evolve in terms of announcements . . . supportive of a Republican contender for office or Republican incumbents." EPA and Justice Department lawyers openly discussed the "political deadline" for completion of negotiations on cleanup of the Seymour, Indiana, site.

This was not politics as usual. While the distribution of federal money for roads, dams, and new buildings sometimes proceeds on a schedule shaped by politics, the administration of Superfund involved protection of health and compliance with the law. Delaying the cleanup of dangerous dumps for partisan political gain put Americans' health at stake.

Yet, party politics was probably not the main reason for EPA's snail-like pace in cleaning up hazardous waste dumps. Rather, it was political ideology. All the evidence points to a top-level decision, both at EPA and at the Reagan White House, never to exceed the five years and $1.6 billion Congress originally set up for the Superfund—whether or not the nation's thousands of abandoned hazardous waste dump sites were effectively cleaned up by that time. Everyone at EPA knew that the job was impossible. Even the nation's 419 priority sites could not be cleaned up within those limits, let alone 15,000 less notorious sites, some of which might turn out to be as bad or worse than the priority sites. But the decision was made: no Son of Superfund.

According to the two highest ranking career civil service professionals in the Superfund program, the decision to close out Superfund lay behind dozens of different reasons given for inaction at various dump sites. Yet no one, either in the White House or at the top levels at EPA, ever frankly announced the policy. Neither the President, nor Edwin Meese, nor Anne Gorsuch, nor Rita Lavelle said to the nation: "We can't spend more than five years cleaning up old waste dumps. And we can't afford to pay more than $1.6 billion for it. Either the states clean up the rest, or we'll just have to live with it." Most of the Superfund —$1.4 billion, or $280 million per year—comes from a special tax on the chemicals industry. The yearly tax amounts to less than one-fifth of one percent of the industry's sales.

In Globe, Arizona, 50 families living not near but *in* an asbestos dump site, thought their problems were solved when Congress passed the Superfund law in December 1980. They believed EPA would quickly buy them out so they could find other places to live without suffering a financial catastrophe. They were mistaken. Joseph Sparks, a lawyer representing some of the residents, told a House subcommittee in May 1983: "As 1981 wore on we began to worry. The flow of information and cooperation that we saw in EPA began to wane. . . . By the summer of 1981 it was impossible for us to get any information. . . . We were faced with a stonewall."

Globe is a century-old copper mining town, 4,000 feet high in the stark, rust-colored Pinal and Hayes mountains 80 miles east of Phoenix. There's not much flat buildable land in Globe; house and land prices are high for a small town. In 1973, when State authorities ordered the Metate Asbestos Corporation's mill on the eastern outskirts of Globe to close because it was violating federal air quality standards, the mill's owner, Jack Neal, had the idea of turning the site into a housing tract. The city—importuned both by Neal and a popular local businessman who wanted to buy a home there—rezoned the tract residential. The Metate mill, still standing in the middle of the proposed development, was supposed to be removed, and the site turned into a mini-park.

After he won the rezoning approval, Neal bulldozed and leveled the tract using asbestos ore scrap and tailings from the mill for landfill. Some of the land, with its burden of asbestos waste, was covered with topsoil. The property was then divided into 55 lots, with mobile homes to be permanently installed on concrete pads.

On a hilltop under the big blue Arizona sky, with a long view of sharp-edged mountains to the south, the Mountain View Mobile Home Estates looked inviting. And the prices were right for people of modest means, around $25,000 to $35,000 in 1973. Neal never did remove the mill; in fact, witnesses at the House subcommittee hearing said he ran it surreptitiously at night for a few months until a sheriff's deputy caught him at it. Nevertheless, the subdivision attracted buyers, many of whom added gardens, fruit trees, desert landscaping, and—in the case of an extended Italian-American family—terraces, fountains, and Italian cypresses. By 1979, 50 of the 55 lots on the 17-acre tract were sold, and 118 people were living there.

Not until October 1979 did Arizona officials discover that the 118 people were living on piles of asbestos waste. A state health inspector who came out to look at the development's malfunctioning sewage system found asbestos all over the place—in the waste water system, in piles around the abandoned Metate mill and nearby railroad tracks, on and in the old mill equipment. Another asbestos mill (run by the D.W. Jaquays Mining and Equipment Corp.) was still operating a few hundred yards upwind from the development, with three large piles of tailings beside it.

The state health officials were alarmed. Asbestos is one of the most powerful of known carcinogens in human beings. It causes lung cancer and mesothelioma, an exceedingly malignant (and, aside from asbestos exposure, exceedingly rare) cancer of the lining of the chest and the abdominal cavities. Moreover, asbestos causes asbestosis, an emphysema-like lung disease, which is irreversible, disabling, and often fatal.

Most of the information on asbestosis and asbestos-caused cancer in human beings comes from studies of workers exposed to asbestos on the job. But several studies published in the 1960's and afterward show that mesothelioma has also killed people who simply lived near asbestos dumps or factories where asbestos products were made, or who lived in the same house with workers coming home with asbestos dust in their clothes. Typically, mesothelioma takes from 20 to 40 years to develop after exposure to asbestos dust; lung and other cancers due to asbestos also have long latency periods.

The federal Centers for Disease Control confirmed that the air, soil, and dust at Mountain View Mobile Home Estates, indoors and outdoors, was contaminated with asbestos. Tailings found within the subdivision and at the active Jaquays mill contained 60 percent asbestos of the chrysotile type. Soil samples from 44 of the homes showed at least 5 percent asbestos, and four contained over 50 percent asbestos. In places, the soil was contaminated nine feet below the surface. In all of the eight households tested, asbestos fibers were found in dust from furnace filters or vacuum cleaner bags. In one air sample, taken while drapes and carpets in a home were being vacuumed, the asbestos concentrations rose to 350,000 fibers per cubic meter. The current federal standard for asbestos workers, set by the Occupational Safety and Health

Administration (OSHA), is two million fibers per cubic meter of air, for an eight-hour workday (time-weighted average); however, the National Institute for Occupational Safety and Health has recommended that the workplace standard be lowered to 100,000 fibers per cubic meter.

"This occupational standard," said the CDC report, "was not designed for the population at large, which may be exposed up to 24 hours per day, nor was it designed to protect children playing directly with asbestos-containing materials, as in Globe."

The CDC report noted that none of the 118 current residents of the subdivision had any known asbestos-related diseases, namely asbestosis, mesothelioma, or lung cancer. It also noted that the families had lived in the subdivision for an average of two years, though a few had been there since 1973. (Since it takes 15 to 40 years for asbestos-related disease to show up, evidence of disease so early after exposure would not be likely.)

The report said there was "heightened concern" about the particular situation at Globe, "because of the ready availability of asbestos to children and other residents, the high respirability of the milled fibers and the continuing environmental contamination. . . . Children are of particular concern, because they were observed playing directly with tailings and because their long life expectancy exceeds the prolonged latent periods for asbestos-related disease."

As the testing began, late in 1979, state health officials warned residents of the Mountain View Mobile Home Estates about the asbestos contamination and the possible dangers. They were stunned. Sarah Luckie had moved into the development two years earlier with her husband Tony (a heavy-equipment operator in the nearby copper mines), her step-daughter, and a younger sister. The Luckies' baby daughter, Holly, was born two months after the family moved in.

"My husband served in Vietnam," Sarah Luckie told the House Subcommittee on Oversight and Investigations in May 1983. "After his discharge from the service . . . we spent several years establishing ourselves economically so it would be possible for us to achieve the American dream, to own your own home. . . .

"In December 1979 . . . our entire world and our hopes seemed to have been destroyed in a single day. We were notified . . . that the material in our yards and surrounding our subdivision was extremely hazardous and could cause severe and permanent damage to health, including cancer. . . .

86

"I spent the entire holiday season in tears. I had recurring visions of my baby playing in the dirt in our yard and then remembering that the men who came to take the samples from our yard wore moon suits."

On January 11, 1980, after reviewing the sampling data, Dr. William Foege, Assistant Surgeon General of the United States and Director of the Centers for Disease Control, called the Globe situation "urgent" and recommended that state authorities evacuate the residents and decontaminate the subdivision. Dr. Suzanne Dandoy, Director of the Arizona Department of Health Services, went a step further. In a letter to Arizona's Governor Bruce Babbitt, she wrote that the subdivision should not be used for residences. "There is no permanent solution," she said. Once covered, the asbestos-contaminated lands should not be disturbed. If people lived there, the land inevitably would be disturbed by such simple acts as planting a garden, or repairing sewer lines. Dandoy also mentioned that the Jaquays mill still operating next door to the subdivision could be a continuing health threat. Even if it complied with all EPA's rules on dust emission, it could break down or malfunction occasionally. Dr. Dandoy recommended that the residents be removed, and suggested that they could later relocate their decontaminated mobile homes onto other land. She noted that representatives of the EPA, the Centers for Disease Control, and the National Institute of Occupational Safety and Health (NIOSH) all agreed with her recommendation.

Unfortunately, part of Dandoy's recommendation was a practical impossibility. The mobile homes, being set in concrete, were no longer mobile. They couldn't be picked up and moved without serious structural damage.

At the time of these events, in early 1980, the federal Superfund law had not yet been passed. In a few cases, such as Love Canal, where President Carter proclaimed a national emergency, the federal government had stepped in to help communities faced with a hazardous waste emergency. But mostly action on hazardous waste sites was left up to the states.

Governor Babbitt took the compromise step of moving the residents out of the Mountain View development, beginning in February 1980. The homes were scoured, the old Metate asbestos mill and all its equipment torn down and buried, and all the open land covered with six inches of soil trucked in from the nearby Tonto National Forest. By summer, the residents moved back in.

This solution, as Dr. Dandoy and the other scientists had foreseen, did not last. In July and August 1980, the "monsoon season" as some local residents call it, heavy rains started washing away the dirt that covered the asbestos-contaminated soil. Residents were again reporting they could see flecks of asbestos in the air. They wrote to the EPA, the Centers for Disease Control, state agencies, and whatever sources of help they could think of, pointing out that the asbestos threat was still there.

When the Superfund law was enacted late in 1980, Sarah Luckie recalled, "We received what we all thought was our first real Christmas present since this horrible nightmare began." The Globe situation was specifically mentioned in the congressional debate over the law as one that the Superfund could help. But then, Luckie went on, "During 1981, we got no reasonable response from EPA. Their responses to our letter and telephone inquiries were sketchy and noncommittal, and they became more so as 1981 wore on. . . . Finally . . . we were so frustrated and fed up that we [filed] a lawsuit against various Federal personnel, including specifically Anne Gorsuch. . . .

"EPA has clearly used more energy in defending against our lawsuit, claiming they don't have to do anything under the Superfund, than it would have taken to bring legal action against the polluters and to implement an emergency permanent relocation."

Another resident, Cathy Scott, described the many letters she and others had written to top EPA officials, and the "noncommittal answers from some low level official who seemed to care less." She added: "Now we are beginning to discover that in fact it was probably low level officials who cared most and that actually it was Anne Gorsuch and Rita Lavelle who could have cared less."

That the "low level officials" cared is certainly true. A midlevel group of EPA career professionals who were assigned the Globe case wouldn't let it drop. One said, "Every time we tried to make progress on Globe there was a new question, a new issue. It was just endless, and very, very, frustrating." But they persevered. Congressman John Dingell of Michigan, Chairman of the House Subcommittee that investigated Globe, gave the EPA staff high marks for concern about the health threat and for trying to get an Agency response. But, he said, "they were sidetracked by top management policies and decisions."

A decision Anne Gorsuch made in June 1982 all but banished mining waste sites from the Superfund program; Globe was considered a mining waste site. Congress, bending to industry pressure, had defined "hazardous substances" in the Superfund law to exclude mining waste, but allowed EPA to spend Superfund money to clean up hazardous "pollutants" or "contaminants"—including those from mining—where they may cause an "imminent and substantial endangerment" of public health and welfare. There is no real legal question that EPA can use the Superfund in such cases. The only unsettled question is whether EPA can force polluters to repay the Fund for the cleanup in these cases.

In 1981 and 1982, three mining waste sites were especially worrisome to EPA staff. One was at the Iron Mountain Mine complex in California. Toxic metals—copper, cadmium, zinc, iron, lead, arsenic, and aluminum—were draining from the mines into the Sacramento River and thence into Keswick Lake, a source of drinking water for summer vacationers. Still worse was the 40-square-mile Tar Creek site, extending from Commerce, Oklahoma, northward to Kansas. Cadmium, lead, zinc, and iron from old abandoned mines had already polluted a shallow aquifer and threatened the deep Roubidoux aquifer. These two sites were among 115 that had made EPA's first cut at a National Priority List in October 1981. Sites on this list are supposed to be the nation's most horrendous known hazardous dump sites, and are entitled to priority attention in the Superfund program.

Then there was Globe. The Globe site was not on the interim priority list, but by early 1982 Arizona's Governor Babbitt asked EPA to name Globe as his state's top priority site. In March 1982 Rita Lavelle's Superfund staff had prepared a letter to Babbitt for Anne Gorsuch to sign, agreeing to put Globe on the National Priority List. Lavelle never approved the letter, and Gorsuch never signed it.

In the spring of 1982, the chemical and mining industries were both pressuring EPA to leave mining wastes out of the Superfund program —the chemicals industry because they didn't want the fees they contributed to Superfund to go for cleaning up mining pollution, and the mining industry because they wanted to be left out of Superfund, period. At the House Subcommittee hearings on Globe, Oklahoma Congressman Mike Synar referred to the industry lobbying and pointed to Rita Lavelle's calendar, which showed that she had 47 meetings with representatives of the chemicals and mining industries in 1982. At the same hearings, the two top civil servants in the Superfund program, William Hedeman and Gene Lucero, both confirmed that Lavelle had a number of discussions with chemical and mining industry representatives on the question of using Superfund money to clean up mine pollution.

Anne Gorsuch settled the matter at a private meeting with Lavelle, Hedeman, Lucero, and another EPA staff member in June 1982. Hazardous mine waste sites, she decided, could go on the National Priority List; but Superfund money could be spent only for investigating and studying them, not for cleaning them up—until "all enforcement authorities" against the responsible polluters were exhausted. Gorsuch stated her decision orally, not in writing. Hedeman announced it a few days later to all of EPA's regional offices. It was never publicly announced. And according to EPA staff members, "Nobody knew what it meant." Except that it obviously meant delay while lawyers fought out the responsibility for the pollution in court. The Globe case never even got that far; and in any event, a prompt rescue of the people living on the asbestos in Mountain View Mobile Home Estates was now out of the question. The Globe victims did not know they were stuck, however, because no one told them about Gorsuch's decision.

According to her associates at EPA, Anne Gorsuch was well aware that the hazardous waste issue was a critical one. She took personal charge of much of the Agency's program, and wrote a good part of the Superfund regulations herself. She knew that she and her agency were going to be strictly judged by the public on how they handled it. Her decision on mine sites had the virtue of not obviously and openly closing the door on cleanup of some of the nation's most threatening hazardous waste dumps. At the same time, it went a long way toward satisfying the chemicals and mining industries. And it fit with the White House and EPA policy of keeping Superfund in a five-year straightjacket. As Hedeman told the House subcommittee: "There was a hidden agenda, if you will, not to set in motion events that would lead to what is referred to as 'Son of Superfund' or the extension of the tax on reenactment of the law beyond the 1985 cutoff. I would include mining waste as part of that. . . ."

At hearings a few weeks earlier, the Senate Committee on Environment and Public Works had begun to dig into the question of a slow-down on Superfund. Here, too, Hedeman and Lucero were the star witnesses. Both men are savvy, personable professionals, though with different styles: Hedeman, the director of the Superfund program, quiet, cautious, and self-contained; Lucero, the head of enforcement for hazardous wastes, rather dashing. Lucero, a Democrat, was ousted from

EPA's highly politicized Denver regional office late in 1981, but landed on his feet in Washington. Hedeman, a holdover at EPA headquarters, got the demanding job of Superfund director after he won the blessing of James Sanderson, Anne Gorsuch's consultant and close adviser. Rita Lavelle depended on both men. They in turn, like most of her staff, saw her as personally pleasant but hopelessly out of her depth in her job. In addition, Hedeman came to be valued and trusted by Anne Gorsuch, and he developed a personal liking and sympathy for her.

At the Senate committee hearing, Maine Senator George Mitchell put this question to Hedeman and Lucero:

Was there any policy explicitly or implicitly to slow down expenditures from the Superfund so that there would be money left in the fund when the law expires in order to support the preconceived notion that no extension of the law was necessary and to minimize the problem?

Both men, under oath, answered yes.

Hedeman said he believed that there was "an implicit policy to at least curtail the progress of the program." Explicit, he said, was "a view that the Agency should not support Son of Superfund."

Lucero said he had no direct instructions to that effect, but there were "policies that slowed down the progress of expending money which . . . we found necessary to try to work around."

Senator Daniel Moynihan of New York responded: "I would like to express my appreciation. . . . [These] are perhaps the first candid responses we have had from your agency in two years."

In closed-door testimony before a House subcommittee, Hedeman said that "in various meetings . . . with both Ms. Lavelle and Mrs. Burford [Gorsuch], there were statements that we would not, the Administration would not, seek reauthorization of the trust fund."

Evidence that the White House knew of and approved the policy to close down the Superfund in 1985 is on the record. At hearings before the House Subcommittee on Oversight and Investigations in September 1983, New Jersey Congressman James Florio made public a December 1982 paper found in Anne Gorsuch's files containing notes for presentation to the Cabinet Council on Natural Resources and the Environment. The Council, chaired by Interior Secretary James Watt, includes several Cabinet members and, ex-officio, Vice-President Bush and Presidential aides Edwin Meese and James Baker. The paper, making a pitch

91

for 40 extra Superfund staffers that OMB had disallowed, warned against cuts that would be "inflammatory" to Congress. After all, the paper argued, Superfund is only a "relatively small and short term investment." Gorsuch's strategy was to keep quiet: "At this juncture, we simply do not need to have the wrong messages sent." The papers stated flatly: "We are trying to avoid 'Son of Superfund.' "

Hedeman and Lucero described in detail the ways in which the Reagan Administration hemmed in Superfund spending. First, Gorsuch tightened a condition that Congress had laid down, that the states put up a ten-percent share of whatever the federal government spent from Superfund to clean up hazardous waste sites. Superfund money is intended for cleaning up sites where no responsible party can be found to pay for it, and also to advance money for cleanups, with repayment to the Fund to be extracted later from polluters responsible for the dumping. Under the Gorsuch rules, EPA could not even spend Superfund money to study a site, or take first steps to stabilize a site, without also collecting from the state.

In 1981 and 1982 many states were on the ropes financially. This was especially true of the states' environmental programs—precisely because the Reagan Administration had sharply cut the federal grants to states, grants which had been established for the very purpose of helping states carry out their duties under federal environmental laws. EPA's unyielding demand for a state ten-percent match, up front, for Superfund spending was a huge impediment to the cleanup of a great many waste sites. That is the judgment, not only of Lucero and Hedeman, but of virtually all informed critics of the program, including the Congressional Office of Technology Assessment in its detailed 1983 report on hazardous wastes.

Hedeman told the Senate committee he had tried to come up with alternative schemes to the ten-percent state match, until "it was suggested that I find something else to do."

"Who suggested that?" asked Senator Mitchell.

"The Administrator," said Hedeman.

Hedeman also described a growing concern among the EPA staff about the thousands of hazardous waste dump sites that kept turning up which no one had yet assessed or even begun to clean up. Originally, there were 11,000 such sites, then the number gradually moved up to 15,000.

Hedeman told the committee: "I was instructed by Miss Lavelle to

[do] rapid assessments of those sites . . . by the end of this year, which was totally impossible to do—in order to verify her view that most of them were not really a problem."

Hedeman didn't think a review of 15,000 sites in one year could give an accurate assessment. But Lavelle told him that if the inventory expanded without EPA's being able even to rate the seriousness of the sites, that "could form a basis for further expansion of the Superfund program." Asked whether she stated that she did not favor an expansion, Hedeman replied, "She made that very clear to me."

Lucero described other impediments to cleaning up the dump sites. One was the Reagan Administration's attitude toward legal enforcement against private business. Enforcement at EPA had come to a virtual standstill. There were no hazardous waste cases filed during Gorsuch's first year in office. Lucero said, "Until the middle of 1982 there was a widespread sense that negotiation was all that was acceptable."

Senator Mitchell, a former prosecuting attorney and judge, said: "I have presided over a lot of cases. The way you get people's attention is to bring an action. If you have a policy of negotiation, you are just not going to get anywhere unless there is some credibility, and the credibility comes from bringing someone into court, winning a case, forcing someone to pay for something."

EPA's definition of a hazardous waste "emergency" was another hindrance to cleanup action, Lucero said. Emergency cleanup actions can be taken swiftly, without extended study and without the state ten-percent match. "But it was very difficult to get an action described as an emergency." As another EPA official who did not testify said, the decision to be "extremely tight" with money to meet emergencies was "a knee-jerk reaction, the day they were presented with the issue." He said their strategy was to keep the reins on Superfund spending held tightly at EPA headquarters until restrictive guidelines for responses to emergencies could be devised. "Their management approach," he said, "couldn't have been more diametrically opposed to the way the Superfund program was set up, which was to move out quickly and make case-by-case decisions."

EPA's regional offices, which had for years made swift decisions on emergencies (under another law, the Clean Water Act), now had to go to the EPA Administrator before making a move to clean up a toxic spill. "They really couldn't believe it at first," said the EPA staff member.

They believed it when two regional offices each cleaned up a spill without asking permission, after which John Daniel, Gorsuch's chief of staff, and Thornton "Whit" Field, her special assistant for hazardous wastes, angrily rebuked EPA staff. Until Rita Lavelle's arrival at EPA, Anne Gorsuch personally took over all decisions on Superfund emergency spending. Centralized control was nailed down.

Then, in July 1981, when the dump at Santa Fe Springs, California, went up in flames, with exploding drums scattering debris on nearby homes, "sure enough, we couldn't respond under Superfund." However, because contaminated water from the dump flowed through the nearby residential area to pollute a local beach and coastal waters, the Coast Guard, legally responsible for U.S. waters and their resources, was able to begin on its own cleanup. Eventually, the California EPA office won permission to assist in the cleanup but only after lengthy telegrams from the region to headquarters and heavy pressure from the EPA staff on their new political bosses. Even then, the cleanup was stop-and-go, while government lawyers fenced with the responsible companies over who should pay and how much.

Another major hindrance to offering emergency help, Lucero told the Senate committee, was that Rita Lavelle refused to see a health threat as an "emergency" unless it involved immediate illness or death. A chronic threat to health—such as a toxic chemical in a water supply that might later produce nerve damage or cancer—was not, to Lavelle, an emergency.

The insistence on what Lucero called "a body count" before perceiving a health threat was an attitude shared by top environmental and health officials throughout the Reagan Administration. In the Superfund program, Lavelle insisted on more studies, more exposure and risk assessments—"an additional quantum of proof to show a health problem," Lucero said. This was a major cause of delay. There never were enough people to pull together the health studies. They had to be taken off other projects, which then were also held up.

Lavelle's hesitancy to believe the generally accepted danger levels to health had most effect, Lucero said, on waste dump cases involving polychlorinated biphenyls (PCBs), dioxin (TCDD), and asbestos.

Asbestos. There is no serious scientific question that it is a killer. Asbestosis was recognized in 1907. As early as the 1930's medical evidence began to accumulate that too many asbestos workers died young of cancer. In the early to middle 1960's an enormous amount of new information became available on the biological effects of asbestos on humans. The leading investigators in this country were Dr. Irving J. Selikoff and his colleagues in the Division of Environmental Medicine at the Mount Sinai School of Medicine in New York. One of Selikoff's associates in studies of asbestos workers from the 1960's to the present has been Dr. E. Cuyler Hammond, vice-president for epidemiology and statistics of the American Cancer Society. A distinguished biostatistician, Hammond helped to analyze the medical after-effects of the atomic bomb explosions at Hiroshima and Nagasaki, and later worked on the large-scale studies, involving more than a million people, which formed the basis for the Surgeon General's 1964 report on the dangers to health of cigarette smoking.

Of the great body of work done by Selikoff and his associates, the most compelling is a ten-year study of excess mortality among 17,800 U.S. and Canadian asbestos insulators, published in 1979. This group of workers have lower and more intermittent exposure to asbestos than workers in a closed manufacturing plant. Even so, the study showed 37 percent more deaths among the asbestos insulators than would be expected on the basis of standard mortality tables. Total cancer deaths in the group were more than three times the expected number—995 versus 320. One hundred sixty-eight of the deaths were attributed to asbestosis. Twenty-one percent of the deaths—486—were due to cancer of the lung; 106 lung cancer deaths were expected. Mesothelioma killed 175 of the workers; this cause of death is so rare in the general population that none were expected.

Studies from the Mt. Sinai group and many others convinced virtually all independent researchers that asbestos is a major industrial cause of cancer and asbestosis. The asbestos industry was harder to convince. The industry strongly resisted even the weak OSHA standard for workplace exposure that is now in effect. Industry spokesmen were particularly insistent that the chrysotile form of asbestos is relatively harmless except at very high levels. Ninety-five percent of the asbestos used in this country is chrysotile. The asbestos at the Globe site is mostly chrysotile, but other forms of asbestos, bought from the U.S. government stockpile, were once milled there.

The industry argument is rejected by most independent scientists. At the hearings conducted by Representative Dingell on the Globe case, Dr. Vernon Houk, Director of the Center for Environmental Health of the Centers for Disease Control, had this to say:

There is no debate about the health hazards of chrysotile asbestos. Those who feel it is not hazardous are uninformed and/or wrong. . . . There is a very substantial literature on this subject. . . . I do not believe there is even room for any informed debate on the issue.

In Globe, there were plenty of people who debated it. The local newspaper, the *Arizona Silver Belt,* the radio station, the Chamber of Commerce, all derided the asbestos threat, and said that talk about it was hurting business in Globe. Tom Anderson, publisher of the *Silver Belt,* remarked that his newspaper plant and City Hall were both built on old asbestos mill sites (both are also built on, and surrounded by, concrete). "There's as much danger right here as at Mountain View," said Anderson.

Two longtime Globe residents—Hubert "Mike" Wood, a semi-retired insurance agent, and Alvin Gerhardt, formerly superintendent of the Jaquays mill—set out to prove that asbestos hasn't killed a single person in or around Globe in the 50 years asbestos has been milled there (the town once had as many as 14 working mills). In 1982, Wood and Gerhardt interviewed 146 miners, millers, transporters and other asbestos workers, 43 of whom were over 70 years old, and reported that none had lung cancer. Of another 486 relatives and friends of the workers, they said, "There has been no illness from Gila County chrysotile asbestos."

"At the time when all the mills were operating," Gerhardt said, "the dust was sometimes so thick you couldn't see in front of you. . . . If this type of asbestos is such a carcinogen, why does Gila County have a lower rate of cancer than the state and national average?"

Dr. James Sarn, until recently director of the Arizona Department of Health Services, said in a television interview that the Gerhardt-Wood information was interesting, but anecdotal. "If . . . you go out and investigate 140 people who are alive, you have not found the kind who are going to die from bronchogenic cancer or mesothelioma." Dr. William Nicholson of Mt. Sinai suggested that any excess of cancers among asbestos mine and mill workers might not show up in Gila County's mortality figures because the workers were probably too few. Nicholson pointed out that only half a dozen people at a time worked at the Metate mill.

Sarn said, "There is overwhelming evidence against chrysotile asbestos." He referred to a 1971 study by Dr. John C. McDonald of

McGill University in Montreal, often cited in defense of the chrysotile form. That study, said Sarn, "was sponsored in part by the asbestos industry in Canada. The initial work did not find any cancer . . . increasing with asbestos. However, a restudy of those people . . . in 1977 and 1978 found that indeed, there was a significant increase. . . . The McDonald study has some 10,900 people that it followed [from] the point of their employment to their final demise."

Some of Globe's 8,000 townspeople, disbelieving the danger of asbestos, have been harshly critical of the Mountain View residents. "People think we're in it for the money, that we're part of the gimme generation," said Cathy Scott. "Some of them said, 'If you're so worried about your health, why don't you move out?' Well, who would we sell the house to? Some other family with small children?"

Sarah Luckie echoed the same thought: "There is no way we could sell the house in good conscience to anyone. No one with any sense would buy it anyway. We are just four years from having paid off that American dream and its value is zero."

John Insalaco, a former upstate New Yorker who moved to Globe with his wife Elaine in 1971, was the first resident of Mountain View and once a strong booster of the development. He was the man who backed up the developer, Jack Neal, in persuading the city to rezone the tract residential in 1973. Insalaco's urging carried weight. He and his family own a music store and upholstery business on Globe's main street, he belongs to business and civic leaders' clubs, and he is a model citizen. His second year in town, he won the Globe "Citizen of the Year" award for his volunteer work in behalf of retarded children.

Insalaco's whole family moved into Mountain View—his father and mother, his wife's parents, a brother. He says he was the last to want to believe there was anything wrong at Mountain View. The Insalaco clan's homes were showplaces. Anna Insalaco, John's mother, still can't resist pulling a few stray weeds from the artfully planted front garden of her former home when she takes a visitor to see the place. Added to the wrench of uprooting the entire Insalaco clan and the fears for their health is the "harassment" John Insalaco gets from townspeople which, he says, is "just tremendous."

In Washington, Rita Lavelle was as hard to convince as the old-timers in Globe that asbestos was a danger to anybody's health. In the summer of 1982, after Anne Gorsuch decided that the Superfund couldn't be tapped for cleaning up mining wastes until "enforcement

97

remedies were exhausted," EPA staff had the job of convincing Lavelle to start enforcing. The necessary first step was a finding by Lavelle that the Globe situation posed a "substantial and imminent" danger to public health and the environment. Then EPA could refer the matter to the Department of Justice. Then, presumably, the Justice Department would seek a court order against the developer and other parties responsible for asbestos pollution of the Globe site, with the aim of forcing them to clean it up or somehow get the residents out of danger. But first Lavelle had to agree there was a danger and sign the paper.

By 1982 it was crystal clear that the state's "band-aid" treatment of asbestos at the Globe site had not worked. Ralph E. Yodaiken, a public health doctor from the Centers for Disease Control who visited the site for the first time in late 1981, was appalled. "The plight of the residents is extraordinary," he wrote. "[I] was amazed to find that asbestos fibers could be picked with ease out of the sand surrounding the homes. . . . The fact that children may be inhaling and ingesting quantities of asbestos fibers must be of concern to any responsible federal agency."

"We were really shocked that anyone would question the danger of living on top of an asbestos pile," said an EPA staffer. Yet Rita Lavelle did. She simply didn't believe the government scientists—in the Centers for Disease Control, in the National Institute for Occupational Safety and Health, or in the EPA—all of whom agreed that the hazard at the Globe site was great. "She had a built-in distrust of anything an EPA scientist said," one staff member recalled. Another added: "She was a visitor." At times she referred to Aerojet (her former employer) as "we" and EPA as "you."

Lavelle hired her own scientific adviser, Arthur Pallotta, who had once worked for EPA as a contractor. In order to make any kind of case to Lavelle, EPA scientists first had to get past Pallotta. "He was the court toxicologist," said one staffer, "and an instant expert on everything —first dioxin, then PCBs, then asbestos." Pallotta did not believe anything that came from Dr. Irving Selikoff and the Mt. Sinai group, according to another staff member. "He thought they were a bunch of environmental extremists."

At one point, Lavelle suggested that the asbestos industry trade association check over the techniques that federal and state scientists had used in sampling the soil and air at the Globe site. A memorandum dated August 12, 1982, from Gene Lucero to EPA scientist Debbie Dalton, said: "Rita asked me if we had considered running the evidence we had on the site by the Asbestos Institute. What are your thoughts?"

Dalton did not exactly accept the suggestion, even though, staff members said, "by that time the people working on Globe would have done almost anything to move the case along." Instead, she checked with EPA scientists, two public health agencies, and the Asbestos Information Association (incorrectly termed the Asbestos Institute in the Lucero memo), and determined that all used the same sampling methods.

"After we argued over [sampling] all summer long," a staffer said, Lavelle then began to raise the argument that chrysotile asbestos is relatively harmless. "She never really said no to the Globe site. She just kept raising new objections." At length, all the questions seemed to be answered. Pallotta was convinced there was a hazard at Globe. Late in the evening of September 30, 1982, the last day for referring that year's hazardous waste cases to the Department of Justice, Lavelle finally signed off.

Then nothing happened. The Justice Department took no steps to bring a court order against the responsible private parties. A spokesman for the department said it would be pointless to proceed against Jack Neal, owner of the Metate mill and subsequent developer of Mountain View Mobile Home Estates, because he had declared personal bankruptcy.

This was Catch-22. You don't get a court order against Jack Neal to clean up the Globe pollution because he's broke, and you don't spend Superfund money because you haven't "exhausted the enforcement remedies." And, as Dingell and others pointed out at the Globe hearings, it is quite an extraordinary interpretation of the law for the Justice Department to refuse to file a lawsuit because "they didn't think the individual concerned had enough money to respond." The congressmen asked, How can the Justice Department know that the defendant has no money unless it goes ahead and files the case?

"They do it every day with regard to people who owe taxes," observed Minnesota Representative Gerry Sikorski. "You have just got people passing the buck all around while these . . . good people are breathing what everyone considers a tremendous danger." Finally, two weeks after the Dingell hearing, the Department of Justice filed the claim against private parties in the Globe case.

Meanwhile, according to Hedeman's testimony, Rita Lavelle was trying to solve the Globe problem in another way. Her solution was to take Globe and the other mining sites off the Superfund National Priority List. Stanley Hulett, congressional affairs director for the Interior Department and a top assistant to Secretary Watt, also favored the idea. Lavelle and Hulett both saw the mining waste issue as a hot potato for western Republican senators who were up for reelection in 1984.

In December 1982 Lavelle and Hulett met to discuss the problem. Also at the meeting were Hedeman, Gene Lucero, and John Skinner, director of EPA's Office of Solid Waste. Hulett, Hedeman says, apparently didn't realize that the three men were civil servants, not political appointees, so he openly talked politics. Hedeman told the House subcommittee, "The discussions of the Republican senatorial races in 1984 . . . made me uncomfortable, frankly."

Lavelle and Hulett agreed that cleaning up mining waste could involve a lot of money because the sites are large, and that the use of Superfund for the cleanup might raise the specter of federal invasion of states' rights. "The last thing [Hulett] wanted was to have the mining issue blow up" in 1984, says Hedeman. Throughout their discussion, Lavelle and Hulett "never got to the question of the best way to deal with the problem from the environmental standpoint."

The strategy Hulett and Lavelle agreed on was to publish the proposed National Priority List with mining waste sites on it for the time being, but to use the preamble to invite comments on whether mining sites ought to remain on the list. Meanwhile, Hulett would try to find legal authority for handling mining sites in the Interior Department. If he found it, Interior could comment on the National Priority List in a way to justify taking mining sites off, cutting them out of EPA and out of Superfund, and shunting them over to Interior. The unspoken understanding was that James Watt's Interior Department would know how to keep mining wastes from becoming an inconvenient political issue.

In December 1982 Anne Gorsuch's chief of staff, John Daniel, gave the strategy his approval. Hedeman's notes from that meeting say: "Leave mining sites on list, but use preamble to let people react to mining question as to whether these fall under CERCLA [Superfund] and whether other authorities may exist"; and "invite people to comment on this policy and identify other authorities that may exist to respond to these sites."

In January 1983 everything changed. The President had ordered

Gorsuch to withhold from Congress documents on Superfund sites. News stories appeared daily on cozy relations between EPA and industry, and on alleged manipulation of Superfund for political purposes. Rita Lavelle's lunches with industry were on the front page. So were stories from Missouri, where EPA had waited months, and still had not used Superfund authority to rescue people threatened by high levels of dioxin.

On January 18—two weeks before Rita Lavelle was fired—Anne Gorsuch reversed the decision on mining wastes. At a meeting that day, Hedeman told Gorsuch about a mining site he had visited in Colorado that had no enforcement remedies to exhaust because there was nobody to sue. He told her that the time had come to focus on the real issue: "Where are we going to spend money out of the trust fund to correct mining sites?"

At last, Gorsuch decided to treat mining waste sites like other waste sites. This policy reversal, and Gorsuch's dramatic offer a few weeks later to buy out the citizens of Times Beach, Missouri, finally cleared the way for action at Globe.

Gorsuch made the Times Beach buy-out offer after a winter flood had washed dioxin-contaminated soil throughout the town, and after Rita Lavelle had been fired. While Lavelle ran the Superfund program, she had never agreed to relocation of victims to deal with hazardous waste dangers. In April 1983 Lee Thomas, Lavelle's replacement as chief for hazardous waste, followed the Times Beach precedent. Responding to an EPA staff petition, he offered the families at Globe the chance to move off their asbestos pile, with the promise that EPA would either buy their homes later or make it safe for them to return. All but five people moved out. EPA concluded in May that a buy-out would be cheaper than any other adequately safe alternative. This made the buy-out offer official. It will cost about $4.4 million, not an exorbitant amount for a Superfund site. At the time, cleanup costs for the average site were about $6.5 million. Three and a half years after state health officials found asbestos at Mountain View Mobile Home Estates, nearly two and a half years after the Superfund law was passed, the Globe homes were finally bought out and boarded up.

The Globe site is just one of hundreds of hazardous waste dump sites that suffered from the Reagan Administration policies of planned neglect. It is one of thousands that need attention, after decades of ignorant or heedless disposal of hazardous wastes. The biggest threat from these old dump sites is that toxic chemicals may leak into the soil beneath and seep into underground water supplies.

Pollution of ground water is a serious business. Half the people in the United States get their drinking water from underground supplies. And once ground water is polluted, it is exceedingly hard to clean it up; so long as it stays in the cool, dark, sterile environment underground, it stays polluted. In a 1983 EPA study of underground drinking water supplies in 945 towns and cities, 21 percent of the 466 random sample sites showed contamination by toxic organic chemicals. In a special sampling of 479 sites chosen for "proximity to landfills, industrial activity, etc.," 27 percent of the water supplies were contaminated.

Without question, hazardous wastes are polluting ground water. Anecdotal evidence is unfortunately plentiful. For example, in Hardeman County, Tennessee, people living near a chemical manufacturing plant waste dump had to stop drinking their well water when they discovered high levels of contamination; the same water was so high in carbon tetrachloride that when they showered in it they had trouble breathing. More systematically, a 1982 study in Connecticut and New Jersey showed that 40 percent of ground water contamination discovered in those states was due to hazardous industrial wastes.

The Superfund dump sites are leftovers from the past. But hazardous wastes continue to mount up at a staggering pace. According to August 1983 EPA figures, industry generates 150 million metric tons of chemical hazardous waste each year (a metric ton is about 2,200 pounds). Estimates from the Congressional Office of Technology Assessment put the total at between 255 and 275 million metric tons. Besides the wastes EPA lists as hazardous, this estimate also includes all the wastes that states define and regulate as hazardous. Altogether we are adding well over one ton of hazardous waste to the environment each year for each person.

In its first months, the Reagan Administration threw into reverse EPA's controls over the mountains of new hazardous wastes generated every day. First, in March 1981, Vice-President Bush targeted for "regulatory relief" the whole of EPA's entire hazardous waste control program.

In the Resource Conservation and Recovery Act of 1976 (RCRA), Congress directed EPA to establish a "cradle to grave" system for managing hazardous wastes safely. EPA's job was to identify and list hazardous wastes; set up a national manifest system to track the wastes from generation to disposal; establish standards for storing, treating, and disposing of wastes; set up a permit system for storage, treatment, and disposal facilities.

The law encourages states to take over hazardous waste controls, so long as they keep up to federal standards. The reason for EPA's running the program in the first place is that most states could not do it without help. Also, as with most environmental programs, uniform federal requirements get states off the hook, in case industries affected by the controls threaten to relocate elsewhere.

In its first four years (1976–1980) of trying to control hazardous wastes, EPA's record was not a glorious one. The Agency repeatedly missed the deadlines Congress had set in the law, and it struggled, often without success, to meet new ones set by the courts when environmentalists sued to compel EPA to act. The job was not easy. The field was new, knowledge was scanty, and industry resistance was high. Also, the Carter Administration's cumbersome attempts at "regulatory reform" often hobbled EPA's already cautious effort. Nonetheless, by the end of 1980—laboriously and belatedly—much of the program was in place. The Bush Task Force directed EPA to reconsider all of it.

First, in tune with OMB and committed to the blitz against regulations most disliked by industry, Anne Gorsuch suspended in June 1981 three protective rules EPA had already issued. One required hazardous waste facility operators to carry liability insurance; the others set standards for hazardous waste incineration and for surface storage of hazardous wastes in ponds and pits. (These last two rules were not precisely "suspended"; instead, EPA announced that it simply would not require operators of incinerators and storage impoundments to get new permits under the new rules. This amounted to the same thing as suspension; so said a U.S. Circuit Court of Appeals, which later ruled the whole ploy illegal in a suit brought by the Environmental Defense Fund.) Other rules that Gorsuch left alone did not take effect for months, because the OMB held up the permit forms, doing a "paperwork reduction" review.

Next, EPA enforcement of the existing rules on hazardous waste disposal virtually stopped. Prosecution of violators almost ceased. EPA had referred 43 hazardous waste cases to the Justice Department in 1980; the 1981 total was only seven. And in February 1982 Gorsuch suspended for a time the ban on burial of drums of liquid hazardous

103

wastes in landfills, a practice that had created Love Canals across the nation.

Liquids standing in barrels in landfills are the worst of hazardous wastes. Far more than dry, immobile materials, they eat through their containers, attack protective liners of burial pits (if there are any liners), spread through the soil when they reach it, and eventually pollute the ground water. Worse yet, drums that have lost their liquid contents are likely to be crushed by the weight of drums stored in layers above. With subsidence of this kind, the whole structure of the burial pit could cave in, crushing all the drums and squeezing out their contents. If this happens after a pit is closed, the cap that seals it will crack, opening the pit to rainwater. Gorsuch's suspension of the ban on burying liquids in drums lasted just under four weeks. After protests from all over the country, she rescinded it.

The liquid-in-landfills decision was doubtless one of EPA's worst fiascos on hazardous waste during the Gorsuch era. But there were others. Suspension of the rules for incineration of hazardous wastes and for surface storage impoundments meant that one more year went by before these facilities had to meet safer standards. (Gorsuch reimposed the rules a year later.) One staff member remarks that EPA could have at least compromised. It could have ordered the worst facilities, the ones that really threatened human health and the environment, to come in for a new permit under the stricter standards. "But everybody insisted on going one step further and letting industry completely off the hook."

Two EPA staff members recall that Gorsuch and her advisers suspended the incineration standard after industry argued that it was impossibly high—technically out of reach for many operators. But when it came time to support that argument with the facts, "The Chemical Manufacturers' Association [the industry lobby] came in and said they didn't have any data to back it up."

Yet, according to her friends and associates, Gorsuch's great ambition as EPA Administrator was to control the dumping of hazardous wastes on the land, and make land disposal safe for the public health and the environment. Under a court order to produce land disposal regulations, Gorsuch wanted to do a good job of it—such a good job, in fact, that EPA could guarantee no discharge of toxic chemicals from landfills. The trouble is, this cannot be done. Putting highly toxic, persistent, mobile organic chemicals into lined pits in the earth is basically a bad idea. Inevitably, they leak.

Rita Lavelle, EPA chief of hazardous waste disposal as well as Superfund director, seemed blandly ignorant of the danger. She said: "We believe that most wastes can be satisfactorily managed in the land and that it can be done with a reasonable margin of safety more cheaply in this manner." Yet in its land disposal regulations, issued in 1982, EPA itself conceded that "any liner [for earthen pits] will begin to leak eventually." EPA gave the liners an active life of 20 to 40 years. The wastes, on the other hand, can last hundreds or thousands of years; many of them hardly degrade at all.

In any case, the 20-year estimate may be highly optimistic. EPA regulations require "state-of-the-art" technology for new landfills. These are covered pits with double liners, made of clay or heavy plastic, equipped with a leak detection system in the space between. Liquid showing up in the space is a warning that the inner lining may be leaking.

In four modern state-of-the-art landfills in New Jersey, liquids appeared in the space just months after the sites opened. A study by Peter Montague, of Princeton University's Center for Energy and Environmental Studies, concluded that the inner linings in all four were leaking. The owners (Monsanto, DuPont, J. T. Baker Chemical Co., and Toms River Chemical Co.) claimed the liquid was rainwater. Montague was not able to determine whether the outer, or bottom, linings of the landfills were leaking. None of the landfills was over four years old, and if chemicals were leaking out they probably would not have reached ground water yet. In any case, monitoring of ground water, which is required by EPA and is supposed to detect leaks from landfills, is notoriously tricky to do. (One difficulty is that the sampling wells may not pick up contamination, because it is hard to predict how fluids will move underground. Another is that ground water sampling data are hard to interpret; serious pollution may occur before the samples show statistically significant increases in pollutants from background levels.)

Everyone, including EPA and the Chemical Manufacturers' Association, agrees that the best choice for managing hazardous wastes is to produce fewer of them, wherever possible. Where that is not possible, the best choices for highly toxic, mobile, persistent wastes, according to the Office of Technology Assessment, are to recycle them, burn them, or chemically treat them to reduce their volume and level of hazard. The residue may then be put in landfills. In some industrial European countries such as Denmark and West Germany, 80 to 90 percent of toxic chemical wastes are said to be treated in this way. In the United States, the OTA report said, land disposal is used for as much as 80 percent of all kinds of hazardous wastes, and that includes toxic wastes. According to a California study, nearly 40 percent of hazardous wastes dumped on the land are highly toxic and very persistent. The same study concluded that 75 percent of the hazardous waste in landfills could be recycled, treated, or destroyed.

The hitch is cost. Recycling, treatment, or waste reduction can cost 50 to 100 percent more than "state-of-the-art" land disposal—in the short run. But, as the OTA report says, "Attempting to minimize present costs will almost certainly lead to a transfer of greater costs to the future." Years or decades from now, cleaning up a hazardous dump site might cost 10 to 100 times as much as the *best* methods of treatment today. Take Love Canal as an example. It is estimated that it would have cost $2 million (in 1979 dollars) to dispose of the toxic wastes there properly. By 1980 the United States and the State of New York had already spent $36 million in cleaning up Love Canal and moving people out. Costs were expected to rise to $100 million, not counting the $2 billion in lawsuits that Love Canal residents have filed.

Actually, some companies that generate hazardous wastes have found they can save money now, in the short run, by recycling and reduction of waste. So far, these strategies have been cheapest and most effective in big firms with centralized operations. Some large volume chemical companies, like DuPont and Dow, have invested in high-technology incinerators that destroy much of their liquid and solid waste. Rohm and Haas, which used to discard leftover chemicals from their research laboratory in Spring House, Pennsylvania, reduced waste through better housekeeping. Now, the lab keeps track of every chemical it uses through a computerized inventory, and generates one-third less waste.

Ten years ago, Monsanto Company's plant at Baxley, Georgia, channeled its caustic chemical wastes into an evaporation pond, and then later dredged out the solids and buried them. Now, Monsanto sells the caustic sludge to a New Jersey waste disposal company that uses it to neutralize acids. Monsanto makes money on the deal, even after paying to truck the sludge to New Jersey. Another device Monsanto has used to reduce hazardous waste was to alter slightly its method of making an adhesive, turning what was formerly waste into a part of the product.

Altogether, through recycling and reduction of waste, Monsanto reported that it saved over $8 million in 1982. The Minnesota Mining and Manufacturing Company (3M), in its ninth year of a "Pollution Prevention Pays" program, said it saved $26.5 million in 1982 by avoiding the generation of 25,000 pounds of waste sludge.

Despite these success stories, a great preponderance of the hazardous waste generated by American industry still winds up on the land because, for the companies that have to pay for it, land disposal is the cheapest and easiest alternative.

In 1981 and 1982, in congressional hearings and in written comments to EPA on the proposed land disposal regulations, numerous critics pointed out the fallibility of landfill liners. They urged that EPA set standards for protective location of landfills, requiring for example that they be sited well away from underground water supplies and in relatively impermeable soils. Some suggested a more fundamental measure: a ban on land disposal of dangerous chemicals that are likely to attack liners and migrate through soils. California has adopted such a ban for certain wastes for which other methods of disposal are available. The rules EPA issued in 1982 did not require either one of these essential safeguards. They put no restrictions on landfilling highly toxic, persistent wastes. Nor did they impose any conditions on where hazardous waste landfills may be placed, except to suggest that they should not be sited in seismically active zones or in 100-year floodplains—or, if they are, to design them to withstand earthquakes or floods.

Gary Dietrich, formerly a senior civil servant at EPA and head of the Office of Solid Waste until May 1982, gives Anne Gorsuch credit for going as far as she did in the hazardous waste landfill regulations. Dietrich says, "I was amazed I was able to sell her on the plastic liner concept." Once sold on it, she stood up for it tenaciously. She personally took the issue to Vice-President Bush, after a standoff with OMB's regulatory relief bosses who insisted on deleting the requirement for liners. "I think OMB was worried that the liner requirement was a step in the direction of requiring liners for old landfills," says Dietrich. "It might be precedent setting." But OMB was no match for Gorsuch on this issue. "She had personally spent much more time on [it] than anyone at OMB," said an EPA staff member. "Not even their staff could argue with her toe-to-toe on the technical issues."

Dietrich concedes that plastic liners in hazardous waste landfills can and do fail. But he believes it was essential to establish the "concept of no exfiltration" (meaning no leaking), which liners represented. Liners, says Dietrich, are the first step. Location standards and limits on the kinds of waste put into landfills should follow, and he believes they will. Then, he says, "we will get to the point where we can guarantee an acceptable level of environment and health protection."

Khristine Hall, attorney for the Environmental Defense Fund, does not agree that EPA's liner requirement is defensible as a first step. "The absence of location standards is inexcusable," says Hall. "They were an issue from the very beginning." She grants that restriction on types of wastes in landfills was a newer issue, but adds: "If California did it, maybe EPA can too."

The EPA land disposal regulations, Hall points out, made "absolutely no technical requirements for existing facilities"—no liners for existing ponds (which could be drained, lined, and refilled), not even retaining walls. "Existing facilities were just completely written off," says Hall. To make it worse, EPA agreed in separate negotiations with the industry to let existing facilities expand by 50 percent before they are officially regarded as a "new facility," which means they escape the more stringent permit controls for new landfills.

To one EPA staff member, it was not even the negatives—the retreats, the omissions, the deals cut with industry—that were the worst of EPA's hazardous waste control program. It was the lack of a positive vision. This staff member said: "With the exception of the land disposal regs, we didn't get anything out. No new listings of hazardous wastes. No permitting—only 25 in two years. Permitting is vital because permit conditions bind the operator of a waste facility to build and run it according to EPA rules. No enforcement.

"We spent huge sums on regulatory impact analysis on existing regulations, which were defensive actions against OMB. Rita wasn't interested in filling loopholes" in the hazardous waste control program, something Congress is trying to do in bills that reauthorize the program.

"No one had a big picture. . . . No one ever asked the question: Where do we want to be five years from now?"

A troubling aspect of EPA's program of hazardous waste control was the connection of James Sanderson, Anne Gorsuch's close personal adviser from March 1981 to June 1982, with the hazardous waste industry. When Gorsuch took him with her to Washington, he kept his Colorado clients. One of his clients was Chemical Waste Management, Inc., manager for the City of Denver of the Lowry Landfill hazardous waste facility, and a subsidiary of the huge conglomerate Waste Management, Inc., of Oakbrook, Illinois.

Chemical Waste Management had vital interests in the hazardous waste issues Gorsuch had to decide. Did Sanderson have any hand in EPA's decisions on these matters? Sanderson himself said certainly not. In a sworn statement to investigators for EPA's Inspector General, Sanderson said that, while he worked at EPA, he walled himself off from decisions that might affect his private clients. Whenever any such matter came up, he told them, "I got up and walked out of the room."*

Others recall the matter a little differently. Gary Dietrich says that Sanderson "very definitely participated" in EPA meetings in January or February 1982 at which regulations for the design of hazardous waste landfills were discussed. At the time, Dietrich was pushing for the landfill liner requirement. Some in the industry strongly opposed it. Asked whether Sanderson participated as an aide to Gorsuch or as an attorney for his client, Dietrich replied: "My impression was that he was acting as a consultant to the Administrator. The subject matter at the meeting was broad. Actually, he supported me [on the liner requirement]. I was kind of amazed."

Then Dietrich mused: "He might have been acting on behalf of Waste Management. Waste Management did want stronger regulations. [Perhaps because] it insulates them from public criticism. [They can say] 'We've got these regulations. You don't have anything to worry about.' "

Dietrich described another EPA meeting on land disposal in April 1982 at which Sanderson was not an ally of his but an antagonist. Dietrich and Sanderson were briefing Gorsuch for a forthcoming appearance before a House subcommittee. Dietrich advised her to assure the committee that she would issue land disposal regulations soon, and would lift the suspension of EPA rules on incinerators, surface storage, and liability insurance for hazardous wastes. Dietrich believed Gorsuch intended to take both actions anyway (in fact she later did), and he thought she might as well do something to improve her environmental reputation with Congress.

Sanderson was angry because Dietrich had discussed the insurance issue in a *Washington Post* interview published that day. "You're up here to make come true what you said" in the newspaper, Dietrich recalls Sanderson saying. Then Sanderson added (according to Die-

---

*In an interview for this book, Sanderson declined to discuss any conflict-of-interest allegations, on the ground that the Justice Department was investigating them.

trich), "Where are you going to be working next week?" At this, Gorsuch reproved Sanderson, but refused to do anything that would appear to be a concession to her critics in Congress.

Asked whether Sanderson, in any of these meetings, ever "got up and walked out," Dietrich said, "No."

No one knows how great a part Sanderson actually took in EPA's hazardous waste decisions. But the simple fact that for fifteen months he acted both as Gorsuch's right-hand man and at the same time as an advocate for industries that EPA was regulating is in itself extraordinary. Law firms do not ordinarily represent two private clients whose interests may conflict. Where public and private interest may collide, is it possible for anyone to switch back and forth between private and public interest hats from day to day (or even, as Sanderson did, in the course of the same day) without losing sight of the separate and distinct interests of each?

Moreover, by January 1982, when Sanderson took part in meetings on hazardous wastes, he was something more than the Administrator's closest adviser; he was also the nominee, selected by Gorsuch and nominated by the President, to EPA's number three position. Normally, it would be entirely appropriate for the man or woman named for that job to attend high-level EPA policy meetings. But Sanderson still had not separated himself from the Denver law firm in which he was a partner and which still represented private clients with interests regulated by EPA.

Sanderson recently described the role he envisioned for himself while he was at EPA: "I approach things from the standpoint that I want the client, or the decision maker, to have all sides of the issues in front of him/her so that they can make a reasoned choice. I've found that normally staffs tend to package things in some direction; and I felt that I had the ability at least to make some impact on making sure that the Administrator had every range of the options laid in front of her, so she knew that it wasn't slanted in one way or the other."

How many citizens, if they were aware of James Sanderson's dual roles, would have felt more confidence in his ability to present unbiased facts to the Administrator than in the EPA staff's ability to do so?

In an interview with a Network News correspondent in December 1982, Anne Gorsuch attacked environmentalists for their "rhetoric" and "misrepresentation" and demanded that her tenure at EPA be judged by its results. She said, "You can say, 'Oh gosh, hazardous waste sites, Love Canals, are horrible things,'—sure they are—now what are you going to do about it, and not the rhetoric. And we've got results. . . . We are going to be controlling hazardous waste disposal sites in this country for virtually the first time. . . . It feels very, very satisfying."

Some of the communities facing new hazardous waste landfills in their backyards were not so satisfied with those results. It came as a real shock to citizens of Cheraw, South Carolina, that the new EPA rules allowed landfills to be built almost anywhere, even on top of a town's water supply. Cheraw is just over the state line from Anson County, North Carolina, where Chem-Security Systems, Inc. (another subsidiary of Waste Management, Inc.), planned to put a "secure" hazardous waste landfill. The spot chosen, deep in the country, was on a hill a few hundred feet from a stream that runs into Jones Creek, which in turn feeds into the Great Pee Dee River. The bottoms of the waste pits, as planned, would have been seven feet above ground water.

People in Cheraw couldn't believe it. They were incredulous that EPA rules would allow a hazardous waste landfill so perilously close to the surface and ground water systems that feed the Pee Dee River. They drink the Pee Dee's water; they bathe in it and cook with it. Any toxic pollutants seeping into Jones Creek would reach the town's water supply intake pipes in just fifteen hours.

Clyde Wallace, an industrial engineer with the Stanley Tools plant in Cheraw, told Cass Peterson of the *Washington Post:* "I asked the EPA regional office in Atlanta how a site seven feet above the water table could be considered safe. They said, 'Hell, those regulations say you could build the site *in* the water table.' " According to Peterson, people in the Anson County area didn't have much use for EPA's liner and leak detection system either. They called the plastic liner "a garbage bag." One asked: "Have they considered that a gopher could bite a hole in it?"

The Anson County site is rural and largely black. Cheraw, population 5,600, is the closest community downstream from the site, and it is in a different state. People in Cheraw believed those were the major reasons that led Chem-Security to choose the site—plus the fact that North Carolina has a law forbidding the state from imposing rules any stricter than the federal EPA's on control over hazardous wastes. Several states, heavily lobbied by the hazardous waste disposal industry, have passed such laws.

In November of 1982, a group of North and South Carolina citizens traveled to Washington, where they met Anne Gorsuch, thanks to the intercession of South Carolina Senator Strom Thurmond. They argued that the waste pits ought to be at least 30 feet above ground water, so that if ground water monitors detected a leak there would at least be a chance of cleaning it up before it hit Jones Creek.

Clyde Wallace recalled that Gorsuch was frostily polite but unsympathetic. She told the group that a rule like that would exclude half of North and South Carolina and the entire State of Florida and that a federal agency cannot write a regulation that will exempt a state from having a hazardous waste site. "But we figure that if it is unsafe it ought not to be built, even if the whole state is excluded," said Wallace.

Wallace voted for President Reagan in 1980; he thought he agreed with Reagan's campaign against overregulation. "I thought he was saying we needed to get off business's back. I thought he meant all those forms people have to fill out. I never thought of it as applying to things like protecting public health and the environment." Wallace added: "I've voted for every Republican presidential candidate since 1960. It's going to be a different story this next time."

In April 1983, Chem-Security announced it was abandoning its plans to build the landfill because of local opposition. Chem-Security's parent, Waste Management, Inc., also abandoned plans to build a 900-acre hazardous waste landfill near Bay City, Texas, along the lower Colorado River. Here, on the Gulf Coast, the water table is practically at the land's surface; the landfill would have been in it. A citizens' group of men and women who had never been activists before—refinery workers, secretaries, housewives, shrimp fishermen—organized Matagorda County against the landfill. They held bake sales to raise money, collected signatures for petitioners to the Governor at rodeos and supermarkets, and threatened to blockade Waste Management company barges carrying hazardous wastes to Corpus Christi with a flotilla of motorboats, shrimp boats, and inner tubes. Waste Management, Inc., gave up.

The story of Denver's Lowry Landfill, managed since 1980 by another subsidiary of Waste Management, Inc., tells something more about land disposal of toxic chemical wastes and how it works in the real world. It also throws an interesting light on Anne Gorsuch's political origins and allies in her home state, where she was a powerful force in the Colorado House of Representatives.

In 1980, after she came to prominence as a leader of the right-wing

"House Crazies," Gorsuch chaired a special committee of the legislature on hazardous waste. The committee's job was to consider whether to establish state control over hazardous dump sites. Gorsuch was against a state program from the beginning. According to a close associate on the hazardous waste committee, she saw waste disposal as industry's own business and she did not like state regulation much better than federal. She selected committee members who shared her views, choosing as co-chairman an arch-conservative State Senator and including among the members another one of the House Crazies, a conservative county commissioner, and Whit Field, then a lobbyist for the Coors brewery, mining, and manufacturing complex.

Gorsuch's strong ideological opposition to a state hazardous waste program prevailed, despite support for it which included state agencies, environmental and civic groups, and the Colorado Association for Commerce and Industry. However, Whit Field of Coors, like Gorsuch, was against it. The Gorsuch committee recommended against a Colorado program on the grounds that the state's authority, versus EPA's under the federal law, would not be clear.

The result was that in 1981 and 1982 Colorado state health officials stood by disarmed, without clear legal authority to stop what they saw as serious violations of good public health practice at Denver's Lowry Landfill. And—what nobody foresaw—the House Crazies were now in control of EPA and thus in charge of the federal hazardous waste program for the region. Gorsuch chose Steve Durham, another former Crazy, as Regional Administrator of the Denver EPA office. In that job, he did nothing to force reform at Lowry. In fact, he contributed to the delinquency.

The City of Denver opened the Lowry Landfill in 1966 on 2,680 rural acres in Arapahoe County, fifteen miles outside the city limits. Lowry was a city dump, and everything went into it, from household garbage to hospital wastes (including some that were radioactive) to toxic industrial chemicals. By the 1970's industries from a wide region around Denver began trucking their wastes to Lowry; Coors was one of the biggest users. In 1972 the state health department estimated that two to three million gallons of liquid waste were poured directly from trucks into unlined pits and open trenches at Lowry. By 1977, the dumping had reached ten million gallons annually. Years later, an official for Hewlett-Packard, another big user, said: "Like so many things, waste disposal being in its infancy, we just didn't realize how much damage could be done. . . . It was basically just not knowing any better."

For a while, the farmers, ranchers, and exurban settlers in the neighborhood didn't realize how much damage could be done either. They didn't even know what was going into the dump. "We thought it was just a trash dump," said Bonnie Exner, who moved out to Arapahoe County in 1974 with her husband, two sons, dogs, cats, ducks, and chickens. The Exners were in the plumbing contracting business, but liked country living.

At first, the worst they noticed from the dump was flies and "privy" smells, when the wind blew the wrong way. But about a year after they moved in, Bonnie Exner said, the fumes from the dump really started getting bad. "There were days when we literally felt like we'd had a bath in oil. And when the wind blew over from the cyanide pits! Sometimes at two or three o'clock in the morning a truck would dump cyanide, and fifteen minutes later we'd jump out of our beds. We couldn't breathe. Our throats were just closed up."

The family also had nosebleeds and headaches, and sometimes tingly hands and feet, or the shakes. Other families had similar complaints. One of the Exner sons had asthma until the old pits were closed over; then he recovered. And Bonnie Exner had the blues. "I'm basically a pretty up person," she said, "but all the time those chemicals were out there I felt like there was no more joy in life."

In March of 1976, the State Health Department began to get seriously worried that toxic chemicals from the dump were seeping into the ground water beneath. Their tests showed that monitored wells were significantly contaminated with inorganic chemicals, not normally found in ground water. As it turned out, they were right to be worried. Later tests of ground water near the old dump, conducted by EPA from 1981 onward, confirmed that toxic chemicals—benzene, toluene, 1-1-dichloroethylene, and others—were flowing in a shallow aquifer underground as far as one mile beyond the disposal site. Seventeen farm wells that draw from the shallow aquifer are located no more than three miles downgradient from the old dump site.

Even more serious was the discovery in 1982 of contamination several hundred feet from the dump site in the deeper Dawson aquifer. This aquifer is the source of drinking water for 5,000 county residents in East Cherry Creek Valley. None of the county wells was contaminated yet, as of 1983, but ten of them were within three miles

114

downgradient of the dump and the district had permits to install ten more wells in the same area (one only a quarter of a mile from the dump).

Ken Waesche, a geologist with the Colorado Health Department, recently recalled that the theory years ago had been that the garbage in the city dump would soak up liquid waste like a sponge and immobilize it. "It's really unbelievable when you look back on it," he said. "There's no way a paper bag was going to soak up organic chemicals."

Despite the Health Department's misgivings, the state took no action at the time. Under Colorado's solid waste law, passed in 1969, landfills were primarily county business. And the federal hazardous waste program was just getting started. So, despite mounting protests from frightened neighbors, the dumping went on until 1980, when interim federal regulations on hazardous waste landfills—in the works for nearly four years—were finally ready.

The new federal rules required Denver to improve the Lowry Landfill or close it. But because so many industries throughout the Denver region were using the dump, closing it seemed to threaten economic disaster. Denver turned to the experts—Chemical Waste Management (CWM). Officials of the parent company, Waste Management, Inc., flew in from Illinois with their brochures and slide shows. They promised to build a "state-of-the-art" hazardous waste facility on the Lowry property that would protect public health and the environment. Denver rushed through a contract with CWM, and the company was receiving wastes by August 1980, in time to qualify as an "existing site" under federal law. That meant CWM did not have to wait, possibly months, for an EPA permit or comply with the stricter standards for new facilities. CWM undertook to meet some of the tougher standards anyway.

Bonnie Exner didn't believe the assurances that the new landfill would be safe. Neither did the other members of CALL (Citizens Against the Lowry Landfill), a group Exner had founded and helped finance from her earnings as a bartender at the local Veterans of Foreign Wars post. "I was working there to support my habit—fighting the landfill," Exner said.

By the end of 1980, the issue was an exceedingly hot one among the 70,000 Arapahoe County residents in the Lowry area. In late November of that year, hundreds of county residents poured into a meeting of the County Commissioners, called to review the CWM plans. The citizens countered that the CWM landfill, already partly built and in business, should have a county permit but was operating without one. They thought the Lowry site, with its porous soil and major aquifers that supply drinking water for thousands of people, was totally unsuitable for a hazardous waste landfill. They wanted it closed. The conservative Commissioners of Arapahoe County agreed. They denied the new facility permission to operate and ordered it closed within ten days. Denver went to court to keep it open. For the time being, it stayed open.

What happened in the next year and a half, while the issue was fought out in court, convinced the people near Lowry more firmly than ever that they wanted the landfill closed. In compliance with the new EPA rules, things at the landfill definitely got better. No longer was a witches' brew of chemicals mixed together in unlined trenches. The reeking old pits were closed and covered over. (Most of the old site now looks like inoffensive rangeland, with the exception of some peculiar-looking mounds covered by thousands of worn-out tires. These are the old pits. Under their covers, they are still seeping toxic liquids into the earth and ground water. Local citizens complain that they still occasionally emit bursts of volatile toxic gases.)

At its new site, Chemical Waste Management built three evaporation ponds, each with double clay linings and a leak detection system between the linings, with pipes and pumps to collect any fluid that accumulated there. Only certain specified kinds of chemical liquids, labeled and segregated, were poured into the ponds. In another section of the Lowry acreage, a huge pit was hollowed out and lined with five feet of clay, as a burial site for toxic wastes in drums.

The first intimations of trouble were at the burial pit. CWM built it around an existing abandoned pit, thus saving $50,000 in construction costs. The Colorado Health Department had recommended against the location, because it was a drainage basin for 90 acres. Not only was there standing surface water in two ponds in the pit—the only ponds on the whole landfill site—but also the Health Department suspected that the pit might actually be in the underground water table. Water in a burial pit for drums is a serious hazard, because it hastens corrosion of the drums and, if chemicals leak out, it can carry them through the lining of the pit and spread them into the ground water.

Without a state law on hazardous waste (thanks to Anne Gorsuch), the Colorado Department of Health had no clear authority over siting. At any rate, CWM did not recognize any such authority and refused to give the health department its plans for review before construction. CWM put the burial pit where it wanted.

According to Chris Sutton, Lowry Landfill project manager for the Colorado Department of Health, CWM would not even allow him or the department geologist, Ken Waesche, on the property while excavation of the pit was going on. The one time they were permitted on the site, the company forbade them to take pictures. "That's because there was a visible pool of water in the pit they were digging," Sutton said.

In the following months, the Health Department kept a watchful eye on the pit. In April 1981 an inspector noted that the company had not yet constructed diversion trenches to keep surface water out of the pit. Seven feet of liquids were detected in a collection area (the sump) at the bottom of the pit. Tests showed the liquids there were contaminated with organic solvents and inorganic compounds, an indication that the drums were leaking and a threat to the integrity of the pit, because the chemicals might eat away at the clay liner. CWM pumped out the liquids, and had to keep pumping. Otherwise, between 35 and 100 gallons a day of liquid continued to collect in the sump. Throughout the year, while the Colorado Department of Health kept after CWM on the water problem in the burial pit, EPA stood aloof.

Another troubling fact was that drums being buried in the pit throughout most of 1981 contained toxic chemicals in liquid form. The industry was on notice that the practice would soon be illegal. The ban had a long history. EPA first proposed it in December 1978, then adopted it with some changes in May 1980, but gave the industry a full year and a half to work out ways to comply. The deadline was November 19, 1981. After that, no more hazardous liquids in drums could go into landfills.

From the time the new Lowry Landfill opened, the Colorado Health Department had urged CWM to cease burial of liquids in drums as soon as possible. CWM agreed. In December 1980 the company's officials told the Arapahoe County Commissioners (and pledged in writing to the Health Department) that by January 1981 they would build an interim facility to solidify liquid waste in drums before burial, and would have a completed facility by the following November.

CWM did neither. Up through the middle of November, the company continued to bury drums containing liquids—over 13,000 of them—and did nothing to construct the solidification unit. The Colorado health officials have a file of letters they wrote CWM during

1981, demanding progress on solidification. CWM ignored the demands. EPA did nothing.

Possibly CWM was confident that the Reagan EPA would not impose the ban. In the summer of 1981, with regulatory relief at full tide, the hazardous waste industry had begun to negotiate with EPA on lifting or weakening the ban. The industry sued EPA in 1980, challenging virtually every aspect of the rules for hazardous waste disposal, including the one on liquids in landfills. Some in the industry wanted simply to rescind the ban. They argued that it was expensive and difficult to squeeze the liquid out of the sludge shipped in drums from waste generators, and dangerous to open the drums for inspection. Others in the industry sought a redefinition of "liquid" to exempt a variety of jellies, pastes, gums, and viscous wastes.

EPA negotiated with the parties to the lawsuit, including dozens of industry representatives and one public interest group, the Environmental Defense Fund. The industry soon coalesced behind the "Vardy proposal." Peter Vardy, a vice-president of Waste Management, suggested that EPA allow landfill operators to bury drums containing liquids in 25 percent of the burial space.

Environmental critics opposed the idea. To them, it looked more like surrender than a compromise. Twenty-five percent of the burial pit area was hardly "minimal," in their view. Gary Dietrich, then acting director of EPA's Office of Solid Waste, proposed a compromise to the industry: no more than 10 percent of the content of any drum could be liquid. Though an improvement over the Vardy proposal, this solution too seemed to the critics a risky one. Ten percent liquid in a 55-gallon drum is five and a half gallons, a very considerable amount.

EPA suggested that the 10-percent solution could be adopted promptly. While the regulation on liquids-in-landfills was being modified, EPA, as a matter of enforcement policy, would simply not take action against operators burying drums that contained less than 10 percent liquid. Thus the change could be made without delaying or suspending the ban on the burial of drums containing liquids. This was a major advantage. Existing rules cannot be changed by fiat; the law requires notice and public comment. Time was running short. It was mid-October, and the ban was to take effect in a month's time.

At a last negotiating session on November 6, 1981, thirteen days before the deadline for the ban, EPA attorneys expected to insist on the Dietrich compromise. But Dietrich himself changed position. After a private caucus, EPA officials accepted, in essence, the Vardy proposal —the 25-percent solution. And they announced they would extend the November 19 deadline 90 days, to leave time for hearings on the new rule. Those who had been expecting for three years that toxic liquids would finally be banished from landfills saw the decision as a bitter defeat. The extra three-month delay that EPA proposed, during which drummed liquids could still be buried at will, was salt in the wound.

A few days before the scheduled ban, Gary Dietrich sent the proposal for a revised rule and a 90-day extension up to Anne Gorsuch's 12th floor office. Somehow, Dietrich's package got lost. Gorsuch didn't sign it before November 19, 1981. The ban went into effect—to the consternation of the hazardous waste industry.

For three months, while Gorsuch and her legal advisers fiddled with details and language, the ban stayed in effect. She lifted it on February 25, 1982. At the same time, she announced the new rule (the 25-percent solution) that EPA was considering. To Dietrich's astonishment, all hell broke loose. After all the years that drummed wastes had been buried in landfills, Dietrich said recently, "I thought another few months wouldn't have hurt—that it wouldn't be that much extra insult to the environment."

Looking back on the uproar that followed the lifting of the ban, Dietrich says now: "I never expected the criticism that developed. We wound up with a horrible problem." EPA's proposed new rule aroused as much indignation as the lifting of the ban. Not only were there cries of protest from Congress, newspaper editorials, and citizen groups; part of the hazardous waste industry was outraged as well—the part that had invested in high technology incinerators to burn liquid wastes.

EPA solved the "horrible problem" by holding an accelerated set of hearings, scrapping the Vardy proposal, changing the absolute ban on liquids in drums to a ban on "visible liquids," and reimposing the ban —all in under four weeks. Environmental groups are satisfied with the rule. The industry is living with it. Today, at Waste Management's facilities, says Dietrich, "they are indeed examining every drum, either pumping out or extruding the liquid [by crushing the drums], and [adding material to] solidify the liquid after they take it out."

Asked whether James Sanderson took any part in the liquid-in-landfills decision, Dietrich says no. But he recalls that Sanderson called him "a couple of times to ask when the ban would be lifted." To the question whether Sanderson made his calls in his role as attorney for

CWM, rather than as aide to Gorsuch, Dietrich replied, "There was nothing in the conversation that would let me make that judgment with any precision. I presume it was in his capacity as attorney" (for the company).

Out in Denver, as the deadline for the ban on liquids in landfills approached and EPA still had not suspended it, CWM took action. Industrial customers still produced wastes every day that had to be disposed of. It would soon be illegal to bury the drums. And the solidification process was still a mirage. Company officials went to Steve Durham for help.

On October 28, Donald Wallgren, Director of Environmental Management for CWM's parent company, asked EPA for permission to add storage capacity on the rim of the burial pit for drums of liquid waste awaiting solidification. On November 13, CWM officials met with EPA to describe the plans for solidifying liquid waste and explain "why the additional storage in containers is necessary." At last, EPA sprang into action. Durham wrote the company on December 11, 1981, giving it permission to increase storage of drums, but "only to implement the solidification process." CWM was allowed to stockpile a huge cache of drums over the next few weeks. CWM's original storage capacity was 200 drums; while the ban on burial was in effect, the company accepted and "stored" 1,434 drums.

Barely a month after getting permission to add storage, CWM once more complained it was running out of space. Solidification was apparently no further along. On January 13, 1982, EPA Denver officials met with Eugene Megyesey, another partner in James Sanderson's law firm representing CWM, and Lowry's general manager, Marianne Walls. They asked permission to bury liquids in drums at Lowry despite the ban. Two days later, Durham wrote a letter giving the company formal permission to "store" drums, not in a storage area on the rim of the burial pit, but *in* the pit. He remarked in the letter that "it is anticipated that there may in the near future be a temporary suspension of [the] ban" on burial of liquid waste containers.

As a practical matter, the CWM people hardly needed permission to store the drums in the burial pit. They were already doing it. On January 11 two EPA inspectors noted that a load of drums from Coors, received that morning, had been placed in the burial pit for storage. Manager Marianne Walls explained that extra storage on the rim was not yet complete, so the burial pit itself offered the next best alternative.

The EPA inspector pointed out to Walls that "it would probably be better from a public relations aspect" to "store" future shipments of liquid waste drums in the "non-working" end of the pit. Walls agreed.

As a legal matter, Durham's letter was important. If anyone challenged "storage" of drums in the pit as a violation of the EPA burial ban, CWM could point to the letter from the Regional Administrator of EPA. By referring to the "anticipated" lifting of the burial ban, the letter also made it fairly clear that the drums could actually be stored for future burial, not for solidification.

On February 25, 1982, five weeks after CWM was given official permission to store drummed liquids in the pit, Anne Gorsuch suspended the ban on burial. In the next four weeks, CWM buried 2,491 drums, including the 1,434 that had been "stored," each containing 55 gallons of toxic wastes, including liquids. Gorsuch reimposed the ban on March 22, after the eruption of congressional, media, and citizen protests. In April 1982 CWM started up its solidification unit.

Then there was more trouble in the burial pit. In May 1982, after spring rains, water in the pit reached flood stage. A citizen's Monitoring Committee, EPA, and the Health Department, making a scheduled visit, were shocked to find rows of drums submerged under two or three feet of water. And a hose from the sump was pouring contaminated water onto unprotected ground outside the pit. This got a reaction out of EPA. CWM was ordered to close the pit, pump it out, build trenches to divert surface water from the pit, and install a closed system to keep pumping out the pit and collect the liquid. EPA levied no fine against CWM and allowed it to reopen the pit within a few weeks.

That summer, the reason for the flood became clear. A contractor for CWM confirmed what the Health Department had suspected all along: the burial pit was in the water table. Four-fifths of the pit's liner was below the ground water level.

In the rainy spring of 1983, the burial pit flooded again, more dramatically. This time, the drums were inundated with five feet of water. The diversion trenches failed. Liquids collecting in the pit surged from 60 gallons a day to nearly 2,300 gallons a day and had to be pumped out. The closed pump-and-storage system CWM had installed the previous year was overwhelmed. Company workers disconnected it and poured liquids from the pit onto a clay pathway leading to a makeshift clay-lined pond. These liquids were contaminated. In the huge volumes now being pumped from the pit, toxic chemicals were present at the same concentrations as in the much smaller volumes pumped out the year before. EPA inspectors also observed that the drums in the pit were leaking badly. After this fiasco, on May 25, 1983, EPA fined CWM $193,000.

Meanwhile, still more trouble appeared at the newly constructed state-of-the-art Lowry Landfill. One of the three huge evaporation ponds in the complex apparently sprang a leak. But no one at CWM reported it to EPA, the state Health Department, or the city. In fact, the company successfully concealed the trouble for fourteen months, until a curious and persistent inspector from the state Health Department ferreted it out.

The evaporation ponds, containing restricted types of wastes in liquid form, are each the length and breadth of a football field and ten feet deep. They are protected by double liners made of compacted clay five feet thick, with a leak detection system (also sometimes called a leachate collection system) in between. The system consists of a sloping layer of sand with a drainage basin at the lowest point (the sump). Any liquid that may seep through the inner clay liner is supposed to collect in the sump, there to be pumped out, treated, and re-dumped. The idea is to keep liquids from penetrating the outer or bottom liner, and from there getting into the earth and ground water.

Liquid in the sump is a sign of trouble. In a new pond or landfill it may very well signal a leak in the inner liner. Clay inner liners are expected to seep small amounts of liquid eventually, but large amounts early in the life of a landfill are extremely suspicious.

Large amounts of liquid (as much as 160 gallons a day) were collecting in the sump of Pond Two at the Lowry Landfill by July 1981, six weeks after the pond opened for business. CWM did not notify the city, county, state, or EPA. Nothing about liquids in the sump, then or afterwards, appeared in the records the company showed to EPA. Only long after the fact did EPA or state officials learn, from privately held company records and consultant reports, what had happened.

In August 1981 CWM started draining Pond Two. The company brought in consultants to study the problem and tried to repair cracks in the pond's inner liner. According to Chris Sutton, Lowry Landfill project manager for the Colorado Department of Health, the investigation and repair were done quietly on weekends. In November 1981, on his regular rounds to Lowry, Sutton asked to look at the standpipe extending from the sump beneath Pond Two. He was told the pond was empty (because its capacity wasn't needed yet), so there was no reason to check it.

This was the beginning of a ten-month runaround. Sutton, a young man with a big curly beard and the open, informal manner of the Colorado outdoorsman, tells the story with relish. By the end of November 1981, Pond Two was patched and back in service. But still (and still unbeknownst to Sutton and EPA) liquid was collecting in the sump, although now in smaller amounts—about 16 gallons a day. In January and March 1982, Sutton asked again to inspect Pond Two's sump. Company employees told him the lock on the standpipe was frozen. In May and July he asked again. Now he was told that the lock had been changed and the company chemist (who had the new key) was off the property.

In September 1982 Sutton got the same story. This time he dug in his heels. Lowry Landfill was now officially closed, and had been for three months. The order to close it, issued by the Arapahoe County Council back in December 1980, was invalidated by the Colorado Supreme Court in July 1982 on grounds of faulty procedure. But at the same time the Court ruled that the CWM facility could not stay open unless it got county approval. Colorado at last had a hazardous waste law, passed in 1981, and county approval is explicitly required under that law. There was no other hazardous waste facility like Lowry in Colorado, nor in the six-state region around it, and the pressure was mounting to reopen Lowry.

Chris Sutton realized he hadn't checked the sumps in all three ponds at Lowry in months. If the ponds were going to reopen, he was going to have a look. So when he was told once again that Brian Culvey, the employee with the key, was off the property and couldn't be found, he said: "We'll just wait till Brian gets back."

He had a six-hour wait. Late that afternoon, Gary Coker, the project's general manager, came down to the pond for the third time that day. Earlier Coker had twice tried to unlock the sump, but his key didn't work. Sutton would not give up. "Normally, I wouldn't be that persistent," he says, "but I knew they were pressuring us to get those ponds open." Sutton told Coker: "We'll just have to find Brian." At that, Coker took a different key from the same ring and opened the lock.

"When it's dry in the sump, it's all dark down there," says Sutton. "When I looked in this sump, I saw my reflection." Sutton turned to Coker and asked what was going on. "He said he had inherited this situation," Sutton reported. (Coker had taken over as manager a few months earlier.) "He didn't like it. He was instructed not to inform the [state and federal] agencies" about the accumulation of liquids.

A few days later, Culvey and Holcomb both told an EPA inspector that Marianne Walls, the former general manager at the site, had told them to keep two sets of books, one a black logbook to be shown to inspectors, which made no mention of the liquid in the sump, and another yellow logbook for company use only, which recorded it. When the two men objected, Walls told them they could show the yellow logbook to EPA or state officials only if the officials specifically asked for it.

Two weeks after Sutton's discovery, top officials from the Denver EPA, the Colorado Department of Health, and Waste Management, Inc., met. Representing EPA was Seth Hunt, who had been special assistant to Anne Gorsuch throughout 1981 and then returned to Denver as EPA Deputy Regional Administrator. (Steve Durham had taken a leave of absence to campaign for Ted Strickland, the Republican candidate for governor of Colorado.)

At the meeting with Waste Management, Inc., Hunt listened with interest to the company's explanation of why there was liquid in the sump and why CWM had never reported the trouble to any government agency. Douglas Wallgren repeated the explanation of the double set of books outlined a few days earlier in a letter from Lawrence Beck, Waste Management's Senior Vice-President, to Dr. Frank Traylor, Director of the Colorado Department of Health.

The company denied that Pond Two was leaking, or had ever leaked. Backed up by reports from a consultant, the company claimed that the 22,000 gallons of liquid pumped out of the sump between July 1981 and September 1982 was rainwater trapped between the liners at the time of construction. Since the pond wasn't leaking, company officials said, there was nothing to report to EPA or the state.

"It was a curious line of reasoning," says Chris Sutton. He pointed out that the space between the inner and bottom clay liners in all three evaporation ponds is connected; the bottom liner is common to all. Therefore, if the water beneath Pond Two was construction water, it should also have been present below Ponds One and Three. But their sumps were dry. "Their argument didn't hold water," says Sutton, chuckling.

EPA and Colorado Health Department tests done in September

and October 1982 detected toxic organic chemicals in the sump liquids that were also present in Pond Two—toluene, dichloroethane, ethylbenzene, tetrachloroethylene. And the chemicals were present in the sump in nearly the same concentrations as in the pond. Ken Waesche, Health Department geologist, said later: "If that's the kind of rainwater we're getting in Colorado, we're all in trouble." Company officials suggested the chemicals might have come from small spills in the pond area during construction, spread around the site by truck tires, and then washed by rain into the sand layer.

After the meeting, according to participants, EPA and Health Department officials reacted to the company's explanations with both indignation and laughter. One said: "What kind of fools do they think we are?" At this, Hunt sharply reproved EPA staff. A witness reported that he said, "Nobody at EPA should give Chemical Waste Management a black eye in the public view."

EPA lawyers and EPA's National Enforcement Investigations Center, located in Denver, met with the U.S. Attorney in Denver in November 1982 to present the evidence against CWM. A week later, the U.S. Attorney officially declined to prosecute the case. Patrick Murphy, the prosecutor in charge, was asked why the U.S. Attorney refused to take action against CWM. After a delay, Murphy replied that he had been instructed to consult with the Justice Department in Washington to get permission to answer the question. The question had not been answered by publication time.

Nonetheless, four months later, after the leaks and the double set of books had been disclosed in the press, and after EPA's failure to deal with hazardous waste had become front-page news nationwide, the Denver EPA office filed a complaint against Chemical Waste Management, Inc., alleging that the company violated the law when it failed to note in the logbook shown to EPA that there were liquids in the sump beneath Pond Two. EPA regulations require that operators of hazardous waste facilities must note in a logbook malfunctions, deteriorations, or discharges that may lead to release of hazardous wastes to the environment.

EPA made other charges: that the company failed to note any actions taken to remedy the condition, that the company's ground water monitoring wells did not meet legal requirements, and that the company's contingency plan was inadequate because it did not deal with

125

"non-sudden" (or gradual) leaks of toxic chemicals. For the four alleged violations, EPA proposed a civil fine of $48,650.

Steve Durham resigned as EPA Regional Administrator in Denver in May 1983. He declined to be interviewed. Seth Hunt, still Deputy Regional Administrator in Denver, talked about the Lowry case in a July 1983 interview. To Hunt, Waste Management's account of the liquid beneath Pond Two was "plausible." Hunt described his reactions at the meeting with Waste Management, Inc., on the Pond Two problem:

"I was sitting there listening to all the pros and cons and I said, 'You know, all this is possible.' All I'm saying is, with all their people, and they brought folks in from all over the country, they have the greatest consultants advising them . . . it was all plausible.

"Our people and the State people—that was a political issue. The State did not want Lowry Landfill there for political reasons. And they had the lead in all of this, and some of their people convinced some of our technical people that it was really bad. And from their point of view —I don't fault them on what their feelings were, what their findings were. And Steve [Durham] took the action."

He paused for a moment and brightened. "I think it will be an interesting court decision. I would love to see and hear what is going on in the mind of the judge. I haven't seen their [Waste Management's] suit. I don't know what they're filing. I'd kinda like to be able to file a suit on their behalf because of all the things that could be, that are big question marks.

"But the bottom line is: there is no danger to the environment. Nothing has leaked out from there."

This "bottom line" was one that both Waste Management, Inc., and Steve Durham emphasized. When Durham announced the civil action against Chemical Waste Management in January 1983, he said: "It is important to note that, while our investigation did indicate a leak in the top liner of [Pond Two], we have no evidence to indicate any release of contaminants into the environment."

This was a curious statement to make. EPA's own complaint said that the company's ground water monitoring system was inadequate, and the Agency's order forbade CWM to receive any more wastes until its ground water monitoring was brought up to par. With an inadequate monitoring system, how could EPA, the company, or anyone else be sure that contaminants had not seeped into the ground water?

As a matter of fact, EPA's Denver office had been warned months earlier that CWM's ground water monitoring wells were not drilled to the right places, and might not detect contamination. An EPA staff review of CWM's monitoring plan, dated June 21, 1982, concluded that test wells downgradient both from the burial pit for drums and from the evaporation ponds were drilled too deep to detect contaminants in the shallow alluvial aquifer that runs closest to the surface. This aquifer would be polluted first if a leak were to occur. At least one of the test wells downgradient from the evaporation ponds was completed in both the mid-level aquifer (the Dawson Formation) and the deep bedrock aquifer (the Denver Formation), "thus not giving a representative sample of the Dawson Formation." The Dawson Formation is the source of community drinking water supplies for 5,000 people in Arapahoe County.

As for the test wells around the burial pit, one was 375 feet away —too far to meet the legal requirement of "immediate detection" of any ground water contamination. The EPA reviewer reported that near the burial pit "at 16 feet a black organic clay with a strong odor was discovered; this clay should be investigated."

Only after Chris Sutton discovered the liquid beneath Pond Two, and the subsequent revelation that CWM had kept two sets of logbooks, did the Denver EPA office crack down on the company's ground water monitoring system.

In March 1983 Waste Management, Inc., was hit with a barrage of news stories charging irresponsible, possibly illegal practices at several of its sites, including Lowry. On March 23, after two days of stories in the *New York Times* and the *Wall Street Journal* alleging misconduct by the company, its stock had dropped one billion dollars in value.

Waste Management officials immediately reacted to the charges, denying some of the most serious ones, explaining others, and announcing that they had hired a law firm to "audit" the company's activities and the allegations against it. In September the law firm reported back, on the whole favorably. It found "no basis" for some charges, "nonserious technical violations" in others, and, in some, "serious noncompliance" with environmental regulations—but not, it said, with any resulting harm to the environment.

As for Lowry, the report said that the company had walked into a "legal and political buzzsaw" in 1980, because of the practices allowed by Denver at the old landfill—"the worst in hazardous waste management." The report also said that Waste Management made a "serious error" in failing to disclose the apparent leak at Pond Two, thus exacerbating "an atmosphere akin to open warfare."

Walter Barber, for years a top career official at EPA and the acting administrator before Anne Gorsuch took over, became Waste Management's Vice-President for Environmental Management in September 1983. In an interview, he said that the company's actions on Pond Two "were not particularly well-advised, in hindsight." The company now expects its operators "to call any kind of abnormal situation to the attention of regulators."

Waste Management, Inc., will implement all of the audit report's recommendations, and more, Barber says. It will have compliance officers at every site, an independent set of environmental auditors to visit each site once a year, and training for operators "in the intent as well as the letter of the law." Barber emphasizes that the company will be moving away from land disposal to incineration and chemical treatment. As for the landfills that already exist, "we're putting in literally hundreds of monitoring wells."

Waste Management is going to live its "longest and happiest life," says Barber, if it is a "model of regulatory compliance."

In mid-1983 Chemical Waste Management gave up on the burial pit at Lowry and agreed to keep it closed. Citizens Against the Lowry Landfill want more than just closure. They want the leaking contents cleaned up and moved out. And they want the whole Lowry complex, ponds and all, to stay closed. Carol MacLennan, now director of CALL, says: "When Lowry shut its doors [in July 1982] Jim Sanderson said that industry all over the region would go belly up. We felt badly at the time. We said we'd consider reopening [Lowry] under certain conditions.

"But we've been without the landfill for over a year. Nobody has closed up shop. Lots of companies have been willing to try alternatives. . . . Our feelings have kind of turned around on whether we need a landfill."

Landfills and evaporation ponds like those at Lowry are a highly visible means of disposing of hazardous wastes. Another form of land disposal, much less visible and far less regulated, is injection of the wastes into underground wells. EPA's latest figures (August 1983) disclose that very large quantities of hazardous waste—far larger than anyone previously suspected—are being pumped underground. These figures came from an extensive, first-time EPA survey of hazardous waste generation and management in 1981. They revealed that the total amount of wastes generated was nearly four times larger than EPA had previously estimated (150 million tons versus 40 million tons per year), and that 57 percent of the wastes reported "disposed" were going underground. Injectable wastes are liquids, often dilute in toxic components. But, according to a staff report by the Congressional Office of Technology Assessment, they "can be quite concentrated and toxic, and they may also contain some fraction of suspended solids." That means that for liquid wastes which are not too viscous or sludgy, injection is an alternative to surface evaporation ponds. It can be a much cheaper alternative. One EPA staff member explains: "You can see the attraction . . . if you start trying to buy a lot of land in New Jersey as compared to having a hole in the ground."

Study of the effects of underground injection is still very much neglected. Most of these wastes, EPA officials say, are pumped into deep wells below the level of any aquifers containing potentially drinkable water. However, the possible connections between deep wells and aquifers located above them are not well understood. Moreover, some liquid hazardous wastes are pumped directly into or above formations that could provide drinking water.

Regulation of injection is limited and bureaucratically confused. It is split up between the states and EPA, and at EPA it is split up into two programs. "It is generally acknowledged," says the OTA staff report, that progress in regulating hazardous waste has been slow "but the situation for injection wells is probably worse than for the other forms of land disposal." An example: with surface land disposal, EPA requires ground water monitoring. With underground injection, it does not.

Most of the hazardous waste injected underground comes from a few large chemical and petrochemical companies, including DuPont, Monsanto, Shell, Atlantic Richfield. It is prevalent in oil and gas well country—where it may present special dangers because of the possibility of upward migration through old abandoned oil and gas wells.

An EPA staff member says that the enormous volume of injected wastes, as revealed in the 1981 survey, "surprised everyone here [at EPA] immensely. It was big news. . . . We're going to have to think differently about the problem."

What people facing hazardous waste sites in Denver and Bay City and Cheraw and elsewhere around the nation want from their government is the assurance that Love Canal will not happen again. They know that there are better ways of handling the worst of hazardous wastes than putting them in the ground. Anne Gorsuch never faced this fundamental fact. The hazardous waste land disposal regulations she developed, with pride and meticulous attention to detail, simply don't do the job. They lack two of the very minimum essentials for protection from leaks of dangerous pollutants—siting controls and restrictions on the kinds of wastes dumped. When you look at the realities of the hazardous waste industry, and consider all the things that can go wrong, and contemplate the fact that these wastes do not degrade in nature but have lifetimes of thousands of years, the present EPA controls look feeble indeed.

To avoid the continuous creation of new hazards, it is necessary to have a larger vision. It is necessary to understand that the costs of dealing with these wastes are not confined to our own lifetimes, but can mount up over years and generations, and that the costs are not just in dollars, but in the health of human beings and the natural environment.

In that light, the unacknowledged decision of the Reagan Administration to strictly limit the program to clean up old waste dumps is indefensible. It was a narrow decision based on the idea that a rather trifling tax on the chemicals industry could not be allowed to continue for more than five years.

What Americans expected from their government was a tough commitment to clean up the mountains of hazardous wastes that had piled up over the years and to keep at it until the job is done.

"GOOD SCIENCE"

From Globe, Arizona, to Denver's Lowry Landfill to EPA's top-floor offices, the federal government's commitment to protecting Americans from dangerous chemical wastes was reoriented under Ronald Reagan. As candidate and as President, Reagan stated the changed position forthrightly. American business had paid too dearly, he said, for our attempts to reduce risks to health and environment. He blamed two factors for the excessive costs: "environmental extremists" and "bad science."

Regulations based on "bad science" had caused "economic trage-dies," Reagan said, and he meant to change them. "We need to review those regulations to bring them in line with all the new scientific knowledge."

Anne Gorsuch took up the same theme in her confirmation hearing. "We can and must improve the scientific and technical basis for the standards and regulations developed." Her deputy, John Hernandez, echoed the thought three days later. EPA science—"in many instances ill-conceived, poorly planned, and hurriedly executed—has been costly to those being regulated," he said, adding this advice: "Good Science makes good economics." To the new leaders of EPA, Good Science led directly to regulatory relief.

It sounded unbeatable—who could complain about better science, less regulation, and lower costs? But in fact, of course, it was not so simple. As applied by President Reagan's appointees to hazardous waste dumps, lead, asbestos, pesticides, toxic chemicals in the air, water, and the workplace, Good Science meant the acceptance of higher risks—sometimes one hundred times higher than the minimal risks previous government policy thought prudent to tolerate. William Hedeman, the EPA civil servant in charge of the Superfund program, says that under Anne Gorsuch and Rita Lavelle "the theme was we've got to be willing to take bigger risks, tolerate much greater exposures." *Science* magazine called the results "EPA's High-Risk Carcinogen Policy."

Another aspect of Good Science was the demand that government should have hard proof of damage to health before stepping in to regulate toxic materials. This approach, reactive instead of preventive, has been described by critics as "counting dead bodies."

How Good Science worked is best shown by example. Consider lead, known since antiquity as a deadly environmental poison. For nearly two years, from a week after his confirmation in May 1981 until his exit from EPA in 1983, Hernandez delayed a cleanup of lead from schoolyards and playgrounds in two Dallas neighborhoods near lead smelters. He wanted proof first that lead had actually entered the bloodstream of children in the neighborhood. When EPA staff in the Dallas regional office appealed his decision and urged action to prevent possible damage to the children's health, his response, they said, was that "we really needed to be concerned about good science. . . . He didn't think we should spend money to remove dirt or have any bulldozers start up before we could identify a specific health problem."

Hernandez's part in the Dallas story stayed submerged for 22

131

months. It only surfaced in congressional hearings during his two-week tenure as Acting Administrator of EPA after Anne Gorsuch resigned. Together with the story that he had, in effect, allowed Dow Chemical to dictate changes in an EPA report on dioxin, it led to his resignation.

Lead is pure poison to human beings. Unlike some other metals that are also toxic, it serves no physiological purpose, even in tiny amounts. It is also pervasive. People today encounter lead at 100 to 1,000 times the exposures in pre-industrial societies (traces in teeth and bones show this).

Experts consider a level of 30 micrograms per deciliter of blood as potentially dangerous, especially in children. According to studies done by Dr. Herbert Needleman in Boston (he is now at the University of Pittsburgh), blood lead at this level in children is correlated with learning difficulties, lower IQ scores, restlessness, and inability to concentrate. At higher levels lead produces damage to body organs and much grosser neurophysiological effects, from headaches to epileptic-like seizures to profound mental impairment, paralysis, and death. Men and women exposed to lead at levels found in the workplace may become sterile. Recent evidence indicates that levels even below the 30-microgram mark can alter small children's brain waves and may subtly interfere with their mental functioning. Lead accumulates in the body. Once there, stored in the bones and liver, it can be released and threaten nerve and brain damage that may be irreversible. And once lead is dispersed in the environment (in the form of small particles that can be breathed or eaten), it stays there. It does not degrade.

A national health survey taken from 1976 to 1980 showed that 4 percent of all American children from six months to five years old had blood lead above the 30-microgram level. Of poor black children living in inner cities, where exposures are intense, 18.6 percent, or nearly one in five, showed blood lead levels above 30 micrograms.

Dr. Vernon Houk of the federal Centers for Disease Control has estimated that half a million children in the United States have elevated blood lead levels. "If we had any childhood disease that approached these figures, a national campaign would be launched to control it," said Dr. Houk. The big casualty is mental capacity. "Lead won't kill these kids," said Devra Lee Davis, who heads the toxicology program at the National Academy of Sciences. "It will . . . make life a little harder. And for many of them, life's already tough."

West Dallas and Oak Cliff, two Dallas neighborhoods near lead smelters, are mostly poor and mostly black. Soil around the schools, day care centers, Boys' Club, and people's homes in these neighborhoods showed exceptionally high levels of lead, in tests reported to EPA's Dallas regional office in February 1981. Between 25 and 30 percent of the soil samples tested contained more than 1,000 parts per million (ppm) of lead, and some were as high as 25,000 ppm. (Soil from other Dallas neighborhoods tested for comparison showed lead at 54 ppm.) EPA considered 10 percent of soil samples above 1,000 ppm as an "action alert level" for lead, meaning that children's health and the environment could be threatened and further study must be done.

Frances Phillips, then acting regional administrator for the Dallas EPA office, called in officials of the companies involved: RSR Corporation, which owned the West Dallas smelter; Dixie Metals, which operated a smelter in Oak Cliff; and National Lead Industries, Inc., owner of a defunct smelter in Oak Cliff. RSR offered to clean up the worst-contaminated areas and help pay for health studies of the neighborhood children; RSR confirmed the offer in writing. Dixie Metals questioned whether lead at 1,000 ppm in the soil was a real threat but offered to contribute to health studies. National Lead made no offer. The Dallas EPA office, under pressure from a newspaper that had a copy of the soil survey, wrote a press notice describing the lead findings and the offer by RSR to remove lead-contaminated soil. "I felt like I had a package tied up in a bow, ready to release," Phillips said. But first, she called Washington EPA headquarters to report on the package. She reached Hernandez. He untied the bow.

Hernandez rewrote the press release. He took out all the references to playgrounds and schoolyards, and obscured the nature of the RSR offer. The version written in Dallas said: "RSR will take remedial measures to reduce the soil lead levels in high-risk areas such as playgrounds, day care centers, and schoolyards where concentrations are over 1,000 parts per million." The Hernandez version: "RSR has indicated it will take remedial measures as necessary to reduce soil lead levels in high-risk areas around its plant." Hernandez also excised the word "schools" from the phrase "samples were taken from residential neighborhoods and schools." He changed the statement that testing had found "marked elevation" of soil lead levels to read simply "elevation."

Later, Hernandez defended his changes, arguing that they left the way open for a more extensive cleanup by RSR. That was not the way it looked at the time to Phillips and others in the Dallas EPA office.

"The press release we got back [from Hernandez] was a softer version of the [RSR] commitment," Phillips said.

Hernandez also quizzed Phillips on the scientific backup for the "action alert level" of 1,000 ppm lead in soil. She provided scientific reports and expert opinion. Hernandez remained unconvinced. He told the Dallas officials to wait for results of blood lead tests of children in the area, to be taken over the coming months, before proceeding on a cleanup based on the 1,000-ppm level.

At this point, the EPA regional staff prevailed on Phillips to call Hernandez once more. "They suggested that I might not have been forceful enough in my discussions with him," she said. She relayed the staff's urging that EPA's primary concern should be for the children, and their plea for prompt action to stop exposure of the children to lead— with possible serious damage to their health—rather than wait for the collection of more scientific proof of the danger. They saw this as a "change of direction" for EPA and a precedent that could undermine enforcement. But, Phillips said, Hernandez turned them down.

Nearly two years later, at congressional hearings conducted by Rep. Elliott Levitas of Georgia, Hernandez repeatedly said he had not been informed about the details of the RSR offer and had not derailed it. He did not recall anything he had done or said that would have prevented the Dallas regional office from enforcing a cleanup while the blood studies were under way.

Phillips and Allyn Davis, another member of the Dallas regional office, remembered it differently. Both understood Hernandez's decision as an order to drop the cleanup efforts and ignore the commitment RSR had made. (RSR actually proceeded on its own with a limited cleanup during the next few months.) Of her first conversation with Hernandez, Phillips said: "Dr. Hernandez was concerned about the precedent that cleaning up at an action level of 1,000 ppm would set. . . . He preferred that we do a health study to determine the action level." Of the second conversation—the callback urged by her staff—Phillips said: "Dr. Hernandez gave me direction and said this is what he wanted us to do. And I said, 'Yes, sir.'" Asked whether Hernandez's role had created or perpetuated a health hazard, Phillips replied: "I don't think I could deny that if we had gone forward . . . we would have reduced the potential exposure of those children."

Representative Levitas put the matter more strongly: "Where there are inexcusably high levels of lead in the environment, why not go forward and clean it up? Why use the children as scientific test animals?" He said: "We are not talking about writing for scientific or medical journals. We are talking about protecting the public health from exposure to toxic chemicals and materials."

Twenty-one months went by before final results of the health tests came in. A first series of tests, conducted by the City of Dallas and available in April 1982, found elevated blood lead levels (above 30 micrograms) in 36 preschool children who lived within half a mile of the lead smelters. This amounted to 13 percent of the children tested in those areas. For Dallas as a whole, where 11,000 people (adults and children) were tested, less than 2 percent had elevated blood lead levels.

Looking at these results, Hernandez again chose to take no action. A panel of scientists convened by the federal Centers for Disease Control (CDC) called the city's tests "inconclusive," because less than one-quarter of the people in the half-mile radius around the smelters had volunteered for testing. Also, the panel said, it wasn't clear how much lead was coming from the smelters and how much from auto emissions. The panel observed that the children's blood lead levels were "markedly below" those around other smelter sites, such as El Paso, Texas, or Kellogg, Idaho. No one suggested, however, that the blood tests were faulty or that the 36 children did not actually have blood lead levels in the potentially dangerous range. Hernandez ordered a second round of tests, to be designed and conducted by the Centers for Disease Control together with EPA.

The CDC test results, available at last in February 1983, were accepted by EPA; in fact, they were ballyhooed. They indicated a lower percentage of children affected than the earlier study had shown—10.5 percent in West Dallas and 4 percent in Oak Cliff—compared with zero in a control group. The study found 30 children who tested above the 30-microgram level. The study definitely established the smelter as the dominant source of elevated lead in the children's blood—over five times as important as auto traffic in West Dallas. (Traffic was so light as to be almost no factor in Oak Cliff.)

EPA's handling of the health study results was bitterly criticized at the Levitas congressional hearings in March 1983. Dr. Norman Dyer, regional EPA chief for toxic substances, and Dr. Bill McAnalley, an ex-EPA toxicologist, charged that comparing the Dallas results with national data was wrong and misleading; the national figures were collected on a different basis. The proper comparison, they said, was the control area, where no children had elevated levels.

But more important, they said, was that the study area was too big. No one had bothered to look at blood lead levels of the children in areas directly downwind of the smelters, where the highly contaminated soil was found. Dyer had proposed doing this a month before the study was released, but EPA headquarters in Washington turned him down on the grounds that the analysis would not be "cost effective." In May 1983 the *Dallas Times-Herald* did that very analysis, without benefit of computer, laboriously plotting by hand the positive test results on a map showing concentrations of lead in the soil in the West Dallas neighborhood. The *Times-Herald* discovered that 34 percent of the children living in areas where soil lead levels were above 1,000 ppm had elevated blood lead levels. Over 18 percent of the children living where soils tested above 300 ppm showed elevated blood lead.

People are more comprehensible than numbers. Not a year before EPA announced "no cases of lead poisoning" in the Dallas lead smelter neighborhoods, the *Dallas Morning News* featured a front-page story about Francine (Cookie) Wells, a West Dallas girl then ten years old, who was in the hospital with serious symptoms of lead toxicity. Her blood lead level tested at an excessively high 65 micrograms per deciliter. She had blacked out in her fourth-grade class at the private Greenhill School, where she was a scholarship student.

Everyone else in the Wells family—her father Shelley, mother Ella, two brothers, and a sister—suffered, like Cookie, from headaches, nausea, trouble in breathing, and cramps in hands, arms, and legs. All are symptoms of lead toxicity. The Wells family lived for 25 years in a small frame home a quarter of a mile north (downwind) of the RSR smelter. Three family members had their blood tested by the city health department in 1981; all three had elevated blood lead levels.

The Wells family home in West Dallas was paid for, and some of the family operated a small gasoline station nearby. When Cookie was hospitalized, her father said: "The only thing we can do is move out of here. But we can't move. We can't afford it."

They did move. In the next year, Cookie missed a lot of school from illness, her high grades began to slip, and she lost her scholarship. Her brother David, a talented basketball player, had to rule out professional sports because of swollen, cramped hands. The Wells family left their West Dallas home (it was still unsold in 1983), abandoned the gas station (now closed), and moved 20 miles away to South Dallas. There, they are struggling to pay a rent of $300 a month on a monthly income of $388.

Alma Shaw is another who decided to move. She was worried about her five-year-old son Derek, whose blood lead tested above the 30-microgram level. The Shaws live in the George Loving Place public housing project north of the RSR smelter, directly in the path of the southerly winds that carry lead pollution, and surrounded by soil with the highest levels of lead.

Some units of the low-rise, sprawling George Loving Place project look unkempt and forlorn, but not Alma Shaw's two-story rowhouse. It is well furnished and well kept, and the rent is affordable for a divorced mother of three who works as a domestic. But when Shaw got Derek's test results, she wasted no time in looking for another place to live, even though she knew rents would be higher elsewhere. "Derek is not really sick," she says, "but his teeth are messed up and he vomits a lot. Once you know it's in his body, you start looking.

"I'm going to move out," Shaw says. "It's just too much when they start messing with my children's health."

Patricia Spears has no intention of moving out. Her four children, aged 8 to 14, all have learning problems. They all have headaches, nausea, and cramps, and one suffers from repeated blackouts. The youngest, Demetria, was tested in the city program in 1981, with results that showed both elevated blood lead and a highly positive finding for lead toxicity. The others were never tested as preschoolers but Spears believes all four were handicapped by the lead they have been exposed to since infancy.

But Spears doesn't want to be forced out of West Dallas. Her roots, home, and work are there. West Dallas, though mostly poor, is not a forbidding city slum. It is an open, countrified, pleasant-looking place with quite a few individually owned homes, a handful of locally owned businesses, and a small middle class, to which the Spears family belongs. Patricia Spears's father, the 72-year-old Rev. W. E. Spears, is a minister in the Progressive Baptist Church in West Dallas and owns one of the neighborhood's two side-by-side funeral homes. Patricia Spears works with her father at the funeral home, lives a few blocks away in her own home, and is a community sparkplug on the lead issue.

"If we lived in [wealthy, white] Highland Park or Northeast Dallas," says Spears, "that lead plant would have been closed in 1981. Why should we have to move? Why don't they shut the plant down instead?"

In the spring of 1983, after the EPA scandals broke, after the congressional hearings, after Anne Gorsuch and John Hernandez and a score of other top EPA officials had departed, something at last began to happen in the lead smelter neighborhoods. Up to that time, the only action (besides the tests) came from RSR, which had voluntarily removed and replaced soil at a West Dallas school and the West Dallas Boys' Club. The Boys' Club is practically underneath RSR's towering smokestack.

At last, EPA and the Texas Air Quality Control Board woke up to the fact that the air around the RSR plant had to be cleaned up; the tests showing violations of the standard were by this time a year old. The State Attorney General filed suit to force the cleanup of the air and soil. The City of Dallas removed contaminated soil from parks and play-grounds. RSR and Dixie Metals (previously recalcitrant) both agreed to clean up contaminated soil near their smelters; their combined costs were estimated at about $260,000. The Dallas EPA office was urging both cleanup of the air and treatment of contaminated soil (by either removing it or putting a barrier, such as asphalt, over it). The city housing authority offered to help anyone who wanted to move out of the public housing project to do so. Cookie Wells, with ribbons in her hair, went to Austin to tell State legislators about her lead sickness. The Texas State Senate made her an "honorary page."

Given strong leadership by EPA headquarters, all of this could have happened two years earlier (or most of it; perhaps Cookie Wells wouldn't have gone to Austin). John Hernandez still believes, two years later, that he did exactly the right thing. Hernandez is surprised and aggrieved at the criticism his actions aroused. In an interview three months after his departure from EPA, he gave several reasons to support his insistence on doing health studies before cleaning up the lead around the smelters—or even accepting the industry offer to do a voluntary cleanup. He pointed to the CDC/EPA study's conclusion that air was the major source of exposure, with the implication that soil was much less important. He characterized the first soil study, back in 1981, as "not well done" because soil was taken not just from the surface in the smelter areas, but from deeper levels. (In reply to a question, he readily agreed that this defect would *understate* the amount of lead in the soil to which children were exposed, not overstate it.) He says he had not expected the blood tests to take more than a few months and that throughout the period of study he had conferred with CDC officials, who assured him that the Dallas situation was not an "emergency." He says that "forcing" people to move out of the smelter areas would have been a drastic and unnecessary step.

However important soil was as a route of exposure in the Dallas neighborhoods, many experts on lead toxicity in children believe that, in general, lead contamination in soil is a serious hazard. Dr. Philip Landrigan, of the National Institute of Occupational Safety and Health in Cincinnati, explains that children don't have to be "dirty" or subject to peculiar compulsions to eat dirt in order to ingest a significant amount of lead in dirt. "Every time a kid drops his toy truck or his lollipop in the dirt and then puts it in his mouth, he's eating dirt," Dr. Landrigan says. In his opinion, soil lead levels of 300 ppm are a matter of serious concern, especially where the earth is bare with no grass cover.

The purpose of establishing a level for action, like Landrigan's 300 ppm in soil or the Dallas EPA's 1,000 ppm, is to protect people by stopping harmful exposures before they happen. This approach values protection and prevention over proof certain that harm has occurred. Rather than putting health and the environment at risk, it establishes limits beyond which risks will not be tolerated. Hernandez's delays in the Dallas cleanup represent another view, which he calls a "sound scientific decision."

The Reagan Administration's determined efforts to allow lead back into gasoline had nothing to do with science, good or otherwise. There is no scientific question that lead is bad for children's health, and the more exposure the worse it is. The argument for putting more lead back in gas was frankly based on the idea that dominated Reagan Administration policy on public health and the environment: regulatory relief.

When Vice-President George Bush took charge of the Presidential Task Force for Regulatory Relief, he invited businesses, trade associations, unions, and states to nominate their least favorite federal regulation as a target for change by the new Administration. Regulated industries jumped at the chance. Anne Gorsuch explained that, when asked to finger "those rules and regulations which they felt were most onerous, burdensome, duplicative, more than one-half of the responses . . . identified EPA rules and regulations." One of these was the EPA rule, first adopted in 1973, limiting lead in gasoline. The lead-in-gasoline rule was a special target of some powerful political supporters of the Reagan

Administration—refiners and blenders of gasoline in the southern and western Sun Belt.

Lead is an anti-knock additive to gasoline, a cheap way of getting higher octane levels. After a lengthy court battle with the lead and refining industries, EPA began limiting the amounts of lead in gasoline in 1977, with a progressive phasedown of amounts of lead allowed per gallon and a temporary delay for "small" refiners to gear up for meeting the general standards. ("Small" was a misnomer for some of these refineries, which were defined as producing less than 50,000 barrels a day. Even Jim Tozzi, OMB regulatory relief honcho, says: " 'Small' doesn't mean small profits. You should be so lucky to be a small refiner.")

In 1978 the Department of Energy tried to stop the lead-in-gasoline phasedown, arguing that it takes more crude oil to produce lead-free than leaded gasoline and that the nation's need for "energy independence" had to take precedence. But Carter White House officials scotched the attempt, after looking at data that showed astonishing parallels between emissions of lead in gasoline and lead levels in children's blood.

The Reagan Administration's Task Force on Regulatory Relief had different priorities in mind. In August 1981 Vice-President Bush promised that EPA would review the phasedown of lead in gasoline, and would look for ways to provide "quick relief" for small refiners and blenders who faced tighter limits right away and, the next year, an end to their exemption from the general standard. The lead phasedown would "impose onerous capital requirements on small refiners," said the Task Force. Bush instructed EPA "to consider relaxing or rescinding the entire lead phasedown rule." For the next fourteen months, until the eve of the 1982 congressional election, the Regulatory Relief Task Force and its crack OMB staff fought to carry out Bush's extraordinary promise.

Anne Gorsuch was more than ready to do her part. In her notorious meeting with representatives of the Thriftway refinery on December 11, 1981, Gorsuch told the company not to worry about violations of the lead-in-gasoline rules because they would soon be changed. Thriftway was a small outfit, selling most of its low-quality, high-lead gasoline in grocery stores and stations on a Navajo reservation nearby. What the Thriftway people wanted was a waiver from the phasedown of lead in gasoline. Without it, they claimed, Thriftway would lose $100,000 a month. In the name of regulatory relief, she told them not to worry, because proposed EPA rules then under review at OMB would drastically revise the rule for a phasedown of lead in gasoline. One participant told investigators later, in a sworn statement, that Gorsuch said that lead phasedown "was a high priority item at EPA and that she hoped that the regulations would be abolished in 1982." Meanwhile, she promised that EPA would not commit resources to "enforce a regulation after changes had been proposed." Before the change in the rules was publicly proposed, before she had seen any analysis of the effects of the change or listened to the comments of independent experts, Gorsuch was committed to the outcome. The Administration had promised relief to the refiners, that was the important fact. Joe Cannon, Gorsuch's special assistant for regulatory relief, recalls that EPA agreed to review the lead-in-gasoline rules "with the implicit assumption that the end result of our looking at it would be to rescind the regulation."

A month and a half after the Thriftway meeting, at about the same time that EPA gave official notice it was considering changes in the rules to allow more lead in gasoline, the story that Gorsuch had essentially given approval in advance to a violation of the law spread across the news media. EPA hearings on the lead proposal opened in April 1982, one day after congressional hearings began on the same subject, including the Thriftway incident. The glare of publicity was the first of several factors that eventually pushed EPA into supporting a tighter, not a looser, gasoline standard. To get it, EPA wound up fighting Vice-President Bush and the OMB team in the White House.

Another essential factor was the behind-the-scenes efforts of career professional staff at EPA. Said one staff member who lived through it: "We were appalled at the idea of subjecting the kids to more lead." They knew, even if their bosses did not, that lead in gasoline is the principal source of lead in the environment—one study for EPA estimated that it contributes nearly 60 percent to the average American's blood lead level—and that it is especially harmful to inner-city children exposed to heavy car and truck traffic in their neighborhoods.

The staff tried to educate the Reagan-appointed policy officials. (One top official was baffled when a staff member told him that "the NAACP will just come unglued" if the lead standard were loosened.) They pointed out the remarkable success, in just a few years, of the Agency's lead regulations. Nationwide, average lead levels in blood dropped 37 percent from 1976 to 1980, as lead used in gasoline dropped from 190,000 tons per year to 90,000. During those four years, EPA rules forced a progressive reduction of the lead content in gasoline. In addition, increasing numbers of cars were outfitted with catalytic converters (pollution control devices that were introduced in 1974), which are "poisoned" by leaded gas; these cars are supposed to use unleaded gas only. EPA staff pointed to nationwide health data which showed, incontrovertibly, that the level of lead in human blood had fallen step by step with the lead emitted from automobile tailpipes. They also calculated that savings to consumers from putting more lead back in gasoline were trivial—about one-tenth of a cent per gallon.

Some top officials at EPA appeared immune to these educational efforts. John Daniel, Anne Gorsuch's chief of staff, told M. R. Montgomery of the *Boston Globe:* "Well, lead phasedown is sacrosanct to these honest, well-meaning people who, you know, spend all their time ministering to inner-city kids. Well, to them it's a serious problem." Of the doctors who opposed any change in the lead phasedown, he said: "I don't think there's any ulterior motive in them when they look at us and say, 'You can't be serious.'"

A more receptive official was Joe Cannon. His high-level EPA job was a reward for work in the 1980 Reagan campaign. Like many other of the Reagan appointees to EPA, he had little experience in environmental matters. His distinction was that he listened and learned. Later, Cannon was the only top official to survive the EPA scandals, when 21 others were fired or resigned.

Another factor in the fate of the lead-in-gasoline proposal was the outrage expressed by doctors and the entire public health community. Dr. Sergio Piomelli, professor of pediatrics at Columbia University and chief physician at one of the country's largest childhood lead poisoning clinics, spoke for many when he told a congressional hearing:

As a physician I am here to express my consternation at the cynical lack of sensitivity to the health of the American children obvious in this proposal; as a scientist I am here to express my surprise at the total lack of understanding of the overwhelming scientific evidence that dictates continuation and not rescission of efforts to remove lead . . . from the environment.

[The] ultimate effect [of the proposed relaxation of the standard] will be intellectual damage to thousands of American children, with enormous costs to society at large. . . . All of this for a modest economic advantage to a very few.

Dr. Herbert Needleman said, pithily: "To go back to where we were before 1977 . . . is insane. That is a professional judgment."

142

State and local public health officials wrote and testified, virtually unanimous in opposition to any weakening of the lead-in-gasoline rule.

Still another factor was the reluctance of the large refiners to line up on the side of more lead in gasoline. Many of them had lobbied EPA strongly for looser standards after the Reagan team took over. EPA records show 32 meetings with representatives of the refining and lead industries between May 1981 and March 1982 on the lead phasedown. EPA held no meetings on the issue with any other groups—neither physicians, nor environmentalists, nor public health officials. Large as well as small refiners were represented in the private meetings with EPA (e.g., Chevron, Exxon, Amoco, the American Petroleum Institute). According to Richard Wilson, in charge of enforcement for EPA's air program, "I suppose the one thing that most of the industry could agree on is it would like to see the rule abolished." Only two refiners (ARCO and Crown) had argued in the private meetings for keeping the tighter standards. However, the big refiners had made substantial investments to get the lead out of gasoline. By the time of the congressional hearings in April 1982, many of them were more interested in applying the same standard to everyone and eliminating unfair competition than in relaxing the standard.

Finally, the exemption for small refiners was coming to an end on October 1, 1982. EPA had a decision to make just a month before the midterm congressional elections.

After the embarrassment of the public exposure of the Thriftway meeting, Anne Gorsuch withdrew from public participation in the lead decision, although she continued to play a behind-the-scenes role. Joe Cannon became the leader for EPA in a struggle against the White House "regulatory relief" team. Jim Tozzi's OMB staff and Task Force leaders, who had also been meeting regularly—at least fourteen times —with refiners, initially pushed for abandoning the regulations altogether, just killing the program. They vetoed EPA's first try at a rule, but as things heated up the OMB team began advocating a rule that would allow an actual increase, nationwide, in the amount of lead in gasoline, arguing that as more cars with catalytic converters entered the nation's fleet, lead use would gradually drop. EPA wanted *no* increase, ever, in total lead added to gasoline and a limit on lead per gallon low enough to cause declining use of lead nationwide, assuming more cars switch to no-lead gas. (Both sides assumed, possibly wrongly, that cars *would* continue to switch to no-lead gas. That depends. The catalytic converter, which is ruined by lead, may not remain the principal device for controlling pollution from cars. Some Japanese cars can now meet the pollution emission standards without a catalytic converter. And the converters already in cars may not continue to work. One survey showed that one out of five catalytic converters have been tampered with and put out of commission, presumably so that car owners can use cheaper leaded gas.)

In the end, EPA—pressed by health leaders, environmental groups, Congress, and the media—won out over the White House team. Seven days before the 1982 election, EPA issued a final rule that is slightly more protective than the old rule. It is still a compromise. Many public health and environmental advocates want a stricter phasedown, with the goal of *no* lead in gasoline. This would recognize the reality that any increase of lead in the environment adds to the body burdens of lead in thousands of children, with the near certainty that some of these children will suffer damage to their mental and physical health.

The Regulatory Relief Task Force also went after rules to protect workers from exposure to lead on the job. About 800,000 workers in 50-odd industries are exposed to lead in the workplace. In 1978 OSHA estimated that 80,000 of the workers had blood lead levels above 40 micrograms per deciliter, which is usually considered the point of potential danger for adults. Over time, with blood lead at this level, workers have experienced progressive loss of kidney function, an insidious loss that doctors may not pick up until two-thirds of the function is gone. A level of 50 micrograms produces anemia; and with blood lead levels at 60 micrograms, a majority of workers show signs of nervous system damage—fatigue, nervousness, sleep disturbance. OSHA also estimated in 1978 that 30,000 workers had blood lead levels above 60 micrograms. Even at 30–40 micrograms, workers have suffered serious loss of fertility, and are at added risk of having stillbirths, genetic mutation, and birth defects in their families.

Worker protection rules on lead that OSHA adopted in 1978 were a compromise. They were limited to what OSHA thought was feasible for most industries most of the time. The goal was to cut back to 30,000 the number of workers with blood lead levels above 40 micrograms per deciliter—ultimately. The controls were to be phased in over as long as ten years depending on the industry. No sooner had OSHA adopted the rules than everybody went to court. Industries sued to relax the standards. The AFL-CIO sued to make them stricter. The next year, the U.S. Court of Appeals for the District of Columbia Circuit upheld the standards for the eight principal lead industries (sending back standards for some 40 minor industries for more analysis of feasibility). In 1981 the Supreme Court refused to review the Circuit Court decision. The OSHA standards stuck.

But only legally, not practically. Under its new director, Thorne Auchter, OSHA stalled on imposing the lead-in-the-workplace rules and threatened to revoke them. First, Auchter postponed a tightening of the "medical removal" rule. Under this rule, lead workers get close medical surveillance, with periodic tests of blood lead levels. If a worker's levels are too high, the company must give him another job away from lead exposure—or even send him home—for as long as 18 months, with no loss of pay or seniority. The "trigger" blood lead level for medical removal was originally a very high 80 micrograms per deciliter, to be phased down to 50. Auchter stopped the phasedown, until ordered by the courts to restore it.

Even after the Supreme Court left the principal lead standards intact, OSHA effectively kept them on hold. The first important step toward meeting the standards was for the big lead-using industries to submit written programs controlling the lead in air in their plants, including engineering controls. OSHA postponed the deadlines for industries to submit these programs for two and a half years. A federal court ordered the original deadlines reinstated.

Early on, the Bush Task Force on Regulatory Relief ordered OSHA to redo the whole lead package. OSHA has taken steps to do so, writing drafts that weaken the rule, sometimes in consultation with industry. At least one company was given a draft of a new standard to review while it was still kept secret from labor unions and the public. After meeting privately with OMB officials of the regulatory relief team, a representative of the St. Joseph Lead Company went over to OSHA, where Auchter's assistant, Mark Cowan, gave him the draft standard. At this, OSHA lawyer Randy Rabinowitz resigned in July 1982. She charged her bosses with changing the lead standards on the basis of private meetings and "without any consideration of the relevant record evidence, as required by statute."

Not until the rout at EPA did OSHA have second thoughts about weakening the lead standards. Said Peg Seminario, occupational health specialist at AFL-CIO headquarters, "After Anne Burford got into trouble, we began to see a change. Auchter got religion." Another OSHA observer put it this way: "The sound of the guillotine falling at EPA just rumbled across the Mall to the Labor Department."

For the first time OSHA invited labor representatives—not just industry—to review proposed changes to the rules. OSHA also took a fresh look at labor proposals for tripartite negotiations (OSHA, labor, and industry) in cases where industries say they will have to go out of business if they are forced to meet the lead standards. Labor prefers to make case-by-case exceptions to deadlines, where there is a proven need, rather than gut the standard.

That labor unions should consider it "getting religion" when OSHA began to include them, as well as industry, in reviewing worker protection standards is revealing. Likewise, labor called it progress when OSHA seemed willing to consider dropping its attack on the existing lead standard. The fact is that, in the first two and a half years of the Reagan Administration, OSHA did nothing to advance protection of health in the workplace.

Instead, OSHA's new officials sandbagged the safeguards already in place. They tried to undo not only the lead standard, but also the cotton dust standard, which was adopted in 1978 to protect textile workers against byssinosis, or brown lung. One of Auchter's first actions as head of OSHA was to ban several worker education booklets and films, including one on brown lung. Pictured on this booklet's cover was a man who had died of brown lung after 44 years in the mills. Auchter said the cover photo made "a dramatic statement that clearly establishes a biased viewpoint in the cotton dust issue." Later, after a public outcry, the booklet was reissued in a plain cover.

Brown lung, a chronic, debilitating respiratory ailment, gets worse over years of exposure to cotton dust in poorly ventilated mills; it can become an irreversible disease like emphysema. Without protection, about 84,000 of 560,000 textile workers—about one in seven—could eventually fall victim to the disease. Astonishingly, even after two-thirds of the industry was on schedule in cleaning up the air in plants to meet the 1978 standard, the OMB regulatory relief team in the White House still insisted on a "cost effectiveness" review. By the spring of 1983, Thorne Auchter himself saw no point in further assaults on the cotton dust standard.

Most important, in two years OSHA added not one new standard to protect workers from cancer. More than ten million American workers are exposed every day on the job to eleven well known cancer-causing substances; no one knows how many are exposed to the 350 chemicals identified so far as possible carcinogens. Whatever risks there are in these chemicals to the public health, workers in the plants that produce them are exposed first and, often, most.

In the first two years under President Reagan, OSHA turned down petitions from labor unions for emergency protection against formaldehyde, an animal carcinogen suspected of causing nasal tumors in workers, and ethylene dibromide, a pesticide used to fumigate grains and fruit that is both acutely toxic and a potent carcinogen in laboratory animals. OSHA also refused to budge with a tighter standard for benzene, a chemical so widespread that one and a half million workers are exposed to it, and a known cause of leukemia. For ethylene oxide—a sterilizer and fumigant, a poison gas in World War I, and a cause of leukemia and other cancers—OSHA finally drafted a standard that would reduce the allowable exposure from 50 parts per million to 1 ppm in air. But not until ordered to do so by a U.S. Circuit Court of Appeals, which called OSHA's long delay in setting the standard "unreasonable."

OSHA's retreat from protection of workers' health was part of a pattern. The same toxic substances that workers breathe or absorb in the workplace nearly always turn up in the wider environment—in air, streams, lakes, soil, ground water, plants, and animals—and through those media the general public is also exposed to them. In a dozen laws passed in the 1970's, Congress charged EPA, OSHA, and other federal agencies to control the toxic pollutants that seriously threaten human health and the environment. In all those programs, "regulatory relief" meant retreat, if not total default.

Underlying the Reagan Administration's approach to toxic pollution was a deeply held belief that previous administrations had exaggerated its risks to satisfy their thirst for government intrusion into affairs of business. The resulting regulation, the Reagan officials believed, stifled progress, strangled industry, deprived the public of the benefit of new chemicals, drugs, and pesticides, and cost too much money.

Inescapably, government regulation of toxic materials must deal with scientific uncertainty. There are legitimate disagreements among scientists on how to interpret both the laboratory tests of animal reactions to toxic chemicals and human experience with the chemicals. Sometimes, available data do not conclusively prove, but only strongly

147

suggest, risk to human health. Conclusive proof could only come at great cost in human suffering. In drafting environmental safety and health legislation, Congress has leaned toward protective standards designed to prevent harm, rather than awaiting proof that harm has occurred. That is because, as Dr. Vernon Houk of the federal Centers for Disease Control has said, "historically, beginning with radiation and for the past few decades with toxic materials in our environment, as we learn more about these substances, we generally find they are more toxic than we thought."

It is not particularly surprising that, in their dealings with government regulators, industry scientists put forward the interpretations most favorable to their employers, or that they often rely on arguments challenged by other scientists. What *is* surprising is that government regulators themselves should adopt the whole industry package and label it Good Science.

EPA's standard bearers for Good Science were John Hernandez, Deputy Administrator; John Todhunter, head of the office of toxic substances and pesticides; and Rita Lavelle, chief of toxic waste cleanup. Anne Gorsuch regarded Hernandez as her chief scientific adviser—"sort of an agency-wide science officer," recalls Todhunter. Together with Todhunter and Lavelle, Hernandez made it his mission to change the basis for EPA's assessment of cancer risks.

EPA and three other agencies (OSHA, the Consumer Product Safety Commission, and the Food and Drug Administration) already had an official cancer policy. It grew out of guidelines EPA had adopted in 1976. In the three years following, the four agencies combed the scientific literature, subjected their policy to scientific peer review, and put it out for public comment in 1979. Most scientists throughout the world subscribe to its principles, which are: Well-conducted tests showing that a substance causes cancer in animals are good evidence that it may do so in humans. We do not need proof of cancer in humans—which is very hard to come by—to conclude that a substance poses a significant risk to people. With our present state of knowledge, we cannot set a safe lower limit for exposure to carcinogens—we have to assume that even very low doses will cause some added cancers. These principles are the basis for a policy that attempts to prevent cancer, rather than reacting after the damage is done—a policy of "better safe than sorry."

148

The advocates of Good Science did not openly challenge these widely accepted principles. It was in their actions, and the memos they wrote to each other, that Good Science was revealed as a policy of less protection and higher risk. Scientists critical of the shift called it a "covert" attempt to radically revise and soften regulations.

Good Science resembled in many particulars attacks published by the conservative Heritage Foundation on previous government cancer policy. (The Heritage Foundation was a source of policy ideas throughout the Reagan Administration.) One author of Heritage Foundation articles on cancer policy was Elizabeth Whelan, director of the American Council on Science and Health (supported in large part by donations from industry); another was Louis Cordia, then a 24-year-old policy analyst for the Foundation. (Cordia left the Foundation for EPA after President Reagan's election.)

Whelan, a good writer and good publicist, called the pre-Reagan cancer policy "regulation at the drop of a rat." She derided "inflexible regulation" that assumes that "laboratory animals are excellent predictors of the cancer-causing potential of a chemical in man"—the inference being, she said, "that mice are little men." Both Whelan and Cordia called for more human epidemiological studies as a basis for regulating carcinogens.

No scientist would disagree that well-conducted epidemiological studies provide the most convincing evidence of human risk. Animal studies are very commonly used instead, for several reasons. First of all, we do not experiment on human beings to test possible carcinogens. Human evidence on cancer-causing substances must be drawn from life experience, and that is very difficult to evaluate, because cancer takes such a long time to develop (typically 15 to 30 years); because people don't stay in the same place, subject to the same environmental conditions, but move around; because humans out in the world (unlike animals in the laboratory) are exposed to a great many different possible carcinogens, not just one at a time; because exposure to possible cancer-causing chemicals is so widespread that it is often difficult to find a control group of humans to compare statistically with the exposed group. Moreover, the sheer number of people needed to demonstrate excess cancers may be very large, even when the risk is extremely high, as it is with asbestos and cigarette smoking. Even the strong connection between cigarette smoking and lung cancer in humans took 40 years to establish.

149

Animal studies are a practical and relatively quick means to identify carcinogens when human evidence is uncertain or lacking. Animal studies provide advance warning that a new drug or chemical may be dangerous to human beings, a warning that can be heeded to prevent human exposure. Experience has taught us what the cost of ignoring such warnings can be. For example, rat studies indicating that vinyl chloride is a carcinogen were reported to an international congress in 1970, but neither government nor industry took any action at the time to protect workers exposed to vinyl chloride at high levels. Four years later, workers in vinyl chloride plants were found to have a rare form of liver cancer (angiosarcoma) in numbers far greater than chance could account for. As the evidence mounted, researchers concluded that plastics workers run 200 times the average risk of getting liver cancer.

The aspect of animal testing that is most often misunderstood is the use of very high doses. A favorite subject of cartoonists is the laboratory rat, replete with 800 times the saccharin found in one bottle of diet soda. The implied question is, Who on earth would drink so much soda?

Scientists reply that this is the wrong question. The reason for using high doses is to get results with a necessarily limited number of test animals. Increasing the dose makes cancers appear more frequently, so they can be detected in a group of 50 to 100 animals. In a group of 100 animals, at least three of the treated animals would have to get cancer, compared with zero in the control group, for the result to be statistically valid. If the dose were the same as people encounter, in the workplace or elsewhere, these results would be horrendous. A 3-percent risk of cancer in a population of 220 million means that nearly 7 million people over a lifetime (or roughly 98,000 a year) would be expected to get cancer from the substance. To detect a cancer risk of smaller, more realistic proportions would require the testing of hundreds of thousands of animals—not a practical possibility. Hence the high doses.

A related misconception is that anything can cause cancer if you give it in high enough doses. On the contrary, the scientific evidence so far is that substances either do or don't cause cancer. Higher doses of carcinogens are likely to cause cancer in more people (or in more animals, in experimental studies). Higher doses of noncarcinogens, like salt, may make people ill in some other way, but they don't cause cancer.

Without regarding mice as "little men," scientists do consider the results of animal tests relevant to human beings. The reason, as stated by David Rall, Director of the National Toxicology Program, is that "basic biological processes . . . are strikingly similar from one mammalian species to another." One piece of evidence for the similarity is that the chemicals and processes that are known to produce cancer in humans also cause cancer in animals. The type and site of cancers may be different, and sensitivity to certain carcinogens may be different in various animal species, including Homo sapiens. But, on the whole, animal tests provide a valid and indispensable cancer warning system for humans.

No one, in fact, directly suggests throwing animal tests out—not even Elizabeth Whelan or Louis Cordia; instead they argued that government regulation relies on positive animal tests too "inflexibly." Yet, in a 1982 decision on formaldehyde, EPA, for all practical purposes, ignored two highly regarded studies showing that the chemical causes cancer in animals. John Todhunter, reversed a recommendation of his staff to give formaldehyde high priority as a candidate for regulation. In doing so, he disregarded reports of three major scientific panels (to the National Toxicology Program, the American Cancer Society, and the International Agency for Research on Cancer) and the conclusions of the Directors of the National Cancer Institute, the National Institute of Occupational Safety and Health, the National Center for Toxicological Research, and many other scientific experts. All the aforementioned experts agreed that formaldehyde is an animal carcinogen and hence is a presumptive human carcinogen.

Disagreement came from the formaldehyde industry. They had a most unusual opportunity to express their disagreement when John Hernandez held a series of "science courts" (so named by an industry lobbyist), at which Hernandez invited industry scientists and lawyers to take a crack at the scientific analysis EPA staff had provided.

Formaldehyde is a versatile chemical used in hundreds of products such as particle board, plywood, paper, home insulation, plastic materials, permanent-press fabrics, preservatives, drugs, cosmetics, and embalming fluids. About 7 billion pounds of formaldehyde are produced in the United States each year; 1.4 million people are exposed to it in the workplace; 11 million people may breathe formaldehyde vapors released from insulation and building materials in the home. Nearly everyone comes into contact with the chemical in one way or another.

In November 1980 EPA received confirmation that earlier data from the Chemical Industry Institute of Toxicology did show that formaldehyde caused a statistically significant increase of nasal cancers in rats—an extremely rare type of cancer in these animals. Experiments at New York University confirmed the results. The doses that caused cancer in the studies were not far above some of the levels reported in the workplace, in mobile homes, and in houses insulated with urea-formaldehyde foam. In February, EPA staff recommended that the Agency give formaldehyde a top priority review, to investigate the human exposures of most concern and decide whether the next step should be to regulate the chemical.

The staff's recommendations, including a draft notice to be published in the *Federal Register*, were waiting for Anne Gorsuch and John Hernandez when they took office in May 1981. A week after his confirmation, Hernandez met with seven members of the Formaldehyde Institute (the industry's trade association and lobbying arm) in his office. "Their scientists told me of a number of technical weaknesses in the [EPA] staff document," Hernandez said.

Soon afterwards, in the summer of 1981, Hernandez convened the "science courts." Groups of industry lawyers and scientists came to EPA to grill the staffers responsible for technical analyses of formaldehyde and another industrial chemical, DEHP (di[2-ethylhexyl] phthalate), and to criticize their results. There were three sessions on formaldehyde and three on DEHP. Attendance at these closed meetings varied from two to three dozen people; of the participants, only two or three could be described as independent scientists. The rest were EPA officials and staff or industry people, including representatives of DuPont and Georgia Pacific and two lawyers from firms representing the industry. Scientists from the Occupational Safety and Health Administration and the Consumer Product Safety Commission heard about the meetings and asked to come but were excluded. No consumer group or environmental organization was invited to attend or even notified. Hernandez told interviewers a few weeks later that EPA "staff represented the consumer."

The atmosphere at the formaldehyde meetings, according to one witness, "began rather tentatively and decorously but deteriorated. By the third meeting, it had turned into a zoo. It was clearly industry people presenting their case. The EPA people were very much on the defensive; they were being knocked down, especially by Todhunter." At hearings of the House Subcommittee on Oversight and Investigations, Richard Dailey, ex-EPA staffer, added details. (Dailey resigned from EPA when

Todhunter dictated changes in the staff report on formaldehyde.) Dailey said:

There was a discussion between the epidemiologist from the Formaldehyde Institute and [Jane] Keller [then an EPA epidemiologist, since departed]. Dr. Todhunter asked Ms. Keller a question. Before she could reply he asked her another question. She never got a chance to answer any of the questions that he asked before he cut her off in a very aggressive manner.

Lester Brown, then a staff member for the House Subcommittee on Environment, Energy, and Natural Resources, invited himself to the last of the science court meetings on DEHP and described the atmosphere of that meeting as "friendly." Hernandez was jovial. At one point, he demanded, looking for the Exxon representative, "Where's my chemist?" "He was joking," says Edwin Clark, now an economist for the Conservation Foundation, then an EPA official. "He never realized at the time how totally inappropriate this whole thing was."

Hernandez was ebullient about the meetings. In an interview with two staff members of a House subcommittee the day after the last meeting, Hernandez described a mouse study of DEHP conducted by the National Cancer Institute in which, he said, "they fed the rats [sic] too much. . . . Wouldn't you know it would take an industry guy to ferret out a thing like that?" No scientist from the National Cancer Institute was present at that science court meeting to explain or defend the study. At a subcommittee hearing a few weeks later, Hernandez described the study differently—as a test in which animals are fed very large amounts of a chemical to find out whether it does or does not cause cancer. This is a standard kind of test in cancer research.

John Todhunter wrote the decision that came out of the meetings. In reversing the EPA staff recommendation, the decision memo not only denied a priority review of formaldehyde, but discarded the basic principles that had previously guided the government's cancer policy. The decision discounted positive, well-conducted animal studies; instead it emphasized a demand for human evidence. And it argued that formaldehyde, though a carcinogen, was harmless in amounts below a threshold dose.

How Todhunter veered from established cancer policy and from the conclusions of eminent scientists on formaldehyde is detailed in a paper in *Science* by Dr. Frederica Perera and in the report of the Gore Subcommittee on Oversight and Investigations, which drew on the testimony of a dozen scientists. Todhunter began by stacking four "negative" animal studies up against "only" two clear positive results. Conservative cancer policy of the last decade has given more weight to positive than to negative studies, for two reasons: The negative studies may be mistaken and action based on a false negative could have serious repercussions on health. Moreover, false negatives, because of the difficulties of detecting cancer in small groups of animals, are more probable than false positives. In addition, the four contrary studies on formaldehyde were *not* in fact negative. The previous expert reviews of formaldehyde had concluded that the "negative" studies were either too flawed for any conclusion to be drawn or else were suggestive of a positive effect.

Todhunter apparently dismissed formaldehyde as a risk to humans because of the lack of positive epidemiological data. He said: "If formaldehyde were a potent human risk, this would show up epidemiologically. There does not appear to be any relationship, based on the existing data base in humans, between exposure and cancer."

The fundamental implication of the formaldehyde decision was that only human data are sufficient to prove a human cancer risk. Todhunter later denied the implication, calling it a "misconception" that EPA had changed its cancer policy. Then he added language that undercut his point: "The fact is, EPA considers formaldehyde to be a carcinogen in the rat by the inhalation route, possibly also in the mouse by the same route, and EPA presumes that formaldehyde may, in theory, pose a risk of cancer to humans."

In theory perhaps, but not in the practical sense of urgently investigating or taking steps to regulate a substance found to cause cancer in animals. To Dr. Ellen Silbergeld, chief scientist for toxics of the Environmental Defense Fund, it was plain that EPA was in retreat from taking animal studies seriously, despite the disclaimers. She called it "creationist" toxicology.

The other major strand of revisionism in the Todhunter document was the insistence that there is a "safe" dose, or threshold, below which formaldehyde does no harm. To support the idea of a threshold, Todhunter produced a theory that cancer from formaldehyde develops only at spots that are first irritated by the chemical and that, at a low enough dose, the irritation does not occur. Even some scientists who represent the formaldehyde industry could not swallow this theory. But the urge to find that thresholds exist was a powerful one at the top levels of EPA. If thresholds exist, then exposures much higher than those currently recommended for many carcinogens—more than one hundredfold higher—are tolerable.

At the Gore subcommittee hearings, independent scientists gave the Todhunter memo very low marks for objectivity and scientific respectability. Dr. Norton Nelson, chairman of the board of scientific counselors to the government's National Toxicology Program and a professor of environmental medicine at New York University, said:

> The document is remarkable in the sense that in each issue examined an extreme position is taken relating to the probable non-significance of the data on formaldehyde. It would perhaps be understandable for such an analysis to be prepared by industry. . . . To be put forward as a dispassionate examination of evidence . . . must be viewed as irresponsible.

Dr. Roy Albert, Deputy Director of the Institute of Environmental Medicine at New York University, head of an EPA scientific advisory committee on Carcinogenic Risk Assessment, said of the Todhunter document: "The exposition of the science was clearly tailored to fit the decision. The document is far too one-sided to be regarded as a balanced assessment of the cancer risk from formaldehyde." In an interview with Tracy Freedman and David Weir for *The Nation*, Albert spoke bluntly: "The sensible part of the scientific community consider formaldehyde a likely human carcinogen and I do too. If you start giving credence to P.R. men and the formaldehyde industry you're losing your grip on reality."

Looking back over the events two years later, Edwin Clark says that Hernandez seemed convinced that a decision in favor of a priority review for formaldehyde "would create serious economic impacts. He apparently thought the review was tantamount to banning the chemical." And indeed a preliminary paper for the Todhunter memo, written to him by the newly appointed director of the toxic substances office, suggested that the formaldehyde review "would create an adversarial relationship with industry at a time when we are seeking industry cooperation."

Clark describes the EPA staff proposal on formaldehyde as "simply to do a bunch of studies." He adds, "I thought it would be an easy

155

decision. I was just astounded when the whole group seemed determined not to make any positive decision at all."

EPA made de facto revisions in cancer policy not only in the formaldehyde case but also in several decisions on pesticides. A special target in the revisions was the principle that there is no safe level of exposure to a carcinogen.

To support the threshold idea, EPA sometimes adopted a theory, held by some scientists and highly popular with industry, that two classes of carcinogens exist, one of which does have safe threshold levels. According to the theory, genotoxic carcinogens directly attack the cells' genetically coded material (DNA) and have no safe level. But epigenetic carcinogens, which attack the cell in a different manner and change the genetic mechanism only in a roundabout way, do have safe thresholds.

The theory would make an enormous practical difference. Applied to water pollutants, for example, the allowable levels of many cancer-causing chemicals would rise by factors of as much as 200 or 300. For heptachlor (a persistent, cancer-causing pesticide), allowable levels could be 13 to 179 times greater; 18 to 285 times as much aldrin would be allowed; 19 to 369 times as much hexachloroethane; 13 to 181 times as much dioxin.

Many cancer researchers agree that some carcinogens may have a threshold, or are many times more damaging at higher than at lower doses. But most believe that there is no simple schematic way of sorting out which carcinogens have thresholds, especially in a large human population with greatly differing sensitivities to different carcinogens. Dr. Norton Nelson said: "We must accept the fact that a demonstration of a threshold in humans or in animals is likely to be difficult and elusive, and at the present time, probably not attainable."

For purposes of protecting the public health, most of the nation's leading experts on cancer reject a scheme that puts carcinogens into two classes and is "softer" on one class. Dr. I. Bernard Weinstein, of Columbia University's Institute of Cancer Research, said it is a "distortion of science" to create greater and lesser risk categories based on the distinction between genotoxic and epigenetic carcinogens. "This distinction is faulty," he said. "My reading . . . is that there is no clear evidence of a threshold for any carcinogen." Because of this, "it is prudent not to assume the existence of a threshold dose for any carcinogen" at all. Dr. Nelson said the threshold assumption is simply "not scientifically supportable."

Dr. Ellen Silbergeld of the Environmental Defense Fund pointed to the example of dioxin. EPA has repeatedly described dioxin as the most potent animal carcinogen known; it has produced cancer in animals at doses as low as 2.2 parts per billion. "And yet dioxin is a classic epigenetic carcinogen," said Silbergeld. "It blows the theory of a threshold completely out of the water."

Todhunter himself denied, in a letter to *Science* in February 1983, that he was "a proponent of the genotoxic versus nongenotoxic segregation for regulatory purposes." Yet Todhunter did in fact use this very distinction, and the assumption of a safe threshold, in approving the controversial pesticide permethrin for use on food crops. In the permethrin decision, EPA also discarded a test showing that permethrin caused liver cancer in mice, accepting a negative study in rats instead.

Further evidence that EPA meant to use the distinction to downgrade cancer risks came in a memo dated October 5, 1982, and an attached draft press release, from Rita Lavelle to John Hernandez. Lavelle reminded Hernandez of a meeting held two weeks earlier at which they agreed to change EPA's position on trichloroethylene (TCE) in drinking water. EPA issues health advisories to states on a number of carcinogens, suggesting levels in drinking water that will keep cancer risks low. TCE causes cancer in mice; EPA had issued an advisory for it. A very widely used industrial chemical (as a solvent, a dry cleaner, a degreaser), TCE is part of the chemical brew leaking from many hazardous waste dumps.

Lavelle said in her memo that TCE "is of paramount importance to us." She wanted Hernandez to follow through on redoing the health advisory to states on TCE, and develop a "threshold model" for estimating its risks. With a threshold model, much higher levels of TCE could be tolerated in drinking water. And the cleanup required at hazardous waste sites could be much less stringent. Lavelle described the draft press release announcing the Agency's plans for TCE as part of an "expeditious, well conceived, planned, and executed communication to the scientific and regulated communities of our plans for the application of 'good science.' "

Gene Lucero, the EPA career professional who served as chief of enforcement for Rita Lavelle's program, observed recently that she came to the Agency "with her own view" on TCE. "That was Aerojet's problem," Lucero said. "I got the impression that, if she had a mission when she came to the Agency, it was the TCE question, as it affected Aerojet."

The draft press release on TCE never went out, nor was a new health advisory on TCE ever prepared. Within six months, Lavelle had been fired and Hernandez had resigned. Had their "good science" prevailed, cleanup of TCE at hundreds of dump sites would have been undermined.

While the change on TCE did not go through, other changes did. They added up to the "high-risk carcinogen policy," as *Science* magazine termed it. For ten years before Anne Gorsuch, John Hernandez, and the other Reagan-appointed officials took over EPA, the Agency's approach had been one of caution. Assuming there was no safe lower limit for exposure to carcinogens, EPA tried to avoid risks higher than one excess cancer per million population. Only in exceptional cases did EPA accept risks of 1 in 100,000. OSHA standards often tolerated cancer risks from occupational exposure higher than those allowed for the general population, because it was considered technologically impractical to get them any lower.

In approving several pesticides, Todhunter and EPA allowed risks estimated at 10 to 100 times the old one-in-a-million standard. For example, EPA decided in November 1982 to allow the continued use of ethylene bisdithiocarbamates (EBDCs), fungicides that are widely used on fruits, vegetables, grains, and nuts and sold under such names as Amobam, Mancozeb, Nabam, and Zineb. A metabolite of this group of fungicides causes liver cancer in mice and thyroid cancer in rats. EPA estimated the added cancer risk to people from residues of the fungicides' metabolite in foods is between 5 in 100,000 and 4 in 10,000. For the people who mix and apply the pesticide throughout a 40-year work-life, the added risk is as much as 1 in 100.

For benomyl, which EPA approved for continued use in October 1982, EPA estimated the risk from traces in food as between 7 in a million to 7 in 100,000. But to make the estimates of risks this low, EPA omitted a standard correction that is virtually always used in applying results of mouse studies to man. The standard correction, a factor of 12.9, takes into account humans' larger size and surface area. If the correction is factored in, the risk is properly figured at 9 in 100,000 to 9 in 10,000 (or practically 1 in 1,000)—an unacceptable risk, according to the old standards.

Regulation deals with one carcinogen at a time, but people do not.

In the real world, we are exposed to many carcinogens. The risks add up and in some cases multiply. The cancer risks of cigarette smoking and asbestos exposure are both high; but, taken together, they are enormous —much more than the simple sum of the two risks. Looking at cancer-causing agents as simply additive, ten carcinogens, each with a risk of 1 in 10,000, add up to a cumulative risk of 1 in 1,000. One hundred such carcinogens add up to a risk of 1 in 100. If a risk of one in 1,000, say, appears tolerable, consider it from a public health standpoint. In a population of 220 million, it means an extra 222,000 cases of cancer over a lifetime of exposure, or roughly 3,000 extra cases per year.

Risk estimates for cancer are necessarily crude; it is a mistake to take these numbers too literally. Because of the uncertainties of applying animal test results—often not very detailed results—to people, the risk estimates could be off by 10 to 100 times, either way. For this reason, it has been the practice to err on the side of caution.

This brings us to the central question about the connection between science and public policy. When the science about toxic chemicals is still uncertain—when the verdict, for many of them is not yet in—which way do we want to take our chances? An anonymous cancer researcher, quoted in the *National Journal,* put it this way: "Do you want to throw out some good chemicals with bad ones and save a few human lives, or do you want to be minimally burdensome to industry and take your lumps when you guess wrong on a chemical? It depends on whether you're a conservative on the economic side or on the human protection side."

Bill Hedeman, the career professional who directed the Superfund program, said recently that Rita Lavelle held a "very very strong view that society was paying for risks we should be prepared to take. . . . The theme of the Superfund cleanups was: We've got to be willing to take bigger risks, to tolerate much greater exposures. Risk of exposure to toxics is a byproduct of the twentieth century that we must be willing to accept."

Dr. Elizabeth Whelan, writing for the Heritage Foundation, stated the conservative economic side of the argument succinctly. Asserting that, aside from lung cancer, there is no cancer epidemic, she concluded that toxic chemicals don't cause any extra cancers among the general public. The springboard for Whelan's leap to this conclusion was the very epidemiological studies—i.e., human evidence—that nearly all other scientists find so fragmentary, contradictory, and hard to read.

Whelan discounted the many studies showing excess occurrence of cancers among workers exposed to hazardous chemicals. High exposures in the workplace have meant that occupational cancer provides the clearest evidence available on human carcinogens. Whelan concluded, however, that occupational risks of cancer may now be close to zero, because "safety measures in chemical plants" are "standard procedure" today.

She concluded:

If modern day chemicals cause cancer . . . then that would be another question. But in most cases no such cause-and-effect relationship exists, and we may soon find ourselves without some very basic, useful items, while we spend more of each dollar in taxes to pay the regulators—all this without preventing even one case of human cancer. This is an enormous price tag for nothing.

Whelan's view that chemicals do not cause cancer in humans is idiosyncratic. Most scientists think they do. They take cancer data from the workplace seriously because those data show that high levels of exposure to certain chemicals cause a high incidence of cancer among exposed workers. The scientific consensus is that the exposure of large numbers of people to lower levels of the same chemicals also causes excess cancer, but we simply cannot yet say how much. The problem is that cancer is a common disease (cancer is the second leading cause of death in the United States) and exposure to cancer-causing chemicals is a common phenomenon.

It is true that except for lung cancer due to smoking and possibly to asbestos exposure, there is little evidence so far of a cancer "epidemic." That was the conclusion of a highly respected 1981 paper by the Oxford University epidemiologists Richard Doll and Richard Peto, based on studies of white U.S. residents under age 65, from 1933 to 1978. However, a recent study of older Americans, ages 35 to 84, concludes that there have been epidemic increases in multiple myeloma and brain cancers as well as lung cancers among older whites.

Actually, Doll and Peto themselves drew no conclusions about the possible influence of chemical carcinogens on deaths from cancer. The really explosive rise in production of synthetic organic chemicals did not take place until the 1960's. Most of the people in the Doll-Peto study were exposed to chemical carcinogens for a relatively short time—far less than the 20 years or more that it takes for most cancers to appear. Doll and Peto said: "Many industrial products have been introduced so recently (and on such a large scale) . . . that even if they do prove hazardous their effects would not yet be apparent. . . . There is too much ignorance for complacency to be justified."

Nicholas Ashford, director of the Center for Policy Alternatives at the Massachusetts Institute of Technology, is a conservative on the human protection side. He believes that strong suggestive evidence of a cancer risk justifies protective action. He points out that science demands a very strict measure of proof for causality—that is, 95 percent confidence that two events are linked by cause and effect, not by chance. For social policy, that criterion is "enormously stringent," Ashford says. To him, the social policy question "would not be, 'Can you publish it in the *New England Journal of Medicine?'*—but, 'Would you let your daughter work with that chemical?' "

Good Science, as practiced by John Hernandez, John Todhunter, and Rita Lavelle, shifted the burden of proof to our daughters. Its premise was exactly the view Ashford rejected, namely that regulatory decisions should be based only on scientific certainties. The public and the Congress have emphatically rejected that approach and its implicit acceptance of the use of human beings as guinea pigs.

To many scientists, the manner in which the Reagan EPA officials made this shift was almost as disturbing as the shift itself. I. Bernard Weinstein called it "a covert attempt . . . to soften regulatory guidelines." Norton Nelson, asserting that there is "no serious question" about the pre-Reagan cancer policy and risk assessment methods, said that we should "not quietly and covertly move away" from those established methods. Ellen Silbergeld said: "This process, being covert and diffuse, is much less easy to recognize, debate, or control."

For an Administration whose top officials, from the President down, had come in vowing to improve EPA's "bad science," John Todhunter's reluctance to describe the shift as a "change" was rather curious. He preferred the word "evolution." EPA's previous policy, Todhunter said in an interview, was "inflexible" and "inappropriate." He added: "Some of the edges were a little rough, so we felt we had to do some fine-tuning."

In fact, their attempts to fashion a coherent statement of revised cancer policy were a failure. New guidelines never got beyond the first draft stage. John Hernandez took a stab at revising the four-agency policy EPA had adopted in 1979. On a Saturday afternoon in June 1981,

161

less than a month after he took office, Hernandez called John Todhunter, then still a consultant expecting to be named as EPA chief of pesticides and toxic substances, and Andrew Jovanovich, who was acting chief of EPA's research and development, into his office to rewrite EPA's cancer policy.

"He sat us down at a table with pencils and paper and asked us to draft a Federal Register notice," Jovanovich recalls. Hernandez remembers the effort as a failure. Contrary to expectations, the Agency's cancer policy could not simply be rewritten or rescinded on a Saturday afternoon. The three were "trying hard" to do it, Hernandez says, but "it was junk. We never got anything out of it." Although the try was "immature and premature," he says, "I did learn something. It forced me to go back and read the old policy."

The EPA effort evolved into an informal working group, made up of Hernandez on occasion, Todhunter, Rita Lavelle's science adviser Art Pallotta, and a few others. Todhunter says they kept "trying to get a coherent policy," but could never pull it off. Gene Lucero, a top member of Lavelle's staff, recalls that problems dogged the group because "they didn't want to have it in an open forum" or to change policies gradually. "They wanted it all in one jump, all at once."

Not long afterward, the White House took over the job. In September 1981, President Reagan's science adviser, George Keyworth, dissolved the group, composed mostly of government scientists, who had written the 1979 cancer policy. Under the auspices of the task force on regulatory relief, a new work group was formed and charged with rewriting the cancer policy. Included in the working group were Hernandez, Todhunter, and their aides.

The group quickly agreed that the 1979 policy was "too conservative" in discounting negative tests, and that it improperly used "sensitive" animals and wrongly rejected threshold theories. A paper from John Morrall of the OMB deregulation team called the 1979 policy "bad science," with a tendency to "err on the side of caution" with the result of "overregulation." Morrall recommended a new "more cost effective cancer policy" with less "regulatory bias."

A year later, the group produced a draft of part of a new document —a policy section on new scientific information. In November 1982, the group sent it to scientists for comments. The comments were never published, but Reagan's science adviser, George Keyworth, who directed the effort, said that most of the 35 scientists were "supportive of our

162

effort while directing criticisms to the . . . substance of the document."
In fact the criticism was heated. Henry Pitot of the University of
Wisconsin for example called the proposal "a blanket attempt to change
policy [when] . . . our present state of knowledge . . . is really not at a
stage where we can, let us say, take the risk." A reviewer from the
nonpartisan Congressional Office of Technology Assessment wrote:
"The document fails to show that changes in scientific knowledge dictate any changes in policy."

In the end (at least as late as 1983), there was no real statement of
the new cancer policy. Instead, EPA produced ad hoc justifications for
decisions on pesticides like permethrin and potential carcinogens like
formaldehyde. Roy Gamse, a career official in EPA's policy office, said
the whole approach to cancer left him "bewildered." He said: "There
was no policy. . . . The message between the lines was that they didn't
want to establish procedures or guidelines because they wanted to maintain maximum flexibility to make any decision on any evidence. They
were trying for situations in which raw data went to Todhunter and
Hernandez without any principles that would lock them into regulating."

The determination not to regulate was the key. Then Good Science
could fashion reasons to show why the risks from not regulating were
acceptable, or maybe didn't exist. EPA's language underwent launder-
ing. Words like "cancer-causing" or "carcinogen" began to disappear
from the Agency's public statements.

Jim Sibbison, formerly a public information officer at EPA, recalled
in an article in *The Nation* that a press release he wrote on the pesticide
DBCP (withdrawn because it caused sterility in humans and was
strongly suspected of causing cancer) came back from Gorsuch's 12th
floor offices heavily edited. All references to cancer were deleted, and the
word "sterility" was crossed out, replaced by "adverse health effects."
Upon proposing a release on carcinogenic chemicals used as wood preservatives, Sibbison said, "I was told not to bother."

"After a while, I simply stopped mentioning cancer, birth defects,
and damage to genes. As a colleague of mine said, 'The Administrator's
office will take the words out anyway.' "

John Hernandez enthusiastically endorsed such changes. He suggested that the Agency "talk about 'degree of mitigation of risk' instead
of 'degree of hazard,' " and promised that "the average citizen is going
to hear that his life is threatened by some chemical many fewer times."

Frederica Perera, a scientist who closely followed and criticized the changing cancer policy, urged straight talk with the public. The "turn-around in the formerly conservative response to scientific uncertainty," she said, showed a willingness to accept higher risks of human cancer "to reach political goals." And political goals are exactly what citizens should know about, and choose.

Perera said: "I believe . . . that it is a mistake to view these revisions as a purely scientific matter and to 'cloak them in science'. . . . Instead, just as a thorough peer review of the scientific basis of policy is essential, so must the philosophical and political basis be openly discussed."

If the issues are openly debated, with all the risks frankly acknowl-edged, it might turn out that the public prefers less regulation and greater risks. Far more likely, as all the polls indicate, is that Americans continue to put the very highest value on protecting human health and the natural environment.

PESTICIDES

Fortunately, Dr. Erik Svenkurud knew what to look for when Maria and Juan Riojas brought their baby daughter, suffering convulsive seizures, into the family clinic at Mercedes, Texas. He looked for pesticide poi-soning. The clue, he said, was the child's pinpoint pupils—a distinct sign of pesticide poisoning which he had only recently learned to recognize, thanks to a training session given by the National Association of Farm-workers Organizations. "In medical schools," Dr. Svenkurud said, "you will hardly hear pesticides mentioned as a possible cause of convulsions."

Recognizing the signs, Dr. Svenkurud wasted no time in starting treatment; the baby began to recover, and blood tests confirmed the diagnosis. Yet the mystery remained of how the child had been exposed to an overwhelmingly toxic dose of pesticide. Dr. Svenkurud knew his area (the Rio Grande Valley of South Texas) and he knew that pesticides drifting from aerial spraying of crops often invade homes of Mexican-American farmworker families living near the fields. Following a hunch, he visited the Riojas family at home, looking for the telltale whitish crust that pesticide residues leave on window sills and table tops. But the surfaces were clean.

The break came when Dr. Svenkurud asked Juan Riojas to describe everything he had done the day his daughter fell ill. Nothing special,

Riojas said. He had worked in the cabbage fields and then pla[?] the baby when he came home. This was enough to tell Dr. S[?] where to look—at the father's clothes. Rio Grande Valley farmworkers, he knew, reenter cabbage fields a very short time after pesticide spraying and often get covered with the residues. The baby had absorbed toxins through her skin when her father held her. The amount of pesticide on his clothes, while not enough to cause acute symptoms in an adult, was sufficient to derange the nervous system of a six-month-old child.

Pesticides, by their nature, are not safe. They are designed to poison and kill creatures whose biological processes are essentially similar to ours. The chemical that disrupts nerve signals in a cabbage worm can do the same to a human being. Some pesticides, if selected and handled with care, may never cause serious trouble, but most are capable of it. Some cause acute illness, ranging from dizziness and nausea to tremors, paralysis, and convulsions, even death. At lower doses over longer times, some pesticides produce permanent nerve or brain damage; some cause heart, blood, or liver disease. Certain pesticides can cause sterility, miscarriages, birth defects, or impairment of genes, which might take two or three generations to show up. Some can cause cancer.

Pesticides entering the air, soil, streams, lakes, and forests have harmed fish and wildlife, sometimes in bizarre ways. Toxaphene, for example, causes "broken-back" syndrome in catfish. DDT caused thinning of eggshells in the American bald eagle, the brown pelican, and the peregrine falcon, threatening the survival of these species.

Pesticides are pervasive. We take them into our bodies in the food we eat, the water we drink or bathe in, the air we breathe. Over 99 percent of us, no matter where we live, carry in our body tissues traces of the persistent organochlorine pesticides DDT, dieldrin, heptachlor, and chlordane (all of them banned for most uses years ago). Toxaphene, once very widely used on cotton and soybeans in the South, has been found at high levels in Great Lakes fish, a thousand miles away.

The other side of the coin, of course, is the importance of pesticides to agriculture. A spokesman for the farm chemicals industry puts it this way: "Our food is not grown, it is manufactured." Pesticides are an integral part of the highly industrialized, mechanized, chemicalized, and enormously productive system of U.S. commercial agriculture. Pesticides also take some of the hardest work out of farming, substituting herbicides, for example, for the hoe and hand weeding. The forest industry, too, depends heavily on pesticides, including herbicides, to keep down underbrush. Power companies and highway departments use chemicals instead of mowers on rights of way. Exterminators are big users of pesticides; so are home gardeners.

Yet chemicals are no miracle cure for insects, weeds, and plant disease. Forty years after the great boom in synthetic organic pesticides began, and after a tenfold increase in insecticide use, farmers are about where they started. Pests still destroy about one-third of their crops. Harvest yields have doubled, but so have the losses. Hundreds of species of insects and mites have become immune to pesticides, and some insects (such as the cotton bollworm) that once were minor nuisances got to be major pests after chemical pesticides wiped out their natural predators. Moreover, most large farms, in the interest of planting higher value crops, have sacrificed crop rotation, which was the main traditional defense against pests.

American agriculture is hooked on chemical pesticides. Farmers depend on them to keep ahead of the game. Many in the farm service business regard them, simply, as indispensable. George Mitchell, the number one crop duster in the State of Texas, says it is a question of "us" (people) or "them" (pests) in a continuing war over farm produce. "Who's going to eat it?" he asks. "Are we going to eat it or are they going to eat it?"

The network of advocates for chemical pesticides includes researchers at land grant colleges, state and federal departments of agriculture, county extension agents, and the industry that manufactures them. The industry lobby is led by the National Agricultural Chemicals Association, with a membership that includes some of the country's industrial giants. DuPont, for example, is eighth on the *Fortune* 500 list, with annual sales of $33 billion and assets of $24 billion. Dow and Union Carbide are in the top thirty, with $11–12 billion in assets.

Environmental critics of pesticides also have a high profile, though with far less money and fewer lawyers and lobbyists than the industry can muster. Rachel Carson's 1962 best-seller, *Silent Spring,* an indictment of indiscriminate poisoning of human beings and their habitat by pesticides, was one of the most influential books on the environment ever written. It led to new scientific studies of pesticide effects, stricter government controls over pesticides, and, eventually, the banning of DDT. For many people, it inspired a new way of thinking about the natural environment and the post-World War II chemical revolution— the production of thousands of man-made chemicals that are not found in nature but are tailored to suit particular narrow human needs. Modern environmental thought was maturing in the 1960's and, thanks to *Silent Spring,* it focused on pesticides.

One of the results was that in 1970 President Nixon and Congress took federal pesticide regulation out of the hands of the Agriculture Department and gave it to the fledgling Environmental Protection Agency. A major theme of *Silent Spring* was the failure of agriculture departments, state and federal, to look at pesticides with any more independent or critical eye than did the pesticide industry itself. Another result was that Congress passed a broad new federal pesticides law, the Federal Insecticide, Fungicide, and Rodenticide Act (FIFRA for short) in 1972, with amendments added in 1978.

Under FIFRA, EPA has to approve all new pesticides before they can go on the market, as well as all new uses for old pesticides. (For example, a pesticide approved for cotton needs a new approval before it can be sprayed on tomatoes.) As a part of registration, EPA sets tolerances (limits on residues) for pesticides on crops that human beings and animals eat. As for old pesticides that were already in use before the law was passed, EPA was supposed to reexamine and re-register them. The law requires that "man and the environment" must be protected against "unreasonable risks" from pesticides. Its principle is a balancing of risks and benefits.

In theory, the system is protective. In practice, it has never worked very effectively. FIFRA is loaded down with compromise. Even at best, EPA has often been hamstrung by the law's unworkable provisions and by industry resistance to what it sees as "delay" of pesticide approvals.

Re-registration of old pesticides, in particular, has been a huge headache. There were tens of thousands of old pesticides in use when the 1972 law was passed; EPA obviously could not review and reapprove all of them at once. Even when the list was whittled down to 600 or so generic active ingredients, EPA did not get around to reexamining them all. Instead, the Agency selects for intensive review only those showing pretty clear signs of substantial risk. Before actually canceling an old registration, EPA has to amass a stack of evidence that the pesticide's risks outweigh its benefits. No more than a handful of pesticides have ever been canceled, or withdrawn by agreement with the manufacturer during cancellation proceedings.

The law also allows end runs around registration. States and local governments can petition EPA for "special" or "emergency" exemp-

167

tions for temporary use (up to one year) of pesticides that are not yet approved—or even for use of pesticides that have been banned or withdrawn as too dangerous to use.

Consider this evidence of how well the law has worked to protect human health and the environment from pesticides: Of 600 registered generic pesticides in common use today, 79 to 84 percent have not been adequately tested for their potential to cause cancer, 60 to 70 percent have not been tested for their potential to cause birth defects, and 90 percent have not been tested for genetic mutations. Thus we are really quite ignorant about the possible dangers of most pesticides. One reason is that modern tests have simply never been done for many of the older pesticides. Worse is the fact that hundreds of pesticide safety tests had to be thrown out a few years ago because they were shoddy or downright fraudulent. Government scientists discovered in the mid-1970's that the biggest laboratory doing tests under contract for the industry—Industrial Bio-Test Laboratory of Illinois—had submitted faked data. The work of some other labs was questioned, but no other fraud on the scale of IBT's has been found. EPA registration of more than 200 pesticides had rested on IBT data. Some of the tests have been replaced, but most have not.

Deficient testing is just one of many shortcomings. Another is EPA's unreliable, inadequate system for assuring that food is kept free of harmful residues. Failure to protect ground water—the drinking water supply for half of our citizens—is still another. Especially grievous is EPA neglect of protection for farmworkers' health.

By the early 1980's, many people concerned with protecting health and the environment from high-risk pesticides were convinced that reform of the law was a necessity. The Reagan Administration had a different idea of reform. In August 1981, Vice-President Bush's regulatory relief task force announced it had selected pesticide registration as a prime target for reconsideration by EPA, to get rid of "burdensome, unnecessary" federal regulations. The task force said the "registration process appears to delay unnecessarily the distribution of new pesticide products and to inhibit new uses of existing products." In other words, lift the regulatory burden from industry and get more pesticides out to the farm as quickly as possible.

EPA's response was prompt. In consultation with the National Agricultural Chemicals Association, the Agency started to redo the whole registration procedure to make it faster and easier. At the same time, EPA promised to "streamline" the registrations that were already in the works. From Anne Gorsuch down, the pressure was on to speed up reviews of new pesticides and new uses of old ones.

Two more themes accompanied streamlining. One was removal of "contention" with industry, the other an upbeat approach to pesticides or, looked at another way, a downplaying of the hazards. John A. Todhunter, the new EPA assistant administrator for pesticide and toxic substances, made these themes the centerpiece of his public speeches. In March 1982, in Columbus, Todhunter told the Ohio Fertilizer and Pesticide Association that the Reagan Administration was trying to bring more "credibility" to the science used in regulation, and that his program would do it "by increasing industry's involvement with my staff in nonadversarial meetings and negotiations." EPA would "speed up" and "streamline" the registration process, he said, through the use of "decision conferences" with industry.

To the Aviation Trades Association (crop dusters) in Kearney, Nebraska, Todhunter complained that "when the media addresses agricultural chemicals, its most common choice of words are 'hazardous' and 'toxic.' " Offering a new word to replace "pesticides," Todhunter said: "What the applicator applies are crop protection chemicals."

John Todhunter was a key figure in pesticide regulation during the Gorsuch years. He believed, he said, in "the use of sound science in the decision process . . . a return of informed professional judgment." What this veiled language apparently meant was that EPA's established policies on releasing chemicals into commerce were too cautious and conservative. As it turned out in practice, Todhunter's science supported quick approvals of new pesticides. But when it came to banning uses of an old one, ethylene dibromide (EDB), Todhunter used "sound science" to justify years of delay.

EDB is one of the most potent carcinogens ever tested in animals. Todhunter refused to accept an EPA staff risk assessment that concluded with a somber warning of the chemical's exceedingly high risk to humans. He produced his own risk figures downplaying the hazard. On at least three occasions, he personally intervened to stave off EPA restrictions on EDB. When he resigned from the Agency in March 1983, EDB was still in wide use.

EDB has been around since the 1950's. By far its biggest use is as an additive to leaded gasoline, although that use is declining as unleaded gasoline takes over. EDB is also an important pesticide. For 25 years, it has been used to fumigate grains that go into the breads all Americans eat and as a fumigant for destroying fruit flies in citrus fruits, tropical fruits, cherries, and plums. Its most important use as a pesticide, and a growing one, is as a soil fumigant, injected underground to kill nematodes (tiny worms that attack plant roots) before the planting of fruit trees, pineapples, peanuts, soybeans, and thirty-odd vegetables.

Federal regulators once believed there would be no traces of EDB left on treated food and set no tolerances (except for the relatively innocuous decay products, inorganic bromines). But EDB does leave residues. They have been found up to six weeks after fumigation in bread made from treated wheat; bread with traces of EDB is sold in supermarkets, and has been given to children in school lunches. EDB residues are also found on rice, on products (like oil) made from treated corn, and on treated grapefruit, oranges, limes, lemons, papayas, and mangoes.

In December 1980, after an intensive three-year scientific review, EPA concluded from new animal studies on chronic effects of EDB that it is a potent carcinogen, interferes with reproduction in both sexes, and causes inheritable changes in offspring. The little human evidence that exists on chronic effects suggests that it has caused sterility in men. In August 1981 California's division of occupational safety and health (CalOSHA) added this: "As a carcinogen, EDB can pose life-threatening danger in a very brief period of exposure."

At higher doses, EDB is acutely poisonous and can be lethal. At high enough levels, it causes respiratory failure and death. It can produce severe damage to internal organs, including the liver, kidney, heart, and lungs. A peculiarity of acute poisoning from this chemical is that its systemic damage to body organs may be delayed up to 24 hours, even at lethal doses.

EDB can be breathed, eaten, or absorbed through the skin. It penetrates protective gear such as rubber gloves, and contaminated clothing—even shoes—can make people ill. At a recent congressional hearing, Dave Smith, a part-time flour mill worker in Minneapolis, told of a brush with death in December 1981, when he spilled liquid EDB from a defective spray gun on his hands and trousers. He washed his hands (he had been told to wash any spills off his skin) but not his trousers. Within an hour, he had a terrible headache, his whole body went numb, and he was so dizzy he could barely make it in the manlift to the ground floor. Rushed to the hospital, he collapsed. His pulse rate dropped from a normal 72 to 29. Not until five days later was it certain he would survive.

EDB in leaded gasoline does not appear to threaten the general public, but is a potential danger to the workers who produce it. The federal limit for worker exposure to EDB is 20 parts per million. That is close to the level at which acutely toxic effects have occurred in humans, it is twice the level that produced cancer in 40 percent of exposed laboratory animals, and it is 154 times the limit of 130 parts per billion recommended in 1977 by the National Institute for Occupational Safety and Health. Some manufacturers take extraordinary measures to keep workers out of contact with EDB: putting workers in "moon suits" with scuba-like breathing apparatus, or using completely closed systems, where workers have no physical contact with the chemical. Manufacturers of EDB are Dow Chemical, Ethyl Corporation, Great Lakes Chemical, and PPG Corporation.

When EDB is used to kill insects and extend the storage life of food crops or to fumigate soil, exposure is far wider. Not only are the fumigators who apply it at risk, so are truckers and food handlers in warehouses; as many as 100,000 workers may be exposed to the chemical. EDB gases penetrate grains and their containers, and the flesh, pits, and packaging of fruits. The foods and their packaging give off fumes for days or weeks afterwards ("offgassing" in the jargon), and in enclosed spaces the vapors can build up to dangerous levels.

For the population as a whole, EPA calculated that the extra risk of getting cancer from eating foods contaminated with EDB is most probably 3.2 in 10,000, with a "realistic worst case" of 1.5 in 1,000. In a population of 220 million people, these risks mean 70,000 to 300,000 extra cases of cancer over a lifetime exposure to EDB in food. For people exposed to EDB on the job (other than in production plants), EPA calculated that the extra cancer risk was 1 in 1,000 for truckers, between 1 in 1,000 and 1 in 100 for fumigation center workers, and between 1 in 10 and 4 in 10 for citrus warehouse laborers. Risks on the job are in addition to those from dietary exposure. "These cancer risks are among the highest risks the Agency has ever confronted," EPA said.

EPA proposed in 1980 to stop the fumigation of grains with EDB immediately and substitute less dangerous chemicals that were just as good and would probably cost less. As a fumigant for citrus, tropical, and some other fruits, EDB is used to prevent the spread of Mediterranean and Caribbean fruit flies. Japan won't accept California's grapefruit unless it has been fumigated, nor will California accept Florida's. To allow time for developing alternatives, EPA proposed to phase out EDB fumigation of fruits after harvest over two and a half years, ending it by July 1983.

The only major agricultural use of EDB that the Agency proposed to continue was as a soil fumigant. In 1980, with another nematocide, DBCP (dibromochloropropane), about to be canceled, some growers were already adopting EDB as a substitute soil fumigant. With this use, there was thought to be little chance of getting residues on the food. Applicators, it was believed, could be adequately protected with rubber boots and aprons and respirators. But recognizing the danger that EDB might seep into ground water, as DBCP had done, EPA did call for monitoring. A well-founded warning, as we shall see.

While the Reagan appointees were moving into EPA, the proposal on EDB languished. But by late summer, during the great California Medfly scare, EDB became a hot issue. The U.S. Department of Agriculture ruled that citrus and tropical fruits exported from California to Japan must be fumigated with EDB. Up to the time, California had forbidden the use of EDB on harvested fruits or grains because of the residues it leaves on food and because of the danger to workers. But now, "We found we'd be in the EDB business in a big way, and we were pretty horrified," said Ellen Widess, a lawyer for CalOSHA. The federal Occupational Safety and Health Administration had never tightened the worker exposure standard for non-farmworkers. It was still 20 parts per million.

California was suddenly forced to build 150 EDB fumigation chambers throughout the state and to find a way of protecting the health of 12,000 fumigators, truckers, and warehouse workers. Lacking adequate protection, truckers and dockworkers refused to handle the fumigated fruit.

The state acted quickly. In September it adopted an emergency temporary standard of 130 parts per billion for workplace exposure and later made the ruling permanent. (Grocery markets with less than 2,000 pounds of fumigated produce on hand at one time were exempted.) California also required reporting of EDB use and monitoring of exposure.

In Washington the response was to do nothing, except begin studies and issue reassuring press releases. Thorne Auchter rejected a request by three unions for an emergency nationwide standard that would reduce occupational exposures to EDB. A personal plea from J. Donald Millar, director of the National Institute of Occupational Safety and Health, failed to move Auchter. Auchter also ignored appeals from his staff. His position was that OSHA did not have enough information on the levels of EDB that workers were exposed to and without that information emergency action would not stand up in court. OSHA Solicitor Frank White explained in a memo to Auchter how an emergency standard could be justified legally, but Auchter opted against it. OSHA and NIOSH already had studies on worker exposure; they were the basis for EPA's risk figures, but Auchter ordered more studies.

Throughout the fall of 1981, Todhunter, Auchter, and other representatives of EPA, OSHA, the Department of Agriculture, and the Food and Drug Administration took part in meetings at the White House on EDB. At the behest of James Lake, a member of the 1976, 1980, and 1984 Reagan campaign staffs and who represented Sunkist, the group met at the White House in October with citrus fruit growers from Florida, Texas, California, and Hawaii who attacked the Cal-OSHA standard and asked the federal agencies involved to issue a statement reassuring the public. In the end, in December, the group decided not to issue a statement because it "would only serve to refocus attention on EDB."

Meanwhile, back in August, while fumigation began in California, EPA had put out its own press release claiming that the EDB use was nothing to worry about. The "note to correspondents" said reassuringly that using EDB for Medfly control "will not pose any undue risk to the consumer. Revised estimates by senior EPA scientists suggest the risk involved in the use of EDB . . . is negligible."

The "senior EPA scientists," in fact, was one John Todhunter. In testimony before a congressional committee, EPA senior science adviser Anne Barton told how Todhunter proposed that she alter her risk estimate according to a scientific theory that she had never heard of, before or since, to get a smaller risk figure. She stuck with the "accepted and standard" way of doing the risk assessment. The press release on EDB risks used Todhunter's method. Todhunter also personally announced that the extra cancer risk from fumigating California fruit for one year was about 100 times less than the risk from smoking one cigarette over a lifetime. Later he amended this, upgrading the risk to the equal of smoking one to 70 cigarettes during a lifetime. In a congressional investigation of this episode, Todhunter's deputy, Edwin Johnson, was asked what he thought of the risk assessment produced by his boss. "An example of Todhunter playing scientist," said Johnson, who added, "Todhunter used poor methods."

Todhunter's statements and the EPA press release provoked M. Adrian Gross, then senior scientific adviser at EPA, to openly contradict his boss. First, he acidly observed that "it would be presumptuous on my part to question the wisdom of assertions made by such authoritative sources as the EPA press office," and then went on to attack the idea that a one-year exposure to EDB was of little consequence. The animal tests of EDB, he said, gave "very persuasive evidence" that cancers appeared after exposure over "a very small fraction of a lifetime."

He then summed up the evidence on EDB. In the experimental results, EDB had all the earmarks of a powerful carcinogen. The studies showed, Gross said, that it caused highly malignant and metastasizing tumors of a very unusual type in both sexes of two species of animals tested. The tumors occurred at an alarmingly high incidence rate at a rather early stage of the exposure period.

Very few other pesticides leaving residues on produce are likely to show such high-risk results, Gross said. If EPA were to discard its cancer risk assessment for EDB, the Agency might as well dismantle the whole process for reviewing pesticides, tell the regulated industry it could stop testing its products for cancer since this would be "largely a waste of time and money," and advise the National Cancer Institute to stop their laboratory tests for cancer as a "similar . . . gigantic waste."

In the fall of 1981, Todhunter explicitly rejected the cancer risk findings of the EPA staff and sent them back to be redone. He also rejected the recommendation of his deputy, Edwin Johnson, the career civil servant who heads the pesticide division, to go ahead with the proposed ban or phaseout of major uses of EDB. Todhunter's special assistant, Bill Wells, wrote in a December 24, 1981, memo to Todhunter that "we should not push for an early resolution" of the proposed restrictions on EDB. He advised waiting for new studies of residues on foods, which might show lower levels of contamination than the current studies because of "improved transport, venting, and storage" of fumigated fruits. Wells said: "This data is likely to allow a softening of our regulatory decisions. If we push to a quick [decision] we may not have as much leeway in softening the position."

When Todhunter's staff came up with the new risk assessment in the spring of 1982, the results were essentially the same as the first one.

"None of Todhunter's questions resulted in important corrections," said a senior EPA staff member. The risk figures were still just as alarming.

On June 10, 1982, EPA staff prepared for Todhunter a decision banning EDB use on stored grains immediately, and phasing out fumigation of citrus and tropical fruits over three years, to end on July 1, 1985. Todhunter did not sign it. Instead, after meeting with Florida citrus growers, he exchanged letters and visits with Florida congressman Andy Ireland, assuring Ireland that EPA was in no hurry to act. Ireland wrote Todhunter, thanking him for "your reassurances that there is no 'rush' to ban EDB, either in 1983 or 1985."

Meanwhile, Todhunter found another reason for delay. At a June 1982 meeting with Mark Cowan, deputy to Thorne Auchter at OSHA, Todhunter agreed not to issue any final EPA decision for a couple of months, until OSHA was ready to issue its new workplace standards. This was called "coordination with OSHA."

Both Edwin Johnson and Paul Lapsley of Todhunter's staff urged their boss not to wait for OSHA. They pointed out that the OSHA rule might be delayed (in fact it did not come out until September 1983). Todhunter refused the plea. And in August 1982 he found still another flaw in the staff's risk assessment figures and sent them back again. Then he waited some more for OSHA. When he resigned in March 1983, he was still waiting.

Dr. Keith Maddy, toxicologist for California's Department of Food and Agriculture, said recently that Todhunter was "relatively alone in the position that EDB was only a modest carcinogen." Maddy's department did most of the testing that found EDB residues on fumigated fruit. He believes that hazardous levels of contamination are unavoidable when EDB is used to fumigate food crops after harvest. "The only scientifically sound position is to stop the use," he said.

Two alternatives to EDB fumigation are refrigeration, which kills the fruit fly eggs and larvae, or gamma irradiation, which sterilizes them. Both work, but both cost more and require more care than fumigation. Florida fruit growers and packers don't trust either one. Florida growers export one quarter of their grapefruit crop—an amount worth $65 million in 1982—to Japan. All of the exported grapefruit has to be treated for the Caribbean fruit fly, which has never been completely wiped out in Florida.

In 1983 the Japanese government accepted cold treatment as an alternative to EDB on grapefruit, and Florida packers sent a test shipment. But they were not sanguine about it. They figured it would cost 60 to 70 cents a carton, compared with 8 cents for EDB fumigation, and that the fruit might not look as good or last as long after refrigeration.

As for irradiation, "the bottom line," says James Emerson, Vice-President of the Florida Citrus Packers Association, "is that the Japanese will never accept irradiated fruit . . . because of the connotation of radiation." Emerson believes American customers would react the same way. "The mood in this country right now is anti-nuclear," he says. Conceding that irradiation works, Emerson insists, "you are running up against public sentiment and you are running up against costs. Costs per carton are prohibitive in comparison to the use of EDB."

The argument that Japan will not accept irradiated fruit was one that Florida growers, Florida senators and congressmen, and John Todhunter all took very seriously. In fact, at one point, EPA hired a consultant to work with Bill Wells on a study of Japanese attitudes. The report concluded that, indeed, "the general attitude of the Japanese people is one of abhorrence of irradiated food." This was all very odd. The fact is, according to expert Jacek S. Sivinski of the CH2M Hill consulting group, "Japan was the first country in the world to commercially irradiate food on an industrial scale." And it is still doing so. A commercial plant at Shihoro, Hokkaido, irradiates an average of 13,000 metric tons of potatoes per season; the potatoes are eaten as is, or made into frozen french fries or potato chips. Japan also took part in an eleven-nation cooperative Asian project, from 1980 to 1983, on irradiation of food.

Dr. Keith Maddy's California Department of Agriculture has sponsored studies in Hawaii to find the right dose of gamma rays for citrus and tropical fruits—enough to sterilize fruit flies but not enough to give the fruit a cooked taste. EPA official Joseph Panetta reports many successful experiments with irradiation of fruit. "It's a good technology," he says, "but it's a little more costly, and it takes fine tuning. . . . As long as EDB is permitted the industry isn't going to shift."

In the fall of 1982, the terrible deaths of two workers at the Occidental Chemical Corporation (Oxychem) plant in Arvin, near Bakersfield, California, underscored the dangers of EDB. Robert Harris, 30 years old and a four-year employee of Oxychem, went into a 7,500 gallon tank to clean it and promptly passed out. James Harris (no relation), 46 years old, a fifteen-year veteran at Oxychem and the plant manager, went in to pull the younger Harris out. Neither man knew the tank contained EDB at an extremely high concentration (reported to be 0.3 percent in water). Normally, that kind of tank held liquid fertilizer. Both men died, their internal organs "completely destroyed," according to Dr. Richard Wade, deputy chief of CalOSHA. "I've never seen any effect of a chemical so horrible in my life," said Wade.

About 30 more people—firefighters, ambulance crew, doctors, nurses, coroner pathologists, other Oxychem employees, and investigators for CalOSHA—got sick as a result of the accident, some just from touching the bodies of the men who had been overcome. The 30 people suffered nausea, blackouts, vomiting and diarrhea, and burning lungs, skin, and eyes. Precautions taken by firefighters—use of respirators and prompt washing after contact with the EDB—probably saved them from worse injury or possibly death. All 30 people are being monitored for longer-term illness.

What happened at the Oxychem plant was an accident. It represents the extreme of danger from EDB, not the norm. Far more significant from the point of view of common widespread usage is the fact that EDB is now turning up in wells and ground water in farming areas where it is used as a soil fumigant to kill nematodes. California, Georgia, Hawaii, and Florida—the only states that have tested for it—have all recently found EDB in well water. By mid-1983, 114 wells in sixteen counties in those states showed EDB contamination, typically in concentrations of 0.05 to 5 parts per billion. Some wells tested at over 100 parts per billion. At 1 part per billion, EPA estimates that the extra risk of cancer (over a lifetime) is 2 in 1,000. At 100 parts per billion, the extra risk is over 1 in 10.

The worst EDB contamination was in Florida, where numerous wells were found to contain EDB, including four community wells supplying drinking water for 10,000 people. The most concentrated use of EDB in agriculture is the injection of massive amounts of the chemical in a "buffer zone" along citrus groves—a sort of underground Maginot Line to block the passage of the root worms. In 1983, while Florida's Commissioner of Agriculture temporarily banned any soil injection of EDB throughout the state, California suspended EDB use in the five counties where the chemical was found in well water. In Florida, contamination of ground water is a particularly serious business since nine out of ten Floridians depend on underground supplies for their drinking water. Once ground water is polluted, cleaning it up is very difficult. As long as it stays underground, it stays polluted.

When farmers turned to EDB as a soil fumigant around 1980, some scientists considered the risk low, because they believed EDB was relatively immobile in the soil. EPA's 1980 proposal did not ban EDB as a soil fumigant. Yet, only three years later, ground water contamination began to show up in all the states that looked for it. This was one reason for renewed public attention to EDB in 1983. Another was the refusal of a handful of environmental groups to let the subject drop and, eventually, the appearance of a rash of stories in the news media that tests conducted by a television station and several states revealed widespread contamination of fruit and grain products by EDB.

In September 1983, two House subcommittees probed the failure to act on EDB by the two responsible agencies, OSHA and EPA. California Congressman George Miller, chairman of the House subcommittee on labor standards, wanted Auchter to explain why he had refused to issue emergency workplace standards two years earlier. When Auchter claimed OSHA could not have made a good enough case in court, Miller replied: "What would have been the great harm if you lost? Your pride? Your agency's batting average? The bottom line is you did nothing and workers are still being covered by a twelve-year-old standard everybody agrees is inadequate."

According to OSHA's own risk estimate and two EPA estimates, a worker exposed to 20 parts per million of EDB throughout his working life would have 999 chances out of 1,000 of developing cancer. This means that the present standard offers no protection at all; it might as well not exist.

Auchter believes, however, that nobody is actually suffering from the lack of an emergency temporary standard. He told the subcommittee: "People are not being exposed to high levels of EDB. . . . There is [not] any grave danger."

At the same hearing, Don Bowman, president of a grain millers' union in Vallejo, California, said the flour mill he works in is fumigated every two weeks, on weekends, with the mill shut down and the windows closed. The place is aired out for only an hour on Monday mornings before the workers arrive. When they get to work, Bowman said, the sweetish odor of EDB is hanging in the air; and the same is true at other mills in other states. According to NIOSH, you cannot smell EDB at all unless concentrations exceed 10 parts per million, which is about 75 times the NIOSH recommended limit. As noted earlier, 40 percent of

178

laboratory animals exposed over their lifetimes to 10 parts per million of EDB got cancer.

The day before the subcommittee hearing, a news leak from OSHA revealed that Auchter was about to propose a new workplace standard of 100 parts per billion. Earlier, OSHA officials had said it would be six months before the proposal was ready. Thus, Auchter's leisurely schedule seems to have been advanced six months by the public and congressional attention. The new standard was still only a proposal, however. It may be years from adoption.

As for EPA action on EDB, six months after Todhunter's departure and three days after a second congressional hearing, the Agency's new Administrator, William Ruckelshaus, issued an emergency suspension of EDB as a soil fumigant. This is the strongest measure EPA can employ against a pesticide. It is the second emergency suspension in the Agency's history. Ruckelshaus cited the widespread findings of EDB in well water as the reason for emergency action. To delay a ban for six months while suspension hearings took place, or up to two years for a cancellation proceeding, would risk further contamination of ground water, he said. EPA also banned other uses of EDB, but with built-in delays. Fumigation of fruit was allowed to continue until September 1, 1984, while all other major uses were ordered canceled. However, these cancellation orders can be challenged in court, and, except for soil fumigation, all the uses can continue while the court cases drag on.

The case of EDB began in 1974 with the first warning from the National Cancer Institute that it was a carcinogen. It continued through three years of EPA review from December 1977 to December 1980, never moved an inch forward during the time Todhunter and his colleagues were at EPA, and is still far from closed.

An emergency exemption granted by EPA in 1982 for another notorious pesticide, DBCP, sheds more light on how streamlining of the pesticide program worked. Emergency exemptions, which get around the usual requirements for pesticide approval, mushroomed under Todhunter. In 1980, EPA approved 249 petitions from the states for one-year "emergency" use of an unapproved or banned pesticide; it turned down 76 petitions and 94 were withdrawn. In 1982, EPA approved 650 emergency exemptions and denied only 18. Fifty-nine were withdrawn.

An EPA staff report published in March 1983 listed several main reasons for the soaring exemptions. Among them were: "Recent policy" that liberalized the definition of emergency to include economic gains as well as losses (in other words, the chance to make greater profits could be defined as an emergency); less voice by the regional EPA offices on whether an emergency exists (which implies more voice by political appointees in Washington headquarters); and "increased pesticide company involvement." The staff report observed that in some cases pesticide companies wrote the states' requests for emergency exemptions, using identical language for different states and simply filling in different numbers for the acres to be treated and pounds of pesticide to be used. Another reason the report gave for the soaring exemptions was that EPA had some pesticides on "hold" until industry submitted new data to replace the worthless IBT tests.

The exemptions were not trivial. They covered literally millions of acres of farmland. And they allowed the use of some extremely dangerous chemicals, notably DBCP.

California banned DBCP in 1977, on the ground that it causes sterility in men, is strongly implicated in cancer, and causes mutations. Further work in California showed that DBCP residues remain on fruit up to a year after treatment. Even when skilled applicators carefully inject the pesticide underground, it still vaporizes into the air and contaminates the fruit. Also, California found widespread DBCP contamination in drinking water wells, including community water supply systems, not just private wells.

After two years of hearings and 7,300 pages of testimony, EPA followed California's lead, suspending most uses of DBCP. Fifteen months later, the Agency and the manufacturers negotiated an agreement to withdraw DBCP completely from the U.S. mainland market. The only use still allowed was for pineapples in Hawaii, where state officials backed two influential growers (Maui Pineapple Company and Castle and Cooke, trading as Dole) in claims that the pineapple industry would collapse without DBCP, and that the growers could use it safely. (Del Monte, another big grower, had stopped using DBCP by 1979.)

In August 1982, with no public hearings and with six days' public notice, EPA approved DBCP for emergency use on 20,000 acres of South Carolina peach orchards. The purpose was to control the ring nematode, which attacks the roots and shortens the life of peach trees.

DBCP was first used extensively in California in the 1950's, especially on grapes and tree fruit. Farmers elsewhere soon followed suit. By the 1970's, farmers, orchardists, and home gardeners were using about 12 million pounds of DBCP per year. Some 2,000 to 3,000 workers were involved in manufacturing it. The major producers were Dow Chemical and Shell.

The first notice anyone took that DBCP causes sterility in human beings came in 1977. A dozen men working in the Occidental Chemical plant near Stockton, California, where DBCP was blended into a finished pesticide, discovered in lunchtime conversations that none of them were having children. This led to medical tests. On examination, nine men who had worked in the plant for fifteen years or more were found to be completely sterile. Many others had abnormally low sperm counts, how low depending to a remarkable degree on how long they had worked at the plant.

The discovery that they were sterile was jolting enough to the men involved. They worried even more about cancer. Ted Bricher, the first of the men to discover he was sterile, said people were asking, "What else does the chemical do to us?" He added, "These guys were scared."

Some of the Stockton workers later sued Dow Chemical and Shell Oil, the University of California, and one of its professors, Charles Hine. They charged that research Hine had done for Shell in the 1950's, for registration of DBCP, showed the chemical caused testicular atrophy in rats and that this finding should have been an early warning that DBCP caused sterility in humans. But neither Shell, nor the University of California, nor Hine had sounded a warning. The research results were not published; they were kept secret as "proprietary information."

Sterility in men exposed to DBCP was found again and again after the first discovery in Stockton, in other DBCP production plants, among pesticide applicators, and recently among banana plantation workers in Costa Rica. Russell Budd, an attorney for workers at a plantation owned by Standard Fruit Company (formerly United Fruit Company) in Rio Fria, Costa Rica, says the workers were exposed to DBCP in the most unprotected ways throughout the 1970's—no gloves, no respirators, mixing of the pesticide in open drums in the fields. A few years later, these workers discovered their sterility in the same way the Stockton men had—talking among themselves about the fact that they didn't have children. Forty of the Standard Fruit workers tested so far are sterile, Budd says. Of the hundreds of others coming in for sperm counts, many appear to be sterile. Because Rio Fria in northeast Costa Rica is so isolated, the family, social, and possibly genetic consequences of sterility and reduced fertility are especially wrenching. Some of the men's wives have left them, and they cannot find other women willing to marry them. For the men who are marginally fertile, genetic impairment is a frightening possibility.

New evidence has also linked DBCP with human cancer. California and EPA banned DBCP partly on the basis of laboratory tests that showed it is an animal carcinogen. In July 1982, the California Department of Food and Agriculture released a study concluding that, in Fresno, increased *human* mortality from cancers of the stomach and from leukemia were definitely correlated with rising levels of DBCP in drinking well water. (Fresno is in the middle of the state's intensively farmed San Joaquin Valley; DBCP was heavily used there.)

The authors of the California study described it as preliminary; it is subject to the same doubts and qualifications as most studies linking human cancer with particular causes. John Todhunter, at a meeting of state farming officials in Sacramento, called the study "sexy" and "cute" but scientifically below par. At the same time, he rejected suggestions that EPA do its own health study of DBCP in ground water.

Dr. Robert S. Jackson, State Health Commissioner for South Carolina, has a special interest in the DBCP matter. When EPA approved the emergency use of DBCP for South Carolina peach orchards in August 1982, the Agency not only failed to consult or warn the public, but likewise did not consult him. "They just put us in [to] be responsible for monitoring," he says.

The state agencies that did know ahead of time about the exemption were the Agriculture Department and Clemson University's College of Agricultural Sciences, which had requested it. Clemson acts as South Carolina's regulatory body under FIFRA, carrying out the state program under the federal law. Clemson did not consult the Health Commissioner either.

Peach growers in South Carolina began using DBCP to kill nematodes in 1972 and within five years were using 800,000 pounds annually on 300,000 acres. Use stopped only in 1979, when DBCP was withdrawn nationally. Not long after, Clemson was trying to get it back. In its petition for an exemption, the College of Agricultural Sciences generated data to show that nematodes had caused $6 million worth of damage to South Carolina peach trees in 1982 and could do twice to four times as much damage in 1983.

Also, Clemson's Dr. George E. Carter, Jr., had conducted experi-

182

ments during the previous year to see whether application of DBCP before the fruit appeared would keep residues off the fruit. The tests were funded in part by Amvac Chemical Company, the only remaining U.S. manufacturer of DBCP. The president of Amvac, Glenn A. Wintemuth, told a reporter: "We sat down with EPA and asked what they would be satisfied with . . . and then we developed a protocol. We asked Clemson to become involved and out of that came the justification by EPA." Thus, it appears that EPA and Amvac company officials, meeting privately together, decided on one or two new studies that would be sufficient to overturn the ban on DBCP. So much for two years and 7,300 pages of open testimony. Neither EPA nor Amvac has opened Dr. Carter's study to public review.

Dr. O. J. Dickerson, head of the Clemson department that prepared the DBCP petition, defends Amvac's support of the research and resents any suggestion that Amvac money determined the experiment's results or the department's attitude. "That's always a criticism of anything we do that somebody doesn't like," he said. "The truth of the matter is that practically all research on pesticides is done or funded by pesticide companies. . . . We have to trust EPA to do the evaluation for us."

Dickerson said that Amvac had put up only $10,000 for the Clemson research, with other companies adding more funds for testing of other pesticides. "The insinuation that we can be bought for $10,000 —that kinda hurts," he said.

The DBCP use in South Carolina that EPA approved never took place. A small environmental group based in Columbia, Grass Roots Organizing Workshop (GROW), got an injunction against it on grounds that it was a threat to public health. Their case rested partly on studies done by Clemson University during 1979 to 1981, some of them under contract to EPA, which showed "widespread contamination of South Carolina ground water" by DBCP, especially in peach-growing areas. Most of the DBCP discovered was at low levels, but some samples were near or above one part per billion, a level that California generally considers unsafe. The previous administration had funded these studies and others in the Southeast as a follow-up to the ban on DBCP.

Brett Bursey, chairman of GROW, says, "There are drinking water wells here in South Carolina that would be closed by the state, if they were in California. Our health department has no authority to do it." Bursey was incensed that neither he nor any other member of the public

183

had an inkling that EPA was about to reopen the door to DBCP. He found out about it from another environmental group in California—after the six-day notice period announced in the Federal Register was over. When his group got the injunction, he says, "Clemson was already giving training sessions to the farmers." Amvac had already gone back into production to make 75,000 gallons of DBCP, worth about $1.8 million, and had shipped it to South Carolina.

Dr. Dickerson of Clemson says the reason the state didn't appeal the injunction was that EPA's exemption contained, in rather general terms, a condition that ground water be checked before and after the use of DBCP. The Department of Health and Environmental Control balked. They didn't have the funds or manpower to do it.

According to health commissioner Jackson, there was more to it than that. "The bottom line," he says, "was that I was going to issue an emergency order prohibiting it [the use of DBCP]. . . . I notified Clemson and EPA of my intention. I felt that what they proposed represented a hazard to the water supply of South Carolina, which it is my responsibility to protect."

Jackson adds with some heat: "The year before EPA had flown down here telling me of their concern about pollution of ground water. . . . Then EPA turns around and issues this exemption. . . . They may be close enough to the political wing of the White House to tolerate such inconsistencies, but I'm not."

What about the peach growers? In 1977, when EPA put emergency restrictions on some uses of DBCP and OSHA clamped down on worker exposure, the National Peach Council reacted with alarm. The Council's executive secretary, Robert R. Phillips, made this ingenious suggestion to assure continued production of the chemical:

If possible sterility is the main problem, couldn't workers who were old enough that they no longer wanted to have children accept such positions voluntarily? Or could workers be advised of the situation, and some might volunteer for such work posts as an alternative to planned surgery for a vasectomy or tubal ligation, or as a means of getting around religious bans on birth control when they want no more children?

California acted before the federal EPA to ban the use of DBCP on peaches. The state's yield of peaches (in pounds per acre) continued to rise after the 1977 ban, despite predictions of economic disaster.

Ralph Lightstone, a lawyer with California Rural Legal Assistance in Sacramento, said recently: "The experts were wrong. Most of those who predicted disaster were getting research money from the chemicals industry." In South Carolina the 1981 crop was 430 million pounds, worth $62.2 million, compared with 350 million pounds and $47.6 million in 1979. But, according to Dickerson, more orchards had been planted "because we did a good job, people made some money, and more people got into it." (The 1982 crop, hit by a killing late frost, was 120 million pounds and sold for $46.3 million.)

In South Carolina, peach growers seem to have accepted the call against DBCP with some equanimity. Dr. Jackson at any rate says the growers have not criticized his decisions, and he consulted them before and after deciding what to do. He says: "The farmers don't want to take the risk of making people fearful of eating peaches that might contain a carcinogen. Reality has an effect on their thinking."

In an interview with Ward Sinclair of the *Washington Post,* Larry Yonce, a major grower and State Peach Council president, reflected something of that feeling. "We told Clemson that we needed control of the peach tree short-life problem, but not at the risk of anyone's health," he said. "We rely on the scientists to tell us what is safe." He had put himself and his workers through sterility and cancer tests when the risks of DBCP were first publicized. All came out okay.

Asked what peach growers used to do before there were chemicals to kill nematodes, he recalled that management techniques were different: root stocks were more vigorous, land was not drained, orchards were cultivated more. Then he added:

Chemicals were the miracle cure for agriculture a decade or two ago, but farmers now realize they have to manage the earth as a precious resource. Many are moving into integrated pest management [which uses less chemicals] . . . because of economics, and it will work. But I am not yet at a point that I can go to no-chemical farming.

Unlike DBCP, DuTer (triphenyltin hydroxide) was never banned or withdrawn from general use. Also, unlike DBCP, the emergency exemptions EPA allowed for DuTer, both in 1981 and 1982, actually went through. And they covered huge acreages. The emergency uses were for rice on three-quarters of a million acres in Texas, Arkansas, and

185

Mississippi in 1981 and on more than one and one-quarter million acres in the same states, plus Louisiana, in 1982.

When EPA granted these exemptions, the existing health studies on DuTer were flawed and incomplete, but troubling. DuTer is an old fungicide, registered in the 1960's and early 1970's to control various fungus diseases of pecans, potatoes, tobacco, sugarbeet, peanuts, and carrots. In 1980 EPA refused to register DuTer for additional crops because of suggestive evidence that it may interfere with the body's immune system (which fights infection), may cause the birth defect hydrocephalus (excess fluid on the brain), and may be toxic to testes (causing a marked drop in testicular weight). EPA asked the manufacturer (Thompson-Hayward) for new studies on these effects, plus adequate studies on DuTer's cancer-causing potential, which had never been done, and on effects of inhaling DuTer. The pesticide is usually applied as a spray mist. The existing incomplete data suggested, EPA said, that breathing the vapor could be a serious hazard.

The next year, 1981, scientific data on DuTer had not changed. But the political situation had. That spring, an aide to newly elected Vice-President George Bush put in a call to EPA's Edwin Johnson (the civil servant in charge of pesticide programs). Bush's aide told Johnson that a group of Texans had met with the Vice-President (a former Texas congressman) and said they were waiting for EPA's decision on a Texas petition for emergency use of DuTer on rice.

"He asked me what the status was on the petition, and asked for a quick decision," Johnson recalls. "I told him it would be a difficult decision."

Meanwhile, an aide to James A. Baker, the White House Chief of Staff, also called EPA on the same subject. Baker's brother-in-law, John (Jacko) Garrett, farms 1,500 acres of rice near Danbury, Texas. He had been calling and writing Baker about the DuTer exemption.

On June 5, 1981, EPA granted the exemption. Again, in 1982, EPA granted the exemption and extended it.

Meanwhile, the California Department of Food and Agriculture was giving serious thought to banning DuTer. Richard Rominger, director of the department, wrote to Congress about the state's concern. California scientists were worried about DuTer not only because of gaps in the data. They also didn't like what they saw in the existing data. "The studies that appear to be acceptable indicate very high toxicity, notably inhalation and reproduction toxicity," said a December 1982 staff memorandum. Even at very low levels, the memo said, breathing the compound causes extreme irritation to nose and throat, chronic bronchitis, loss of balance, and skin abnormalities. The memo questioned whether present tolerances for DuTer on foods were protective enough. "It is doubtful that this pesticide can be used safely on any food crop considering the currently inadequate data base and the extremely low effect levels. . . ." The memo said that "for a product this toxic," registration should be supported by studies on exposure of mixers, loaders, and applicators, on medical management of poisoning, on absorption of the pesticide through the skin, and on possible exposure of field workers from residues on leaves and in soils.

John Todhunter never openly acknowledged any problem with DuTer other than outmoded data. In a letter to Congressman George E. Brown, Jr. (D-CA), Chairman of a House Agriculture Subcommittee, Todhunter said, "Because the existing data base on this fungicide did not meet current standards for new product registrations, the Agency has asked the registrant to submit additional data." This is not quite what EPA said. Its 1980 letter to the manufacturer described suggestive evidence that DuTer could cause birth defects, damage to immune and reproductive systems, and other damage to health, and it called for new data to clear the matters up.

As for the conditions justifying emergency use of DuTer, Todhunter did not argue that rice farmers faced a sudden catastrophic loss. Rather, he emphasized the potential for economic gain with the new use of the pesticide on rice.

No one denies that politics played a part in the DuTer exemption, and some defend it on the ground that politicians are supposed to convey their constituents' concerns to federal officeholders. Senators, governors, and members of Congress often push hard for "emergency use" of unapproved, banned, or withdrawn chemicals, for example, for the use of ferriamicide against fire ants in the South. But it is rare for top Administration officials to take a hand in the matter. The DuTer exemption involved considerably more than politics as usual. EPA had been asked, in the normal legal way, to extend the use of DuTer to two major new crops, soybeans and rice, and the Agency called for more data to assure its safe use. A few months later, long before the new data were ready or could be ready, aides to the top Texans in the White House —Vice-President Bush and chief of staff Baker—pressured EPA to approve the rice use de facto anyway, but privately, with no public notice or chance to air both sides of the issue. The requirements of law (FIFRA) for a careful weighing of the risks and benefits in a major new use of the pesticide—the first new use under modern testing requirements—went out the window.

While emergency exemptions allowed scores of unapproved chemicals on the market by the back door, streamlining of registration let dozens more through the front. Under the speedup ordered by the Bush task force and carried out by Todhunter, EPA scientists were under intense pressure to rubber-stamp approvals of the pesticides that industry was eager to market.

Consider the result in the case of the herbicide Harvade. Herbicides are the hot sellers in the pesticide business; their sales are now outstripping sales of insecticides. Many herbicides are used for weed control. Others like Paraquat and Harvade are systemic plant poisons designed to make cotton picking easier. Applied a few days before harvest, they cause the cotton plants' leaves to shrivel up, leaving the boll within easy reach of mechanical pickers.

In 1982 Harvade was waiting for approval. The manufacturer, Uniroyal, had sent voluminous test data to support its application for approval of the product, together with summaries and evaluations of the data. (The industry, not EPA, conducts the health and safety tests that EPA uses in deciding whether to register a chemical; EPA evaluates them.) An EPA scientist reviewed the report, gave it a thumbs-up decision, and sent his affirmative review along to his superiors. The approval came in August, in time for the cotton harvest.

The trouble was, the scientist's review was not original. It was a copy, almost word for word, of the evaluations and summary submitted by Uniroyal. The review omitted data on an unusual brain tumor in rats that point to a possible threat to human health, and failed to discuss suggestive data on lung cancers in mice. These data were in the report but didn't make it into the industry-submitted summary, nor into the EPA review.

Evaluation of industry test data is no mechanical job. Assuming the laboratory work has been done well—and it generally is nowadays, according to a comprehensive report on EPA's pesticide performance, issued by a House Agriculture Subcommittee in December 1982—there are still plenty of opportunities for differences in interpretation of what the raw data mean.

EPA scientists, in private talks with the Subcommittee's staff, did not fault all the reports submitted by industry. Some manufacturers and laboratories were given high marks for consistently good, straightforward, well-organized reports. But some reports repeated old, discredited arguments in an attempt to explain away adverse test findings. Worse, some omitted statistical analysis that would have flagged possible threats to health.

In the interviews, several EPA scientists said they had to spend extra time on reviews of some industry-submitted reports, to stay alert to "manifestations of pesticide toxicity which are not mentioned or properly analyzed in the studies submitted to the Agency." One scientist commented that "while he thought he had encountered 'every trick in the book' during his career evaluating chronic toxicity experiments and data, he has recently been amazed by new levels of 'ingenuity and cleverness' employed by some pesticide registrants."

The job of review became more demanding as a new flow of studies came in, especially in 1980 and 1981, to replace tests which had been done by the discredited IBT laboratory and other suspect studies. While the workload increased, the Administration cut the money for the pesticides program and the people to staff it from $70.5 million in 1980 to less than $52 million in 1983, and from 829 employees to 537. At the same time, top EPA officials pressed for more approvals. Less than a month after her confirmation, Anne Gorsuch wrote the pesticide unit: "We intend to assure that introduction of new pesticides into commerce is not impeded by delays in processing." A memo circulated to scientists in the pesticide program bore the heading: "BACKLOG REDUCTION—OUR MOST IMPORTANT PRODUCT." Managers began to rate employees' performance on how many reviews they turned out. "We all depend on [EPA toxicologists] to review these things properly," said one EPA scientist, "but they [top management] don't care how you review. They grade you on how many you make." Another said, "The scientists were given quotas [which were] tied to supervisors' performance standards."

The cut-and-paste Harvade review was detected, quite accidentally, by an EPA scientist during an audit of the laboratory that had done the testing for Uniroyal. The scientist was M. Adrian Gross, a doughty warrior who is best known for having uncovered the nature of the work coming out of the IBT laboratory back in 1976. In 1982, after his clash with Todhunter over the EDB risk assessment, and several other disagreements with Todhunter and his subordinates over pesticide decisions, Gross was demoted to a small laboratory audit division and denied access to data on pesticides that were currently under EPA review.

The Harvade case was not unique. There were other EPA cut-and-paste reviews. The House Agriculture Subcommittee report first exposed this fact, and in an interview in May 1983 pesticide chief Ed Johnson confirmed it. At least one other of these reviews had missed important health data, Johnson says; in this case the pesticide (which he declined to identify) was still unregistered. Johnson insists the streamlining had nothing to do with the carbon-copy reviews. "I think it was a case of two individuals," he says. "It had been going on for quite a while." To clear the matter up, Johnson contracted with an independent firm to spot check EPA scientific reviews.

It was too late, though, to undo the Harvade approval, according to Johnson. EPA interprets the pesticide law to say that once a pesticide is registered, the registration sticks—even if EPA approval was by accident. Johnson says the only way to get Harvade off the market, if EPA decides that is warranted, would be to start lengthy, cumbersome cancellation proceedings. And EPA can only start to cancel a pesticide if there is evidence of "unreasonable adverse effects." Lawyers for environmental groups don't agree with this interpretation of the law. They argue that if a registration was never valid it should be withdrawn.

Part and parcel of streamlining was a new, exclusive relation between industry and EPA on decisions affecting pesticides. John Todhunter created a system of "decision conferences," limited to EPA and industry representatives meeting behind closed doors. To Todhunter, these conferences were a "nonadversarial" and expeditious way of conducting the pesticide regulation business. In April 1982, he told a meeting of the National Agricultural Chemicals Association: "I'm pleased to report that we have had several [decision] conferences since last October, all of which resulted in conclusions and decisions. This type of activity saves both you and me a very important commodity—TIME. Instead of going around the merry-go-round for months, even years, we come to a resolution. It makes a big difference."

To public interest groups—environmental, labor, and farmworker organizations—the big difference was that they were now shut out of the decision making. Formerly, public interest groups had a chance to comment before EPA made decisions at the end of long, intensive scientific reviews of old pesticides—such as EDB. Now EPA and the industry were disposing of these cases themselves, in private. More was involved here than the legitimate and necessary exchange of ideas between the Agency and the industry it regulates. As Todhunter said, the industry and government were making real decisions. To those left outside the system, it looked like a new version of an old story—the "blurring of any distinction between the regulator and the regulated," according to Maureen Hinckle of the National Audubon Society.

The case of pentachloraphenol (PCP), a pesticide and wood preservative used in homes and farms across the country, offers an exceptionally clear example. PCP and its salts are suspected of causing cancer, birth defects, and genetic disorders. EPA proposed in 1980 to ban many of its uses. EPA's Scientific Advisory Panel, which reviews the Agency's pesticide actions, suggested in July 1981 that EPA's proposals did not go far enough in controlling or banning wood preservatives. In a unanimous report, the panel delivered an unusual, strongly worded rebuke, which "deplored the lack of scientific objectivity of the presentations by industry concerning biological hazards of wood preservatives." Within three weeks of his confirmation, John Hernandez met with representatives of the industry. John Todhunter met with them a week after his confirmation in November 1981. In March 1982, George Eliades, president of a wood preservatives industry group, wrote Todhunter thanking him for "personally reviewing the scientific data on PCP." A week later, EPA staff held the first of at least 21 closed meetings with industry representatives on the chemical. On March 30, 1983, EPA announced a decision to continue most of the uses. After protests by environmental and farmworker groups, EPA held a single public meeting to allow the public to comment on the decision. The proposed EPA decision, circulated at the meeting, was printed on the industry group's letterhead.

In this way—not only for PCP but for lindane and a number of other pesticides—EPA officials and industry representatives agreed among themselves to reverse protective decisions the Agency had made earlier after intensive scientific reviews. They also agreed not to start any new reviews to decide whether pesticides in use should be limited or banned. Not one new scientific review of old pesticides was begun in 1982. Several already planned were abandoned. After meetings with industry, and with no public comment, EPA dropped plans to review terbutryn, suspected of causing cancer, mutations, and reproductive failure.

Judging from his speeches, Todhunter saw public concern about the dangers of pesticides as misplaced, and a public role in pesticide decisions as unnecessary. In a speech at the University of Massachusetts in Amherst, in October 1982, he said that the use of the words "hazardous" and "toxic" in connection with pesticides "conveys a lack of trust in the producers of the chemicals, the government which regulates the industry and the applicators who apply those chemicals."

When the pesticide industry attempted to change the pesticide law, making industry reports on the health and safety of pesticides much less accessible to the public, it found an ally in Todhunter. Until 1978, the industry health and safety reports that underlie EPA registration of pesticides were considered proprietary—something that companies had paid for and were entitled to keep to themselves as a trade secret. The laboratory scandals in the mid-1970's rocked public confidence in the scientific basis for pesticide approvals. In its 1978 amendments to FIFRA, Congress provided for public scrutiny of the health and safety data.

The Industrial Bio-Test story shows why public interest groups and independent scientists want the right to look over the health and safety data industry provides. IBT was once by far the biggest independent lab testing pesticides for industry. But behind its prosperous front—the business was worth $9.5 million a year in 1975—were some appalling conditions. Among IBT's "laboratories" was a large concrete-floored room which came to be called "the Swamp" because the test animals kept there died by the hundreds from neglect and mishandling and decomposed in their cages. In an article in the *Amicus Journal*, Keith Schneider described the scene: "Dead rats and mice . . . decomposed so rapidly that their bodies oozed through wire cage bottoms and lay in purple puddles on the dropping trays. It was in conditions like these . . . that IBT conducted thousands of critical research projects for nearly every major American chemical and drug manufacturer, dozens of foreign concerns, and several federal agencies as well."

In May 1981, a special Federal grand jury indicted IBT's officers for fraud. They were charged with wholesale falsification of reports, including replacement of test animals that died in the Swamp, and fabricating results with the new animals. A tip-off to conditions in the lab was the fact that the health and safety reports coming from IBT were too good to be true.

The ex-president of IBT, Joseph Calandra, and three other former

192

officers were brought to trial in Chicago in 1983, accused of fraud.* One of the indicted officers was Dr. Paul Wright, who had gone to IBT from Monsanto in 1971, stayed eighteen months while one of Monsanto's products, the anti-bacterial agent TCC, was tested, and then returned to Monsanto. Until IBT was shut down, Monsanto remained one of the laboratory's best customers.

After the IBT scandal broke, EPA first gave pesticide manufacturers the task of auditing the laboratory's studies. But the industry audits proved unsatisfactory; according to EPA, they "routinely overlooked some areas of concern." Ultimately, EPA and its counterpart in Canada shared the arduous job of unearthing and evaluating all the IBT studies. It took five years to wade through the data. In July 1983 EPA finally announced there had been 801 IBT tests supporting registration of 140 pesticides and that three-quarters of the tests were invalid. As of September, only 10 percent of the invalid tests had been redone and accepted by EPA.

The 1978 changes in FIFRA, opening pesticide health and safety reports to public view, recognized the public's stake in the trustworthiness of the scientific work on pesticides. The industry, complaining that their proprietary interest in test data was not adequately protected, challenged the provision in court. Their suits kept the data bottled up for three more years. Even after most of the suits were settled, EPA continued to block public access.

For months, EPA stonewalled on a request for health and safety reports made in September 1981 by a group of Texas farmworkers. The farmworkers sued EPA for release of the data. Then, early in 1982, a coalition of the AFL-CIO, several environmental groups, and a California farmworker organization requested that EPA release studies on eleven widely used pesticides, including two (toxaphene and captan) that had used IBT studies as an important part of their registration record. Again EPA stalled. The labor and environmental groups also took EPA to court, charging not only that the Agency was illegally delaying release of the data, but that it had quietly agreed to industry demands for a moratorium on disclosure until Congress had time to change the law more to industry's liking. A congressional staff member

---

*Calandra was granted a mistrial because of a serious heart condition. The other three IBT officers were convicted of fraud in October 1983.

(Charles Benbrook of a House agriculture subcommittee) reported that Todhunter conceded, behind closed doors, that EPA was observing such a moratorium.

On the day before a federal judge was scheduled to order Todhunter to submit to questioning under oath, EPA capitulated and denied an industry petition to withhold reports from the public. In September 1982, the plaintiff groups signed an unprecedented consent agreement with Union Carbide, one of the producers of the eleven pesticides. This agreement finally opened at least one company's health and safety reports to public examination.*

The promises EPA made in 1981 to speed up pesticide approvals and cooperate with the industry were kept. John Todhunter in particular did not seem to believe that pesticides presented any real danger to human health and the environment. To him, "fear and ignorance" were the problem. Where previous administrations had compromised, this one saw no need for it.

So there were real changes. But in one respect—protection of farmworkers from injurious pesticides—there was little change at all. EPA had taken charge of federal standards to protect farmworker health and safety in 1973, after winning a highly political turf battle in which EPA was the compromise candidate, with the Occupational Safety and Health Administration on one side—more protective—and the Agriculture Department on the other. Except for a very few, very minimal rules, which EPA adopted in 1974—rules which have never been enforced— the Agency has done practically nothing to shoulder its responsibilities for protection of farmworkers.

Hired farmworkers, mostly migrant, mostly Hispanic and black, do the bulk of what is left of intensive hand labor on American farms— harvesting tomatoes, picking grapes, clipping onions, hoeing cotton, detasselling corn. They work in the midst of plants that are coated with pesticide residues. Some of them mix and apply pesticides at the foreman's or owner's direction. Next to production plant workers, they have the highest exposures to pesticides of anyone in our society. But they

---

*The farmworkers, represented by Robin Alexander of Texas Rural Legal Aid, won their case against EPA too, but the company they were suing (FMC) settled without releasing the health and safety data.

have nothing like the health and safety protection that industrial workers have under federal and state laws, imperfect as that is.

Migrant farmworkers, as a class, are not healthy. They are among the poorest people in America, and, like very poor people everywhere, they die prematurely. In 1970 the life expectancy of migrant farmworkers in the United States was reported to be 49 years, compared with the U.S. average of over 70 years.

No one has systematically studied whether farmworkers' lifetime exposure to pesticides has led to an unusual incidence of cancer, birth defects, sterility, long-term brain or nerve damage, or premature death. There is some evidence that farmers (the term includes farm owners, and they are a far richer and healthier group than farmworkers) do run a higher-than-normal risk of getting certain kinds of cancer that may be related to chemicals exposure. Evidence from about 50 studies, evaluated by Dr. Aaron Blair of the National Cancer Institute, suggests that farmers get more leukemia than do people in general. The same is true, to a lesser degree, of cancers of the lymphatic system, stomach, prostate, and brain.

Dr. Emiel Owens and Clarence Owens have investigated signs of health damage in farmworkers that may be related to pesticide exposures. Following two of the major migrant streams up the East Coast and the Midwest, they examined 100 farmworkers. Fifty-six percent, they found, had abnormal kidney and liver functions. Although these effects may follow contact with certain pesticides, they could be related to other causes as well. Significantly, the Owens team also found that 85 percent showed lowered or depressed levels of cholinesterase; all of the workers continuously in the fields showed lowered levels. Cholinesterase is the enzyme that regulates the transmission of nerve signals and is attacked by two major classes of pesticides—organophosphates and carbamates—and some others as well. The Owens brothers also found that 78 percent of the workers had skin rashes, ranging from mild and transient to persistent burning sores. Skin rash follows contact with too many different kinds of pesticides to name, from weedkillers to fungicides to insecticides.

A 1980 health survey of 260 farmworkers in the Rio Grande Valley in South Texas turned up similar results. Over 50 percent had experienced dizziness, 40 percent chronic headaches, and 23 percent blurred vision—all symptoms of pesticide poisoning that affects the

195

nervous system, of which cholinesterase inhibition is one kind. Eighty percent of the workers reported skin disorders linked with their work.

These symptoms are not usually life threatening or crippling in the short run. For a time at any rate, they just make people miserable. They demonstrate the persistent, almost universal, very often illegal exposure of farmworkers to toxic chemicals, some of which can cause birth defects, mutations, or, in the longer run, cancer.

Acute pesticide poisoning that brings farmworkers to doctors' offices or hospitals is rarer. In California, the only state that requires doctors to report pesticide poisoning, there were 1,388 cases reported in 1982. Acute pesticide poisoning seems to be worse in California than in the other big agricultural states, because the hot, dry, still summer weather there tends to turn residues of toxic pesticides into even more toxic breakdown products. Shocking cases of mass "picker poisoning" in the early 1970's led California to adopt far more stringent protection for farmworkers than other states have done, or than the minimal protection EPA has imposed.

Even so, pesticide illnesses persist in California, and the reported incidents almost certainly understate the actual occurrences. Farmworkers are paid by the piece, and, like other poor people without sick pay or insurance, they often work when sick. Especially in seasonal work like harvesting, workers are loath to miss even a day. Some workers fear they'll get into trouble with the crew leader if they even mention illness. Some are illegal aliens ("undocumented aliens" is the euphemism in south Texas), and they want nothing to do with anyone in authority.

In addition, most doctors are not trained to look for or recognize pesticide poisoning. Many of the symptoms—headaches, nausea, blurred vision—mimic flu or other common illnesses. Dr. Erik Svenkurud, who diagnosed the convulsions of the Riojas baby as pesticide poisoning, was the exception. Altogether, Dr. Ephraim Kahn, a California specialist in farmworkers' poisonings and consultant to the Department of Health Services, estimates that, among workers in the field, as little as one or two percent of pesticide poisonings may be picked up and reported. Of the acute pesticide poisonings reported in California in 1982, 362 involved fieldworkers.

In the Rio Grande Valley of south Texas, serious acute pesticide poisonings of farmworkers appear to be less frequent than in California, but exposure, and milder forms of poisoning, could not be more widespread. Half of the farmworkers surveyed in the region in 1980 said they had actually been directly sprayed with pesticides while working in the fields. Spraying workers in the fields violates federal law.

Robin Alexander, then a lawyer with Texas Rural Legal Aid in the Rio Grande Valley, told an investigating committee of the Texas legislature in 1982 that she had talked to literally hundreds of farmworkers and their families in the Valley and all, without exception, had been exposed either to direct pesticide spray or to drift (also illegal) from neighboring fields.

In 1980 and 1981, Alexander collected dozens of depositions from farmworkers in the Valley, most of whom did not want to reveal their names but wanted to tell their stories about pesticide exposure and illness.

"I am 28 years old and have always worked in farm labor. I usually have headaches and a very severe burning rash that started five years ago. This was when a duster plane was spraying the same [cabbage] field we were working in. . . . Ever since then, between the months of March and June, I get this rash and headaches. They start as soon as I smell the pesticide. The doctors . . . just tell me I'm allergic, yet they don't know to what."

"Last year . . . we were clipping onions [when] a duster plane suddenly appeared and started spraying while we were working. No one ever instructed us to leave. Ever since then I have had trouble walking, frequent headaches, blackouts, and blurred vision. I have gone to [a doctor] but all they tell me is that it's the climate and the dirt."

"When we work in the fields, our whole family goes, my children ranging from six years to one year. While we were working . . . a duster plane started spraying the field right next to us. The wind started blowing the pesticide toward us. We were hoeing cotton and were at one end of the field, and my children were playing outside the car at the other end. There was no way to tell them to get inside the car. That day when we got home I felt very dizzy and had a lot of blurred vision. . . . My children . . . got a lot of burning sores all over their bodies."

Many migrant farmworkers make their permanent homes in the Rio Grande Valley, working there in the fall, winter, and early spring months and migrating in the summer. Some of them, when they can save enough, buy a little plot of ground in a rural development tract—a "colonia"—and build their own house with the help of friends.

On a blowy, sunny April day, the colonias look very attractive. Flowers bloom around the houses and fences, the yards are neatly kept, the billowing curtains well starched. What is not so readily apparent is that most colonias, being next to fields, are regularly drenched with pesticide spray.

A 54-year-old farmworker says:

"The field that is located just across the street from our neighborhood . . . is always sprayed and the spray is always carried to our house by the wind. Every morning the grass is all white from the pesticide and when I step over it, my shoes get wet and I immediately get sores all over my feet. I constantly have headaches, dizzy spells, blurred vision, and usually cough up blood. I have gone to see a doctor; all they tell me is that it's the weather and my nerves."

Dr. David Kibbe, then working at a family health center near McAllen, did a pilot study in 1980 testing people who lived in a colonia next to a frequently sprayed lettuce field. The study looked for evidence of pesticide exposure. In two runs involving 20 to 25 people (out of about 100 living in the colonia), he found detectable traces of pesticide in 30 to 60 percent immediately after the fields were sprayed.

Dr. Kibbe's findings were no surprise to the people living in the colonia, but it was important to demonstrate their exposure as objective fact. Some growers, pesticide salesmen, and others in the Valley find it hard to believe that the ailments so common among farmworkers and rural residents—headaches, nausea, blurred vision, and especially rashes —could be caused by pesticides. A frequently heard comment in the Valley in explanation of the rashes is, "You should see how these people live."

Besides being racist and insulting, this comment doesn't reflect reality. Anyone who visits a few Mexican-American farmworker families at home in the Valley must be struck by the fact that "these people," despite poverty, are house-proud. Jose Torres, formerly a migrant worker, now a paralegal aide at Texas Rural Legal Aid, says: "The two things that mean most to our families are for the children to get an education and for us to have homes of our own."

Josefina Castillo's home—rented, not owned—is, typically, spotless. Pictures of children and grandchildren (some in high school graduation gowns), typically, hang on the walls. Josefina Castillo is a little unusual, though, in her willingness to speak out, under her own name. Starting out in the fields at fifteen, she is now in her fifties and has become an outspoken fighter for decent working conditions for farmworkers—clean drinking water and enough of it, water for hand washing, portable toilets, protection from pesticide spraying. She has gone to Austin to testify before committees of the Texas legislature and to Washington to ask for help from Congress and federal agencies. Do crew leaders retaliate and refuse to hire her? Some won't give her a job, she says. But others—"If somebody says I have been to Washington, the crew leaders don't believe it. What does this woman know?"

Most important to Castillo is that "growers should not make you work during or after they spray. They should plan it so there is enough time between when they spray and the time they make you go in the fields so that you will not get sick." She is especially afraid of what pesticides may do to the farmworkers' children, who play in the dirt while their families work, and to pregnant women. Like most other workers in the Valley, she herself has been drenched with pesticides many times, from crop dusting directly overhead, from crop dusting over nearby fields, from picking in orchards where pesticides droplets cling like dew to the fruit and leaves.

None of this is legal. These common everyday practices in the Valley blatantly violate the few regulations EPA has ever established to protect farmworkers' health from pesticide hazards. EPA's rules state: "[N]o owner or lessee shall permit the application of a pesticide in such a manner as to directly or through drift expose workers or other persons except those knowingly involved in the application." Under EPA rules, farmworkers may not go back to work in pesticide-treated fields until the spray dries or the dust settles, except with protective clothing. For twelve pesticides that were considered most toxic when the rules were adopted in 1974, farmworkers may not reenter fields for specified times, up to 48 hours. "Appropriate and timely warning," either oral or by posted signs, must warn farmworkers when spraying will take place. The rule doesn't specify who is to give the warning, but EPA officials say the responsibility is the grower's.

These protections are frail compared to California's. But for whatever they are worth they are meaningless when no one enforces them. The states now have the responsibility for enforcing the requirements of FIFRA within their borders. In Texas, the Department of Agriculture has the enforcement authority. In 1981, the Texas Farmworkers Union and local branches of the Sierra Club and Audubon Society documented the gross misuse of pesticides in the Valley and the failure of the Texas Department of Agriculture to enforce the law. They accused the Department of "blatant disregard" for the health of farmworkers, area residents, and the environment. They petitioned EPA to use its oversight powers to correct the state's failure to act, or else to rescind the agreement under which the state administers the federal pesticide law. EPA did neither. It rejected the petition for reform and simply ignored its own duty—the federal government's duty—to call the state to account and make sure that farmworkers get the adequate protection of health and safety that federal law guarantees.

Farmworkers who mix and apply pesticides usually run the worst risks of damage to health. Certain pesticides are so acutely toxic that EPA has ruled that only certified applicators, or people they directly supervise, may apply them. Unfortunately, EPA exercises no control over how the applicators are trained and certified, much less how they supervise others. In Texas, a certified applicator needs to do nothing more than pass an open-book exam on a 49-page booklet, of which 8 pages deal with safety precautions and one or two sentences mention fieldworkers.

Damacio Cano, a licensed pesticide applicator in the Rio Grande Valley, said the class he took to get his license gave almost no instruction on rules to avoid exposure or symptoms connected with exposure. "We were just told if we felt nauseous to see a doctor." Cano added: "When telling workers how to apply pesticides, farmers usually just say mix so many quarts of pesticides to so many quarts of water and leave the workers there to do it. I believe these workers generally do not have enough information about pesticides. One way you can tell is that the ones who are spraying are usually just wearing ordinary clothing and no masks, gloves, or rubber boots."

The story of Vicente Rodriguez, a 27-year-old employee of the Reina del Sol Ranch, is not really unusual. One day in August 1981, Rodriguez said, he turned the irrigation sprinklers on a field treated with a pesticide he believed to be Temik—"little black balls that are spread a little under the ground." He had no protective gear, nor did he know to take any unusual precautions. He sloshed around the field adjusting the sprinklers, getting mud and water in his boots. By the end of the day, he was prostrated by vomiting, diarrhea, and pain in the back of his head.

Temik (Union Carbide's brand name for aldicarb) is one of the

200

most acutely toxic pesticides in use in the United States. It is a cholinesterase-inhibitor, and while it remains in the body it can cause the gamut of symptoms of nervous-system disruption, from vomiting, headache, tremors, paralysis, coma, to death. EPA toxicologists are satisfied that aldicarb does not have lasting or cumulative effects; if you survive a poisoning without damage to internal organs, you should recover.

Vicente Rodriguez recovered, but not without a terrible fright. As he lay ill, he remembered that his brother Raul, who had also worked at the ranch, had a similar attack two months before and had died shortly afterwards in Mexico.

"My brother had just died, and I felt I was going to be the next to die," Rodriguez said. He spent five days in the hospital, where he was treated for pesticide poisoning. Back at work, he found he could no longer tolerate working with pesticides. The smell of the stuff made him ill. He finally left the ranch because he couldn't work with pesticides.

The unusual part of the story comes next. Most farmworkers in south Texas are hired by a crew leader for a particular job and are paid by the piece. They are legally defined as "contract laborers" and thus get no Social Security, unemployment compensation, or other social insurance. Rodriguez, however, was a ranch employee. With the help of the United Farm Workers union local and a private lawyer, he collected damages and payment of medical expenses through workers' compensation. Another unusual feature is that he found another job. Unemployment is fearfully high in the Valley. But Rodriguez was young, he got his citizenship papers, and he found work as a roofer.

This sequel to the story was news to the Dallas regional office of EPA. The Rodriguez pesticide poisoning incident was well known in Texas, because David Hanners of the *Dallas Morning News* had written a front-page story about it in August 1982. The Dallas EPA office made no inquiries and took no action, although the case appeared to involve violation of EPA rules for use of restricted pesticides under the direct supervision of a certified applicator. In response to an inquiry months later, a staff worker in the Dallas EPA office called the Texas Department of Agriculture to find out what had happened in the Rodriguez case. He reported back that Mr. Rodriguez had never filed a complaint with the Department and had died in Mexico. The Department, he said, "was never able to find the man, though they tried down in Edinburg." In fact, a phone call to the United Farm Workers local readily turned up the information that Mr. Rodriguez was alive and working in Edinburg.

Changing jobs is a very different matter for an older farmworker, especially for one who holds a regular, year-round job as a hired employee. There are very few of these "ranch hand" jobs, and they are highly prized. Hector Sanchez (not his real name, he doesn't want it used) has worked for seventeen years at one of the largest farms in the Valley. He is 54 years old; he has one grown son who has cerebral palsy and is semi-dependent, and two younger daughters. He drives a tractor, mixes pesticides, applies them through a boom extending from the tractor, irrigates, and does a dozen jobs on the farm. For several years he has had asthma, which clears up a bit on weekends when he doesn't work. Recently he has been almost crippled with a burning rash that covers his arms and extends from his ankles up to his thighs. He knows the rash is due to pesticides. The doctors at local clinics have told him so. But he can't do the only thing that would clear up the rash and possibly the asthma as well—get away from pesticides. "I cannot get another job at my age," he says. "My youngest daughter at home is only seven. How would my family live?"

Carlos Ramirez—that is his real name—knows what it is to lose a ranch hand job late in life. When he was 60 years old, he was dismissed from Pioneer Hybrid International, Inc., a seed corn company, where he had worked for eight years.

Ramirez and two other employees of Pioneer had done something very unusual. After they and eight other workers were overcome by pesticide poisoning while detasseling corn in the summer of 1980, they sued for damages. The pesticide was liquid Furadan (carbofuran, a cholinesterase-inhibiting chemical made by FMC), which had been sprayed on the corn by tractor. Robin Alexander of Texas Rural Legal Aid took the case. She asked for the industry health and safety reports on Furadan but ran into the roadblock Todhunter had imposed on release of the data. After a federal judge in south Texas ordered EPA to release the studies, FMC quickly settled the suit out of court.

"The funniest thing was," Ramirez said painfully, "that right after we got the settlement, the boss and the foreman and the boss's son, they got together and they fired me. They said it was misconduct. They just threw me out."

The settlement was signed July 10, 1982. The company managers fired Ramirez on July 15. They charged him with using bad language

202

and were supported by depositions from several other workers. There was nothing in Ramirez's personnel file on misconduct or bad language, nor had the company ever before taken any disciplinary action against him. The company did not fire the other two workers who had sued; one was later promoted. Ramirez, said Robin Alexander, had been the leader in the suit and was "maybe the most courageous of all the farmworkers I ever met in the Valley."

Carlos Ramirez says he has worked in the fields all his life, but he cannot find another job because he can't get a reference from Pioneer.

Because most farmworkers have little chance to change jobs or otherwise escape pesticide exposure, strong laws strongly enforced are doubly important for their protection. But all the people in the Rio Grande Valley, and the natural environment they live in, are regularly exposed to pesticides at rates much above the national norm. Farm use of pesticides in the Valley approximates thirteen pounds per person per year, compared with about four pounds (farm use) averaged across the country. The growing season covers twelve months of the year, and the big crops—cotton, vegetables, citrus fruit—are those that farmers generally treat heavily with pesticides.

Winds are frequent and strong in the Valley. Nearly anyone you talk to has occasionally been caught by pesticide drift on the highway, or in a ball park, or at a picnic. For people who live next to farmland, exposure to pesticides is far more frequent. Among these are not only Chicano families in colonias, but also a growing population of Anglos known as "winter Texans." They are retired people, mostly blue collar workers, from the Middle West "frost belt"—Michigan, Indiana, Illinois—who spend the winter months in the Valley, often in palm-shaded trailer parks directly adjoining farmland.

Rural residents who don't have air conditioning to cope with the Valley's stifling heat (this includes most of the families in colonias) leave their windows open most of the year. They are the ones at greatest risk —especially if they live near cotton fields, which are sprayed up to fourteen or fifteen times a season. Some of the pesticides sprayed on cotton are highly toxic organophosphates, such as ethyl and methyl parathion.

"It would not be surprising," said one medical scientist in the Valley, "to find out that levels of these pesticides in homes near cotton fields exceed the OSHA criteria [the federal standards that protect production plant workers]. OSHA standards are based on eight hours at work and sixteen hours off. What about women and children here in the Valley, home all day and getting exposed for all twenty-four hours?" The scientist asked not to be identified because sentiment that pesticides are entirely safe is strong among growers in the Valley and criticism is fiercely resented.

The Pesticides Laboratory in San Benito, Texas, runs a hotline for reports of pesticide poisoning and also conducts studies on lower-level exposures and effects. Dr. Tony Mollhagen, director of the lab, believes that incidents of extreme acute pesticide poisoning are less common than they were fifteen years ago because people have learned to be more cautious in handling agricultural chemicals. He cited a study that documented 118 cases of acute pesticide poisoning in the Valley in 1968 and a 1978 follow-up showing about one-fifth as many cases. He added, "We're not averaging one crash a year for crop dusters anymore."

Mollhagen agreed, however, that the absolute numbers of pesticide poisoning cases mean little. They are almost certainly undercounted, first because doctors often don't recognize the symptoms and miss the diagnosis entirely, and second, even if they recognize pesticide poisoning, it is hard to document, because traces of many pesticides in the blood and urine disappear in 24 to 48 hours. "We are probably getting reports of only a small minority of the cases," he said.

Like others in the field, Mollhagen is concerned about lower-level exposures and longer-term effects. In a study funded by EPA, the Pesticides Lab is currently monitoring pesticide traces in soils, water, and leaves, and in the urine of farmworkers, at a few farms in the area. In these studies, growers and crew leaders are observing legal reentry times; in fact, the purpose of the study is to find out if the existing reentry periods for certain pesticides are valid. Still to be systematically studied are exposures and effects under the real-life conditions of the Valley, legal and illegal.

Cyndy Chapman, President of the Frontera Audubon Society and a leader in a citizens' coalition against the misuse of pesticides, is constantly aware that, as Valley residents, she and her husband Jim and small daughter Stephanie are absorbing loads of pesticides in their bodies much above "normal" for the United States. Besides valuing wild birds and animals for their own sakes, Chapman sees wildlife as an early warning system of what is happening to human beings with rising exposures to pesticides. It worries her that biologists of the U.S. Fish and Wildlife Service discovered a peculiar change in the short-lived, rapidly reproducing, live-bearing mosquito fish that inhabit shallow ponds and ditches in south Texas. Scientists found that mosquito fish living in irrigation drainage ditches in the Rio Grande Valley could withstand far greater doses of the pesticide toxaphene—60 to 160 times as much—as previously unexposed mosquito fish from the nearby Arkansas National Wildlife Refuge. Toxaphene is toxic to fish and wildlife and may be a human carcinogen; it was heavily used on cotton in the Valley until insects became immune to it. The astonishing tolerance that Rio Grande Valley mosquito fish developed to toxaphene reflects their high exposures. This development may be good news for species survival of the adaptable mosquito fish, but it is unsettling news for the human beings—long-lived, slow to reproduce, and far less adaptable—living in the same environment.

Cotton farmers in the Rio Grande Valley know about resistance to pesticides in boll weevils and budworms, if not in mosquito fish. Texas cotton farming virtually collapsed in the early 1960's due to insect attack, and not for the first time. Cotton farming had almost gone under 70 years earlier when the boll weevil first crossed the border from Mexico.

After half a century of struggle against this ravenous pest, farmers greeted DDT and other synthetic, long-lasting, broadscale insect killers as a magical cure. For a few years, they were. But with repeated sprayings weevils that had an inborn immunity to the pesticides multiplied and susceptible ones died out. Insect populations can develop resistance very rapidly, because individual lives are short and new generations breed quickly. The continual, increasingly frequent spraying of pesticides also decimated natural predators of the tobacco budworm and pink bollworm, neither of which had previously been major cotton pests but now rapidly became a double menace. By 1962, the budworm and bollworm, now resistant to pesticides themselves, destroyed more cotton than the boll weevil.

Cotton farmers in central and south Texas, where the weevils and worms easily survive mild winters, were almost wiped out. The attempt to destroy cotton pests with escalating doses of pesticides was an economic as well as ecological failure. Texas A&M University was one of the first of the nation's land-grant colleges to develop a substitute system: integrated pest management (IPM), a new system of insect control that gets away from overwhelming reliance on chemicals. Texas cotton farmers were pioneers in IPM. The IPM system combines preservation of beneficial insects with restraint in pesticide spraying and old-fashioned good agricultural practice, such as plowing under the cotton stalks and litter where boll weevils like to take refuge during the winter. IPM may also include novel biological controls, such as spraying hormones that stop insect growth in the nymph stage, or dropping sterilized males from airplanes to crowd out the fertile males in mating with the females. Farmers using IPM don't try to eradicate every last insect, but rather try to keep them at low enough levels that farm profits are not sacrificed.

Most cotton farmers in the Valley are sold on the system of "spray as needed" control of pests, which is one aspect of IPM. After an early spraying to kill overwintering boll weevils ("That's the one that eats your lunch," a Valley farmer says), further spraying is delayed to give beneficial insects a chance to multiply. Then, scouts check the fields twice a week to see whether pests have gone over an established "economic threshold"—that is, the point where it costs less to spray than to let the pests destroy more cotton. Even with this modified system of relying on chemicals, cotton farmers in the Valley spray seven or eight times in good years, and as many as fifteen times in bad years, in a growing season that lasts about twenty-two weeks.

Hans Hansen, who grows cotton, corn, grain sorghum (an animal feed), and tomatoes on a 700-acre farm near Weslaco, works with the local A&M-State of Texas agricultural extension agent in a modified IPM system. This system, he says, is the only way for a cotton farmer to survive nowadays. "Years ago we didn't have near the pests. You could get by without much spraying. Now they keep increasing on us all the time. You have to keep on using something different on them. . . . If my daddy was alive now, he couldn't farm."

Hansen sees chemical controls as a tricky business for the farmer to manage, but absolutely essential. As for threats from pesticides to farmworkers' health, he said, "I don't know of any farmer that will let anybody go into a field right after it's been sprayed." He was not aware of any incidents of farmworkers being sprayed in the fields.

Hansen was indignant about a bill in the 1983 Texas legislature that would strengthen the right of people injured by pesticide spraying to sue for damages. Already, he thought, protests against pesticide drift had begun to tie the farmers' hands. The times for spraying are crucial for a crop like cotton, he explained. Delay a few days and you've lost the fight to the weevil. And with the way the wind blows in the Valley, it's not always possible to get ideal conditions for spraying. Hansen said some crop dusters are now reluctant to spray near homes because of the protests and possibility of suits, so that farmers may have to plant sorghum (which requires less spraying but is less profitable) instead of cotton in fields near homes.

John Norman, the IPM cotton expert at the Texas A&M–State of Texas station in Weslaco, believes that monocultures—planting the same crops in the same large areas year after year—are simply innately vulnerable to pests. Cotton farming in the Valley is a monoculture, and it is even more so across the border in the vast latifundias of northern Mexico. Even with the considerable extent of integrated pest management practiced by Texas cotton farmers, cotton still soaks up more insecticide than any other crop in Texas, and the boll weevil is still the state's number one pest.

Norman is interested in any practical idea for cutting back on insecticides; he knows that insecticides don't last. Right now, he is trying to warn farmers against the impulse to lavish the new synthetic pyrethroids on everything that gets worms—sorghum, corn, all sorts of vegetables, as well as cotton—because of the danger of repeating the DDT "experiment." Synthetic pyrethroids (Ambush, Pounce, Pydrin) mimic the traditional pyrethrin, made from chrysanthemums, but are more effective insect-killers—for now. Reportedly, the diamondback cabbage moth in India, where pyrethroids have been heavily used in the last few years, is already resistant.

John Norman believes it is realistic to cut insecticide use on cotton 20 to 30 percent by using known methods of boll weevil control: Plant heavily infested cropland to something else. Make sure farmers actually plow under cotton fields after harvest, as Texas law requires, to destroy winter habitat for weevils. The Valley Cotton and Grain Association and the Texas and U.S. Departments of Agriculture mobilized together after the disastrous weevil year of 1980 to identify unplowed fields through aerial surveys and to crack down on offenders. Norman also has hopes for some farther-out remedies—using sex lures to draw the weevils into traps, spraying hormones to stop insect development, growing cotton without irrigation so that foliage is not so lush and inviting to pests. "After all, cotton is naturally a desert crop," Norman says.

The citrus fruits and vegetables grown in the Valley are next behind cotton in pesticide application. According to John Norman, 90 percent of that application is for cosmetic purposes. He made an exception for fungicides, which, he said, control diseases that could wipe out a whole orchard or cabbage field. But most of the pesticides lavished on citrus and vegetables are for the purpose of producing a blemish-free product. "Otherwise, the consumer won't buy it," Norman said. Aaron Welch, a DuPont representative in McAllen, estimated the cosmetic use of pesticides at a lower but still substantial figure of 25 percent.

In a 1979 report, the Congressional Office of Technology Assessment estimated that, in time, IPM could reduce the need for chemical pesticides on major crops by 75 percent. Each crop is different, however. Commercial growers rely much more on chemicals for some (apples, peaches, onions, tomatoes) than for others (wheat). Professor David Pimentel of Cornell University says it is the nature of IPM research to be slow going, compared with industry and academic research on spectacular broad spectrum chemicals. "With IPM, you have to work out a technique for each insect, for each natural enemy for each crop. It's not easy." Unfortunately, IPM research has lagged most on the fruit and vegetable crops, which require the closest work by large numbers of people. Much more effort has gone into the big cash crops like cotton.

Meanwhile, the great majority of farmers are sold on chemicals and are using pesticides in ever larger amounts. In the 1980's, Texas state officials at last began to pay attention to the growing occupational hazard from pesticides.

Two labor unions in the Valley, the Texas Farmworkers Union and the United Farm Workers (AFL-CIO), were both organized in the 1970's and were often at odds on leaders and tactics, but both began to push strongly for better protection of farmworkers' health. Doctors and nurses at family health clinics, legal aid lawyers, the Audubon Society, and the Sierra Club joined the unions in an informal coalition of Valley residents against misuse of pesticides. Texas newspapers and television news shows discovered the pesticide issue. And representatives of the Valley area in the Texas state legislature responded.

In 1982 committees of the Texas legislature held hearings in Austin and in the Valley in which field workers, pesticide mixers and applicators, doctors, lawyers, and others described the common experiences of people in the Valley with pesticides. One of the witnesses was Norma Adams. She is a federal wage and hours inspector based in Harlingen, who regularly goes out to the fields to interview workers. Like most of the fieldworkers, she has been sprayed several times. Once, after a pilot sprayed in the next field, "so close that he couldn't avoid spraying everybody out there," she was outraged enough to put in a complaint to the Texas Department of Agriculture. Nothing happened. The inspector who took her complaint said he had two reasons not to act: first, the complaint was not timely (it had been held up for weeks in the Department's regional and state offices); second, there was conflicting testimony (Mrs. Adams and the workers said the plane had sprayed them; the sprayer said he had not).

With a new Texas Commissioner of Agriculture, Jim Hightower, elected in November 1982, the response of the department may be different. Hightower is a populist politician and agricultural reformer from years back; both the United Farm Workers and many owners of Texas family farms backed him strongly in the election.

To Ron White, Hightower's deputy for pesticide regulation, it is obvious that growers and farmworkers have a common interest in protecting their health and their environment from dangerous pesticides. "I don't honestly believe there are many growers who want to have a health hazard," he said. "It's not a question of our imputing ill will, or being out to get anybody." Instead, he hopes to get growers, farmworkers, crop dusters, and chemical companies working together on the problem.

He also expects his staff to react when they hear about farmworker pesticide poisonings. He was chagrined that in 1982 (before Hightower's election) department inspectors had done nothing to follow up the notorious case of Vicente Rodriguez simply because nobody had filed a formal complaint. "Frankly, the level of diligence was not what you'd want it to be," he said.

White welcomed the modest improvements in labeling of pesticides that EPA issued in March 1983. Long in the works in EPA's tiny farmworker protection office, the improved labeling rules call for a simple warning in Spanish on containers of toxic pesticides. They also require manufacturers to print on the label EPA's rules for farmworker protection, e.g., "Do not apply this product in such a manner as to directly or through drift expose workers or other persons. The area being treated must be vacated by unprotected persons." In theory at least, having these rules on the label makes it easier for state authorities to enforce the rules and prosecute violators.

White added, however, that the overall direction of EPA's pesticide program has made his job much tougher. "What's going on in Washington with EPA makes this whole thing harder to do. We have no faith anymore in what EPA is saying. We used to rely on them."

The fact that Texas is waking up to farmworkers' needs for protection from pesticides, as California did a few years before, does not remove the need for strong national standards strongly enforced. Certainly, health protection for migrant farmworkers, who travel from Texas to Michigan or from Florida up to Maine or from California to Washington, is an interstate problem.

Pesticides, altogether, are a national problem. Compromises in regulation that leave some states unprotected are usually a mistake. When William Ruckelshaus imposed the emergency suspension on EDB in October 1983, he observed that contamination by DBCP, that other hazardous nematocide, has now been found in Oahu's Pearl Harbor basal aquifer. This aquifer is a major source of drinking water for Honolulu. When EPA exempted Hawaii from the nationwide ban on DBCP, one of the reasons given was that nobody had yet found any DBCP in the basal aquifer. Three years later, somebody has.

Another compromise exempted Hawaii from a nationwide ban on heptachlor. Four years later, heptachlor turned up in Hawaii where it never should have been: in 95 percent of Oahu's milk supply. In the butter, cheese, yoghurt, and ice cream made from the island's milk. In mother's milk.

Heptachlor is a powerful insecticide of the chlorinated hydrocarbon class, which also includes DDT, chlordane, aldrin, and kepone. It has been linked with kidney and liver damage in human beings and causes cancer in laboratory animals. It is also a nerve poison in insects and in higher animals.

EPA action against heptachlor involved a long and bitter fight. The manufacturer, Velsicol of Chicago, insisted the product was safe and came up with studies to show it was not a carcinogen. Five EPA scientists checked Velsicol's studies and concluded that damning data had been omitted. A federal grand jury indicted six officers and ex-officers of Velsicol on charges of concealing information, but the case was later dismissed on procedural grounds. After nearly five years and 147,000 pages of testimony, EPA finally banned most uses of heptachlor in 1978.

Except for Hawaii. Hawaii's powerful pineapple growers, led by the multinational companies Del Monte and Castle and Cooke (Dole), joined forces with the manufacturer, Velsicol, to demand continued use of the pesticide on the grounds that there was no alternative to it. As with DBCP, EPA made an exception. Use of heptachlor on Hawaii's pineapples was allowed for four more years, until the end of 1982.

Pesticide use in Hawaii, with its tropical climate and monoculture of pineapples and other crops, is simply enormous. The state uses 9 million pounds of pesticides each year, six times as much per acre as California. As for heptachlor, pineapple growers use it as a weapon against mealybug wilt, a disease that withers the roots of the plant. Rather than attacking the mealybug directly, heptachlor destroys ants, which are its natural protectors. Ants love a substance called honeydew that the mealybug excretes and will fight off the mealybug's enemies—wasps, ladybugs, lacewings—to save their honeydew supplies.

Heptachlor got into Hawaiian milk by a circuitous route. After harvesting the pineapple fruit, growers send in a machine that cuts the plants' tough spiky leaves to the ground and chops and shreds them. Then this "green chop" is sold as feed for the island's dairy and beef cattle. Federal rules require that growers wait a full year after the last heptachlor application before harvesting green chop, a precaution that is meant to keep the pesticide out of milk and meat.

The precaution didn't work, whether because growers did not observe it or because the theory behind it was wrong is not known. In January 1982, during a random twice-a-year test of milk sold in Honolulu, the State Department of Health found high readings of heptachlor. Unwilling to take "irresponsible" action against the dairy industry, state officials delayed and retested. Finally, on March 18, under pressure from a Honolulu newspaper, the Department announced a limited recall of milk. A week later, the Department recalled ice cream. The next week, the director of the Department of Health resigned. His successor announced there would be no more recalls. The next day the state recalled yoghurt. A week later, it was cottage cheese.

The federal Food and Drug Administration then banned Hawaiian milk products on airplane flights, and military commissaries in Oahu took all milk products off their shelves. By the end of April, the state had recalled all milk products from one of Honolulu's two milk processors. Then, tests of nursing mothers' milk showed high levels of heptachlor. On May 15, testimony before the state legislature revealed for the first time that heptachlor had been detected in hamburger meat as well as in milk back in January, but the state had neither recalled the meat nor informed consumers.

Use of heptachlor on Hawaiian pineapples finally ended in 1982. But to some of the people exposed to high doses of the pesticide the story isn't over. Beverly Creamer, a reporter for the *Honolulu Advertiser*, was pregnant when the pesticide story broke. After following the revelations for a month, she picked up the latest story, "And it hit me. This stuff could have been in the milk I've been drinking for five months. . . . I started crying. I'm frightened something might be wrong with my baby.

"No one really knows what heptachlor does to babies. Unborn or not. And whether the pesticide their mother ingested . . . will give them cancer when they're ten. Or kidney failure when they're twenty.

"But I'm trying not to overreact, not to become hysterical about this. I'm trying to believe that the doctors who say the heptachlor will wash out of our bodies and our babies' bodies, causing no harm, really know what they are talking about.

"But I can't help being haunted by the memory of thalidomide and DES [di-ethylstilbestrol, a hormone given mothers in the 1950s to prevent miscarriage, which, years later, was found to cause cancer and genital abnormalities in their children].

"Most of all, I'm trying to believe that my baby is all right."

Creamer's baby daughter Jennifer, born July 8, 1982, is all right so far. But, said Creamer recently, "The scary thing is you don't know what effect it's going to have down the road."

Another exception to the 1978 ban on heptachlor came back to haunt American families a few years later. Together with two other pesticides banned for most uses—chlordane and aldrin—heptachlor is still legal for termite control. In fact, chlordane and heptachlor are still Velsicol's biggest sellers despite their cancellation for most agricultural uses years ago. These dangerous pesticides are supposed to be safe for termite control if applied properly; that is, injected under pressure, either straight into the soil under a house or through holes drilled in the foundation and then sealed.

The unfortunate fact is that "termite treatment" has contaminated hundreds—maybe thousands—of homes across the country with chlordane, heptachlor, and aldrin. According to the industry, every instance of contamination from termite treatment is due to misuse. Yet when misuse becomes widespread enough it approaches a general condition of use and may seriously threaten public health. And most misuse has been practiced not by careless or ignorant homeowners but by licensed exterminators.

Contamination from termite treatment isn't new. It was first noticed in the early 1970's in military housing at Ohio's Wright-Patterson

Air Force Base. Strange smells in the houses alerted the families to the contamination. Chlordane, injected into concrete slab foundations, was seeping into the houses from cracks in the slab. In some cases, applicators had unwittingly drilled through heating ducts in the slab; afterward, each time the heat went on, air currents carried the pesticide to every corner of the house. The Air Force tested 753 of its older homes at various bases and found two-thirds tainted with chlordane. Astonishingly, every new house of 800 tested was also contaminated. It cost nearly $1 million to clean up the houses.

In 1978, 53 more houses at Scott Air Force Base in Illinois were found to be contaminated. In 1980, another 200 were discovered in Kansas. The Air Force finally banned chlordane for houses with ducts in or under concrete slabs and banned that kind of construction in termite-prone areas.

The Air Force warned EPA of its chlordane experience as long ago as 1974. The General Accounting Office repeated the warning in 1980, observing that in its 1978 settlement with Velsicol EPA "did not consider" the Air Force experience.

Private homes on Long Island were next. By the early 1980's, complaints to the state Department of Environmental Conservation were averaging 250 per year. One in five turned out to involve serious contamination, mostly with chlordane and aldrin. In 1982, seven homes turned out to be so badly contaminated that the Department advised the families to evacuate their homes.

The Jeffrey Lever family was one of these. In the spring of 1983, the Levers had their house tested after Mrs. Lever suffered a miscarriage and the two Lever children developed skin and mouth rashes. The family discovered that an exterminator had soaked their whole house with aldrin—walls, floors, closets, wooden beams. After this spectacular misuse, their house was uninhabitable. With the blessing of their insurance company, the Levers called a bulldozer to tear the house down and push everything—clothes, furniture, house, foundation and all—into the swimming pool, where it was all buried.

After this, hundreds of families on Long Island began to find the same kind of contamination in their houses. Usually, the tip-off was the smell. Some family members in contaminated houses suffered from headaches, lassitude, nosebleeds, dizziness, weakness, and confusion. All of them suffered from fright. Chlordane, heptachlor, and aldrin are all carcinogens as well as nerve toxins.

New York Congressman Tom Downey said his Long Island constituents were flooding a local hotline with calls—as many as 600 a day, 11,000 in all, with nearly 1,000 requiring investigation. "They ask just who *is* in charge in such emergencies," he said. "The EPA will explain that the state is immediately in charge. However, the state . . . can only advise evacuation of houses which they finally establish as dangerous." Testing houses for contamination normally takes four or five months; with the logjam of complaints in 1983, it could take years to finish testing. "People have a justifiable question in asking how their federal watchdog, the EPA, could have taken a role in preventing this and how the EPA can help now."

Too often, the federal watchdog has lain down on the job. This is nothing new. The neglect of farmworkers' health; the compromises on DBCP, heptachlor, and aldrin; failures to protect food and ground water from pesticide pollution—all these took place before Ronald Reagan was elected President and put Anne Gorsuch and John Todhunter in charge of EPA's pesticide program. The wonder was, however, that these people were blind to the failures and compromises of the past and their continuing responsibility to protect the public health from chemicals that are inherently and necessarily dangerous. The only victim they saw was the pesticide industry. The only responsibility they undertook was to clear more chemicals for quick use.

214

3
OUR
LAND

THE TRESPASSERS:
DRILLING IN THE WILDERNESS

Bob Burnett was hunting quail that morning. He had crossed a mesa and was standing at its rim looking north when, about a mile away, he saw them—a drill rig, a Cat (bulldozer), a water truck, and a vehicle used for hauling bulldozers called a lowboy. They definitely were on the national wildlife refuge. But what really bothered him was whether they were on the land within the refuge which had been designated as a wilderness by the United States Congress. He just was not sure.

That question nagged at Burnett like a chigger bite for the rest of the day (November 1, 1982). After bagging his limit of quail, he returned to his home in Roswell that afternoon. The first thing he did was pull out his maps. "Yes, by God, they were on the wilderness, where they had no business being." Bob Burnett has been a hunter and a conservationist for over 40 years in eastern New Mexico. He understands that not everyone finds the land along the Pecos River, with its salt grass, sage, and mesquite, all that inviting. Certainly the place names are none too inviting—Bitter Lake National Wildlife Refuge, Salt Creek Wilderness. But Bob Burnett loves this open country and his views on the wilderness do not lack starch. "I believe we ought to leave some land as we found it, so our grandchildren and their grandchildren can enjoy

215

it too. It's the Good Lord's gift to us all." In the coming weeks, he was to learn how many other people believed as he did.

Bob Burnett wasted no time. He first called the local office of the Fish and Wildlife Service—the federal agency responsible for looking after the refuge and the wilderness. Did they know there was a fully-equipped oil-gas crew out on the Salt Creek Wilderness? No. Had they issued a permit allowing road-building and oil and gas development on the wilderness? No. Next, he called the local office of the Bureau of Land Management (BLM). The land that surrounds the refuge and the wilderness is also owned by the United States—public land that the BLM is supposed to manage in the public interest. Had they given an oil-gas crew a right-of-way to the wilderness? No. Then, Burnett alerted some of his fellow conservationists. They, in turn, spread the word to others. Burnett is active in the National Wildlife Federation. Before nightfall, word had spread of the intrusion into the wilderness to members of the Sierra Club, the Wilderness Society, the Audubon Society, and Earth First in the Southwest.

The next day, November 3, was an eventful one. Burnett went out to the wilderness to see for himself what was happening and to talk with the foreman of the oil-gas crew. He learned that the trespasser was Yates Petroleum Corporation. The previous day Yates had bulldozed a road, approximately 20 feet wide, across the public land, had cut through a fence that keeps cattle out of the wildlife refuge, installed a cattleguard, and continued bulldozing the road onto the wilderness for about a half a mile. Then, Yates stripped and leveled an area on the wilderness of about a quarter to a half acre in size for use as a drill pad. By November 3, the drilling had begun. When Burnett returned to Roswell, he called the Fish and Wildlife Service and the BLM to find out what they planned to do about the Yates trespass. He was informed that they had issued trespass citations to Yates. In fact, the U.S. Fish and Wildlife Service had issued a citation after overcoming resistance by the Secretary's office and the BLM.

Yates stopped working for about an hour—apparently to consult with their lawyers, and then took up where they had left off. When Burnett and other conservationists learned that Yates had resumed operations, they were back on the phone with the Fish and Wildlife Service and the BLM inquiring what they were going to do next. But now they were informed that the local offices of these federal agencies had been ordered by Washington not to comment further on the incident and to refer all calls to their Albuquerque offices. The Albuquerque offices of the Fish and Wildlife Service and the BLM referred the callers to Washington. The bureaucratic runaround had begun.

Bob Burnett notes: "The local BLM and Fish and Wildlife Service people were scared. They didn't want to lose their jobs. Hell, you can't blame them. They knew which side their superiors in the Department of the Interior were on—Yates's. Many of these people are my friends." What really struck Burnett was the contrast in attitudes between the civil servants, who are the custodians of the land, and the trespassers. "That drill crew was cocksure of itself."

Since the government was taking no immediate action to stop Yates, the conservationists decided they would try. They checked with the Fish and Wildlife Service and found that it would be legal for them to camp on the road that Yates had bladed across the wilderness. So the morning of November 7, that is what they did, blocking the entrance that Yates had cut into the wilderness. They also alerted the media. By late afternoon, a small convoy of Yates vehicles was piling up at the gate—a tankload of water, a truckload of drilling mud, a reel truck with a towering spool of 4-inch plastic pipe, and a flatbed with two more reels. All day long, the Yates foreman, Mike Slater, had assured Burnett there would be no violence, so Burnett, who had guided the campers to the site, returned home. But then a lowboy carrying a bulldozer appeared on the scene. Ed Burns, a retired civil servant from Las Cruces, who was one of the conservationists at the scene, describes what happened next:

"Now the bulldozer was brought up to the cattleguard. The scene was brilliantly lit by the headlights of the vehicles and the spotlights of the TV crews. . . . Slater confronted me, 'You've done your bit for God and country,' he said. Now he warned us to get out of the way or we would be hurt. The bulldozer was coming through and the driver was not going to stop for anything.

"In a ringing voice Slater shouted, 'Go.' The dozer moved forward. Employees poised for the purpose yanked up the tents and threw them into the ditch. John Colburn, who had been sitting on a foam pad inside the wilderness boundary, did not move quickly enough. . . . Slater seized John, wrestled him to the side of the road, then claimed credit for saving his life.

"Three others snatched Mike Colburn and threw him aside. He was the 16-year-old boy. I stepped out of the path; I did not get to be 65 years old by standing in front of oncoming bulldozers. Leonard apparently exercised similar discretion. Then the convoy roared through. . . ."

Millions of Americans watched it all on the evening news. Burnett was interviewed by the TV reporters, and was flooded with calls afterward. "They were all very supportive. These were ordinary people like me from all around the country, and they wanted to know what they could do to help us keep oil and gas developers out of the wilderness. Some of them were real mad. One guy was so mad he wanted me to give him the name of that bulldozer driver so he could take care of him. I said, 'Whoa, brother, that is the worst possible thing you could do. We're starting to win this fight.' "

In a sense, he was right. But before the Salt Creek Wilderness trespass case was over, it took some very strange turns.

The day after the confrontation at the gate the Yates lawyers, moving with an alacrity not matched by the federal lawyers working on this case, went into a local court and convinced a judge to issue a restraining order against the conservationists. They must not obstruct Yates access to the wilderness drill site. That same day, federal officials were asked why no BLM or Fish and Wildlife Service agents had been present to prevent the confrontation. They replied that they had orders "from above" to stay away from the Yates drill site.

The Yates trespass generated so much public interest that, on November 10, Bob Burnett, as one of the chief protagonists in the case, found himself in Washington, D.C., testifying before the United States Congress for the first time in his life. Burnett hardly fits the image of the "left-wing environmental elitist" portrayed by Secretary of the Interior James Watt. He was born on a ranch in west Texas, and his father moved the family to Roswell, New Mexico, during the Depression. Burnett works for himself—he installs and services pumps, water pumps and oil pumps. In 1980 he voted for Ronald Reagan. But his congressional testimony reflected the profound frustration of conservationists with the Reagan Administration. He told Rep. John Seiberling, Chairman of the Subcommittee on Public Land and National Parks, Committee on Interior and Insular Affairs, that "it is beyond belief that the most powerful nation in the world cannot stop the illegal drilling going on in the wilderness, in the Salt Creek Wilderness area, and yet they walked into a court, Yates Petroleum people walked into a courthouse, and in a very few hours, in less than half a day, they obtained a restraining order against the people that were legally and lawfully on the public lands."

He contrasted the kid-glove treatment Yates had gotten to how the federal government dealt with trespassers on the Gila Wilderness in western New Mexico a couple of years ago under another Administration. These trespassers were off-road vehiclists. They were required to leave their four-wheel drive rig and were escorted off the wilderness on foot. They then had to hire pack horses and trek back into the wilderness, disassemble their vehicle, and remove it piece-by-piece from the wilderness. They also had to pay a stiff fine.

No one from Yates appeared at the hearing, but the company did present written testimony which was illuminating. First, though, a little history.

When the federal government in the late 1940's acquired the land for the Bitter Lake National Wildlife Refuge from private owners and from the State of New Mexico, the state retained its mineral rights. In 1972, the state issued an oil-gas lease to Yates for the site that is now a designated wilderness. Under the terms of the lease, Yates had to drill sometime before midnight, November 1, 1982, or its lease would expire. For almost ten years, Yates did nothing. Then, faced with the imminent prospect of losing its lease, it acted. In early September of 1982, the State of New Mexico, responding to Yates's request, issued the company a permit to drill. Yates then applied to the U.S. Fish and Wildlife Service for a right-of-way and surface occupancy permit and to the BLM for a right-of-way permit.

At this juncture, the Department of the Interior had at least two options open to it for protecting the wilderness. It could have acquired Yates's lease outright, or it could have made a trade with Yates, giving Yates a comparable oil-gas lease on non-wilderness public land in return for this one. The Department of the Interior did neither. Indeed, there is no indication that Interior officials ever considered these options. One option the Department did *not* have was to issue the permits Yates sought. The Congress had prohibited expenditures to process permits or leases for energy development on wilderness areas. The Congress had passed this unusual measure because the previous year Secretary of the Interior James Watt had approved oil-gas leases for the Capitan Wilderness in the Lincoln National Forest in New Mexico, to the west of the Salt Creek Wilderness. The leases had been issued before an environmental assessment was done and without any public notice. When a lowly but conscientious G-7 in the Forest Service blew the whistle, quite a ruckus ensued. The Wilderness Act of 1964 allows oil and gas leasing

219

on the National Wilderness Preservation System until the end of 1983, but it does not require leasing. In fact, no Secretary of the Interior since the act was passed twenty years ago had adopted a policy of issuing oil and gas leases on wilderness lands. Oil and gas development was considered incompatible with wilderness values.

The centerpiece of Yates's testimony before the House committee was a letter dated October 25 from Alexander H. Good, Associate Solicitor, Energy and Resources, Department of the Interior:

The purpose of this letter is to inform you of the status of your application to the Bureau of Land Management and the Fish and Wildlife Service for access and drillsite permits for exploration on your lease on State-owned minerals in the Salt Creek Wilderness. *The Solicitor's Office has determined that there is no legal objection to the approval of the above requests.* However, recent appropriations legislation has prohibited the obligation of funds for "any aspects of the processing or issuance of permits or leases pertaining to exploration for or development of coal, oil, and gas" in certain areas, including Salt Creek Wilderness, §126, P.L. 97-276. In short, due to the restriction in the appropriation legislation, we cannot process or issue the applications at this time.

Yates did the underlining. This is a curious letter in several respects. Good seemed to be straining to offer Yates a legal loophole, instead of simply advising the company that Congress had prohibited the issuance of drilling permits for wilderness areas, and, lacking a permit, Yates could not legally proceed. That was the explicit reason, after all, for the congressional prohibition.

After receiving the Good letter, Yates explained, it was

faced with the imminent loss of its lease, and having been effectively denied the permits requested, on October 31, 1982, Yates erected a well sign in accordance with the requirements of Paragraph 16 of its lease and conducted other activities on the surface of its lease in preparation for an entry to the surface of its leasehold. On November 1, 1982, Yates spudded its well by drilling a hole 40 feet deep in which a conductor pipe was cemented. On November 2, 1982, Yates commenced operations by constructing its roads and drill pad necessary for its operations. On November 3, 1982, Yates moved onto its location the remainder of its necessary equipment and drilled out from under its surface conductor pipe.

According to Yates, it acted "reasonably to protect its existing private right." According to Fish and Wildlife Service and BLM employees in New Mexico interviewed for this book, "Yates took the law into its own hands."

Another bit of information revealed in Yates's testimony was that Yates had actually consulted with the BLM and Fish and Wildlife Service about its proposed access road into the wilderness. Two weeks before Yates bulldozed the road across the public land, it was out on the land with BLM and Fish and Wildlife Service officials, seeking their advice on the best course for that road to follow, and indeed Yates altered its planned route to avoid a potential archaeological area. So it should have come as no surprise to anyone in the Department of the Interior when Yates acted.

One week after Bob Burnett told federal officials that Yates was trespassing, federal lawyers obtained a temporary restraining order against Yates. Yates immediately appealed but had to cease operations on the wilderness pending the decision of the appeals court. By that time, however, Yates was already well over halfway done, having drilled some 2,800 feet. The federal judge in Albuquerque followed up his temporary restraining order with a rather vigorously worded injunction against Yates on November 18.

In late December, a few days after the congressional prohibition against the processing of oil-gas permits on wildernesses expired, the Fish and Wildlife Service and the BLM issued Yates the necessary permits. It was done without fanfare. Congress was not in session. There was no press release. Under their own regulations, the BLM and Fish and Wildlife Service are not supposed to issue right-of-way or occupancy permits to someone like Yates, who has an outstanding trespass, but they did anyway, on orders from the Secretary's office.

Yates resumed operations in January, drilling another 1,400 feet. On February 7, 1983, Yates capped the gas well it had found and vacated the wilderness site. There are, incidentally, hundreds of new gas wells in this part of eastern New Mexico that are capped. The reason they remain capped at a time when natural gas prices are climbing rapidly is that they do not hold enough gas to justify the capital investment required to hook them up to existing pipelines.

The BLM reached an out-of-court settlement with Yates in its trespass case. BLM agreed to revoke the trespass decision as well as the trespass damages ($1,558.40) against Yates. In return, Yates will pay the federal government $37.50 for rental of the road between October 31 and December 28 and an additional $500 for the administrative charges of processing the right-of-way permit. Before it is final, the BLM-Yates agreement must be approved by the Interior Board of Land Appeal, and that approval is expected. The Fish and Wildlife Service trespass case against Yates is still pending. Roswell Magistrate Ray Phelps is awaiting word from the Fish and Wildlife Service regarding their negotiations with Yates over an out-of-court settlement.

The trespassers are gone now from the Salt Creek Wilderness, and the damage is done, but questions remain regarding the Department of the Interior's handling of the case.

Interior knew that Yates had received a drilling permit from the state. It knew that Yates did not want to lose its lease. It knew it could not process Yates's right-of-way and surface occupancy permits. Why didn't Interior buy out Yates's lease or exchange it for another on non-wilderness public land? Certainly the conservationists would not have objected. As Burnett testified, "The New Mexico Wildlife Federation has no objections to Yates being reimbursed for any moneys that it could have lost. . . ."

Interior knew that Yates had already prepared plans for an access road and drill pad site. And it knew that the lease was about to expire. Why did the Solicitor's Office send Yates such an ambiguous letter seeming almost to invite Yates to proceed on its own?

After Yates ignored the trespass citations issued on November 3, why didn't federal agents simply escort the Yates crew off the wilderness? At one point in the congressional hearings, Rep. Hank Brown asked a Department of the Interior official straight out: "What prohibits your law enforcement people from taking those trespassers by the arm and escorting them off the property?" Answer: "Nothing." Then, the exasperated Brown, a Republican from Colorado, asked: "Why don't you do it?" The response: "We were in a very complicated situation as far as we were concerned and were not too sure that we were on the right ground at that moment." That was more than Rep. Pat Williams from Montana could swallow. After observing that he understood how Yates may have been confused by the October 25 letter from the Solicitor's Office, Williams noted: "The proper response for the corporation should have been through the courts rather than jumping on a bulldozer. . . . If a young fellow downtown conducted himself in the manner that this corporation has conducted itself, he would be apprehended and thrown into an overcrowded jail and begin to serve his time, but we don't

222

treat corporate criminals that way, and we allow the illegal activities to continue. . . ."

Bill Curtis, an attorney for the Sierra Club Legal Defense Fund, puts the matter in this perspective: "If someone busted into the Secretary of Interior's office and started chopping up his desk, the government would hardly diddle around for a week drafting a petition for a temporary restraining order before taking action; they'd call in the U.S. Marshals and have them haul the offender out posthaste."

Why did Interior issue Yates the necessary permits when Yates had outstanding trespass violations against it? And why was Yates only given a slap on the wrist after committing so blatant a trespass?

Bob Burnett thinks he has the answer to all of these questions. Based on his off-the-record conversations with Department of the Interior employees in New Mexico and his reading of the sequence of events as they unfolded, Burnett is convinced that Yates talked with high-level Interior Department officials in October and that they gave Yates a green light or at least an amber light, i.e., assurances that the government would go easy with them if they bulldozed their way into the wilderness.*

Burnett does not see this as an old-fashioned case of political back scratching. He thinks the Administration acted as it did or failed to act for ideological reasons. "Ever since the Reagan Administration came to office, they have tried their darnedest to 'open up' the wilderness system to oil and gas development, and every time the Congress or the courts have gotten in their way. They saw this case as an opportunity to set a precedent establishing the rights of an existing lessee to drill in the wilderness. They did it for the principle of the thing. Of course it backfired on them real bad."

Burnett's interpretation is interesting because it brings the pieces of the puzzle into a coherent pattern. Other interpretations are of course possible. This one comes from a career employee inside the Department of the Interior in Washington: "I think the politicos in the department were asleep on this one. They just weren't paying much attention until the very last moment and then they sent that October 25 letter to Yates,

*An Interior Department spokesman, Harmon Kallman, concedes that Yates did "have some conversations" with political appointees at Interior, but denies Yates was given "any kind of go-ahead."

hoping it would cover their collective asses if Yates took matters into its own hands. Of course, it only made matters worse. Then Yates climbed on its bulldozers. . . . Once Yates acted, the Reagan appointees were forced to do something, especially after it got on television and Congress got stirred up. Their hearts weren't in it, though. These, after all, weren't welfare chiselers they were dealing with. So they fumbled around with the case until the heat was off; then they quietly handed Yates the permits they wanted and gave them a little slap on the wrist."

Despite the fact that Yates seems to have gotten away with trespass, Burnett comes away from the whole episode not one bit discouraged, even though his involvement in it has cost him business out in the oil fields. "The oil and gas industry may have won the battle, but the conservationists won the war. Now, even Watt is talking about no oil and gas development in the wilderness system.

"I'm going to continue fighting for what I believe in as a conservationist until they throw dirt on my face when I'm six feet under," Bob Burnett declares. "And I'll tell you something else. I voted for Ronald Reagan last time and it was the biggest mistake I ever made in my life, but it's not one that I'm about to make again."

THE HARD LESSONS OF A HUNDRED YEARS

Our land. Seven hundred and twenty million acres—forests, scrublands, prairie, tundra. Not Yates Petroleum's or Exxon's, not AMAX's, Louisiana-Pacific's, Bank of America's, Interstate Land and Cattle Company's, or Sunshine Development Corporation's land. Ours. Managed for us by the federal government. Before examining the Reagan Administration's record as our land manager, it is worth recalling how this land became ours.

From 1781 to 1867 the United States government acquired 1,840,709,120 acres of land and water from other nations. These lands were paid for with dollars from the U.S. Treasury and, in some instances, with the lives of soldiers from the U.S. Army. They came to be known as the public domain.

Our Constitution states, in Article IV, Section 3, Paragraph 2, that "the Congress shall have Power to dispose of and make all needful Rules and Regulations respecting the Territory or other Property belonging to the United States. . . ." Throughout much of the nineteenth century,

Congress tried to dispose of the public domain. There were two motives behind this disposal policy—one economic, the other political. It was hoped that the promise of free or very cheap land would stimulate the development of the West and this in turn would strengthen and stabilize the young nation's roller-coaster economy. And it was feared that a large mass of propertyless people would make for a very unruly republic. Both Thomas Jefferson and James Madison had emphasized this point, and disorders, such as Shay's Rebellion, which broke out after Independence, drove home the point. Provide public land to the propertyless and they will not be tempted to separate the propertied from their wealth.

In 1837, a year of financial panic, Congress passed the Preemption Act. It allowed a frontier settler to buy 160 acres of public land for $1.25 per acre. In 1847 and 1855 it passed the Military Bounty Acts, which authorized the payment of land scrip to every veteran of a foreign or Indian war since 1790—160 acres per veteran. All you had to do to qualify was to have served in the military for fourteen days during one of the wars. The lands disposed of by these measures were merely the *hors d'oeuvres*, though, compared to the great land banquet that began in the 1860's. The passage of the Homestead Act and the granting of huge tracts of free public land to railroads such as the Great Northern and the Union Pacific signaled the serving of the main course.

The lure of virtually free land, not to mention the virtually free minerals, forage, timber, water, and soil that came with it, brought the mining corporations, ranching enterprises, lumber companies, and land speculators to the public land table. Homesteaders came, too, but the government proved more proficient in distributing land to the haves than to the have nots. Over the next 60 years, the U.S. government disposed of more than one billion acres of public land, and genuine homesteaders, under the Preemption Act or one of the several home-stead acts, probably got no more than 15 percent of it. About 55 percent went to corporations, and 30 percent was given to states to encourage the building of schools and general economic development.

The original Homestead Act of 1862 offered a settler a quarter section of public land (160 acres) for a filing fee of $10. Live on the land for five years and it was yours; you didn't have to pay another cent for it. Or, if you were in a hurry to acquire the title, you paid $1.25 an acre after only six months' residence. But at the same time the U.S. land offices were handing out homestead titles, or patents as they were called, they were also holding public land auctions. Conse-

225

quently, as historian Frederick Merk observes, "The man of wealth continued to have the privilege of buying unlimited quantities of public land at an auction or following an auction at a district land office." Moreover, it did not take the mining corporations, et al., long to learn how to use the Homestead Act to their advantage, just as they had the Preemption Act. A company would have a "dummy" go into the U.S. land office and file for a homestead. After six months, the dummy would come back, pay the $1.25 an acre, collect the patent, and then turn it over to the company. Dummies worked for anything from 10 cents for a shot of whiskey to $10. The land office clerks were underpaid and overworked. They seldom had time to verify homestead claims, and, if they did, a small bribe usually persuaded them not to. Historians Charles and Mary Beard reported that "millions of acres of valuable timber, mineral, and grazing lands were literally stolen under the eyes of dishonest or negligent officials in the federal land offices." They added: "In the history of political corruption, seldom if ever had there been transactions on a scale so prodigious or conducted with more brazen effrontery. Thousands of great fortunes in the East as well as the West were built out of the resources wrung from the government for a pittance or for a bribe. . . ."

During the 1870's, Congress passed a series of laws which accelerated the disposal of public land to vested interests. The Mining Law of 1872, for example, enabled a mining company to buy public land on which it had found gold, silver, copper, or some other valuable mineral. The price? Just $2.50 or $5 an acre, depending on whether it was a placer or lode deposit. Then there was the equally generous Timber and Stone Act under which the U.S. government sold prime timberland in California, Oregon, and Washington for $2.50 an acre, about the price of a good log. Or the Timber Culture Act that allowed the purchase of 160 acres of public land over and above a free homestead at $1.25 an acre if the purchaser promised to plant a fourth of it in trees. Ranchers, in particular, found this a handy way to expand their holdings, and never mind about the trees. Or the Desert Land Act of 1877. You could buy 640 acres of arid public land for $1.25 an acre on the condition that you irrigated it. Historian Frederick Merk says that "95 percent of the titles obtained under this law were fraudulently obtained by or for corporations."

Ironically, just at the time when the public land banquet was in full swing, a very different idea about the public land took root: Don't give it all away; keep some public land public. It was a tiny seedling of an idea at first, but it drew support from two growing forces in American life—populism and the conservation movement. In 1872 Congress set aside some two million acres of public land in the northwest corner of the Wyoming Territory as a "pleasuring ground for all the people" and designated it Yellowstone National Park. By 1900 Congress had created three other such reserves—Yosemite, Sequoia, and Mount Rainier. And during the 1890's a couple of million acres of public forest land was set aside and the Secretary of Agriculture was empowered to regulate their use. A few years later, President Theodore Roosevelt took an even bolder initiative—he signed orders that reserved some 141 million acres of public forest land. His action touched off a political squall, instigated by the mining and lumber interests. There was even talk for a while of impeachment. But Roosevelt had the spectacle of what had happened to the forests on once-public lands in northern Michigan, Wisconsin, and Minnesota as a reminder of what could happen to the western public forests. Lumber companies had bought the land cheap, clear-cut almost every inch of the virgin forest, and then moved on, leaving behind an ungodly mess and an erosion-scoured land. (The same thing is happening today in Third World countries, especially those with tropical rain forests.)

The 141 million acres Roosevelt reserved became the foundation of the National Forest System, which now includes 191 million acres. Roosevelt also moved to save America's rapidly disappearing wildlife. He set aside some crucial habitats, especially for migratory fowl, on the public domain. Moreover, he took an important step, now long forgotten, to keep the public rangeland public. Enterprising ranchers on the Great Plains had simply fenced in vast stretches of public range as their own. Fearing that if the U.S. government continued to look the other way the ranchers would become de facto owners of the public range, Roosevelt insisted on prosecuting some outstanding offenders. Will Comstock and Bartlett Richards, owners of the huge Spade Ranch and well-known cattle barons, were taken to court and convicted for fencing in 212,000 acres of public range. Although they drew very mild sentences, their case attracted widespread publicity, and it spelled the end of this practice, which is one reason there is public rangeland today.

The disposal of public land continued, even under Roosevelt. It remained the overriding public land policy for the first three decades of this century. The idea of retaining some land, however, spread and evolved. More places were set aside in the public domain to protect their extraordinary natural beauty, places such as the Grand Canyon and Glacier National Park, or to protect their archaeological riches, places such as Mesa Verde and Chaco Canyon. In addition, the U.S. government was beginning actually to buy private land to add to the public domain in order to protect valuable public natural or cultural resources, places such as the Everglades or the Gettysburg Battlefield. The U.S. government also began to buy land that had been terribly abused by private owners in order to initiate the recovery process through reforestation, gully control, and runoff abatement. In fact, many of the National Forests in the eastern half of the United States got their start this way. While the policy of disposing of public land remained dominant until the 1930's, the idea that some land must be preserved from exploitation by private interests had gained considerable ground.

But if the government was going to retain and obtain land, how should it be managed? Here, too, ideas were evolving. It became obvious that land set aside as a wildlife refuge should be used primarily for wildlife conservation. Other uses should be allowed only if they are compatible with that objective. It made no sense, for example, to make the Okeefenokee Swamp a National Wildlife Refuge and then allow a development company to drain it, bulldoze it, and turn it into a soybean plantation. Tougher questions arose where society seemed to demand both resource conservation and exploitation. In grappling with such issues, especially on the National Forests, public land policy thinkers and managers, through trial and error, developed three basic management guideposts. *Multiple use*—decide which uses are legitimate and then regulate them so that they do not interfere with one another and see to it they do not permanently impair the land's productivity. For example, over half the flowing water in the arid West originates on the National Forests. Hence, watershed is an important use of the forests. Timber harvesting, another legitimate use, has to be controlled so that it does not cause floods downstream or pollute that water with mud (soil erosion). *Sustained yield*—manage the harvesting of renewable resources such as trees and grass so that the next generation and many thereafter have the same output from them as we had. *A fair return*—when a public resource such as oil or timber is exploited, the public should be fairly compensated, just as a private landowner would be.

The wholesale disposal of public land had pretty well petered out by 1930, even though the major giveaway laws were still on the books.

228

The Depression had dampened the demand for land, especially the depression in agriculture, which had begun well before 1929. Besides, much of the prime, economically exploitable land had already been given away.

There were, though, millions upon millions of acres of public land left. No one had taken them and they had not been set aside as National Forests, Parks, Monuments, etc. Outside of Alaska, these were mainly drylands in the eleven western states. They really were a commons, but on a much bigger scale than we usually associate with the word commons. Ever since the western livestock boom that began after the completion of the intercontinental railroad, ranchers had been grazing their sheep and cattle on this public commons, as many as they wanted and free of charge. It was a nice arrangement for the ranchers—they did not have to pay property taxes on this land because it was public; they did not have to pay rent because the U.S. government charged none; and they did not have to follow any rules or regulations because there weren't any. It was a very poor arrangement, however, for the grass. Over millennia, some very tough native grasses had adapted splendidly to the frequent droughts and the constant bullying of the sun. It was these grasses that brushed up against the bellies of the conquistadors' horses and the pioneers' oxen. Buffalo grass, blue grama, Indian ricegrass, and bunchgrasses with some marvelous names—*Sporobolus aeroides*, *Elymus condensatus*, *Andropogan scoparious*, and *Poa tenuifolia*. But for too long, too many sheep and cattle had been eating away at these grasses. The grasses that survived were thin and weak. And where they had not survived, inferior species of plants moved in, a little like scavengers moving into a city after it has been sacked by an army. Russian thistle (*Salsola kali*), which came to be known as tumbleweed, filaree, and cheatgrass. Or the ground was bare.

When the terrible drought struck in the early 1930's, millions of acres of public rangeland were in a sorry state, easy prey for windstorms. Soil swept off the rangelands, joined with soil from the parched wheatfields, and formed what was called, on the Great Plains, "black blizzards." On May 11, 1934, a terrible windstorm blew over the Great Plains and kept right on going eastward. A man in Chicago at midday said, "The sun looks like a blue steel ball." Over the whole Ohio River Valley that afternoon, the huge dust cloud blotted out the sun entirely. The next day it was over Washington, D.C., and fine yellowish dust seeped into the committee rooms of the United States Congress. The government's neglect of the public rangelands then began to end. That same year, Congress passed the Taylor Grazing Act, its very first attempt to control grazing on the western commons. This legislation withdrew millions of acres of rangeland from the major public land disposal programs, including the Enlarged Homestead Acts of 1909 and 1916, and established a system of grazing allotments and grazing fees.

The Administration of Franklin Delano Roosevelt took a number of other steps as well to retain and extend the public domain. The President signed executive orders that closed virtually all the rest of the public domain to homesteading, real or bogus. And the Administration launched an aggressive effort to buy up badly abused private land. Some of the worst overgrazed rangeland, public and private, was purchased, creating National Grasslands. Badly eroded forest land in southern Ohio, Indiana, and Illinois as well as in Appalachia and the Piedmont was purchased, and the Civilian Conservation Corps (CCC) was put to work on it. The idea of keeping public land and conserving public resources had now fully replaced disposal and neglect as a national policy. During the 1940's and 1950's, the conservation programs of the New Deal were consolidated. Only the CCC was disbanded. This was a period of stability for the public domain. Of course, not all public land problems had been solved; conflicts between different uses still existed and probably always will. But by the early 1960's the question of how to manage the National Forests, Parks, Monuments, and wildlife refuges was spelled out in various laws such as the Multiple Use–Sustained Yield Act for the National Forest System.

Doubts still lingered, though, about what to do with the public lands that had not been set aside as National Forests, Parks, etc. In the 1960's, the Congress established the Public Land Law Review Commission (PLLRC) to decide once and for all what to do with those lands. In 1970, after several years of testimony and deliberation, the PLLRC issued its report, *One Third of the Nation*. Its 137 specific recommendations can be boiled down to: (1) keep most of the public land, allowing only "modest disposals"; and (2) manage them for multiple use and sustained yield.

In 1976 Congress passed the Federal Land Policy and Management Act (FLPMA for short), and it stated that "the public lands be retained in Federal ownership, unless as a result of the land use planning procedure provided for in this Act, it is determined that disposal of *a particular parcel* will serve the national interest . . ." (emphasis added). The law

requires "harmonious and coordinated management of the various resources without permanent impairment of the productivity of the land
and the quality of the environment."

WILDERNESS LOST

For nearly three years, James G. Watt served as Secretary of the Interior,
chief steward of most of our public lands and resources. Controversies
swarmed about him from his first day to his last. He wanted to make
more land and more resources available for development. He was neither
tentative nor stealthy in his approach. He ploughed ahead until he could
go no further and then he backed up and tried again. He had little
respect for those who did not agree with him and often questioned the
motives of those who actively opposed him. James Watt became a
symbol and a spokesman for the reaction against environmentalism.

A great deal has been said and written about Watt, so much that
he hardly needs introduction. A brief sketch will do: He was born and
raised in Wyoming and graduated from the University of Wyoming
Law School. Then for fifteen years he worked in Washington, first as
an aide to Wyoming Senator Milward Simpson, then as a lobbyist for
the Chamber of Commerce, and finally as a middle level political appointee at the Department of the Interior.

When Watt left Washington, Joseph Coors selected him to direct
the Mountain States Legal Foundation, which Coors had just founded.
He became a leading advocate for western energy, ranching, and development interests battling against federal environmental restrictions.
The purpose of the Foundation, Watt testified, is to "defend individuals
and the private sector from illegal and excessive bureaucratic regulation.
The foundation is dedicated to the values and concepts of individual
freedom, our right to private property, and the private enterprise system."

He saw his mission as a battle in which the future of the country
was at stake. His opponents were the enemy, and in them he saw many
evils. Environmentalists in particular he perceived as dangerous and
subversive, suggesting they sought to weaken America and to undermine
freedom. He called them extremists and likened them to Nazis. The
strength of his political convictions was enhanced by his "born again"

Christian fundamentalism. James Watt burned with the ardor of a conviction unchecked by doubt.

At the urging of Joseph Coors, Ronald Reagan selected Watt to head the Interior Department and to chair the Cabinet Council on Natural Resources. There was an anecdote about his appointment that Watt relished. He retold it often to reporters. At one of his very first meetings with the new President, he had ticked off the things he wanted to do as Secretary of the Interior and reminded the President how controversial his agenda would be. There was bound to be flak, lots of flak. Was the President prepared for it? Would he support Watt when it came? Ronald Reagan looked him square in the eye and replied, "Sic 'em."

That is what he did. Unlike Anne Gorsuch, he knew his way around his agency very well. He had spent fifteen years in Washington, half of them at Interior. Unlike Gorsuch, he chose his own top aides. He was quickly confirmed and started right in on the process he described as making the bureaucrats "yield to my blows." He quickly fired, demoted, or transferred employees who did not share his views. It was early in the Administration. Resistance was swept aside. "We are going to get ahold of this thing fast," he said in a speech. "If a personality is giving you a problem, we're going to get rid of the problem or the personality, whichever is faster." One campaign he began early was the effort to open up wilderness lands for development.

Of our land, only about 7 percent has been designated wilderness or is being considered for wilderness designation. But the stewards Ronald Reagan appointed to tend our land seem preoccupied with the notion that there is too much wilderness. Sometimes they almost seemed possessed by an atavistic fear of wilderness as if it were the looming ominous threat it was 200 years ago.

Ronald Reagan came to office believing that a significant part of the nation's mineral wealth and energy resources had been "locked up" on the federal lands by wilderness or other environmental restrictions. The basis for this belief appears to be an article published in 1975 in the *Mining Congress Journal,* which reported that two-thirds of the federal lands have been "effectively withdrawn" from mineral development. The energy industry, which at that time was trying to explain to the American consumer why their prices were going through the roof, picked up this report and expanded upon it. Energy company "public service" ads in magazines and newspapers and on television warned that

232

much of the federal land had been "effectively withdrawn" from coal and oil and gas development.

Congress directed its Office of Technology Assessment (OTA) to look into the matter. OTA's independent analysis, which went little noticed, showed that in fact about 13 percent of the federal lands had been permanently withdrawn from mineral and energy resource development. OTA traced these withdrawals back to their origins. Interestingly, over half had been withdrawn for non-wilderness or non-environmental reasons. Many had been withdrawn for use by the military—it is not a good idea to have an oil well or a coal strip mine in the middle of a missile firing range, for instance.

Nevertheless, the contention that much of the federal lands had been withdrawn from mineral and energy resource development for wilderness and other environmental reasons lived on. It was useful ammunition in the battle for the hearts and minds of the American consumer—and voter. Presidential candidate Ronald Reagan repeated it several times during the campaign, including during a televised debate with President Jimmy Carter. It became an article of faith for Reagan and for the mining and oil and gas industries.*

The Reagan Administration seems to have miscalculated the amount of popular support for wilderness. In its push to turn more of our public land and resources over to private economic interests—the oil and gas, coal, hard rock mineral, timber, ranching, and off-road vehicle industries—the Reagan Administration did anticipate some resistance on Capitol Hill. Hence, it sought to accomplish its objective through a kind of bureaucratic sleight-of-hand. Rather than trying to change the law, the Administration concentrated on trying to change the procedures and regulations created to implement the law. But the Administration's tactics did not escape public notice, especially when it came to wilderness.

A career employee in the Department of the Interior in Washington observes: "These people [the Reagan appointees] are not political bozos. . . . But they have a blind spot when it comes to some issues such

---

*Further studies have demonstrated that, even if you assume that all of the land under study for wilderness designation is actually added to the existing National Wilderness Preservation System by the Congress (which will not happen), then our total wilderness would contain less than 5 percent of the nation's potential coal, natural gas, or oil resources and less than 5 percent of its major hard rock mineral resources, except uranium. It would contain slightly more than 5 percent of the nation's potential uranium resources.

as wilderness. Every time they've launched one of their anti-wilderness initiatives, they've been genuinely surprised at the fuss they've stirred up. Even in Wyoming. I mean, when you have the entire Wyoming congressional delegation, conservative Republicans to the core, proposing legislation to prohibit mineral and resource development in Wyoming wildernesses, then you know some of the folks back home are getting on their case."

The Reagan Administration's anti-wilderness moves have inspired a surprisingly widespread defense of wilderness in the press—from the urbane *Esquire* magazine to the small-town *Contra Costa Times*. In *Esquire*, Geoffrey Norman wrote that in a land without wilderness "too many kids grow up wanting to be Mick Jagger or the president of IBM or the hottest hand in town at Pac-Man." The *Contra Costa Times*, in Walnut Creek, California, editorialized that wildernesses have a "very real economic value" as living gene banks. "Biologists are just beginning to unravel the secrets of the cell and the genetic coding every creature bears. . . . The living things which have taken millions of years to evolve may soon become of immense value in ways we scarcely now imagine. That's a value in preserving wilderness quite aside from the soul-refreshing sense of peace and perspective our harried, urban populations can glean from these untrammeled spaces."

One of the strongest supporters of wilderness in the U.S. Congress and one of the staunchest critics of the Reagan Administration on the issue is Rep. Jim Weaver. He has been elected four times from a district in southwest Oregon, most recently garnering more than 60 percent of the vote. Weaver's success is interesting because his primary constituency is rural blue collar: "The lumber workers live up the draws. . . . They like to hunt and fish, but they do not consider themselves environmentalists." For years, western conservative Republicans and Democrats have portrayed wildernesses as areas set aside for the enjoyment of a tiny elite—those with the leisure time and money to back-pack into them—set aside at the expense of workers who need the jobs that would have been created by development of the areas or who want to drive their off-road vehicles on that land. Weaver, who unabashedly describes himself as "a populist," finds working-class people support wilderness once the facts are known. "The lumber industry says a lot of timber is being locked up in the wilderness system. So when I go into one of those lumber towns and someone at a meeting asks about wilderness, I call for a show of hands. How many people here are in favor of setting aside 50 percent of the public timberland in the State of Oregon for wilderness? Well, nobody raises their hands and you can hear some grumbling. How about 25 percent? A few hands go up. How about 15 percent? More hands. How about 10 percent? Almost every hand in the room is up now. Then I explain to them that 1 percent of the timberland in Oregon is now in the wilderness system and that I am sponsoring legislation to put another 2 percent into wilderness." The Reagan Administration is opposing that legislation.

Overall, the Reagan Administration has concentrated on (1) opening wildernesses and potential wildernesses to oil and gas leasing, and (2) cutting back the amount of land under consideration for wilderness designation. The Yates Petroleum trespass story is just one illustration. Secretary of the Interior James Watt issued oil and gas leases for some quite spectacular wilderness candidate areas, like the Palisades in Targhee and Bridger-Teton National Forests in Idaho and Wyoming and the Deep Creek area in Lewis and Clark National Forest, near Glacier National Park in Montana. Most of these initiatives are being challenged in the courts by conservation groups, and there they are stalled at this writing. Oil and gas development cannot begin until the courts rule. In addition, as already noted, Watt issued two leases for the Capitan Wilderness in the Lincoln National Forest in New Mexico, but the companies involved have agreed in an out-of-court settlement with the Sierra Club Legal Defense Fund to surrender those leases.

As a lawyer in the Solicitor's Office of the Department of the Interior at the time the Reagan Administration assumed power, Dale Goble had an inside view of the Administration's efforts to undermine the wilderness designation process. The law requires that the BLM inventory the public land it looks after in order to identify those with wilderness characteristics. This was accomplished in the late 1970's and, by the time Reagan took over, the BLM had some 24.3 million acres in Wilderness Study Areas (WSAs).

In July 1981, the Secretary of the Interior launched a major initiative to amputate, on technical grounds, most of the WSAs. At the time, Interior Deputy Secretary Donald Hodel, who has since moved up to become Secretary of Energy, was the Department's chief wilderness surgeon.

The task of explaining to Hodel that what he was trying to do was neither legal nor administratively practical fell to Dale Goble. "One of the major characteristics of a wilderness, under the law, is that it be a roadless area of at least 5,000 acres. Now the law itself does not define 'roadless' or a 'road,' but Congress's intent is made clear in the law's legislative history. What Hodel wanted to do was not consistent with Congress's intent. For example, he proposed dropping a 117,000-acre area in the California desert from wilderness study status because it had a half-mile road running into it at one point, a so-called 'cherry stem.' That was ridiculous. He also sought to expand the definition of a road to include even a jeep track." Furthermore, to apply these new technical criteria would require re-inventorying the 24.3 million acres in the WSAs. That, Goble calculated, would take every BLM field employee one full year of work and cost about $125 million to accomplish.

Hodel heeded his advice, according to Goble, "probably because of the extra cost involved; the legal problems didn't seem to faze any of them." But Goble was branded "a troublemaker, not a team player."

Then Secretary Watt and his advisers decided the President could, with a stroke of his pen, simply release large areas from wilderness study status. But the Congress had not given the White House that authority; rather, it had instructed the Executive Branch to: identify areas technically eligible for wilderness designation; study those areas to assess the trade-offs between wilderness values and exploitable resources; and manage them to preserve their wilderness character until Congress decides whether or not to designate them wildernesses. By releasing areas eligible for wilderness designation from wilderness study status, the White House would prevent Congress from making that decision.

Goble was called upon, by his immediate superior, Alexander Good (the man who signed the Yates Petroleum letter), to write a legal opinion on the Presidential release strategy, and he did. Goble saw his job as a government attorney in straightforward terms: If your boss asks for your legal opinion about X and you think X is not legal, you should tell him so, even though he may want very badly to do it. So Goble told Good directly—and Secretary Watt via Good—that what they wanted to do was not legal. Indeed, he told them that the release maneuver would not even pass the red face test—"You couldn't get up in court and argue the case for it without getting a red face."

"At the time the release maneuver was proposed," Goble recalls, "the Administration people in Interior wanted just a few of the wilderness study areas to go to Congress for its consideration, the ones none of the special economic interests cared about. I was told, 'We don't want

236

most of these areas getting to Congress because then compromises and deals will have to be made.' "

Soon thereafter, Goble was transferred out of the Solicitor's Office in the main Department of the Interior building to the Geological Survey, 25 miles away in Reston, Virginia. He was informed that to reenter the Interior building he would need the permission of the Solicitor himself. Meanwhile, Alexander Good wrote the opinion, a favorable one. Alexander Good, a conservative Republican from southern California, is a Reagan appointee.

On December 30, 1982, while Congress was out of town, Secretary Watt released 660,000 acres of public land from wilderness consideration. The press dubbed it "Watt's midnight raid on the wilderness," and members of Congress exploded in outrage. Watt was undeterred. By mid-August 1983, he had released a total of 1.7 million acres from wilderness consideration (and protection). Members of Congress, several states, and environmental organizations were challenging his actions in court, but Dale Goble was gainfully employed elsewhere. The day he left the government, he posted the following announcement in several places in the Department of the Interior where it could be read:

DALE D. GOBLE

IS PLEASED TO ANNOUNCE

that he has accepted a position with

THE UNIVERSITY OF IDAHO COLLEGE OF LAW

and

that he is no longer obligated

to create legal-sounding lies allowing

JAMES GAIUS WATT,

his cronies, henchmen and flunkies

to break the law,

rape the land and

give the public's resources away.

As disagreeable as Dale Goble's experiences were with the Reagan Administration's Department of the Interior over the wilderness issue, he had an even worse one involving litigation brought by Sagebrush Rebellion, Inc.

The case began in 1980 after the Department of the Interior

released an environmental impact statement (EIS) on a proposed expansion of the Snake River Birds of Prey National Conservation Area into adjoining public land, managed by the BLM. The Snake River Canyon, southwest of Boise, Idaho, contains one of the largest concentrations of golden eagles, prairie falcons, and hawks—red-tailed, marsh, and Swainson's—in North America. Sagebrush Rebellion, Inc., representing agribusiness interests in southern Idaho, sued, charging that the EIS was inadequate. The proposed action would withdraw the land from possible use for irrigated agriculture. Under the Desert Land Act and the Carey Act, the last remnants of the U.S. government's old policy of disposing of public land very cheaply, there are pending applications for 100,000 acres of land in the addition to the Birds of Prey Area. Plowing up this brush and grassland would wipe out the Townsend ground squirrels and jackrabbits upon which the eagles, falcons, and hawks feed. Later in 1980, Secretary of the Interior Cecil D. Andrus made his decision, issuing an order adding 483,000 acres of land to the Birds of Prey Area. He said we had protected the birds of prey's bedroom or nesting area, now we had to make sure they had a dining room. Uses of the land other than irrigated agriculture, such as livestock grazing and recreation, may continue under the Andrus order because they do not endanger the birds of prey's habitat.

After the change of Administration, the plaintiffs filed an amended complaint in what was now *Sagebrush Rebellion, Inc. v. Watt*, challenging the withdrawal. Dale Goble and another attorney in the Solicitor's Office were called on to draft an answer to the new complaint. They did so and sent it on to Alexander Good. A short while later, Goble was summoned to Good's office and informed that the response he had drafted was "unacceptable." When Goble asked why, Good replied that "Runft had found it totally unacceptable." This was a curious bit of information because Runft, or Mr. John L. Runft, happened to be the attorney for Sagebrush Rebellion, Inc. It was a little like a football coach being handed back his game plan before the big game and told the opposition coach doesn't like it. Good even supplied Goble with a list of the points which Runft found objectionable. Goble and the other government attorney reworked the response, sharpening as best they could the government's (not Runft's) case. In the midst of all this, a letter which an Idaho congressman had written to Secretary of the Interior James Watt showed up in Goble's in-box. The letter thanked Secretary Watt for meeting with a group of citizens from southern

238

Idaho, among them John L. Runft, to discuss public land issues. "Isn't it a small world?" Goble mused.

The second draft was also found unacceptable and Good gave it to another attorney in the Solicitor's Office. Watt et al. were thwarted, though, and this time it was not by the Congress or the courts. The Justice Department had gotten wind of Interior's dealings with Runft and threatened to withdraw its representation of Secretary Watt if Interior continued to deal with the attorney for the plaintiffs behind Justice's back. This led Interior Department officials to question whether Justice "was on board," and attorneys in the Interior Department's Solicitor's Office were set to work writing defenses of the Administration's federal land policies for the benefit of the Justice Department.

To date at least, the U.S. government is holding firm in the *Sagebrush Rebellion, Inc. v. Watt* case; it has not caved in. The court is considering whether to allow the National Audubon Society to join in as a defendant in the case. Joining Sagebrush Rebellion, Inc.'s counsel is Mountain States Legal Foundation, James Watt's previous employer.

Another threat to the wilderness study process, unlike Watt's "midnight raid," attracted little public notice. John B. Crowell, Assistant Secretary of Agriculture, the man President Reagan has put in charge of the Forest Service and our National Forests, decided to reexamine all the wilderness recommendations that the Forest Service had already made.

The Forest Service's wilderness study process, called Roadless Area Review and Evaluation (RARE), has creaked along for almost a decade. RARE I was replaced by RARE II, and then RARE II hit a snag in the courts. The State of California and the Natural Resources Defense Council sued the U.S. government, arguing that the Forest Service had inadequately evaluated 46 areas within that state which it had designated "non-wilderness." The state did not challenge the areas which the Forest Service had designated "wilderness." The court ruled that the Forest Service had acted improperly in rejecting many areas for wilderness protection. But Crowell turned the decision on its head. He scrapped all RARE II recommendations, including the seven million acres recommended for wilderness, although the court had found only the "non-wilderness" recommendations illegal. All RARE II lands (62 million acres) will be restudied in what has been described as "RARE

II ½," or "medium RARE." That gives the Reagan Administration an opportunity to lop off some of RARE II "wilderness" recommendations and to build roads into roadless "non-wilderness" RARE II areas for timber cutting, thereby disqualifying them from future wilderness designation. In fact, Crowell's plans call for the harvesting of some 1.5 billion board feet of timber in such roadless areas during fiscal 1984.

Before Crowell sent them back for restudy, the RARE II wilderness recommendations were under attack in other places besides California because some outstanding wilderness areas had been overlooked. One such area is the Middle Santiem on the Willamette National Forest in Oregon. The Middle Santiem represents one of the last expanses of old-growth Douglas fir forest left in the Pacific Northwest—20,000 acres of roadless land in the foothills of the Cascades. It has escaped the bulldozers and chain saws so far because its soils are subject to avalanche, massive slumps, and earthflows, especially after road building. Roads are costly and precarious in the Middle Santiem; they have a way of disappearing after heavy rains. Nonetheless, the Forest Service is currently planning to build roads into this area and allow clear-cutting. So much for the wilderness. A good many of the Douglas fir *(Pseudotsuga menziesii)* trees in the Middle Santiem are over 200 years old, 200 feet tall, and five feet in girth. And the taxpayers will pay for the roads, subsidizing the destruction of the ancient forest.

Crowell's zeal matches Watt's, but his style is subtler. Unlike Watt, he does not attract attention to himself or his policies with public utterances about the end of the world, the Holocaust, or the Beach Boys, or jokes about race and religion. Nor does Crowell seek confrontations with conservationists. Rather, he invites them into his office for coffee and a chat. His image may be soft, but his policies are harsh.

GETTING OUT THE CUT

John Crowell was vice-president and general counsel for Louisiana Pacific when Ronald Reagan named him Assistant Secretary for Natural Resources and Environment in the Department of Agriculture. Louisiana Pacific, one of the giants in the lumber industry, buys more timber from the National Forests than any other company. Crowell named as his deputy Douglas MacCleery, the chief lobbyist in Washington, D.C., for the National Forest Products Association. Together, Crowell and

MacCleery are setting policies that will affect our National Forests long after they have left government.

The Forest Service budget for fiscal 1984 provides a road map to where Assistant Secretary Crowell is headed with our forests. There will be more money than ever to support timber production: $193 million for the preparation and administration of timber sales, *up* 8 percent from the last non-Reagan budget (fiscal 1981); $211 million for Forest Service road construction, *up* 4 percent; plus a $291 million credit for lumber companies to build roads on the National Forests, *up* 38 percent. And there will be much less for recreation and conservation: $94 million for recreational and cultural resources, *down* 12 percent from fiscal 1981; $34 million for wildlife, *down* 16 percent; $28 million for soil and water conservation, *down* 42 percent; $8 million for trail maintenance, *down* 43 percent.

The shift toward spending for exploitation and development is a theme that runs through the budgets of all the federal agencies that manage public resources. All tilt toward the production of marketable resources and away from the conservation of non-marketable resources. The Administration values resources that have monetary value—oil, coal, timber, etc.—more than those that do not—golden eagles, clear streams, forest trails, etc. This bias runs beneath all the Administration's public resource policies like a warped floor beneath a pool table and explains why so many of the taxpayers' balls end up in those few pockets.

The Forest Service budget provides funds to build 12,000 miles of new roads in the National Forests, primarily to accommodate logging equipment, but not enough to maintain one-third of the existing trails in the National Forests, used primarily for hiking. Over 36,000 miles of trails in the National Forests will deteriorate; some will become impassable. But public use of hiking trails in the National Forests increased 99 percent over the last decade. Today hikers spend more than 12.3 million visitor-days per year in the National Forests. The trails have become overcrowded. More, not fewer, are needed. The same holds for campgrounds. Tens of thousands of Americans are turned away each year from campgrounds in National Forests such as the Hoosier in southern Indiana and the Wayne in southern Ohio because they are full up. Total recreational pressures are mounting on our forests, with all uses (hiking, camping, hunting, fishing, etc.) now exceeding a quarter million visitor-days per year. Twice as many Americans visit National Forests each year as visit the more publicized National Parks.

241

The recreational pressures on forests near big urban sprawls are acute. One such sprawl is the one that stretches along the east face of the Rockies in Colorado—from Fort Collins down through Boulder, Denver, and Colorado Springs. The nearby National Forests—the Roosevelt, Arapahoe, Pike, and Isabel—are, on long holiday weekends, starting to resemble New York City's Central Park. The same is true for the forests near the Los Angeles basin. So it really makes no sense for the Reagan Administration to beggar recreation in order to pay for increased support of timber production, especially at a time when the market seems a lot less eager to produce public timber than Mr. Crowell is to sell it.

Throughout the first three Reagan years, the gap between timber sold by the Forest Service and timber harvested by the lumber companies has widened. Today the backlog of sold but uncut public timber comes to about 40 billion board feet, almost a four-year supply.

On the National Forests of the Northwest, there are approximately one billion board feet of public timber that has been sold, but not removed. That timber was sold before the recession hit the wood market —when Douglas fir was going for $450 per thousand board feet. Then came the recession and Douglas fir dropped to $80 per thousand board feet. Some of the lumber companies who had bought the timber found they couldn't afford to remove it at those prices. Under Forest Service regulations, they do not actually have to pay the U.S. government for the timber until it is removed from the National Forest. They have sought relief from the Administration, which has agreed to extend their contracts, giving them another five years to harvest, remove, and pay for the timber they purchased more than two years ago. At stake are contracts worth about $4.5 billion to us, the owners of that timber. And, because the Administration will not charge the companies interest, this timber industry relief measure will cost the U.S. Treasury about $500 million annually. Louisiana-Pacific, by the way, has more than 1.5 billion board feet of public timber under contracts worth $212.5 million. If the Administration had not extended the contracts, the company would have had to pay immediately about 20 percent of that amount, or, if the Administration had charged interest, it would have had to pay about $4 million a year.

Despite the huge backlog of sold but uncut and unpaid-for timber, Crowell plans to sell even more public timber in 1984: 11.6 billion board feet, up 600,000 from the previous year. As a consequence, timber sale

and production costs will consume over half the Forest Service's budget
—seven times more than recreation and watershed and wildlife conservation. If the U.S. government recovered its sale and production costs,
such a policy might at least be comprehensible. But it will not.

Over half the National Forests spend more to produce timber than
they can sell it for. Take the San Juan National Forest in southern
Colorado, for instance. There, in fiscal 1981, the Forest Service spent
$3.5 million in total on timber production—sale administration plus
reforestation plus roads—and its receipts from timber sales totaled
$461,158. An analysis of timber production costs versus receipts for
three other National Forests in Colorado—Grand Mesa, Uncompahgre,
and Gunnison—over a five-year period reveals that, for every dollar of
taxpayer money invested in timber production, we got 35 cents in
return. The Reagan Administration inherited this policy of subsidizing
timber production on our forests, but Crowell has not moved to eliminate the subsidies; he has pushed for increased production and more
subsidies.

Crowell proposed to double timber production from the National
Forests by the 1990's. He and spokesmen for the lumber industry argue
that the American consumer will be the big beneficiary. Increased output from the National Forests, they say, will enhance the nation's wood
supply and thereby lower consumer costs, especially when it comes to
buying a new home. There are a couple of problems with this argument.
For one thing, only one-tenth of the nation's timber production comes
from the National Forests. Any large increase in production from the
National Forests will simply be offset by a decline in output from private
forests. The overall effect on lumber prices will not be dramatic. For
another, lumber costs account for only about 15 percent of the cost of
a typical wood frame house. Other factors account for the other 85
percent—land prices, interest rates, non-wood material costs, and labor
costs.

Darius Adams, an economist with Oregon State University, and
Richard Haynes, an economist with the Forest Service, did a computer
simulation of a doubling of output from the National Forests to assess
its economic effects. Their analysis shows that private forest owners,
responding to the lower price for standing commercial timber induced
by the increased supply, will reduce their cut by over half. Therefore,
a doubling of the National Forest harvest will mean a *net* increase in
the nation's timber supply of about one percent. By the time the results

243

of the reduced timber prices trickle down to the consumer, lumber and plywood costs will decline about one-eighth of one percent as a result of a doubling of production from the National Forests. It amounts to a discount of about $100 on the cost of a $75,000 wood frame house.

On the other hand, some parts of the forest product industry will profit handsomely. Assuming that the increased output comes from the Douglas fir forests in northern California, Oregon, and Washington— the plan advocated by Crowell—it will increase the profits of Douglas fir lumber producers by 12 percent and plywood producers by 8 percent because of the subsidies built into the production of timber in the National Forests. The companies best situated to reap increased profits will be those like Louisiana-Pacific that rely more on the public timber and less on privately held forests. Companies such as Weyerhaeuser that depend on their own forest lands will see the value of their timber decline. Smaller lumber companies that cut timber on their own land or the land of other private owners and then sell it to the big companies will be badly hurt by the increased production from the National Forests.

To double production, Crowell plans massive sales of the old-growth Douglas fir forest of the Pacific Northwest. The marginal stands in the dry Rocky Mountain states will not yield enough timber soon enough to meet Crowell's goal.

In the narrowest economic sense, old-growth Douglas fir is prime timber. But the massive harvest planned by Crowell reverses a policy that has guided the scheduling of timber sales for over 60 years: nondeclining even flow, sometimes known as nondeclining yields. What this means is simply that you do not harvest more timber this year than you can harvest next year or 25 years from now or in perpetuity. Nondeclining even flow is a fundamental forest conservation measure. It insures that some wood will be available to those who come after us, and it helps to maintain the ecological continuity of the forest.

It is not possible to clear-cut an old-growth Douglas fir forest, such as the ones that grow on our land between the Pacific coast and the west side of the Klamath Mountains in northern California and the Cascades in Oregon and Washington, and maintain a nondeclining even flow. These so-called old-growth surplus forests have more board feet per acre than the second-growth forests that replace them will have for many, many years. That is why many big lumber companies have lobbied for years against the nondeclining even flow policy—the more board feet per acre they can harvest, the greater their profits. The National Forest Management Act of 1976 opened a small crack in the nondeclining even flow policy:

. . . in order to meet overall multiple use objectives, the Secretary of Agriculture may establish an allowable sale quantity for a decade which departs from the projected long-term average sale quantity that would otherwise be established; provided further, that any such planned departure must be consistent with the multiple-use management objectives of the land management plan. . . .

Crowell is trying to drive a juggernaut through that crack. And woe to anyone in the Forest Service standing in the way. The Mount Hood National Forest staff in Oregon drafted a forest plan that favored reduced timber harvests. They were summarily ordered by MacCleery to go back, start from scratch, and do it all over again. On January 19, 1983, Crowell sent a memo to the chief of the Forest Service warning that multiple use may be "unduly impacting efficient use of priced resources." He wrote: "I continue to feel that there is much more compatibility between economically optimal levels of timber production and important environmental values than is often assumed, even by professional foresters." He then warned that "appropriate changes will be made" unless the draft plans "begin to improve significantly soon." There is no doubt in anyone's mind in the Forest Service what Crowell means by "appropriate changes" or "improve significantly." If you come up with a forest plan that does not significantly increase the "allowable cut," you will find yourself counting caribou in Alaska or, worse, at a desk job in Washington.

Most of the line officers in the Forest Service are professional foresters, and they tend to be predisposed toward timber production above all other uses of the forest. "Getting out the cut," it is called. As one forester who used to work with the Forest Service explains, "It's partially education. I got a degree from one of the best schools of forestry in the U.S., but I had just a one-semester course in wildlife management, one in soil science, and none in hydrology. The whole emphasis was on growing and harvesting commercial timber. And, it's partially organizational conditioning. If you want to move up the career ladder in the Forest Service, you'd better get out the cut. In addition, though, there's a strong macho element to timber production and all that it entails. This accounts, I think, for foresters' genuine enthusiasm for aerial spraying of herbicides—I've heard them say, 'Let's lay down some T'—that's 2,4,5-T, a very toxic chemical. It also explains the gusto they bring to road building and clear-cutting. The conservation-oriented tasks offer no such emotional charges. It's really like war except no one is shooting at you."

And yet, as Crowell's memo suggests, he is meeting some resistance even from among professional foresters in the agency. They have trouble with Crowell's objectives because they do not square with the rules or with reality. The Forest Service professionals are the ones who have to do the cost-benefit analyses; they have to come up with the justifications for the departures from nondeclining even flow as well as for the harvesting of timber at a loss. This means confecting some very dubious, sometimes even silly numbers and cranking them into the computer. One draft forest plan, for example, assumes considerable recreational "benefits" from the increased number of clear-cuts on the forest because they "open up" the forest for camping. As one forest planner quipped, "Presto, we created a whole legion of heretofore nonexistent people who love camping on clear-cuts." Another plan projects that an increase in fishery values of the forest will accompany increased timber production, although fish biologists point out that the exact opposite will in fact happen. Another plan makes the production of economically marginal timber cost-effective by assuming that the price of timber will double in this decade, although there is no evidence to support such an assumption.

The frustrations of the Forest Service planners bubbled to the surface at a meeting of the Western Forest Economists in early May 1983 near Mt. Hood, Oregon. Andy Stahl, a former Forest Service consultant and lobbyist for the Associated Oregon Loggers, who is now a forester for the National Wildlife Federation, describes what happened: "Doug MacCleery organized what was called 'a fluid session' after the regular meetings were over. It was one of those speak-your-mind-without-fear-of-reprisal sessions. The fluid was alcohol. Well, MacCleery found himself facing about 50 very disgruntled Forest Service planners—economists and systems analysts. These are mostly young, well-educated people, hired by the Forest Service over the past five or six years to make the computerized planning process work. They jumped down his throat. They told him they were fed up with having to create bullshit—numbers that had no relationship to reality—and with the whole politicization of what was supposed to be an objective evaluation of management alternatives."

But it is clear, Stahl adds, that "unlike Watt, Crowell and Mac-Cleery understand that you cannot simply announce you are going to rape this acre of land—you have to say, 'As a result of our rational and analytical planning process, we are going to rape this acre of land.'"

While Crowell intensifies the pressure to cut more timber on the National Forests in the Northwest, output from *private* forest lands in that region is declining. It peaked in 1976 at 8.4 billion board feet and is expected to decline steadily to one-third that amount by the year 2030. This is particularly noteworthy because some of the most productive timberland in the Pacific Northwest is private land. The Forest Service-managed land tends to be that which was left over after the big land grab by the lumber companies in the late nineteenth century—forest land in the Cascades and the Coastal Range mountains, which are steeper and harder to log. The output from the private forest land is declining both because timber companies did not manage for nondeclining yield and because some lumber companies lose interest in the land after the big mature trees have been sawed down. In western Oregon alone, there are now some three million acres of private, cut-over forest land that is not being managed for timber production. When Georgia-Pacific, one of the giants in the lumber business, moved its corporate headquarters from Portland, Oregon, to Atlanta, Georgia, it epitomized to people in the Northwest, such as Congressman Weaver, that company's "cut-and-run policy."

Still, the question remains: Why not cut down the old-growth Douglas fir forests, which now constitute only five percent of the Pacific Northwest's land base, and reap the economic benefits? After all, that is what we did to the great climax hardwood forests in the East, to the mature pine forests across northern Michigan, Wisconsin, and Minnesota, and to the old-growth Douglas fir on private land in the Pacific Northwest.

The best answers yet to that question come from the Forest Service itself. *Ecological Characteristics of Old-Growth Douglas Fir Forests*, written by scientists with the Forest Service, the BLM, Oregon State University, and the University of Alaska, ties together many pieces of research. Although technical in nature, their report presents a clear, even loving portrait of its subject: "Some general attributes of an old-growth forest are immediately apparent to an observer with even a moderate background in natural history. Trees typically vary in species [Douglas fir, hemlock, spruce, and cedar] and size; dominant specimens are truly impressive. Some large species differ in color and texture as well as in size. The multilayer canopy produces a heavily filtered light, and the feeling of shade is accentuated by shafts of sunlight on clear days. The understory of shrubs, herbs, and tree seedlings is often moderate and is almost always patchy in distribution and abundance. Numerous logs, often large and in various stages of decay, litter the forest floor, creating some travel routes for wildlife and blocking others. . . . It is quiet; few birds or mammals are seen or heard except perhaps the melody of a winter wren *(Troglodytes troglodytes)*, the faint song of golden-crowned kinglets *(Regulus satrapa)* in tree canopies, or a chick-oree *(Tamiasciurus danglasi)*.

"Small to moderate streams flowing through old growth are shielded from the sun by the canopies of adjacent trees. The smallest streams may be choked with organic debris; as size and volume of streams increases, clear, cool water runs through gravel beds behind old log dams and spills into plunge pools. . . ."

The old-growth forest nourishes the land. In its great canopy live lichens, especially *Lobaria oregania*, which extract nitrogen from the air and inject it into the trees. Then through leaching, litter, and decomposition, this absolutely essential nutrient is distributed to the whole forest, most importantly to the soil. No artificial fertilizers are needed here. Young-growth forests, on the other hand, have no such nitrogen-fixers. Also, the many rotting logs on the old-growth forests' floor recycle other nutrients such as phosphate and calcium to the soil. The water stored in the great canopy—about 264,000 gallons per acre—moderates temperature extremes winter and summer. And it sustains the trees during prolonged periods of drought.

The roots of these giant trees anchor the land. This is a vital function in the Pacific Northwest where many of the sloping soils are highly susceptible to what scientists call "mass erosion processes." There is creep—the slow downslope movement of the soil mantle. There is slump—the slipping of a block of earth over a broadly concave surface. There is earthflow—the glide downslope of broken-up soil material. Slumps often turn into earthflows. There are debris avalanches—rapid, shallow-soil slides down hills. Logging operations—specifically roads and clear-cutting—can set off one or another of these mass movements, depending on the local geology. Enormous quantities of soil that took centuries to build ends up in streambeds where it smothers the salmon and trout eggs that have been laid in the clean gravel—literally shutting off the embryo fishes' oxygen supply. The eroding soil muddies the rivers, increasing their destructive force during floods.

Old-growth forests produce superb water. The water is clear because the soil stays put and it is soft because the forest holds onto its minerals. It is cool because of the shade provided by the forest's canopy. And the forest supplies the water with an abundance of organic nutrients so that a rich variety of aquatic insects and vertebrates, such as cutthroat trout, tailed frogs, and Pacific giant salamanders, thrive.

The watershed and fishery values of old-growth forests, unlike board feet of timber, do not lend themselves to quantification in dollars. Hence, they seldom get their due. Crowell did not invent this problem, but his pressure to make timber production supreme has severely aggravated it. What dollar figure does one affix to the cool, clear water flowing from an old-growth Douglas fir forest? Or even to a coho salmon? The latter does have a value in the market, but does that dollar figure reflect its full value to an angler? The arbitrary numbers which are created to solve this problem always devalue such resources; they never seem to incorporate their intangible worth.

The same problem arises with wildlife. The old-growth Douglas fir forest provides some rather uncommon creatures with a home. These include the northern spotted owl, the silver-haired bat, the northern flying squirrel, and the red tree vole. Biologists tell us that if we destroy the old-growth forests we will destroy these creatures. A pair of spotted owls with young needs a one-mile radius of old-growth forest around their nest to survive. They eat flying squirrels, snowshoe hares, and dusky-footed woodrats. In one of his speeches, Crowell asked, "How many pairs of owls can we afford to protect?" He claimed that the spotted owl management plan which he had inherited would cost about $3.6 billion in lost timber sales. But we do not *lose* the resource if it is not harvested now—it is still there for future use if we so choose. And the market doesn't *lose* $3.6 billion worth of timber—if there is the demand, it is available elsewhere and can be produced from private forest land.

Crowell's plans are bitterly opposed by many professionals in the Northwest. Jim Hutchinson, a fish biologist in the Oregon Department of Fish and Wildlife who often works with the Forest Service, is one of them.

"I try to get them to draw circles around the old-growth stands in their allowable cut areas, especially those on the steep slopes and along the riparian habitats, so they don't get cut down. I badger them. The Forest Service's people are good people, but they've always been under the gun to get out their allowable cut. Now it's even tougher for them to do their multiple-use job because of the pressure on them from Washington to increase the cut and to relax conservation practices developed over the years."

Hutchinson tries to teach sound management techniques to those who use the forests. He will spend days trying to trace the cause of the latest mud flow that has smothered trout and salmon spawning beds. "I follow them back upstream. When I locate the source of the mud, I try to talk to the person responsible, explaining to them about riparian buffer zones, road construction techniques to prevent sluicing, and other conservation measures. If it's a Forest Service person, they are quite receptive. The Forest Service moves its field people around a lot, though, so it's a never-ending process of education." If it is private land, the owner or logging company may or may not be receptive to Hutchinson's suggestions. "The Reagan Administration's lax attitude toward conservation has made it harder persuading private operators to cooperate."

Often, when Hutchinson is out tracking mud flows, people will stop him and ask why they don't see the salmon runs like they used to when they were kids. If there's a gravel bar in the nearby stream, he will wade out to it and stomp up and down. "Clouds of silt rise from it into the water and I say, 'See that, that's why there aren't those big salmon runs anymore.' Then I tell 'em about logging and road building."

What worries Hutchinson in particular now is that "much of the flatter terrain has been logged and only the steep forest land remains." He has had some first-hand experience with steep-slope logging. In the mid-1970's Hutchinson worked in the Coastal Range where the soils are thin, the slopes are very steep, and the rainstorms are fierce. They can dump as much as four or five inches of water in a 24-hour period. "After one such storm, my colleagues in the Forest Service went out onto the Siuslaw National Forest and they counted some 200 landslides. About 70 percent were from clear-cut areas, about 20 percent were caused by roads, and 10 percent were natural."

And just in case you may think that storm was one of those once-in-every-hundred-years events, Hutchinson refers you to the *Reedsport Courier* and an account of what a 1982 rainstorm did to a stretch of

Scofield Creek, which runs through private, state, and federal (Siuslaw National Forest) land. John Johnson, another biologist with the Oregon Department of Fish and Wildlife, writes: "I drove six miles on Scofield Ridge and counted 26 slides. . . . Damage to the spawning areas was massive. Huge torrents filled the creek with tons of silt debris and logs. Gravel bars, where I had watched some of this year's few returning adult coho spawning, were covered with two feet of silt. I counted ten major logjams in the two miles of stream. The usable spawning gravel for coho and steelhead [a rainbow trout which, like salmon, migrates to the sea and returns to fresh water to spawn] was estimated to be 24,000 square yards in 1960; my January 1982 estimate was only 1,000. . . . Returns of adult salmon and steelheads will be adversely affected for several years." Clear-cuts accounted for 57 percent of the slides, roads for 38 percent; 5 percent were natural.

"When are they going to manage the forests for all the American people, not primarily for the timber industry?" Hutchinson wonders aloud. "When are they going to manage the forests for all the uses— fishing, hunting, hiking, camping, watershed, and so on—and not primarily for the timber dollars?"

Jim Hutchinson now works in the Cascades in and around the Willamette National Forest, and, while the damage caused by logging operations here is less spectacular than on the Siuslaw, it is apparent when you get off the main highways. If you have any doubts, Hutchinson will guide you up Highway 126 out of Eugene, up the beautiful McKenzie Valley, to Nimrod. There you take a right on Quartz Creek road. The leveler land where Quartz Creek flows into the McKenzie River has obviously been cut-over years ago. The weeds and the young alder trees are flourishing here. About five miles up the road, where the Douglas fir start looking a lot taller than church Christmas trees, you see the first clear-cut. It's on private land. From the ridge top right on down to the creek's tumbling water, everything has been cut. You can see where rainwater has carved sluices into the treeless slope and carried soil down to the creek. Also, there are some spoon-shaped depressions which indicate debris avalanches have occurred. Climbing further up the road, you see a sign announcing that you are now on the Willamette National Forest, and another one warns you to watch for logging trucks. There are more clear-cuts, but they definitely look circumscribed—much narrower across and not running right down to the creek's edge—a strip of mature Douglas fir has been left along the water. The slopes, though, are even steeper—like the sides of a V, with the stream at the bottom. Also, it looks as if some of the landfill on the downslope side of the twisting road has slid into the creek. Then, off to the left, up Lytle Creek, a tributary of Quartz Creek, there is a tremendous clear-cut; both sides of this V have been logged. Further up, the same is true along Indian Creek. There is no evidence of avalanches or slides and a lot of logging debris remains on the slopes, but these are recent cuts and the period of great vulnerability lies ahead. In about a year or two, the roots of the felled trees will rot and lose their holding power.

We are supposed to receive fair market value for our timber. Part of how it happens that we do not was explained in the spring of 1981, in a federal judge's decision in favor of a small company that sued two timber giants.

In 1975, Reid Brothers Logging Co., one of the last small, independent logging enterprises left in southeastern Alaska, filed a private antitrust action against Alaska Lumber and Pulp Co., a subsidiary of Alaska Pulp Company, Ltd., of Tokyo, which is owned by 16 Japanese companies, and Ketchikan Pulp Co., a subsidiary of Louisiana-Pacific, the firm for which John Crowell had been general counsel before he took charge of the National Forests. After five years of pre-trial evidence gathering and a trial that lasted almost half a year, Judge Barbara J. Rothstein found in Reid Brothers' favor and awarded them damages of $496,672. The Ninth U.S. Circuit Court of Appeals upheld the decision. Louisiana-Pacific has appealed the case to the Supreme Court.

The case is important because it reveals a grisly picture of the machinations of two companies seeking to get a lot of public timber at a very low price and of the failure of the government to do anything about it.

The Tongass National Forest in southeastern Alaska is the largest forest in the national system. Ketchikan Pulp and Alaska Lumber now hold contracts that run past the year 2000 to harvest over 13 billion board feet of timber on the Tongass. They are currently paying $1.48–$3.07 per thousand board feet, less than 5 percent of the rate paid for Tongass timber sold competitively. In a study of the contracts, Kaid Benfield and Peter Mathers calculate the United States will lose $1.28 billion. Most Forest Service timber contracts run only 3.5 years and involve a million to a few hundred million board feet.

Judge Rothstein ruled that the Louisiana-Pacific subsidiary and the

Tokyo company's subsidiary had conspired to restrain trade in the southeast Alaska lumber market and in fact had monopolized that market in violation of the Sherman Antitrust Act.

They did it with the help of the federal government. In an effort to stimulate the economic development of Alaska, specifically to create pulp and paper industries, the government signed 50-year agreements with Ketchikan Pulp Co. (KPC) and Alaska Lumber and Pulp Co. (APC) in the 1950's, guaranteeing them a vast timber supply from the Tongass. The companies, as Judge Rothstein noted, "utilized this advantage as a starting point for concerted and combined efforts to control the Alaska timber market, to eliminate competition and to maintain and exercise monopoly power."

KPC and APC resorted to some classic market-monopolizing techniques, ones which John D. Rockefeller used to build Standard Oil. They squeezed their rival mills by reducing their supply of timber and then, when those mills foundered, bought them out. When KPC and APC bought logs from purchase loggers—a logger like Reid Brothers, who buys lumber from the Forest Service, cuts it down, and sells it to a mill—they paid, by mutual agreement, extremely low prices. The purchase loggers had no other outlets after awhile because KPC and APC had gobbled up the other mills. Also, KPC and APC were very eager to lend the hard-pressed purchase loggers money. That way, they could pull the financial rug out from under them if they showed any signs of trying to outbid KPC and APC for the more profitable timber on the Tongass during the Forest Service's "competitive" sales. Eventually, all of the purchase loggers, except for Reid Brothers, were driven out of business or became strictly contract loggers—a logger who cuts trees already purchased by the mill and is paid a flat fee dictated by the mill.

So that they would not bid against each other during Forest Service sales, KPC and APC sat down beforehand and divvied up the Tongass National Forest into the territories each was most interested in. They also set up dummy corporations for "public relations purposes," that is, to make the bidding during a Forest Service timber sale appear competitive and to disguise the fact that they were ending up with all the timber. They also used the dummy companies to bid against competitors. That way they could remain committed to the lower price which they paid purchase loggers while keeping timber away from rival mills.

Under such conditions, there is no chance that we, the owners of the timber, could receive fair market value for it. KPC and APC controlled the prices and because they functioned primarily as suppliers to the entities that they owned, it was, as Judge Rothstein observed, "impossible to accurately determine the value" of the product. Moreover, they apparently maintained two sets of books for transactions in which they sold Tongass timber to buyers not owned by them in Japan. One set of books recorded fictitiously low prices. These were open to scrutiny by the Forest Service or the Justice Department. The others were confidential and in them were recorded the real prices—the higher prices—actually received by them in the resale of our timber.

The most remarkable thing about all of this is that most of the devalued timber from the Tongass National Forest ends up in Japan, benefiting the Japanese economy, not ours. It is shipped to Japan in the form of cants—logs cut into slabs to satisfy the federal requirement that all National Forest timber undergo "primary processing" before being exported. Or it goes to Japan in the form of pulp. With the Tongass National Forest, the United States finds itself in the kind of commercial arrangement which has long victimized underdeveloped countries. We sell our raw material cheap to another country and then buy it back in the form of finished products at much higher prices. In such an arrangement, the maker of finished products invariably profits at the expense of the raw material supplier.

Not only are we being economically exploited, but the environmental costs are high as well. The salmon population on the Tongass—coho, pink, and chum—has dwindled due to the muddy runoff from lumber roads and clear-cuts. Also, the cutting of old growth timber at low elevations has, the Alaska Chapter of the Wildlife Society reports, imperiled the populations of brown bear, otter, mink, marten, bald eagles, and numerous species of waterfowl.

Obviously, the Reagan Administration cannot be held accountable for the past failures of the Justice Department to enforce the Sherman Antitrust Act or the Forest Service to get a fair market value for our timber. But now that the facts are out, thanks to the Reid Brothers case, now that it is clear what the subsidiaries of Louisiana-Pacific and the Tokyo conglomerate have been up to in Alaska, decisive action is needed to set matters right.

Instead, the Reagan Administration does nothing. Timber on the Tongass continues to be sold at ridiculously low prices to the monopolists. And the U.S. government continues to subsidize timber production on the Tongass: we get about 15 to 20 cents return for every dollar we spend on Tongass timber production.

The Antitrust Division of Reagan's Justice Department investigated the whole matter after Judge Rothstein made her decision and the Department reported:

. . . [W]e do not believe that an antitrust proceeding by the Department of Justice against either of the two companies is warranted. We have not found evidence of antitrust violation, occurring within the past five years, of a character sufficient to support a criminal prosecution under the antitrust laws. With regard to a possible civil action seeking injunctive relief, we have concluded that, despite evidence of past antitrust violations by the two companies, there is at this time no realistic prospect of obtaining effective and meaningful injunctive relief. . . . We have also examined the possibility of a civil action by the Government seeking monetary damages, but have concluded that the Government would be unable to demonstrate financial injuries or losses, compensable under the antitrust laws, occurring within the applicable four-year period of limitations.

Bill Brizee, an attorney in the office of general counsel at the Department of Agriculture, parent agency of the Forest Service, told the *Washington Post* that USDA was puzzled by the Justice Department's refusal to take criminal or civil action.

USDA, however, need not wait for the Justice Department to act. Under the Code of Federal Regulations and the National Forest Management Act, the Secretary of Agriculture could cancel the government's long-term contracts with Ketchikan Pulp and Alaska Lumber and Pulp, and the Secretary could bar these companies from any future sales of Tongass timber. To date, the Secretary of Agriculture has taken no such action and there is no indication that the Reagan Administration is interested in changing the Tongass status quo. There is interest in the Congress, though, in amending the Alaska National Interest Lands Conservation Act, which provides for over $40 million per year to be spent to ensure an annual harvest on the Tongass of 4.5 million board feet.

Not all the federal forests in jeopardy are managed by the Forest Service. The Department of the Interior's BLM looks after 2.1 million acres of public forest land in Oregon. Called the O&C land, it has an odd history. It was given to the old Oregon and California Railroad

Company after the Civil War, but Congress took it back in 1916 because the O&C had not developed it. Twenty-one years later, Congress passed the O&C Act which governs the land's management. The Act's language lacks precision, but it does say that the land should be managed "for permanent forest production" and for water, recreation, and the stability of the local economies.

It took Reagan's Department of the Interior a while to realize that it actually managed forest land. In July 1982, BLM Director Robert Burford set forth the Administration's cut-first policy for the O&C lands. "Management of other nontimber values, required by law," Burford declared, "will be provided to the extent possible by allocation on nontimber or nonsuitable forest land. If nontimber management needs are not met by this initial allocation, mitigating measures may be applied to the timber management program. Only if the first two steps are not adequate will management constraints, such as extended rotation, be applied to timber production. Finally, as *the last resort*, consideration may be given to withdraw lands from the allowable cut base" (emphasis added). In other words, all values other than commercial timber take a back seat.

Forester Andy Stahl points out that "the BLM was already overcutting the O&C lands and generally doing a much poorer job of managing the nontimber resources than the Forest Service, so Burford's new policy is really a matter of jumping from the frying pan into the fire." The impact of Burford's directive was swift. BLM's Coos Bay District, which manages 326,000 acres of public land, drastically revised its timber management plan upwards. It had planned to reduce timber harvest by 7 percent; timber sales were boosted to 254 million board feet, an increase of 9 percent. A proposal to set aside 36,000 acres of forest land for diversified wildlife management, especially for cavity nesting birds such as the spotted owl, mammals such as the furbearing marten and fisher, and tree nesting raptors such as the bald eagle, was trimmed to 25,300 acres. The National Wildlife Federation estimates that under the new timber management plan for the Coos Bay District the population of Roosevelt elk will decline 70 to 80 percent.

"Goodbye, multiple-use management; hello, tree farm," a state biologist concludes. Burford's directive states: "Allowable cut declaration levels will be based on the use of intensive management practices. . . ." Among other things, this means intensive spraying of herbicides such as 2,4-D.

In early 1983, Ronald Reagan went to Oregon to give a speech to timber company executives. He did not stop to talk to the foresters who see a resource being senselessly abused. He did not visit the clear-cut sites where the earth is sliding into Quartz Creek and Scofield Creek and the South Fork of the Salmon. He did not talk to the executives about the subsidies they enjoy from the Forest Service or their obligation to leave a living regenerating forest for future generations.

What he did say reveals a great deal about the premises for the policies of his Administration. To put some land in wilderness was fine, he said, "but not to go out on the wholesale amounts they are talking —because that wasn't the intention and the private sector has not been guilty of rape of all the natural resources. There is today in the United States as much forest as there was when Washington was at Valley Forge."

The President was off on his facts (by about a quarter of a billion acres) and his forest policies show it. They are based more on illusion and ideology—comfortable conservative mythology—than on reality and the needs of the nation.

SELL IT, LEASE IT, SURRENDER CONTROL

All told, the Bureau of Land Management is responsible for 340 million acres of public land—47 percent of all federally managed lands. Three hundred and forty million acres. That's an area 85 percent as large as the entire United States east of the Mississippi and larger than many countries. It's bigger, for instance, than Cuba, Nicaragua, and El Salvador combined—a lot bigger.

The public lands lie in the big blank spaces on the map of the western USA—the big blank spaces west of the statelines of the Dakotas, Nebraska, Kansas, Oklahoma, and Texas, and the big blank spaces in Alaska. The National Forests and Parks and the military bases are marked on the map. Not the public land managed by the BLM.

Drive, say, from Los Angeles to Las Vegas, or from Reno to Salt Lake City, or from Tucson to Albuquerque, or from Grand Junction to Sheridan, and that open landscape that rolls by hour after hour is it. You won't see signs posted saying "Public Land—Managed For You By The Bureau of Land Management, U.S. Department of the Interior," you won't see information centers with nice brochures or rangers in crisp green uniforms and Smokey Bear hats, but that's it.

It seems barren, but there is a Galapagos out there of strange and fascinating survivors from another age—the desert tortoise, the leopard lizard, the lungless salamander, the spadefoot toad, and the fairy shrimp. And out there live most of our remaining bighorn sheep, kit foxes, and wild mustangs, as well as over half of our antelope and mule deer.

Native art treasures are out there, too, carved into rock (petroglyphs) and sculpted onto the earth (intaglios). Our past is out there—over a hundred areas on the National Register of Historic Places and another five hundred eligible—and the earth's past. Near Cleveland, Utah, for example, is one of the world's major dinosaur graveyards where recently two new species were unearthed—*Stokesaurs clevelandi* and *Marshocaurs bicentesimus*. In northwest New Mexico is the Bisti Badlands, which about a hundred million years ago was a swamp. Its petrified sequoia and bald cyprus tree trunks, its dinosaur bones and clam shells, its wealth of fossils—snails, fishes, turtles, and crocodiles—may hold the answer to the tantalizing question of why the dinosaurs' reign on earth ended so abruptly (in geologic time) and the mammals began their takeover. Was there a dramatic shift in the earth's climate? Did a giant asteroid collide with the earth as some scientists have conjectured? Paleontologists hope to be able to complete their explorations of the Bisti before the Secretary of the Interior leases it for coal strip mining.

And, there is out there "refuge," as western novelist and historian Wallace Stegner notes, "from the industrial termite-civilization we have created." In 1982 over 58 million Americans spent an estimated 317 million hours of R&R on the public, BLM-managed land—photographing wildflowers, camping, backpacking, fishing, etc. There's elbow room out there. Solitude. You can go to sleep under a sky no longer seen from our cities—a deep black dome filled with shimmering stars and streaked by meteorites.

The Reagan Administration wanted to sell vast tracts of the public land. The plan was announced in February 1982, and by the summer Secretary Watt was saying that as much as 5 percent of the public land, 37 million acres, an area the size of the State of Michigan, just slightly smaller than all of the New England states combined, could be sold. The land sale program was managed by the White House. President Reagan issued an Executive Order establishing a Property Review Board chaired by Edwin Harper, an assistant to the President. Members of the Board included Presidential counselors Edwin Meese and James Baker, Budget Director David Stockman, and National Security Adviser William Clark.* The mission of the Board, according to David Stockman, was to "initiate an active disposal program designed to identify federal holdings that are not being put to highest and best use and to expedite disposal of these properties. All executive agencies [would] be required to conduct a review of real property holdings and to report to the Board within 60 days. . . ."

The Board acted in secret without established rules or public accountability. The members did not consult with representatives of state or local government or with the owners of the land—the public. There was no public discussion of the meaning of "highest and best use," although economic productivity seemed to be the basic rule of thumb. "I want to open as much land as I can," Secretary Watt told the *New York Times.* "The basic difference between this Administration and the liberals is that we are market oriented. . . ." Only six years earlier, in response to a century of abuse of the public land, Congress had passed the Federal Land Policy and Management Act, declaring the policy of the United States to be that "the public lands be retained in federal ownership . . ." and that these lands be managed "in a manner that will protect the quality of scientific, scenic, historical, ecological, environmental, air and atmospheric, water resource and archaeological values. . . ." But the Property Review Board had a very different goal: to dispose of all lands that could be sold "without adversely affecting the activities of the agency" that managed the land. In the case of the Forest Service and the BLM, by 1982 "activities of the agency" generally meant making public resources available as quickly as possible for private exploitation. There was nothing in the Board's mandate about avoiding adverse affects on the land's values protected by law. It was almost as if, having won an election, the Administration believed the law had been superseded by the greater truth of their mandate.

The determination to sell off vast tracts of public land was rooted in two strong elements of the philosophy that both the President and James Watt brought with them to Washington. One element was the notion that federally owned resources should be made economically

---

*Clark, a long-time friend of the President, was named Secretary of the Interior after James Watt was forced to resign.

productive to help put federal fiscal policy in order. There was much talk of reducing the national debt through the sale of public lands, and the President's budget projected seventeen billion dollars of income from such sales over five years beginning in 1983. Like the profligate Prince Stephan Arkadyevitch Oblonsky in Tolstoy's *Anna Karenina,* we were to sell off the family estate to pay our debts.

The other element was hostility to the federal government and especially to the federal government as a western landlord. Campaigning in 1980, Ronald Reagan had said federal ownership of western land "is contrary to the Constitution. It's contrary to the basic law when the 13 colonies first came into the union."* The federal government had owned those western lands since before the states they lie in became part of the Union, but only in the last decade had it begun to manage what it owned and to place some restrictions on use of the land. That was what James Watt meant when he spoke of "the arrogant and heavy-handed policies of the federal government," and the resistance to federal management efforts was what Reagan was playing to in his 1980 speech.

In the late 1970's, after a lawsuit by the Natural Resources Defense Council forced the BLM to take a hard look at the environmental effects of grazing on the public land, after Congress passed the Surface Mine Control and Reclamation Act, FLPMA, and the Public Rangeland Improvement Act, and after two Executive Orders were issued on the control of off-road vehicles on the public land, the federal government took some steps to reduce the environmental damage caused by grazing, mining, and off-road vehicles. Although those steps were tentative, even rabbit-like on occasion, they did signal an end to the status quo for the special interests who used the public land. Coupled with President Carter's famous hit list of federally subsidized western projects, which was compiled without consultation with any governor, senator, or congressman from the region, these initiatives ignited something called the "Sagebrush Rebellion." James Watt, as he has said on numerous occasions, was part of the Sagebrush Rebellion. So were a number of other men whom Reagan brought with him to Washington.

The Sagebrush Rebellion was, as Wallace Stegner observed, "the

---

*He was wrong. Article IV, §3, of the United States Constitution explicitly recognizes federal authority to manage land holdings: "The Congress shall have Power to dispose of and make all needful rules and regulations respecting the Territory or other property belonging to the United States."

voice of a regional elite, an economic and political oligarchy." The man President Reagan named to run the BLM and 340 million acres of our land, Robert Burford, epitomizes that elite. At the time of his nomination, Burford was described as a rancher, but, as his financial disclosure statement revealed, he was, like many big ranchers in the West, a lot more than that. He held grazing permits for 32,000 acres of public land in western Colorado. (He transferred them to his son before becoming BLM Director.) He also owned more than $250,000 worth of private land in Colorado and $100,000–$250,000 worth of cattle. In addition, he had a $100,000–$250,000 interest in Central Colorado Banks, Inc., and was a director of that corporation. He also had $100,000–$250,000 deposited in the First National Bank of Grand Junction, Colorado, and held oil-gas interests worth $50,000–$100,000. But these were only some of his assets. Others include an owner partnership in Paradise Mobile Home Park valued at over $250,000 and a $250,000-plus interest in Little Parks Ranches. Burford is also the former Republican Speaker of the Colorado House of Representatives.

The Sagebrush Rebels were elusive on the question of what should happen to the public land. Some advocated turning it all over to the states, and indeed several western states passed legislation declaring their right to public lands within their borders. And Senator Orrin Hatch introduced legislation in Congress to turn over all BLM-managed land and all National Forest land to the states. Among the senators who joined him as co-sponsors were Laxalt of Nevada, Garn of Utah, Wallop of Wyoming, and McClure of Idaho. Others advocated "privatizing" the public lands by "assigning title to existing permittees" and thereby capturing "individual incentive and initiative for using rangeland efficiently . . . [and ensuring] response by profit-maximizing land owners to changing market demands for range use."

Major industrial interests, those represented by men like J. Robert Fluor and Joseph Coors, who had helped to bankroll the Mountain States Legal Foundation while, under James Watt's leadership, it became a leading advocate of the Sagebrush Rebellion, wanted above all to see federal lands opened for development and exploitation. As J. Allen Overton, Jr., President of the American Mining Congress, put it, the United States had been on a "massive regulatory binge" that had "locked up" natural resources on the public lands. "Our society is built on stuff that comes out of a hole in the ground and if we don't unplug the red tape stuffing the hole, this country is going to be in a hell of a mess." Selling the public lands was a response to a variety of interests angered by federal restrictions on their use of publicly owned resources.

The Property Review Board set preliminary acreage targets for each agency. BLM prepared an initial "inventory" of 4.4 million acres for disposal. The Forest Service found 60,000 acres immediately available and announced a review of another 140 million acres that could potentially be deemed "unneeded." On July 2, 1982, the Property Review Board announced a list of 307 parcels soon to be sold to the highest bidder. Suddenly opposition mounted, and much of it took the Administration by surprise.

When it became clear which forest lands might go on the sales block, even Administration loyalists such as Senators Jesse Helms and James McClure balked. Helms vowed that, as long as he chairs the Senate Agriculture Committee, the Uwharrie National Forest in his home state of North Carolina would not be sold. The Forest Service had targeted 41,000 of the forest's 47,000 acres for study for possible sale. Any sale of National Forest land will require legislation. McClure warned Assistant Secretary Crowell to find out precisely which acres were excess and their worth before talking any further about selling Forest Service land. The Forest Service had targeted 187,000 acres in his home state of Idaho.

Secretary Watt heard from one of the Administration's staunchest group of supporters—the western livestock industry—the soul of the Sagebrush Rebellion. Many ranchers who graze their cattle and sheep on public rangeland enjoy an advantageous arrangement with the government. The U.S. government does not charge ranchers the market rate for grazing on public land. Grazing fees are based on something called AUMS, animal unit months—one AUM is the forage for one cow or horse or five sheep or goats for one month. Under the current system, which the Reagan Administration did not invent but has done nothing to change, ranchers pay the BLM or Forest Service an average of $1.40 per AUM, while on comparable private land the rate is $8.83. Moreover, the U.S. government pays for range "improvement." This usually includes the killing of brush, the seeding of forage grasses such as crested wheatgrass, and the building of livestock watering facilities. A recent study done of grazing on BLM-managed public land in Oregon and Washington found that the U.S. government receives 54 cents in grazing revenues for every dollar it spends on range improvements. This, coupled with the lower than market level grazing fees, means that each rancher who uses the public rangeland nets an average subsidy of $2,117 a year. Ending the subsidies and selling the land to the highest bidder was not quite what these Sagebrush Rebels had in mind.

Two months after the initial list of parcels to be sold was announced, the governors of Arizona, Colorado, Idaho, Montana, New Mexico, North Dakota, South Dakota, Utah, and Wyoming adopted a resolution opposing the land sale program and decrying the Administration's failure to consult with the public or to abide by the requirements of the laws governing use of the federal lands. Elected politicians from Sagebrush Rebellion territory challenged the basic premises of the Administration's policy:

> We believe that decisions regarding the use of the public lands should be based on sound resource management principles and should not be motivated solely by efforts to achieve predetermined revenue goals. We believe that the public domain must not become a one-time marketable asset but should remain a manageable resource for the benefit of future generations as well as the present.

The program went forward, but under political and legal attack it progressed slowly and little land was sold. On July 18, 1983, Secretary Watt wrote to the western governors to inform them that he had "secured from the Chairman of the Property Review Board a letter that clearly states that Board was not to 'become involved in the operational functioning of the agency [Interior] in regard to the management of public lands.' " He did not promise to halt the sale or transfer of lands, however, and local BLM land managers continue to solicit nominations of land that the local interests would like to see privatized.*

There are many other ways of relinquishing government control of public assets aside from selling them, and the Reagan Administration has pursued these with much more success than its Assets Management Program.

One way is to slash the funding for the monitoring and regulation of resource users. Under the Reagan Administration, the money in the

---

*As a revenue-raising scheme, the President's Asset Management Program has been a bust. In three years, the government has sold 13,057 acres of public land and made $9,400,661. There has not yet been a full accounting of what the program has cost the various land management agencies, but they have certainly spent at least twice the amount earned identifying lands to sell and administering the sales. So the major accomplishment of the Asset Management Program has been to divert scarce financial resources away from public land conservation programs.

BLM budget for grazing management and for off-road vehicle management has declined by more than one-third, although these are, along with strip mining, the major causes of environmental damage on the public land. Less money is also available for soil and water conservation and for wildlife habitat management. Their funding in the BLM budget under Reagan has been cut almost in half. There is more, however, for mineral and energy resource development and for the management of public land sales.

The Reagan Administration has taken a number of steps to turn control of the 170 million acres of public land on which livestock are grazed over to ranchers. These steps, as Guy R. Martin, a former Department of the Interior official, notes, "transfer effective control of public rangeland to private owners without the formality of a sale or direct compensation to the United States." The Administration has relinquished federal control of new water rights on BLM-managed land. Under the Watt policy, ranchers or other private interests such as mining companies can acquire, from the states, those water rights not specifically reserved to the federal government. In the dry West, a water right is a precious asset. As James Watt said while he was head of the Mountain States Legal Foundation, "whoever controls our water, controls our land."

The Administration also abandoned the process of evaluating the environmental conditions of the public rangelands and adjusting grazing to the land's carrying capacity. Where the land is in poor shape due to overgrazing, the BLM now simply maintains the grazing staus quo instead of trying to reduce the amount of grazing. There is now a sentence, supplied by Director Burford's office in Washington, that crops up, almost verbatim, in every BLM grazing plan in the West: "Initially, the livestock numbers will remain unchanged unless an adjustment is mutually agreed upon by the permittee and the BLM."

There are two fundamental problems with this approach. First, ranchers seldom reduce the AUMs in their grazing allotment voluntarily. A federal grazing allotment is an asset, and to do so diminishes its value. When a rancher goes to the bank for a loan, he can use his grazing allotment as collateral. He can sell it, pass it on to his heirs, or he can use it to cover a bet in a poker game. If the public range his cattle or sheep are using is in poor shape, it is of course in his long-term interest to cut back on grazing and let the grasses recover, reseed, and stabilize the soil. Then forage will be more abundant in the long run. But, like many of their fellow humans, ranchers tend to live in the short run. They agree with economist John Maynard Keynes: "In the long run, we'll all be dead." Cut a rancher's allotted AUMs and in the short run it will cost him. He will either have to plant more alfalfa or barley on his own land or buy more feed on the market, or rent private grazing land, or sell off some of his livestock, perhaps at a loss if the market is soft at that time. So ranchers usually resist bitterly when the government tries to reduce their AUMs. And ranchers have more political influence than their numbers suggest. About 13,000 ranchers graze livestock on the public land, but within their ranks are men such as Robert Burford, with financial tendrils reaching well beyond their fence lines and with solid political connections in their communities and states as well as in the Congress. That is why trying to reduce a rancher's AUMs has been compared, within the BLM, to walking naked through the cactus. A BLM district manager, for example, confers with a rancher about cutting his AUMs. The next day a U.S. senator may well be on the phone with the head of the BLM discussing the district manager's "uncooperative attitude" and how it might affect the BLM current budget request. And the day after that, the district manager might well receive a call from the BLM personnel office in Washington informing him that he is being transferred to a nice windowless office 400 miles away to spend a couple of years writing a manual on tar sands development. It happens. Indeed, one of the first acts of the Reagan Administration's BLM was to remove Bob Buffington from his post as BLM state director for Idaho. Buffington, who is now in Africa as a range consultant for the U.S. Agency for International Development and is widely respected in professional land management circles, had rubbed some influential Idaho ranchers the wrong way by suggesting reduced grazing of overgrazed public rangeland.

The second problem with maintaining the grazing status quo is that large stretches of the public land need some rest. The Taylor Grazing Act slowed the rate of decline of the public rangeland but for the most part did not reverse it. At the time the Reagan Administration took office, about one-third of the public rangeland, over 50 million acres, was still in poor or worse condition. But, for the first time in its history, the BLM was beginning a serious effort to reduce grazing on the most badly overgrazed public land. That effort has come to a dead stop. For example, a court-ordered analysis of the 800,000-acre BLM Reno District found that over half of the public land is in poor ecological condition and that riparian and aspen communities, especially valuable in an arid region because they sustain diverse plant and animal life, have been devastated "due to overutilization by livestock." To the south, another court-ordered analysis of BLM land in Clark County, Nevada, found that 89 percent of it was in poor condition and that all major washes, which play a vital role in maintaining the land's biological diversity, were in poor condition. And yet, in both the Reno and Clark County areas, the BLM now plans to maintain current grazing levels indefinitely.

It has been a long time since the Dust Bowl and even longer since many of the streams in the West changed from perennial to intermittent flow, but it is still true that what happens on arid rangeland affects more than just grass. Soils from denuded rangeland can and do end up in cities as dust pollution—cities such as Phoenix, Bakersfield, Las Vegas, Grand Junction, Fresno, Winnemucca, and Roswell, to name only a few. And denuded rangeland loses its ability to absorb water. This loss has a drastic effect on stream flows and ground water tables. When it rains, the water runs off the land in a great rush, instead of soaking into the ground. This, in turn, causes flash floods and gully cutting as in the Rio Puerco area of north central New Mexico. Once-perennial rivers such as the Santa Cruz in Arizona become dry riverbeds, except during floods, or they become loaded with sediment like the Rio Grande.

Another step taken by the BLM that transfers control of public rangeland without transferring ownership is to expand use of ten-year Cooperative Management Agreements with ranchers. A remarkably candid briefing paper prepared by Burford's staff explains what these are: "A cooperative management agreement is a formal, written agreement between the BLM and a livestock operator that recognizes the operator as the steward of an allotment." The purpose, as the briefing paper explains, is to provide livestock operators "with (1) recognition of good stewardship, (2) *a larger role in managing grazing on the public lands,* and (3) the assurance of tenure . . ." (emphasis added). It continues: "Generally, cooperative management agreements cannot be transferred and will automatically terminate with the transfer of base property. Exceptions may occur when the allotment remains in control of the family, corporation, or partnership upon death of the livestock operator." Under a cooperative management agreement, a rancher will be able to increase his livestock grazing on the public land at will, so long as he pays for it. What, one might ask, is in it for us, the public? Well, in return for control, the livestock operator agrees to finance "new range improvements." That's it. One hopes that whoever in the Reagan Administration worked out this bargain with the livestock industry will not be involved in negotiating our next trade agreement with Japan or the Soviet Union. Otherwise, the Japanese could end up with IBM and the Russians with Kansas.

A number of veteran public rangeland experts outside the Reagan Administration have commented on the Cooperative Management Agreement scheme. They point out that while Burford has been promising that agreements will only be signed with operators who graze livestock in allotments with "satisfactory resource conditions," he has also been gutting the BLM's existing inventory data system and slashing funds for collecting new allotment-specific data. Hence, the BLM may well not have a factual basis for knowing whether an allotment is in "satisfactory condition" or, when a rancher's cooperative management agreement is up for renewal, whether he has maintained it in "satisfactory condition." Without such facts, it will be difficult to deny a rancher a cooperative management agreement, especially a big, politically influential rancher. William Meiners, who was with the BLM for ten years before retiring as Chief, Division of Resource Management, Boise District Office, and is now an environmental consultant, states that the cooperative management scheme is based on a categorization of rangeland environments and their associated resources which has no basis in reality. To condone these agreements would be "a travesty—a travesty assuring ultimate desertification of the rangelands of the eleven western states and loss of our land heritage." Russell W. Heughins, a public land historian, writes of the cooperative management agreements: "In essence, the permittee has supplanted the Bureau and Secretarial authority and perhaps even Congressional power. What some feared in 1934 may well come to pass, proprietorship by a select number of public grazers and without the encumbrances of private ownership."

It is also worth noting what has happened to the BLM's citizen advisory councils under the Reagan Administration. Nobody ever said that multiple-use management of the public land was going to be easy, and in FLPMA the Congress created the advisory councils to help the BLM over some of the rougher resource conflicts. The councils are organized at the district level and they are supposed to represent a balance of user interests. Under the Reagan Administration, they have become as lopsided as the land management agencies' budgets. A close look at the people the Reagan Administration has named to the advisory councils gives a good idea of how the Administration defines "multiple use" and for whom it is managing the public lands. The Boise District Advisory Council is fairly typical. All the seats are now filled with Reagan Administration appointees:

Walter Yarbrough, a rancher and a contractor, is chairman of the council. He is also a Republican state senator.

Harry Bettis, a rancher and a director of the Idaho First National Bank, is supposed to represent the "public at large" on the council.

Logan Lanham, a public relations man for Idaho Power Co., is also on the council to represent the "public at large."

Rayola Jacobsen, a substitute teacher, wife of a rancher, Sagebrush Rebellion, Inc., activist, and opponent of the expansion of the Snake River Birds of Prey Conservation Area, is supposed to represent "environmental protection interests."

Dick Bass, a rancher and Cattlemen's Association officer, is on the council to represent the "renewable resource interests."

Eugene Davis, a rancher and Cattlemen's Association officer, is also supposed to represent the "renewable resource interests."

Douglas E. Bean, executive director of the Idaho Petroleum Council, an oil industry interest group, is supposed to represent "nonrenewable resource interests."

Glenn Youngblood, a public relations man for Boise Cascade, a big lumber company, is on the council to represent "recreation interests."

E. J. Smith, a planning consultant who was recommended for the council by the Idaho Farm Bureau, is supposed to represent "transportation."

Robert Salter, a biologist and retired employee of the Idaho Department of Fish and Game, is on the council to represent "wildlife interests."

Note the preponderance of ranching and corporate people and the absence, save for Robert Salter, of any conservationists. Or of any representatives from citizen groups such as the League of Women Voters. The bias is clear.

Among the experts who have kept a close eye on the Reagan Administration's public land policies as they have unfolded is Earl Sandvig. No one alive knows more about public rangeland than he.

Sandvig grew up on a ranch in northeastern Montana and, after going out on his own, "cowboyed" for several years before deciding to attend the University of Montana and study range science. After graduating, Sandvig joined the Forest Service and, over a career which spanned more than 35 years, he worked his way up to become an Assistant Regional Forester for Range and Wildlife and one of the most respected range managers in the U.S. government. He was the kind of range manager who spent more time on horseback than behind a desk. He taught a whole generation of Forest Service range managers in the Rocky Mountain states how to read the land for telltale signs of overgrazing such as soil scalping, rilling, and gullying. He dreamed up a simple but very effective test of a range's health. Cut the top and bottom off an ordinary coffee tin, put the remaining tin ring onto the ground and pour water into it. Then watch what happens to that water. On flat, overgrazed rangeland it will just sit there, and on sloped overgrazed rangeland it will rush to the downslope side of the tin ring and then just sit there. In either case, it will take long minutes for the water to soak into the ground. But on rangeland that has not been overgrazed, it will soak right in. Closer inspection of the ground reveals why. Beneath the healthy grass plants is a mat of dead grasses with obvious water-absorbing capacity, and below the surface is a network of hairy roots which both keep the soil permeable and suck up the water. A couple of years ago, Sandvig was on a BLM tour for conservationists and state officials of public rangeland in eastern Oregon. The local BLM man was bragging about what good shape the range was in. He pointed out that grass all around looked just like the grass in a small fenced-in enclosure that had not been grazed for several years. So Sandvig got his coffee tin out of his knapsack. He picked a spot right next to the enclosure. Everyone gathered around. He poured water from his canteen onto the ground and it made a beeline for the downslope side of the tin. After it had finally soaked in, he climbed over the fence and repeated the test. Even though the slope was the same, the water soaked right in. Sandvig, incidentally, has given Robert Burford's grazing allotment on the public land in western Colorado his tin ring test, too. It flunked.

Sandvig was also the kind of range manager who was not content to report poor range conditions to his superiors and then leave it at that. He fought to reduce grazing. "When I saw violation of solid principles of range ecology, I felt it deeply that this can't go on, that it defeats everything we've been taught, and violates natural laws." Eventually, it got him in hot water with his superior, Ed Cliff, Regional Forester. Cliff told him to take it easy making grazing reductions; he told him that it took 50 years to ruin the ranges on the National Forests in southern Wyoming and western Colorado and to go slow in making changes; he told him that the stockmen were powerful politically and the timing wasn't right to oppose them. So Sandvig retired and Cliff went on to become chief of the Forest Service.

After his retirement, Sandvig maintained a keen interest in the public rangeland and increasingly focused his attention on BLM-managed public land. "The Forest Service still has seriously overgrazed areas, but nothing like the BLM. The majority of BLM rangeland is terribly abused." He thinks that after the passage of FLPMA the BLM started to make progress. "It reduced grazing by about 10 percent overall, but it will have to cut grazing by at least 20 percent to make any headway." Sandvig thinks the Reagan Administration has stopped that progress in its tracks and set the BLM back about 50 years. "All the grazing plans coming out under this Administration will have to be totally redone."

Sandvig draws an interesting contrast between BLM's Cooperative Management Agreement program, which abdicated control to the rancher, and its continued low grazing fees, which subsidize the rancher, with recent grazing policy implemented by the Defense Department. In eastern Oregon, near Boardman, there is a Naval weapons-testing facility with about 40,000 acres of rangeland which the Department of the Navy has leased to ranchers by means of competitive bidding. This is arid land, with average annual rainfall of from eleven to eighteen inches and almost all of that falls between December and March. The land is subject to high winds and dust storms. Most of the livestock forage is annuals, especially cheatgrass and filaree. Nonetheless, the lowest bid the Navy received for the grazing season of 1982 was $6.10 per AUM and the highest was $12.16. The BLM, which does not use competitive bidding, charges $1.40 per AUM for nearby public land.

Sandvig notes that in fiscal 1981 federal agencies collected $24.9 million in grazing fees while paying $58.5 million for the costs of managing rangeland and sharing grazing revenues with local governments. He estimates that, if all federal agencies, especially the BLM and the Forest Service, went to a competitive bidding system, they could get an average of at least $10 per AUM. That would turn the existing grazing deficit of $33 million into a surplus of $82.9 million.

Sandvig also points out that the Navy is a far more diligent land manager than the BLM. Its soil and water conservation plan for the weapons-testing facility near Boardman requires the lessee (the livestock operator) to install range analysis study plots at systematic intervals over the range. These enclosures will provide the Navy's range manager with excellent reference points for determining the condition of the range and how much grazing to allow the next season. The lessee is reimbursed for the costs of installing the necessary fences and markers. There are some enclosures on BLM-managed land which have been installed by the BLM, but they are not systemic; hence the agency often has difficulty evaluating the condition of grazed land because of the lack of base data. In addition, the Navy requires lessees to stabilize wind-eroded "blow areas" on the range and to reseed the range with perennial grasses and annual legumes each year. The lessee is required to make certain range improvements at his own expense: repair and maintain existing fences and livestock watering facilities, control noxious weeds and rodents—but "indiscriminate" killing of coyotes, bobcats, or badgers is strictly prohibited. No such requirements exist on BLM-managed public land. Moreover, the Navy's range manager retains the right to reduce the number of allowable AUMs in any lease year if conditions such as drought demand it. The BLM range manager must have, for all practical purposes, the livestock operator's agreement in order to reduce AUMs.

Sandvig describes the Navy's soil and water conservation plan as "a honey" and thinks it should be a model for all public rangeland. "Unfortunately, the Administration is moving in exactly the opposite direction with the BLM's grazing plans, which do nothing but endorse the status quo, and its Cooperative Management Agreements, which leave all important decisions up to the ranchers. It's disgraceful."

Of the Administration's efforts to dispose of public land, Sandvig snorts, "Hell, freedom is the issue. Have you ever tried fishing, horseback riding, or camping on private land? Nine times out of ten the owner will kick you off. If the Administration has its way, only the privileged few who own land will have access to our great outdoor resources in the West. The rest of us will have to wait in line to spend a couple days on some overcrowded National Park. There are damn few private land owners who practice real multiple-use management. Private forest land is managed for timber production; private ranches are managed for livestock production. The public lands are our heritage. They're owned by 240 million Americans. We ought to hang onto them."

OUR COAL WILLINGLY SOLD

A little north of Teapot Dome in Wyoming and Montana is the Powder River Basin. There, on April 28, 1982, the Department of the Interior, with considerable fanfare, held the largest public coal sale in United States history. Some 1.6 billion tons of public coal were put on the block; that is almost twice the amount of coal produced in the entire United States in 1981.

In such a sale, we are supposed to receive "fair market value" for our coal. It is the Secretary of the Interior's job to see that we do.

Including a follow-up sale held October 15, 1982, Secretary Watt leased twelve tracts of public land, about 37,000 acres, in the Powder River Basin. Bearing names such as South Duck Nest Creek, Keeline, Colstrip C, and West Decker, these tracts contain coal beds that are thick—in some places over 100 feet thick—and close enough to the surface to allow surface mining operations on a huge scale. The coal here is classified as sub-bituminous, which means that when it burns it gives off more heat than peat or lignite but less than the bituminous coal mined in the Midwest and Appalachia, but its sulfur content is lower, which means less air pollution.

Coal companies paid a total of $67.2 million for the Powder River leases. That is a lot of money, but is it the fair market value for the coal? That question bedeviled Secretary Watt and his subordinates, who orchestrated the sale. It ultimately contributed to Watt's downfall. Watt and his staff steadfastly insisted that fair market value was received.

According to the U.S. General Accounting Office (GAO), they are wrong. According to GAO, Secretary Watt undersold our coal in the Powder River Basin by roughly *$100 million.* In other words, he got a lot less than half its value.

Of all the investigations into the Powder River Basin (and there have been a number), GAO's is the most telling because GAO is an independent, nonpartisan agency with no political axe to grind and because its auditors are experienced in the complexities of determining fair market value. They actually went to the trouble to figure out what the coal is really worth.

The sequence of events immediately preceding the sale is crucial to understanding how Secretary Watt came to undersell our coal by $100 million.

On February 22, 1982, Secretary Watt decided to sell 2.5 billion tons of coal in the basin, with the first sale occurring April 28. The Federal Coal Leasing Amendments Act of 1976 requires the Secretary to sell the coal by means of competitive bidding, and the public announcement of the sale was set for March 25.

On March 2, the Interior Department's Minerals Management Service's office in Casper, Wyoming, transmitted to the Service's headquarters in Reston, Virginia, outside Washington, D.C., its assessors' estimates of the fair market value for the coal to be sold April 28. The long-standing Department of Interior policy for insuring that fair market value is obtained in such a sale is for its assessors to establish the fair market value for each tract *before* the sale and to make that figure the "minimum acceptable bid."

Sometime between March 2 and March 8, the two men in charge of the Powder River Basin sale for Secretary Watt—Garrey Carruthers, Assistant Secretary for Land and Water Resources, and his then Deputy, David Russell, both Reagan appointees—concluded that the fair market value estimates prepared by the career employees in the field were way too high. They worried that the minimum acceptable bid figures would scare off would-be bidders and that the first major coal sale under the Reagan Administration's much-publicized push to "get federal coal into the marketplace where it can do some good" would be a flop. As Russell told a congressional investigator, "Why risk the largest coal sale in American history with minimum acceptable bids that are too high?"

On what basis did Carruthers and Russell decide the assessors' estimates were too high? The answer remains murky to this day. Carruthers claims that they "had not been comfortable with the information flowing in from the field for some time" and points to a scatter diagram prepared by a BLM economist to back up their conclusion that the estimates were too high. That diagram shows the range of values received for all federal coal sales over the past two years. It does not, however, contain any Powder River coal data. Much more pertinent would be a diagram showing the results of private coal sales in the Powder River Basin, but neither Carruthers nor Russell had such a diagram.

Critics have expressed concern that the staff estimates were rejected because of coal industry pressure. Russell and Carruthers categorically deny this happened. However, a leak of the minimum acceptable bid

273

estimates apparently did occur. In a report by the Interior Department Inspector General that finally became public in January 1984, a coal industry lawyer is quoted as saying that Russell passed the information to him more than a month before the auction. Although the report was referred to the Department of Justice, as in the case of the investigation at EPA, they declined to prosecute. The GAO also investigated the leaks and found evidence that other coal industry representatives also got early access to minimum-bid information. The evidence noted by GAO comes from Douglas Hileman, an employee of the Minerals Management Service. On March 25, he has reported, a representative of Carter Coal Company contacted him and during the conversation revealed two of the minimum acceptable bids "down to three decimal points."

One of the great ironies of this whole affair is that the government assessors had, indeed, miscalculated in making their fair market value estimates, as GAO later discovered, but they had erred on the low side and not, as Carruthers and Russell insisted, on the high. They had undervalued the coal.

At a meeting on Friday, March 19, just 39 days before the biggest sale was scheduled to occur, Russell and Daniel Miller, Assistant Secretary for Energy and Minerals, and his Deputy, William P. Pendley, decided to scrap the minimum acceptable bid system and try an "entry level" bid system which relied on post-sale analysis to determine whether fair market value was obtained. This rather momentous decision was made without benefit of any supporting documentation—there were no background papers, no impact analyses, no staff or consultant reports. And no minutes were kept of the meeting, so there is no record of the rationale for scrapping the old system. The Minerals Management Service staff in Reston was given that weekend to work out the details of the new system to determine how over a billion tons of public coal would soon be sold.

The Minerals Management Service staff took the minimum acceptable bid figures, cut them by about 40 percent—a total decrease of $46.8 million—and renamed them entry level bids. The chief economist for the Service modeled the new system on a stamp auction he had once attended. To get things rolling, the auctioneer had allowed bidding to begin at well below fair market value and then let competition among bidders drive up the price to fair market value.

On Monday, the new entry level bid numbers were rushed to the printer to be incorporated in the sale announcement, and, on March 25, as scheduled, a 26-page "BLM Lease Sale Schedule and Notice of Coal Leasing Offering, Powder River Federal Coal Production Region" was released.

On April 28, the bids came in. Three of the tracts attracted two bids each, eight got only one bid each, and two received no bids at all. The "high" bids were, in every instance but one, very close or identical to the entry level bids which had been conjured up over that weekend in Reston. Recall that those entry level bid numbers were never intended to represent fair market value, but rather to operate as a floor from which competitive bidding would rise.

Nonetheless, Interior's post-sale analysis, through a process which no one outside of Carruthers's office has yet been able to fathom, found that the bids on ten of the eleven tracts represented fair market value. And Secretary Watt accepted those ten bids and declared the sale "a great success."

On October 15, the follow-up sale was held. The one tract, Rocky Butte, whose April 28 bid had been rejected by Interior, went up for sale again along with another tract. Each attracted one bid. The Rocky Butte tract's history is instructive. The original minimum acceptable bid estimate was $27.6 million. That was slashed to $11.7 million at the weekend Reston meeting, and on April 28 the one bid received for Rocky Butte was for $11.17 million. On October 15 a bid was received for $22.2 million. One wonders what would have happened if Interior had rejected all of the "high" bids received on April 28, as it did the Rocky Butte bid, and put them up for sale again in October?

The Powder River Basin coal sale turned out to bear no resemblance to the economist's stamp auction. Overall, there was only one bidder for nine of the twelve tracts, and the other three had only two bidders each. The new bidding system, however, is predicated on there being genuine competition. "Absent competition," as GAO noted, Interior did not have "a sound basis for determining fair market value." GAO concluded that if Interior had used the original value estimates, revised upward to correct the technical errors, it would have had a benchmark for judging the reasonableness of the bids. "Had this been done, we believe most of the bids would have been rejected."

One year minus a day after the April 28 sale, Assistant Secretary Carruthers was summoned before a subcommittee of the House Interior Committee to answer charges made in a 121-page report done by the Surveys and Investigations Staff of the House Appropriations Committee. The report charged that the Secretary had sold the Powder River Basin coal at "firesale prices." The small hearing room in the Rayburn building was packed with people and overheated by the television lights. As the day wore on, Carruthers was grilled about every aspect of the Powder River Basin sale by a number of congressmen. Finally, Congressman Sidney Yates asked outright whether the absence of competition concerned him. The exasperated Carruthers replied: "Yes, competition is nice in a market. We and the Justice Department would like to see more competition. But so long as you have one willing buyer and one willing seller, you have a market."

Yates tartly replied: "We want to make sure you are not too willing."

Several factors contributed to the absence of competition at the Powder River Basin sale. Coal demand was depressed, interest rates were high, and in at least one instance Interior actually eliminated the competition for a tract. At the request of AMAX Coal Company, BLM Director Burford agreed to divide the Duck Nest tract in two and the South Duck Nest tract went up for sale on April 28. It had just one bidder: AMAX. ARCO spokesman Harold Craig told *Washington Post* reporter Dale Russakoff that "once they divided it, the tract wasn't attractive to us. . . . Until then, we intended to bid, and had we won we certainly intended to mine it." He added: "If you've got a tract that's competitive, obviously that drives prices up, and makes the entire bidding process more favorable from the government's point of view." AMAX bid $3.6 million for the South Duck Nest tract. What the North tract will bring when it is sold remains to be seen, but, before it was divided and there was still competition, the whole tract was worth about $15.8 million.

Before he resigned, Watt set in motion plans for more big coal sales. He targeted some 15 billion tons of public coal for possible sale by 1985. Following Powder River came the sale of about 540 million tons of lignite coal in the Fort Union area of Montana and North Dakota. No bid was received on 428 million tons and the remainder, in five small tracts, received one bid per tract. Next is supposed to be the San Juan Basin in northwestern New Mexico—over a billion tons of coal—followed by another big Powder River Basin sale—five billion tons.

Over the years, before Watt, the federal government had leased 16.5 billion tons of publicly owned coal reserves. In 1982 production from federal coal leases totaled about 104 million tons, 12 percent of all

U.S. coal production. There are approved mine plans or pending mine plans for 9.9 billion tons of already-leased federal coal. In other words, production could be increased substantially in a relatively short time if there were more demand. Enough public coal has already been leased to meet even the most extravagant coal demand projections for many years to come.*

Governor Tony Anaya of New Mexico recently noted that the federal government has already leased enough coal in New Mexico to meet demand for the state's coal for the next 80 years and that the Administration's proposed sale of 1.3 billion tons from the San Juan Basin would raise it to a 117-year supply. What, the governor wants to know, is the rush?

The arithmetic of the Administration's coal leasing program certainly provides no answer to his question. One must look elsewhere. Brant Calkin, Deputy Secretary for Natural Resources in New Mexico, offers this explanation: "The Administration's coal leasing program, like almost all of its major public resource programs, is certainly not based on economic or environmental logic. I think it's ideological zeal—government is bad, the market is good, ergo, dump all the public resources you can onto the market before those damn 'socialists' take over again. The Watts and the Crowells don't want to manage resources, they want to dispose of them."

The massive coal lease sales have had the same impact on federal resource management as massive timber sales and land sales. Other values have suffered. Interior has ceased trying to decide which coal *should* be developed and which should, at least for the present, be left alone. That, they say, is for the market to decide. But the market pays no attention to such other values as wilderness, wildlife, agriculture, and watershed protection. That was the job Congress assigned to the stewards of the land at the Interior Department, and they have refused to do it.

After the release of the GAO report on the Powder River Basin sale, a move was made in Congress to impose a four-month moratorium on federal coal leasing to give Interior a chance to unsnarl its new leasing system and do a better job analyzing the human and environmental impacts of future sales, but it failed in the Republican-controlled Senate

---

*There is reason to lease coal where development is already under way and it makes both economic and environmental sense to mine all the coal at the same time.

by a vote of 51 to 48. The industry's National Coal Association, which has staunchly supported Secretary Watt throughout the Powder River Basin controversy, sent 50 lobbyists to Capitol Hill to work against the moratorium. Carl Bagge, president of the National Coal Association, stated: "This assumed monumental importance. We're working for coal, God, and America. All we want is to make a buck and develop coal resources and bring fuel to America." After the Fort Union coal sale fiasco, however, the Senate reconsidered and voted to halt more coal lease sales until a special commission could review Watt's coal leasing practices. Watt, in an off-hand crack to the Chamber of Commerce, characterized that commission as "a black . . . a woman, two Jews, and a cripple." This remark was, of course, his undoing.*

Not since Warren G. Harding was President have we seen an Administration so willing to dispense public resources to the vested interests—the big mineral, oil and gas, coal, lumber, and livestock interests—at the public's expense. Venality and old-fashioned cronyism characterized Harding's Administration. Ideological zeal characterizes Reagan's. But the effect is still to enrich the few at the expense of the many, and to injure our land. And there is a sense of atavism, a throwback to an age in which our resources seemed so boundless that plunder hardly seemed to matter. Since that age, most of the nation had come to view our land as a resource to be managed and protected and believed that the law now required such protection.

But, while it is true that the courts, the Congress, the states, and sometimes simply the force of public opposition have halted or delayed some of the Administration's policies, the basic substitution of exploitation for protection in the institutional value system of the government agencies that manage our land has continued unabated. It continues to affect the scores of decisions the agencies make each day that ultimately determine the fate of our land.

---

*While on the subject of fair market value, one must not forget that the Mining Law of 1872 is still on the books. This means that the public receives no return from the exploitation of valuable minerals such as gold, silver, copper, zinc, uranium, and molybdenum on the public land. Not a penny—there are no lease sale revenues, no royalty payments. The law has long been recognized by experts as an anachronism—a throwback to another era when the giveaway of public resources was the norm. The last three Administrations have sought its repeal. However, the Reagan Administration has not lifted a finger to do so and is apparently content to let the giveaways continue.

4

THE
NATIONAL
PARKS
PUT AT RISK

"The best idea we've ever had."
Wallace Stegner

Driving up the San Diego freeway toward Beverly Hills, on a clear day you can see that the vast urbanized Los Angeles basin is rimmed on the north by mountains. To the east, miles away, are the lofty snow-topped San Gabriels. Stretching from the heart of Los Angeles to the west are the Santa Monicas.

The Santa Monica Mountains are a young, jagged, narrow coastal range, rising steeply from the sea on the south and dropping on the north into the San Fernando Valley. As you go westward, more and more of the mountain range is still wild. The peaks are bare rock or grassland dotted with sage, the flanks spread with manzanita, sugarbrush, wildflowers, and centuries-old live oaks. In the streamsides and canyon bottoms are thick stands of sycamore, willow, and valley oak. It is a hospitable environment for birds (240 kinds) and mammals (over 60 species, including deer, bobcat, and coyote). Four pairs of golden eagles nest in these mountains. Twelve to twenty mountain lions live there. The track of a mountain lion was recently sighted in the Santa Monicas within the city limits of Los Angeles, about three miles from Sunset Boulevard.

This superb mountain range is a relic. It is almost the last natural area in greater Los Angeles that is not yet built on, paved over, or swallowed up by a hundred miles of urban sprawl. As scenery, the Santa Monicas rank almost with the Marin headlands that rear up over San Francisco's Golden Gate. As open space close enough for ten million Angelenos and millions more visitors to use, as habitat for wild animals on the doorstep of a great metropolis, as a refuge from Los Angeles smog, and as a fine, spacious, still unspoiled example of the Mediterranean chaparral ecosystem—the largest of its kind left in the United States—the Santa Monicas are unique.

For these reasons, Congress established the Santa Monica Mountains National Recreation Area in 1978 as part of the national parks system. The boundaries of the Recreation Area enclose 150,000 acres, including the homes of 30,000 people, some prime beach property (e.g., the movie stars' colony at Malibu Beach), and a finger of mountain ridge poking into Beverly Hills and Hollywood. Nobody planned to buy all of it. Instead, the idea was to coexist with the people living there and to combine land purchases with land protection.

In 1980 the National Park Service started to buy land. In 1981 the Secretary of the Interior ordered it to stop. James Watt clamped a freeze on land purchases throughout the park system. He said: "We must be stewards of what we have before we reach out for more." And despite the fact that Congress kept providing moderate sums to continue parkland purchases, Watt mostly did not spend it.

Whether the Reagan Administration intended a temporary or permanent freeze on adding parkland was not clear. (Watt said at one point that most of the "truly unique" park areas were already in the system.) But even a temporary freeze involves permanent losses. Land intended for parks, to preserve or buffer unique natural areas, is lost to developers. And inevitably land prices rise. This is exactly what happened to the Santa Monica Mountains National Recreation Area.

When the Santa Monica park was established, its first superintendent, Robert Chandler, and his staff worked out a plan that would link 40,000 acres of federal parkland with 40,000 acres of existing parks and public beaches owned by the State of California, the City and County of Los Angeles, and Ventura County. The Park Service would try to protect the rest through easements, or by working with local governments for protective zoning. A fragile structure perhaps, but the best that could be done with limited money and some mighty expensive California real estate. In 1980 Congress provided a first installment of $35 million out of what was supposed to be $155 million over five years. Superintendent Chandler first went after acreage that was under the threat of development. Later, he meant to buy cheaper, more remote land.

One choice property the Park Service wanted was the Currey-Riach ranch. Five hundred and twenty acres of rolling oak-studded grassland, it was ideal both for a recreation center and as an important entranceway to the park. Another highly prized site was the Quaker-Ross property, a gentle, well watered bowl surrounded by grassy hills and a rampart of mountains—a little Shangri-La in the middle of the park. The Park Service owns a small plot in the bowl and wanted the rest for a headquarters and visitors' center. As of January 1981, the Park Service was in serious negotiations to buy both sites. In February, with the Watt freeze, negotiations stopped. In the next two years, 1982 and 1983, Santa Monica got just $5 million for buying parkland—more than the zero recommended by the Interior Department but far from enough to carry out the program Chandler and his staff had planned.

The Currey-Riach ranch was lost to the park. When the Park Service had to stop negotiating to buy the tract, the owner got permits to develop it. As John Reynolds, assistant superintendent of the park, says, "The same land that's most suitable for recreation is also most suitable for building houses." Eight hundred homes and condominiums and one million square feet of commercial and office space will be built on the former ranch.

As of 1983, the Quaker-Ross property (the little Shangri-La) was going through the permit process for real estate development. Some individual lots on the hills enclosing the bowl had already been sold; a mansion as big as a motel was erected on one commanding site. If the park ever manages to get the remaining land, it will be at a much higher price than the one being negotiated before the freeze.

It is single-family houses, says Reynolds, "that have eaten up more land than anything else." These new houses—typically pseudo-Norman castles or Roman villas on huge lots leveled like helicopter pads out of the mountains—are appearing farther and farther up the mountainsides. "On some very important parcels, we're in a race with the developers," Reynolds says. The developers have plenty of potential customers.

281

When the *Los Angeles Times* published a cartoon showing the whole Santa Monica NRA divided up into building lots and labeled "Wattville," some people thought it was a real estate ad. They called the *Times* asking how to reach the Wattville sales office.

Reynolds thinks it isn't too late to save the park. Before the freeze, the park was able to buy three out of five tracts needed for recreation. There is still land left for a 50-mile "backbone" hiking and riding trail from Hollywood to the western end of the mountains, and for connections between wild areas so that the park's animals will not be herded into little "islands" that cannot sustain them. It is still possible to protect Zuma Canyon, the last natural major waterslope from the Santa Monica Mountains to the sea. And much of the park's magnificent scenery is still intact. From winding Mulholland Drive, you can still look across ranks of wild silent peaks and steep valleys to the pale violet clouds hovering over the sea. Indeed, a massive lobbying campaign by park advocates and environmental groups resulted in a $15 million appropriation for land acquisition in 1984.

The people of Los Angeles appreciate the park. Even the small acreage that the Park Service already owns (about 6,000 acres) had nearly half a million visitors in 1982, and that does not count seven million people just driving through or 29 million visitors to the state and county beaches and the three state parks up in the mountains. The park staff helps school and community groups bring 40,000 children a year —mostly inner-city children—into the park for environmental field trips. "We've had kids out here that had never seen a natural stream, never seen the ocean," says Reynolds.

The staff, exceptionally weighted toward resource management and research, has proven adept at taking care of the park's land and educating neighbors. The high chaparral ecosystem of the park is adapted to naturally recurring fires. If fires are suppressed for too long a time, the dry brush builds up and when, eventually and unavoidably, some fire does get out of control, it becomes a roaring holocaust. The park's staff have sold many of their neighbors on the need for controlled burns and have conducted several.

Elsa Leviseur, an architect living in the city of Santa Monica, is one of many citizens who have dedicated years of volunteer work to saving the Santa Monica Mountains. Leviseur says that much of the area is simply unsuitable for real estate development because of its fire ecology and its geological instability. Some of the soils are naturally unstable, with a tendency to slide off their clay base. Building on canyon slopes or mountainsides—especially bulldozer-type development on flattened-out terraces—makes the erosion worse. Mammoth mudslides and earth-slides are regular occurrences in the Santa Monicas. "The Pacific Coast Highway [at the base of the mountains] is closed for a week to six weeks every year," says Leviseur, "because the land is moving across the high-way."

No one has the figures for the Santa Monica area, but federal and state disaster relief for victims of fire and earthslides in the Los Angeles basin can run into millions. Leviseur thinks it makes more sense to spend federal and state money to preserve what is left of the Santa Monica Mountains in a natural state, than to bail out private landowners.

It's a question, she says, of whether the Santa Monica Mountains "should provide recreation for the many or should be owned and enjoyed exclusively by those who are able to afford it."

This question did not trouble James Watt. On the contrary. The Santa Monica NRA had an extra strike against it precisely because it was an "urban park." And that was anathema. In an aggressive speech to the concessioners of the national parks in March 1981, Watt said: "I do not believe that the National Park Service should run urban parks. I have strong views on that." And: "We will use the budget system to be the excuse to make major policy decisions." In an Associated Press interview a month later, Watt added details. He said that parks such as "Gateway East and Gateway West" (the Gateway National Recreation Area in New York and New Jersey, and California's Golden Gate) are "play-grounds . . . where there is the ranger pushing the kids in swings." Those "playgrounds," he said, "should be maintained by those that play in them."

The Gateway and Golden Gate NRAs, both established in 1972, were the first "urban parks" to join the national park system. Not without controversy. Over the objections of some park professionals, Congress and Richard Nixon's Secretary of the Interior, Walter Hickel, enlarged the concept of national parks to include the best of our remaining wild lands near cities, serving millions of people who may never get to the Grand Canyon or Yellowstone. In the next six years, Congress established four more of these new parks near cities: Cuyahoga Valley National Recreation Area (between Akron and Cleveland) in 1974, and, in 1978, Chattahoochee River National Recreation Area (Atlanta), Jean Lafitte National Historical Park and Preserve (New Orleans), and Santa Monica.

To anyone who visits them, the idea that "Gateway East and Gateway West" are mere "playgrounds" must seem a strange one. Golden Gate NRA is 68 square miles of tawny hills, redwood groves, beach, and blue ocean. In one continuous expanse, it links San Francisco harbor with the redwood forest enfolded in Muir Wood National Monument, with Mt. Tamalpais State Park (from the peak of Mt. Tamalpais you can sometimes see the Sierra Nevadas, a hundred miles away) and with Point Reyes National Seashore. No part of the park is more than an hour's drive from San Francisco or Oakland, and it offers boating, camping, fishing, and swimming as well as its spectacular scenery. Yet it is so spacious that a visitor who wants seclusion can usually find it, on a headland above the crashing Pacific, with a view of the city gleaming in the distance. Today, Golden Gate NRA is the most frequented place in the national park system, with 20 million visits in 1982. This compares with about 2.5 million visits apiece to the old "crown jewel" parks —Yellowstone, Yosemite, and Grand Canyon.

Gateway NRA, around New York harbor, is not just a Coney Island either. In Brooklyn, in addition to the very well used Jacob Riis Beach, it has 9,100 acres of wildlife refuge on a major bird migration route in Jamaica Bay. The refuge includes seven miles of trails, two ponds, marshlands, and 318 species of birds. Gateway's Sandy Hook unit in New Jersey has rugged beaches beloved by fishermen, a unique 200-acre Holly Forest, and historic Fort Hancock as well. Robert Cahn, the Pulitzer Prize–winning writer on the national parks, calls the Sandy Hook unit "a small national park in itself." Altogether, more than eight million visitors a year use the Gateway National Recreation Area.

Secretary Watt and other officials appointed by President Reagan to the Interior Department tried to get rid of certain urban parks. Without publicly saying so (it is always politically unpopular to take parks away from people), they compiled a hit list of parks to be rooted out of the park system. In an interview with Associated Press, Watt said that some parks—he did not name which ones—should be deauthorized. "Candidly that needs to be done. I don't know if we have the political leadership to do it, the courage to do it now." That he meant urban parks was clear from the tenor of the whole interview, which was an attack on "playground" parks.

Two confidential memos from G. Ray Arnett, the Interior Department's assistant secretary for fish and wildlife and parks, to Russell Dickenson, National Park Service Director, made Watt's intent unmistakable. The first memo, in April 1981, asked Dickenson to comb the files of the past ten years for evidence of Park Service opposition to national recreation areas, seashores, or lakeshores that Congress had created. Arnett singled out Santa Monica NRA for attention first, then Cuyahoga Valley NRA, then Fire Island National Seashore (near New York), Indiana Dunes National Lakeshore (on Lake Michigan near Chicago), and Sleeping Bear Dunes National Lakeshore (also on Lake Michigan, more rural, but easily reachable from Chicago and Detroit). Governors, senators, and congressmen from the affected states erupted in anger at the suggestion of a hit list. Interior Department spokesmen denied there was one.

In a second confidential memo, a few weeks after the first, Arnett wanted to know the procedure for turning over Cuyahoga NRA to Ohio. He also wanted to discuss "an accelerated divestiture program" for Santa Monica. Again, members of Congress angrily protested and again Watt denied there was a hit list.

If the hit list was dead, it had a lively ghost. In the fall of 1982, both the Inspector General and the Office of Management and Budget proposed deauthorization of parks. Watt's spokesmen disavowed the proposals.

Meanwhile, Watt had refused to accept a gift of 176 acres of Army surplus land to be added to Gateway's Staten Island unit—scenic shorefront land with a view of New York Harbor, and with two historic forts. The Gateway Citizens Committee took Watt to court and eventually forced him to accept the Army's surplus land.

Among the most effective protests from Congress on doing away with parks were those of Ohio Representative John Seiberling and Illinois Representative Sidney Yates. Both men have a personal concern, on behalf of their constituents, for urban parks. Both are also vigilant protectors of all the parks and all the federally owned public lands. Seiberling is chairman of the House Interior subcommittee on public lands and national parks. Yates is chairman of the House Appropriations subcommittee on the Interior.

Congressman Seiberling, who led the move in 1974 to preserve a pastoral stretch of the Cuyahoga River corridor between industrial Akron and Cleveland, argues that it is elitist to save only the spectacular national parks in remote parts of the United States. "We need to take care of the people who can't afford to go the long distances and give them a high-quality park experience," he says. Nathaniel P. Reed, a lifelong Republican and Assistant Secretary of the Interior under Presidents Ford and Nixon, said he had once had some reservations about urban parks. "But the overwhelming attendance figures have convinced me that these areas are bringing outdoor recreation to millions of people who would otherwise be frozen out of the park system."

This point of view is at the opposite pole from Watt's "playground" remark. Implicit in the Interior Department's hit lists is a regional as well as a class bias—a denigration of the populous east and west coasts and the industrialized Great Lakes area. Los Angeles, Cleveland, Chicago, and New York were good targets for a give-back of recreational parks. But nobody ever mentioned the almost purely recreational character of Nevada's and Arizona's Lake Mead NRA and the Lake Powell area in Utah's Glen Canyon NRA. Both were created by huge dams built by the Interior Department's Bureau of Reclamation for the main purposes of storing water and generating electricity. Both are parts of the national park system. Neither pretends to a major purpose of preserving natural wonders; what they provide is a spacious, scenic, non-commercial setting for water recreation in desert country. Both are meccas for people who enjoy motorized boating. Lake Mead and Lake Powell offer the kind of recreation James Watt said he enjoys ("I don't like to walk and I don't like to paddle"); they serve the part of the West that Watt comes from—the part that is also Ronald Reagan's strongest political base; and they were never even thought of for a give-back. These recreation areas are not "urban," of course. They serve people from the lightly populated surrounding areas plus millions of people throughout the Southwest from Los Angeles to Phoenix to Salt Lake City, who can afford to drive to them.

While the hit list of urban parks was apparently dropped, the freeze on acquisition definitely took hold. In its first three years, the Reagan Administration bought land for the national parks only when compelled by Congress to do so. This policy was very different from its predecessors. Visits by Americans to their national parks started to skyrocket in the 1950's, with increased prosperity and the construction of interstate highways. Park visits rose from 30 million a year in 1950 to over 300 million a year in 1982. Up until 1980, all the Secretaries of the Interior favored adding to the parks. And they had the means to do it.

In 1965 Congress set up a special fund for buying parkland, fish and wildlife refuges, and forest land, and for grants to states to help them establish their own parks and recreation projects. The Land and Water Conservation Fund gets most of its money, specially earmarked, from the nation's royalties on offshore oil leases. This means the money for buying parks does not come directly out of the taxpayer's pocket but rather from the sale of "a nonrenewable resource which belongs to the whole nation." Congress wanted some of the proceeds spent for "other resources which will also be used for the benefit of the whole of the American people." The fund was supposed to provide a reliable source of money for adding to the parks. The House Interior Committee said at the time: "[I]t is not the sort of program that can be effective if it is subject to being turned on and off like a water tap."

The Reagan Administration turned off the tap. Each year he was in office, Watt asked Congress for only enough purchase funds to pay for court awards for land previously bought. Every year, Congress appropriated more than Watt asked for. Altogether, Watt spent only about half the amount Congress provided and spent it largely on the court awards at that, not on acquiring additional lands as intended by Congress.

Watt claimed that the parks we already own were in "shameful" condition and should be "restored" before we add any more. He announced a plan to spend one billion dollars over five years fixing up park facilities—water and sewer systems, roads, bridges, tunnels, visitor centers, lodges, even a swimming pool. During that time, not a cent would go for new parkland.

Watt's talk about "shameful" conditions made a lot of people quite angry. While nobody denied that some parks, especially the older ones, needed repairs, few park professionals agreed that park facilities were an unholy mess. In fact, spending on maintenance and operations had grown steadily in the previous few years. Congressman Yates was particularly incensed that Watt called this period a time of "ruin" for the parks, and he collected the figures to refute Watt's claim. He told the House of Representatives: "Any resemblance of Mr. Watt's testimony [on that subject] to the truth . . . is purely coincidental."

Watt also continued to quote a figure of $1.6 billion needed to correct "health and safety" hazards in the parks, long after the Park Service itself announced it could find no more than $577 million worth of repairs that needed doing and the source of the original figure, the

287

General Accounting Office, had accepted the lower Park Service estimate.

In light of the park's fundamental needs, Watt's plan had some critical shortcomings. Parks professionals have worried since the 1950's that the popularity of the parks is doing them in. Overcrowding, pollution, and traffic threatened—still threaten—to make slums out of some of the best-loved parks. Part of the answer is to add worthy new parks, taking some of the pressure off the old ones. From 1968, when offshore oil revenues began to fatten the Land and Water Conservation Fund, until the end of 1980, 82 new park areas were added to the national park system. At the same time, park visits more than doubled.

By February 1981, when Watt froze parkland acquisition, money in the fund stood at over $1 billion. At the same time, the Park Service had selected 423,000 acres, about eight percent of the privately owned land within the borders of the national parks, for purchase at a cost of $800 million. Going along with the budget-cutting by the new Administration, Congress was willing to postpone some of the buying. But some purchases cannot just stay on hold.

Santa Monica was not the only park threatened with the permanent loss of essential tracts of land. Some of the older parks were hit hard too. In Grand Teton, for example, Park Service officials wanted to buy properties within the park and were turned down by their Interior Department superiors. In 1983 two houses had already been built on the land, and one owner was threatening to subdivide.

Another critical deficiency in Watt's plan for the parks was that it ignored threats to the very natural features that make the parks unique. Damage from too many people—trampling plants, compacting the earth, sometimes illegally collecting fossils or prehistoric art, or tearing up dunes and beaches in dune buggies—is only a part of it. Still harder to manage are threats to the parks from outside—from power plants spewing pollutants, or dams that destroy a park's natural water supply, or urban encroachment. Today, one hundred days of the year, the view in the Grand Canyon is smudged by air pollution, most of it coming from industries and smelters hundreds of miles away. Tomorrow, if geothermal energy development goes ahead on the border of Yellowstone, the park's geysers—even Old Faithful—might peter out.

A 1980 report, *State of the Parks,* prepared by national parks superintendents in response to Congress, made it clear that *all* the parks, even the most remote, are suffering natural resource damage. But scientific knowledge about the natural norms in and around the parks—the flora and fauna, the natural condition of the air and water and soils—is scanty. For most of the resource threats, park managers need more knowledge to identify and deal with the intrusions. Watt's plan for "restoration of the parks" ignored these needs. In his budget additions of about $100 million a year for restoration, nothing was earmarked for preservation of natural resources. In fact, in his 1982 budget, Watt deleted $5 million originally promised for natural resource projects (such as management of habitat of the endangered grizzly in Yellowstone). What is more, Watt's own actions in managing the federal lands and their coal, oil and gas, and geothermal energy intensified some of the worst threats to the parks.

Sometimes, conflicts between mining or logging or the generation of power and the clean air, fresh water, beauty, and silence of the parks are tough to resolve. Pollution from our industrial society is not easy to contain, and the parks are not immune to it. But if the government is going to sacrifice national parks, most Americans want to know that there is a pretty compelling reason to do so. The Administration's rush to sell off the nation's energy resources had no apparent compelling reason. There was no practical economic sense to it, in a depressed market for oil, gas, coal, and uranium. And no one, it seemed, was counting the cost to the parks. Secretary Watt told Russ Dickenson, his National Parks director, that when it came to external threats to the parks, "You're on your own."

All over the West, national parks have got massive coal leasing to worry about. For example, Watt put up 1.3 billion tons of coal for strip mining in the San Juan basin, with leasing scheduled to begin in December 1983. In the middle of the San Juan basin is Chaco Canyon National Historical Park, a great center of the ancient pueblo culture of the Anasazi. Until the end of the twelfth century, when its occupants mysteriously departed, this place, with its huge multistory apartments housing as many as 1,200 people, its underground kivas for religious ceremonies, its pottery and textiles, its extensive agriculture, was something like a city-state, connected by road with 75 outlying communities. Strip mining in the public lands of the San Juan basin would endanger the remnants of this impressive civilization. It could aggravate the serious erosion in Chaco Canyon itself, pollute the air, and load the water in the park with toxic wastes. It would threaten the thousands of archaeological sites outside the park's boundary, including at least 40 of the old outlying pueblo communities.

Bryce Canyon National Park in southern Utah is another park bordered by strippable coal. There, Watt attempted to reverse a decision by the previous Secretary of the Interior, Cecil Andrus, to keep strip mining out of sight of the park. Andrus banned surface mining on 9,000 acres of the Alton coal field, which lies in the green hills below Bryce Canyon's famed Yovimpa Point. It is a spectacular outlook. Below its windy height stretch miles of cliffs, canyons, and pinyon-and-juniper-covered mesas. In the entire Colorado plateau, which extends westward from the Colorado Rockies to the Nevada desert, Yovimpa Point is the best place to view the "Grand Staircase," a mighty series of steps that descend across 150 miles, from 11,000-foot Mt. Dutton to the bottom of the Grand Canyon. The steps drop 1,000 to 2,000 feet at a time in cliffs of stunning colors—salmon pink, gray, white, vermillion, chocolate. Much of this geological extravaganza is visible from Yovimpa Point. On a clear day you can see the Grand Canyon more than one hundred miles away.

Strip mining, if it ever takes place in the Alton field, will cover an eight-mile swath of the view. Dragline shovels, with their 300-foot booms, will be fully visible. Dust from the digging will hang in the air. The noise of explosives will compete with the wind in the sage. Robert Benton, superintendent of Bryce Canyon National Park, keeps in his office a photograph that amuses him. It shows a wooded mountain slope, a dragline, and, about 500 feet away, a blazing fireball. "This mining company wanted to prove they could make a quiet blast, and it fireballed on 'em. It jumped several hundred feet, all the way over the dragline, and, we understand, started a forest fire," says Benton, chuckling quietly.

To Benton's mind, "the point has largely been made that, without Secretary Andrus' decision, the Alton coal field would have a number of negative impacts," not least on the park's visitors. Answering a park questionnaire, one of them wrote, "If I wanted to take my family to see a coal mine, we would have gone to Pennsylvania."

Coal from the strip mine, if it ever opens, will be shuttled to a slurry plant in 120-ton dump trucks—enormous contraptions, bigger than a locomotive, the size of a house. At the slurry plant, the coal will be pulverized, mixed with pure well water drawn from the Navajo aquifer, and pumped to a power plant—possibly in Nevada, possibly to a new plant near St. George, Utah, seventeen miles from Zion National Park.

The proposed use of well water for coal slurry worries the local ranchers. Water supplies in southern Utah, as in most places in the West, are scarce and prized. Sylvan Johnson, an alfalfa farmer in Johnson Canyon (named for Sylvan Johnson's Mormon pioneer grandfather), said at a hearing on the Alton coal field proposal, "God Almighty, we'll all be dry in five years!"

Soon after James Watt took office, he asked a federal court to void the Andrus decision so that he could remake the decision himself. The court turned him down. Still in court are two legal challenges to the decision, one by the major leaseholder, the Utah International Mining Company, which wants to mine; and another by a coalition of ranchers and three conservation groups who believe that the Andrus decision did not go far enough to protect the environment, and should have covered more acreage.

On the other side of the country, at Florida's southern tip, Everglades National Park has been trying to control threats from special interests to its air and water, its fish and its marvelous wading birds. Commercial fishermen want to go on fishing in the biologically impoverished Florida Bay. The operator of a hunting camp in Big Cypress National Preserve, next door to the Everglades Park, wants continued air boat service through the park in an area designated wilderness. Florida Power and Light wants to burn cheaper, higher-sulfur oil at its Turkey Point Plant near the park. In 1981, Interior Department officials who supervise the parks began to champion these special interests.

The Interior Department officials were G. Ray Arnett, assistant secretary for fish and wildlife and parks, formerly a petroleum geologist, founder of a trophy hunters' lobbying group, California director of fish and game when Reagan was governor, and an advocate of hunting, commercial fishing, and snowmobiling in the parks; Arnett's special assistant Ric Davidge, formerly managing director of the National Inholders Association, a group which represents owners of land within park boundaries and which often battles the Park Service on their behalf; and Roy Spradley, associate solicitor for conservation and wildlife, formerly an attorney for Florida Power and Light. These officials all tried to undo plans the Park Service had adopted up through 1980, after years of work and several public hearings, to conserve the natural resources of the Everglades. As of 1983, the Park Service plans were still holding up.

Congress authorized the Everglades National Park in 1934; in 1947 President Truman opened it. Everglades is the "mother" park for biological conservation. It is one of eight places in the world designated an

International Biosphere Reserve, a World Heritage site, and a National Park. Its 1.4 million acres make it the second largest national park (after Yellowstone) outside Alaska. Its vast level expanses of sawgrass marsh, broken by little pine-covered hummocks and bordered by mangroves, are home to over 300 species of birds, including herons, ibises, bitterns, and the spectacular roseate spoonbill. The wood stork nests here. A large white bird with black head and black-edged wings, the wood stork on land looks comically incapable of flight; in the air it is all fluid grace.

Wood storks are getting rather rare in the Everglades. Since the park was authorized 50 years ago, its whole wading bird population has declined as much as 90 percent, some biologists say. A major reason for the decline, according to Rick Smith, assistant superintendent of the park, is that the entire fresh water supply of south Florida, from the Kissimmee River basin down, has been dammed, channelized, and regulated for the needs of the large-scale agriculture and urban growth in Florida's southern tip.

"Aside from the rain that falls on the Everglades, hardly a drop of water arrives in the natural way without passing through a manmade structure," says Smith. "The drastically altered water regime has radically altered the productivity of the estuaries." As fresh water is diverted to farms and cities, less of it reaches Florida Bay and other estuaries of south Florida. This makes the estuarine water saltier—too salty to serve as a hatchery and nursery for some fish and shellfish. As the quantity of fresh water in the estuaries declined, so did the fish. And so did the wading birds.

The wood stork has a special problem. Its young hatch in early spring before Florida's rainy season. Under natural conditions, water bodies gradually shrink at this time of year, and food for the bird's young is concentrated into smaller and smaller pools. Human regulation of water behind levees interferes with this natural cycle. In drought years, the gates in levees are kept closed, hoarding water for irrigation of farms and for city water supplies late in the season; in this case, water bodies dry up and food disappears. In flood years, the gates are opened, and water levels stay high for too long, so the storks' food is too dispersed. In either case, the chances of nesting failure are great. "In the last twelve years the wood storks in the park have had only two successful nesting seasons," says Smith.

By the late 1960's, sport fishermen in southern Florida began to complain that fish were disappearing from the Everglades. As reports of the decline accumulated, the Park Service started to investigate. Unlike most parks, Everglades has an excellent scientific institution, the South Florida Research Center, right in the park.

In 1978 and 1979, the Everglades staff worked out a resource management plan based on information gathered at four workshops and four public hearings. Smith says: "Our first priority was to have enough fish for the eagles, the ospreys, the herons—all the components of the ecosystem—they get first shot. The second priority, consistent with National Park Service policy, was recreation, or sport fishing. In last place was commercial fishing." The plan the Park Service adopted in 1980 set a bag limit on popular varieties (redfish, snapper, and sea trout) for sport fishermen. It established a large sanctuary in northeast Florida Bay, excluding motor boats, for the endangered crocodile. And it phased out commercial fishing in Florida Bay over the following five years. The commercial fishermen challenged the plan in court. A federal district judge in Miami, denying a temporary injunction against the plan, remarked there was little chance the plaintiff would win its case on the merits of the argument.

What happened next is pieced together from leaked memos and information from Park Service insiders. First, the newly appointed assistant secretary of the Interior, G. Ray Arnett, met with commercial fishermen, with farmers who were seeking leases in the park, and with the operator of a Big Cypress Preserve hunting camp. Then, Roy Spradley wrote the Justice Department, asking its lawyers to seek a compromise in the suit the commercial fishermen had brought, because "as a matter of policy, this department [Interior] no longer supports the commercial fishing regulations. . . . Specifically, the Department intends to revise the regulations to provide for commercial fishing in Everglades National Park."

However much the new officials at the Interior Department might wish to void regulations not to their liking, the law does not allow rules that have been duly adopted simply to be swept off the books. Therefore, Arnett ordered the Park Service to hold new public hearings on commercial fishing. Ric Davidge came down to Florida to chair the hearing. He got an earful. The Park Service received 11,276 public comments, orally and in writing. Nine thousand three hundred and sixty-five were against any changes in the regulations.

The change in regulations was put on hold. "But Arnett didn't give up," says Destry Jarvis of the National Parks and Conservation Associa-

THE NATIONAL PARKS PUT AT RISK

tion. Over the objections of Russell Dickenson, the Service's director, Arnett sent a team of biologists from the Fish and Wildlife Service to redo the study of the fish population in Florida Bay. "He sent the wrong people [freshwater instead of saltwater fish biologists], with the wrong equipment, under impossible time constraints"—that is, to complete the study before the end of 1985, when commercial fishing was to be ended. Because of the extreme pressure of this deadline, said Jarvis, the first research proposal the new group made "was so destructive—it would have killed so many fish in order to study them," that it had to be abandoned. The deadline for the study stood, however.

Meanwhile, Arnett's office ordered the Park Service to solicit public comment on a proposal to open the "stairstep" airboat trail to general recreation, including all kinds of boats. The trail crosses parts of the wilderness area in the Everglades Park. The reaction was vociferous. "Man, I tell you people did not want the airboat trail opened again," said a Park Service employee.

Arnett then ordered the Park Service to explore ways of giving operators of hunting camps in the Big Cypress Preserve lifetime rights to keep their camps open. The Park Service's plan had required an "orderly phaseout" of these camps. But, said Jarvis, "this Administration is paranoid about hunting camps" and was determined to keep them open. This turned out not to be legally possible, basically because the operators did not own the land their camps were built on. They had simply occupied the land years back and built on it. Legally, they were in trespass. In ordinary language, they were squatters.

A Park Service insider in Washington remarked: "When an Administration changes, [the new] people tend to be naive. They think everybody must agree with them. . . . That's the danger of listening to small interest groups—they think those values are shared by a large group of people, and it just isn't true. . . .

"They got burned and got burned bad. Not just by people with a strong environmental point of view but the general public. They've made promises and then they can't get out of it." With relish, this oldtimer described how the operator of one hunting camp "made life miserable for them. Hell, I bet there's been days she called Ric Davidge ten times."

Another special interest with an ally at Interior Department headquarters was Florida Power and Light. The utility was stymied in its plan to burn cheaper higher-sulfur oil at plants near the Everglades Park, because the Clean Air Act and EPA rules protect major national parks from degradation of air quality. Florida Power and Light proposed a rejuggling of south Florida's air quality areas to allow extra pollution in the park.

When the park's professionals wrote testimony for a public hearing opposing the change, pointing out that the higher-sulfur fuel could damage the park's vegetation, they got word from Washington that their testimony was "unacceptable." Who had blocked it? None other than Roy Spradley, the former lawyer for Florida Power and Light who was now associate solicitor of the Interior Department. Just hours before the public hearing, the testimony was unblocked. And a Dade County, Florida, board turned down the utility's request. It was close. One Park Service official says, "Energy we should be spending on conservation is going into trying to fight through the department."

As for the biggest problems in the Everglades, Park Service professionals agree that they are not the making of commercial fishermen or any other small special interest group, but of society's decisions over the past 50 years to adjust the south Florida environment to human needs and desires, rather than the other way around. Park officials have approached the state's South Florida Water Management District with ideas to restore to some degree the natural water flows, and have met with an interested response. One member of the Park Service says he feels a personal responsibility to try to restore the health of south Florida's ecosystem.

"There are plenty of people to speak for manipulating the environment to suit human beings—the city of Miami, the real estate developers, the sugar cane growers. The Everglades National Park speaks for the wood storks."

At the Everglades National Park, a combination of public protest and steadfast professional competence within the park service has so far staved off attacks by special interests on the Everglades resource management plan. At other parks, special interests have been more successful. For example, assistant secretary Arnett opened Lassen Volcanic National Park in northern California to "limited" snowmobile use—despite overwhelming opposition at three public hearings by California citizens, and despite the fact that large parts of Lassen National Forest, bordering the park, already allowed snowmobile use.

Arnett's office also overruled the Sequoia superintendent, who had banned a demonstration by snowmobiles because it could damage the park. Arnett's special assistant, Ric Davidge, reversed a recommendation by Olympic's superintendent for purchase of a privately held lakeshore property. The owner then proceeded to clear-cut the lot and sell the timber—an illegal action in a national park. After that, Davidge instructed the Park Service to buy the now denuded property and give its owner the use of a government-owned $70,000 house on the lakeshore for 25 years. The owner, by the way, eventually had to pay a $100 fine for illegal logging.

According to Robert Cahn, the prize-winning writer on the parks, "morale [in the Park Service] is at an alltime low." The reasons are the overruling of professionals by the Administration's political appointees; the demotion of senior Park Service professionals who had served in Alaska and had been criticized by Alaska's Republican senators and congressmen; and a "reorganization" of top Park Service management that put political appointees in places formerly occupied by career Park Service professionals. Author of this plan was Ric Davidge.

In 1983, before his resignation, James Watt instructed the top civil servants in the Department of the Interior to go about the country and put on a media show justifying the Secretary's program, especially the parks program. Watt personally did his part, taking every opportunity to portray himself as the rescuer of the parks. On television Watt said: "We've restored the parks. The parks were abused by the past Administration and past Congress, and we have turned that around." To a congressional committee, Watt said: "Every single year of the . . . four years [before Watt came in], Congress cut the budget which was supposed to take care of the national park system. No wonder it was hurting." And he said: "When I came in, I believe we were flushing raw sewage water into the streams and lakes of our national parks."

None of these statements, in fact, was true. The parks were not "abused" by a stingy government before Watt came to the rescue. Spending on park maintenance actually rose every year but one from 1977 to 1981. And there was no raw sewage flushed into park streams. Neither Russ Dickenson, the national parks director, nor anyone else in the Park Service, could recall any such thing when Congressman Yates asked them about it.

Watt's manipulation of the facts about the parks was actually a backhanded compliment—a tribute to their enormous popularity. We Americans invented the idea of national parks. We are exceedingly proud of them; we think, with Wallace Stegner, they are "the best idea we've ever had"; and we will not tolerate any abuse of them. Watt was trying to cash in on our special attachment to our national parks.

What is the truth of the Reagan Administration's record in the parks? Watt actually did raise spending for park maintenance and construction, not as dramatically as he claimed but at a rate rather faster than the increases of the previous four years. His "restoration" program made money available for some big-ticket items, such as road reconstruction, that managers in many parks welcomed. Bryce Canyon, for example, got repairs to its sewer system. Yellowstone got more money to rebuild the park's water systems (this work started in 1977), to fireproof and shore up the Old Faithful Inn (started in 1980), and to move cabins away from the border of Old Faithful. Certainly, such projects are worthwhile. And they are about the only pluses in Watt's management of the national parks.

Consider the minus side. The Watt restoration plan ignored thousands of threats to natural resources that Park Service professionals had documented in the *State of the Parks* report. It skimped on everything from a management plan for the feral, non-native goats in Hawaii's Haleakala Park to studies of how coal strip mining on public lands in Utah would affect underground water that feeds the springs and streams of Zion National Park. Catering to special interests in parks like the Everglades multiplied the threats to the parks' natural resources. So did the "fire sale" of energy resources on publicly owned lands in the West, even more so.

The Administration's refusal to touch the more than $1 billion in the Land and Water Conservation Fund to fill out the national park system did very real harm. Privately owned lands inside these parks were lost, and the losses cannot be regained. Under the Watt approach, the chances of adding new parks that represent distinctive features of the American landscape—Mono Lake in California, for example, or a tall grass prairie park—are about zero. With millions more Americans wanting to visit their national parks every year, it is peculiarly shortsighted to regard the park system as complete, or to rule out a whole class of parks—urban parks—as unfit. A generous vision of the parks has to include natural wonders from one coast to the other, in places as remote as Alaska's Brook Range or as accessible as New York's Gateway, varied enough and spacious enough so that every American at least once in his or her lifetime can have the experience of visiting a national park.

5

REPEATING

OUR

MISTAKES

"Can't repeat the past?" he cried incredulously.
"Why of course you can."
Jay Gatsby, 1925

"WHOOPS"

The Bonneville Power Administration is the federal agency that markets the electricity generated by the many federal dams on the Columbia River system in Washington, Oregon, Idaho, and western Montana. Bonneville wholesales electricity to utilities who retail it to customers. It is the fourth largest supplier of power in the country. In late June of 1976, Bonneville sent each utility it serves a letter, a warning.

It said Bonneville would not be able to supply in full their "firm energy requirements" as of July 1, 1983. The letter was signed by Donald Paul Hodel, then the administrator of Bonneville, now President Reagan's Secretary of Energy.

For the recipients, the letter was a chiller. Most of them were small public utilities, entirely dependent upon Bonneville. From their vantage point, they had few options. They could challenge Bonneville's projection of what their "firm energy requirements" would be in 1983, but who were they to do such a thing? Bonneville was the biggest electricity supplier in the region. It had the experts, the computers, the sophisticated forecast data. Besides, Bonneville sold a good thing—electricity —very cheaply; it was in fact the cheapest electricity in all the United States. So, if you were going to question Bonneville's projection of your future electricity needs, your inclination was to ask for more, not less. Or the public utilities could start drawing up plans for curtailing their customers' supply of electricity. Not too surprisingly, no public utility is eager to do such a thing. It means telling your neighbor you're cutting them off at a certain point. And Hodel understood this. That same month, he told an electric utility trade association meeting in San Francisco: "[I]n the Pacific Northwest the shortages we project are so serious that we have encouraged our utility customers to draw up contingency plans for curtailing services within their own systems. What we have found is a deep reluctance to come to grips with the problem of which specific loads should be dropped or which feeders should be cut off. The utilities don't want to make these kinds of decisions—they much prefer to leave them to the governors, the regulatory agencies, or to the state legislatures."

The public utilities did have another option. Although their financial resources were too scant to build the electricity-generating plants necessary to meet the increased demand Bonneville projected for them, they could band together, issue tax-exempt municipal bonds, and with the proceeds build some big power plants and share the output. That was the option Bonneville had been pushing them to take since the late 1960's.

By 1976, the utilities' consortium—the Washington Public Power Supply System (WPPSS)—already had three nuclear power plants in the works. To get those plants (WPPSS 1, 2, and 3) off the ground, Bonneville had sweetened the deal for both the sponsoring utilities and the would-be investors. Bonneville was not expressly authorized to finance or operate such plants, but it could buy and sell electricity, and through some very creative accounting and legal maneuvering Bonneville created the "net billing" concept. It allowed Bonneville to commit itself to buying the output from WPPSS 1, 2, and 3 and cover the cost by spreading it out over all the utilities who bought electricity wholesale from Bonneville. This was necessary because it was recognized that the electricity from these nuclear power plants would be at least three or four times more expensive than from existing hydroelectric plants (it turns out to be nine times more expensive), and there was real concern that no utility would buy it. And if the plants were never completed, Bonneville was committed to paying off the bondholders and charging the cost to its wholesale electricity customers.

Those three nuclear power plants were just the beginning. Bonneville was projecting that some 50,000 megawatts of non-hydroelectric generating capacity would have to be built to meet the region's rising electricity demand during the next two decades. That meant at least 50 new power plants (nuclear and coal) would have to be built before the year 2000.

WPPSS, with Bonneville's backing, was ready to push ahead with nuclear power plants 4 and 5 when trouble arose from unexpected quarters. In 1973 the Internal Revenue Service ruled that Bonneville could no longer effectively underwrite any more tax-exempt municipal bond projects like WPPSS's nuclear power plants 1, 2, and 3 through the net billing mechanism. And without Bonneville to assume the risks, the public utilities were reluctant to sponsor WPPSS nuclear power plants 4 and 5. They would have to sign what are known in the business as "take-or-pay" contracts with WPPSS. Otherwise, WPPSS would not be able to sell its bonds. Take-or-pay contracts are used by builders of electric power plants to assure that the utilities that buy electricity from these plants pay off the bonds floated to finance their construction. In effect, the customers of the power plant agree to pay whether or not the plant is finished and electricity is ever received. Thus, the risk is shifted from the builder and the bondholders to the customers, who in this case of course were the public utilities.

Hodel's warning letter was intended to impress upon the utilities the gravity of the upcoming electricity supply situation and to nudge them into supporting WPPSS 4 and 5. It worked. Some 88 utilities signed up. They knew those plants would not be on line in time to forestall the Bonneville-projected shortages, but Hodel reasoned that the plants would be ready in time to cut that unhappy electricity shortage period short—to only a few years. Most of the public utilities bought his line of reasoning.

Not Seattle though. In July 1976, the Seattle City Council voted 5 to 4 against allowing the city's public utility, the largest public utility in the region, to participate in WPPSS nuclear power plants 4 and 5. (The Seattle public utility had been one of the sponsors of WPPSS plants 1, 2, and 3.) The decision was based on a twelve-volume study prepared by three consulting firms. The bottom line was that Seattle could meet its future electricity demands more cheaply through conservation and the use of alternative energy sources. Eugene, Oregon, also declined to participate in WPPSS plants 4 and 5.

That same month, the architectural and engineering firm of Skidmore, Owings and Merrill delivered a report to Bonneville, a report which found that conservation was a technically feasible and cheaper alternative than nuclear power plants. Bonneville rejected its findings. Six months later, an environmental group—the Natural Resources Defense Council (NRDC)—published a study detailing how the region's electricity demand could be filled through existing plants plus energy conservation and less expensive small-scale sources. WPPSS nuclear power plants 4 and 5 could be postponed until at least 1995, NRDC concluded.

But WPPSS, at Bonneville's urging, pressed ahead, and in March 1977 investment brokers across the country began selling bonds to build nuclear power plants 4 and 5. Before year's end, WPPSS had five nuclear power plants under construction.

By the time Ronald Reagan moved into the White House, WPPSS was in deep, deep trouble. Few people outside of the Pacific Northwest had noticed, though. WPPSS bonds were still being sold by major brokerage firms such as Merrill Lynch, Prudential-Bache, Smith Barney, Harris Upham, Paine Webber, and Shearson/American Express. (The brokerage firms earned fees of 2 to 3 percent on the bonds.)

On May 29, 1981, a newly installed WPPSS management team released a new figure for what the five nuclear plants would end up costing: $23.9 billion, up from the $6.7 billion WPPSS had originally budgeted. (Critics were calling the whole enterprise "Whoops.") Soon thereafter, WPPSS halted all construction on nuclear power plants 4 and 5 because it was apparent the bond market could not sustain the level of financing required to keep all five nuclear plants under construction. WPPSS was now using a large portion of the proceeds from its most recent bond sales to pay the interest on previously issued bonds. Normally, power plant bonds are repaid out of the revenues earned from the sale of electricity. As the costs of these plants soared, the public utilities began to doubt whether they could afford the electricity rates that WPPSS would have to charge to cover costs.

In January 1982, WPPSS abandoned nuclear power plants 4 and 5. Now the public utilities were faced with the grim prospect of repaying the $2.25 billion in principal and $4.75 billion in interest on the bonds sold to finance nuclear power plants that would never generate a kilowatt of electricity or a dollar of revenue. They balked. And WPPSS's intricate web of financial support started to unravel.

Bonneville itself was now threatened with bankruptcy. It had backed the bonds for nuclear power plants 1, 2, and 3 and some $6.1 billion in bonds had been sold to finance their construction. More was needed to complete them, however. But with default imminent on the plant 4 and 5 bonds, the market had dried up for additional WPPSS bond issues. In April, Bonneville advised WPPSS to stop construction on nuclear power plant 1, which was 67 percent complete. It has been mothballed for at least five years. And in June Bonneville advised WPPSS to do the same with nuclear power plant 3. It was 76 percent complete and has been mothballed for at least three years. Work continues only on nuclear power plant 2, which is 97 percent complete and is supposed to generate electricity sometime in 1984, unless further problems arise. Bonneville had to provide the $150 million needed to complete plant 2 because financing was not available.

On July 25, 1983, WPPSS defaulted on its $2.25 billion of bonds for nuclear power plants 4 and 5. It was the largest municipal bond default in American history—larger than New York City's much publicized bond default would have been several years ago. At this writing, Bonneville insists it will back the $6.1 billion in bonds sold to finance nuclear power plants 1, 2, and 3, and it has raised its rates almost 1,000 percent to do so.

What went wrong? Why did WPPSS collapse?

A good place to begin looking for answers to those questions is in Bonneville's electricity demand projections. All five nuclear power plants were built upon them. Actually, the regional electricity demand projections which were behind Bonneville's WPPSS initiative and Hodel's dire forecast of electricity shortages were not done by Bonneville at all. They were worked on by the Pacific Northwest Utilities Conference Committee, a regional industry umbrella group. Their projections were based on the assumption that electricity demand in the region would grow at an average rate of about 4–6 percent a year through the end of the century.

Where the utility executives and Hodel erred was in their underestimation of what real energy conservation, i.e., more efficient energy use, could accomplish. It is not that they opposed energy conservation. They definitely did not. They spoke out in favor of it on numerous occasions.

But they did not realize how much energy can be made available for future economic growth from conservation. Hodel still does not.

The reason the predicted electricity shortage never materialized—and will not materialize in the foreseeable future—is that, as Bonneville and the utilities raised their rates, electricity consumers adapted. Ever since the building of the big federal hydroelectric projects in the 1930's and 1940's, electricity in the Pacific Northwest has been very cheap. There has been little incentive to use it efficiently. The cost per kilowatt hour was half the national average and the region's per capita consumption of electricity was twice the national average. Electricity demand grew at an average annual rate of about 7.5 percent. With prices rising, though, consumers are becoming conservation-conscious.

In fact, conservation has created an electricity surplus in the Pacific Northwest of about 2,000 megawatts. That is enough electricity to supply Seattle's total demand for two years. And Bonneville now projects that the surplus will extend well into the 1990's. Ironically, the big worry today is what to do with the electricity generated by WPPSS nuclear power plant 2 when it comes on line. Even with all the recent rate hikes, the electricity from this nuclear power plant will be more expensive than what consumers are now paying in the region. Who will buy it? British Columbia too has a big surplus of electric generating capacity, so they are electricity sellers, not buyers. Maybe California will buy it in order to displace electricity still generated by oil or natural gas. That is the hope, at least.

Between 1974 and 1981, the utility industry projections for future electricity demand in the Pacific Northwest dropped by about 8,300 megawatts. In other words, the industry projections were shedding the equivalent of one WPPSS nuclear power plant per year. And in 1982 Bonneville finally did its own independent forecast. It projected an average electricity demand growth rate of 1.6 percent a year.

Since the default, much of what has been written about WPPSS has stressed its management problems. An editorial in the *Washington Post,* for example, calls WPPSS's default "the financial counterpart of Three Mile Island" and states: "[A]s Whoops demonstrates, it is unwise to leave the management of nuclear systems to amateurs and people whose previous experience is limited to operating dams." And there is no question that mismangement occurred. From 1977 to 1981, the cost overruns on the WPPSS nuclear power plants averaged half a million dollars per hour.

303

But if you look at the record of other nuclear power plants, ones not managed by "amateurs," you will find cost overruns worse than WPPSS. For example, the new Millstone 3 nuclear power plant in Connecticut is coming in eight times over its original budget. The new Shoreham nuclear power plant on Long Island has cost ten times more than its original budget. When Millstone and Shoreham are turned on, electricity consumers will begin repaying their costs through increased rates. According to Long Island Lighting Company, it will need a rate increase of 56 percent to pay for the Shoreham nuclear power plant—electricity consumers on Long Island already pay an average of 10.95 cents per kilowatt hour, over four times as much as electricity consumers in the Northwest.

The fact of the matter is that even managers who are not "amateurs" rarely keep large-scale nuclear power plant costs within budget. Such plants are subject to the more or less normal cost-inflators that affect any big construction project—rising interest rates, supply interruptions, equipment failures, labor disputes, etc.—*plus* some very special ones that stem from the nature of the technology.

A nuclear reactor is a very complicated machine for boiling water to make steam to power a turbine to generate electricity. Heat for boiling the water comes from splitting—or fissioning—uranium atoms. In the process, tremendous temperatures are reached, requiring constant cooling. This cooling is crucial because the fission process produces vast amounts of deadly, long-lasting radioactive waste products. Today's typical large reactor, after six months of operation, contains about 1,000 times the radioactive materials released by the Hiroshima A-bomb. If the reactor core is not kept properly cooled, it will disintegrate, releasing the radiation. During the Three Mile Island nuclear power plant accident in March 1979, the reactor core did overheat and it began to disintegrate. What happened next is fascinating. As Eliot Marshall reported in *Science,*

. . . [G]ood luck had as much to do with averting a catastrophe as good engineering. For 13½ hours, it appears, the reactor was left partially exposed above the cooling water, while temperatures inside the reactor vessel climbed off the recording chart. Engineers in the control room realized that something inventive had to be done. As one NRC [Nuclear Regulatory Commission] staffer said: "There was speculation that there were voids or perhaps bubbles in the system." Fortunately for Harrisburg, in trying to collapse these imagined voids, the technician repressurized the system and raised the water level to cover the reactor core. Had this decision not been made when it was, gas would have continued to fill the reactor vessel, ultimately reaching the pumps and threatening the only viable cooling mechanism. As it was the damage was extensive, although not enough to trigger an irreversible meltdown.

It is that combination of large scale and technical complexity that conspires during construction of nuclear power plants to escalate costs and that provides such fertile ground for Murphy's law—if something can go wrong, it will. The nuclear power plant at Diablo Canyon, near San Luis Obispo, California, is a prime example.

Pacific Gas and Electric (PG&E), the nation's second largest private utility, began construction of the plant back in 1967, when Ronald Reagan was still in his first term as governor. It was supposed to cost $350 million. In 1969, two petroleum geologists surveying a couple of miles offshore from the Diablo site discovered an active fault, one which the designers of the nuclear power plant had known nothing about. The geologists informed the U.S. Geological Survey (USGS), but their report about the fault, called the Hosgri fault (using the first three letters of each geologist's name), was not published in a scientific journal until 1971. It is unclear when PG&E learned about the fault. Its first official acknowledgment that it might have a problem came in 1973. PG&E had devoted two paragraphs in its thirteen-volume Final Safety Analysis Report to the Hosgri fault. Later that year, the Atomic Energy Commission (the NRC's predecessor) asked the USGS to study the fault and assess the earthquake risk to the Diablo nuclear power plant. The USGS concluded in 1975 that the nuclear power plant could be subjected to a 7.5 Richter scale earthquake centered 2½ miles offshore on the Hosgri fault. For a year, the staff of the NRC lobbied the USGS to lower this figure, but the USGS scientists refused to budge. The trouble was that the two 1,000-megawatt-plus nuclear reactors being built at Diablo Canyon had been designed to withstand a 6.5 Richter scale earthquake centered twelve miles away. USGS ruled that the reactors might undergo an earthquake-induced shock of 0.7 g's. Originally, PG&E said they could withstand 0.4 g's, but after some recalculations came up with the figure of 0.5 g's. That still left PG&E with a big problem. They did not want to tear down what was already built and start over with a more earthquake-resistant basic design. So, under orders from the NRC, they set about retrofitting the original design with braces and other devices to absorb the shock.

Meanwhile, other problems arose. The plant is being built on an Indian burial ground, and it is almost as if the spirits of those old Indians were coming back to haunt PG&E for disturbing their resting place and hauling their bones off to a museum in San Luis Obispo. In 1973, a "once-in-a-hundred-years" rainstorm touched off massive mudslides behind the construction site, blocking the only access road into Diablo Canyon. Then, the next year, during a routine test, the cooling system pipes were flushed out. The outflow killed every abalone and almost every other marine creature that happened to be in Diablo cove at the time. It seems that water flushed out of the cooling system was highly toxic. The basic coolant—salt water pumped from the ocean—had corroded the copper tubing through which it flowed in the plant. PG&E had to replace hundreds of miles of copper tubing with titanium tubing. Also, there were labor strikes in 1975 and 1976. For the remainder of the decade, the retrofitting problem preoccupied PG&E.

In 1981, PG&E announced that Unit 1 was ready to go. The NRC granted it an operating license, only to withdraw the license two months later when an independent consulting firm found 7,472 technical defects in need of correction in Unit 1. In addition, a PG&E technician discovered that the braces that had been installed on Unit 1's pressure vessel had been put on backwards. Apparently, the brace installation instructions for Unit 2 had been used for Unit 1, and the braces had been transposed because Unit 2 is a mirror image of Unit 1. At this point, PG&E was estimating the plant's cost at $2.3 billion.

A new contractor—Bechtel Corporation—was hired to speed the work of correcting the defects and finishing the plant's "remodeling." In 1982 and 1983, the work went on at a furious pace, often in two ten-hour shifts, seven days a week. That of course is expensive. The plant cost is now about $4 billion and PG&E is reapplying to the NRC for an operating license. Then a Pacific storm in the late winter of 1983, the same one that demolished movie stars' homes at Malibu, tore up about 200 feet of concrete breakwater protecting the Diablo cooling water intake plant.

After sixteen years and $4 billion, the Diablo Canyon nuclear power plant has yet to generate a kilowatt of electricity. But the brownouts that PG&E once predicted if the plant was not on line by the 1980's have yet to occur. If there are further delays, PG&E can always buy surplus electricity from WPPSS.

Near Diablo Canyon, on the very busy north-south Highway 101,

PG&E operates a well-appointed information center for the public. Not too long ago, PG&E changed the name of the center from Nuclear Information Center to Energy Information Center.

Just as WPPSS was unraveling, the Pacific Northwest received some welcomed news. The Northwest Power Planning Council, a non-partisan group created by a 1980 Act of Congress, issued its twenty-year Conservation and Electric Power Plan for the region. It was a refreshing contrast to past utility industry-Bonneville-WPPSS plans; this one emphasizes the development of flexible, short lead-time, least-cost resources. Its guiding principle is: "All resources must be cost-effective—buy the cheapest resources first." And, according to the Council, the cheapest resource is conservation. It is also "the most flexible," and the Council stresses the importance of flexibility. "As recent events have shown, there is a high cost in being wrong. The major challenge, therefore, is reduce the probability and the consequences of being wrong." In other words, do not commit your limited capital to huge, costly nuclear power plants which take years to build unless there are no other alternatives. Instead, invest in the following resources:

First, conservation;

Second, renewable resources, in particular, the development of smaller hydroelectric sites;

Third, cogeneration—using industrial waste heat to generate electricity—and high-efficiency combustion turbines;

Fourth, conventional thermal plants.

The Council favors coal-burning plants over nuclear plants because of their shorter construction time, smaller unit size, and lower risk exposure. But it concludes that neither new coal nor nuclear plants will be necessary until the late 1990's, and then only if the region follows a high-growth path.

LOST OPPORTUNITIES

A fascinating experiment now getting under way in Hood River, Oregon, will provide the Northwest Power Council with invaluable conservation cost data. Funded by Bonneville, Pacific Power and Light Company (PP&L), an investor-owned utility, and the publicly-owned Hood River Electric Cooperative will weatherize, free of charge, every home that lets them in this 536-square-mile county. There have been similar experiments elsewhere: for example, the Public Service Electric and Gas Company had a free weatherization program in some small New Jersey communities, but the Hood River experiment is far more ambitious in scope and the weatherization undertaken will be far more intensive. It will involve high-level insulation and window-glazing. Many homes in Hood River are heated electrically and the average home consumes about 13,000 kilowatt hours per year. After the weatherization, they are expected to consume 6,000 kilowatt hours. The saved kilowatts can then be used to meet new electricity needs *without* building new generating capacity. The experiment has implications that reach far beyond Hood River and the Pacific Northwest, because the same potential to save money by using energy more efficiently instead of spending to build new plants exists everywhere.

Ronald Reagan does not understand or believe in energy conservation. He said that conservation meant being "too hot in the summer and too cold in the winter" and would "at best" only make us "run out of energy a little more slowly." He spent years as a paid lecturer for General Electric and is convinced that the nation had to build more nuclear plants quickly. "I believe that [nuclear power] offers our greatest hope for the solution of our energy problems over the next two or three decades." The problems of the nuclear industry he blames on government regulators. President Reagan appointed men who shared his view to run the Department of Energy.

James Edwards was President Reagan's first Secretary of Energy. A dentist and ex-governor of South Carolina, Edwards, during his confirmation hearing, revealed a less than rudimentary understanding of energy conservation. And after Edwards was in office for several months he was testifying before Congress in a budget hearing, trying to explain why he thought the market was doing a good job of providing consumers with useful energy efficiency information, when he had the following exchange with Congressman Sidney Yates:

EDWARDS: I just happened to buy a refrigerator the other day. . . . Right on the front was a big yellow label and it had the cost basis of so much per kilowatt hour, and how much it would cost to operate that particular refrigerator for a year.

YATES: Weren't you glad to have that?

308

EDWARDS: It was a pretty good thing.

YATES: . . . the reason you have it is because it was required by Congress. . . . It will not be there if your reduction goes through. . . . One of the items being cut back is the department that is responsible for requiring that information to be put on that refrigerator.

Edwards's chief asset seemed to be that he was an outspoken booster of nuclear power. As governor, he had bragged that South Carolina was "the world's nuclear energy capital." (In the state are the Department of Energy's Savannah River facility where nuclear weapons are made, eight conventional nuclear power plants, and the now-abandoned Barnwell nuclear fuel reprocessing plant.) As Secretary of Energy, he told a reporter that he would like to "get rid of these strident voices" that are blocking nuclear energy development because "subversive elements are using these people." He added that "there are a lot of people who would like to do to us economically what no military force in the world could do: bring us to our knees [by halting nuclear power and other forms of energy]." "The Soviets," he warned, are "building these [nuclear] installations as fast they can."

To the number two spot in the Department of Energy (DOE), Reagan named W. Kenneth Davis. He came from the Bechtel Corporation, the world's largest nuclear power plant construction firm. Davis had been Bechtel's vice-president for nuclear development. And he, in turn, installed J. Hunter Chiles, the Market Research and Analysis Manager for Westinghouse's nuclear power division, which has manufactured more nuclear reactors than any other company in the world, as director of the Energy Department's influential Office of Policy, Planning and Analysis. Under Chiles's guidance, DOE produced a report that seems to be modeled on WPPSS. It calls for the expenditure of two *trillion* dollars to build more than 400 coal and nuclear plants in the United States between now and the year 2000 to meet skyrocketing energy demands.

Edwards, Davis, and Chiles seemed not to have grasped what was happening to WPPSS or to the industry in general. Not only was WPPSS canceling plants because they were too expensive and not needed, power companies across the country were doing the same thing. Eighty-one reactor orders had been canceled—more reactors than are now in operation in the United States. No new reactors had been ordered in five years. Energy conservation, however, was booming, because Americans had noticed it was the only way to reduce energy costs. New power plants produce more energy, but it is more expensive energy.

In 1973 the automobiles on American roads and highways averaged 13 miles a gallon. Today they average 23 miles a gallon. In 1983 the average American home uses 20 percent less energy than in 1973 because of weatherstripping of windows and doors, insulation, improved efficiency of furnaces and hot water heaters, and because we are adjusting our thermostats to avoid overheating in the winter. Many industries have improved their energy productivity dramatically. The 3M Company, for example, has reduced its energy consumption per unit of output by almost 24 percent, and Dow Chemical has cut its by 40 percent. Since 1973, the volume of AT&T's business has grown 97 percent, but its energy usage has decreased 13 percent—a $2.3 billion savings. Overall, the U.S. economy consumes 19 percent less energy per dollar of gross national product (GNP) than it did in 1973. Ten years ago, energy forecasters in government and utilities assumed energy consumption and GNP were inexorably coupled.

And these efficiencies are just the beginning. A massive study done by the National Academy of Sciences reported we can cut our energy consumption per dollar of GNP in half by the year 2000. That would sharply increase productivity while virtually eliminating the need for imported oil. Which is why energy technologists and scientists issued a collective groan when Ronald Reagan made his crack about conservation.

The growing success of energy conservation efforts in the United States was primarily due to increased energy prices. When energy was cheap, we did not think about it very much and waste was built into our buildings, our cars, and our habits. The sharp rise in prices got the attention of industry and the public in a hurry and provided a strong incentive to conserve. Another factor, however, was governmental action. Selective government intervention in the market to encourage energy efficiency has been quite effective. Federal fuel economy standards for cars and miles-per-gallon labeling requirements have expedited the switchover to more efficient cars, helping to reduce our reliance on imported oil. And federal labeling requirements for refrigerators, air conditioners, and hot water heaters have stimulated the market for more efficient appliances.

Federal assistance helped create extraordinary community-based programs from Buffalo to Minneapolis to Seattle. Federal conservation

310

and solar tax credits helped individuals make the initial investments needed to yield huge future savings. The Oak Ridge National Laboratory estimates that, as a result of federal government conservation programs functioning during the late 1970's, the nation will save $41 billion in residential fuel costs by the end of the century.

As for what could be accomplished in the years ahead, physicist Art Rosenfeld at the Lawrence Berkeley Laboratory likes to use the example of energy use in buildings. In 1982, the U.S. energy bill was about $400 billion, and about $120 billion of that went to pay for heating, cooling, and lighting of buildings and for running equipment and appliances like pumps, fans, refrigerators, washers, dryers, and computers. Rosenfeld calculates that, of this $120 billion, about $60 billion was wasted. "That is, it could be saved, with no change in our life-style, if we made the optimum investments in lighting and daylighting, heating and cooling systems, controlling infiltration or supply of outside air, insulating, buying the most efficient appliances as our old ones wear out, reducing hot water waste, and so on. Most of this $60 billion saving will eventually be achieved by market forces, but the lag is probably twenty years. If we can reduce market lag from twenty years to ten years, we'll save $300 billion over the next twenty years. . . . In addition, the conservation investment would permit us to defer construction of 200 standard 1,000-megawatt power plants, costing $1.5 billion each, which pays for the entire conservation investment all by itself."

The new Administration was not impressed. They sought an immediate 80 percent cut in federal conservation programs, proposing to eliminate virtually every energy program providing information or assistance to individuals or small businesses. The low-income weatherization program helped install insulation, storm windows, and caulking in the homes of low-income families. It was reaching 400,000 homes a year premised on the belief that it was more useful to reduce the energy bills of the poor than to continue to help the poor pay high bills. The Administration asked Congress to eliminate the program. (Congress said no.) The Solar and Conservation Bank was intended to provide low-interest loans to consumers and small businesses for conservation and solar energy investments. The Administration asked Congress to eliminate the Bank, too, and, when Congress refused, the Administration simply ignored the law setting up the Bank until ordered to proceed by a federal judge.

Maxine Savitz ran the conservation research and development program at the Department of Energy when the Reagan team took over. She was not unduly concerned. True, their public utterances about energy conservation had hardly been enlightened, but Savitz, a scientist with a doctorate from MIT and a non-ideologue, thought that once the Reagan people became better acquainted with the facts, they would support the energy conservation program. It was, after all, the most cost-effective program in DOE. For every dollar spent, it was yielding an annual return of about $2.50 in energy saved. Furthermore, the program had been launched under the Ford Administration. "Energy conservation was a bipartisan issue," Savitz thought.

Her new boss, the man Reagan appointed to be Assistant Secretary for Conservation and Renewable Energy, was Joseph J. Tribble. He was a conservative Republican from Savannah, Georgia, who worked as an engineer for a big paper company, Union Company. He knew a lot about boilers, a little about energy conservation, and nothing about managing a several-hundred-million-dollar R&D program. Maxine Savitz soon learned that Tribble's mind was already made up. He was not interested in hearing the facts. Nor were his superiors—Edwards and Davis. Indeed, they seemed to resent it when, at staff meetings, she tried to introduce relevant facts into the discussion. "I thought my job, as a professional, was to lay out the options. But the Reagan appointees' minds were closed tight. All they wanted to do was cut the budget and turn everything over to the market." Savitz, though, is no troublemaker. Rather than going public to the press or to some congressional committee, she concentrated on salvaging what she could of the conservation program as Tribble and company dismantled her staff and slashed her budget.

Savitz's program had provided seed money for the development of a number of energy-efficient technologies now on the market that private companies had not been interested in investing R&D money in. These include a high-frequency fluorescent light, which produces the same amount of light as the old fluorescent but uses 15 percent less electricity; the first heat-pump water heater; and an ingenious technique for using paint fumes as a fuel in the sheetmetal curing process. The conservation R&D program's first 23 completed projects accounted for energy savings in 1983 of $85.6 million, and they had cost the government $34.3 million. The project's current annual rate of return is about 250 percent.

Tribble one day informed Savitz that she was being transferred out of the conservation program to an obscure DOE office in Colorado. She refused to move to Colorado because her husband works in Washington, D.C., and her children are in school there. She offered to take some other position in Washington and was even prepared to take a cut in pay. Instead, they fired Maxine Savitz. She had been a civil servant for over a decade and her efficiency ratings had been uniformly outstanding, even under Reagan.

Surveying the wreckage that the Reagan appointees had made of DOE's energy conservation R&D program, the department's Energy Research Advisory Board, made up of experts from industry and academia, had this to say: "Personnel shifts and losses, low and shifting funding levels, and lack of planning have had a disastrous effect on the Department of Energy's ability to conduct an effective energy conservation R&D program."

Other Reagan Administration initiatives at DOE have included an effort to squelch a federally funded study which evaluated energy conservation possibilities, using only available technologies, in each sector of our economy. Done by scientists and engineers at Lawrence Berkeley Laboratory, Carnegie-Mellon and Princeton Universities, the Environmental Protection Agency, and the Solar Energy Research Institute, the study was completed in early 1981. It concluded that the United States could reduce its energy consumption by 25 percent while the economy continued to grow at historical rates. The new Administration did not like the conclusion and tried to prevent its publication. It was published instead by a congressional committee and then by a private publisher —Brick House—appropriately entitled *A New Prosperity*.

More recently, DOE scuttled plans to establish energy efficiency standards for six major household appliances—refrigerators, electric water heaters, furnaces, freezers, room air conditioners, and central air conditioners. The standards are required by a law passed in 1975 during the Ford Administration. Some states, such as California, have gone ahead and set their own standards, but only because the federal government was studying what national standards to set. The 1975 law says no state or local standard can be more stringent than the federal standard —even if the federal standard is no standard. Hence, the Reagan Administration decision not to issue any standards undercut standards already working in many states.

The California Energy Commission calculates that its appliance standards, which are the toughest in the nation, will save the state $26 billion in fuel bills by the year 2002. California and other states will now have to go to court in an effort to save their standards.

One scientist who helped to draw up the California energy efficiency standards recalls: "The American appliance manufacturers lobbied and testified against the standards. They fought us tooth and nail. But the Japanese appliance manufacturers came in and said, 'You decide the energy efficiencies you want and we will meet them. Just tell us what you want.' "*

Countering the Reagan Administration argument that energy efficiency standards should be left up to the market, state energy officials point out that the appliance market is different from the normal market. Over half the appliances in homes and commercial buildings are purchased by developers or contractors, and are *not* purchased by the people who pay the energy bills. In other words, they are purchased by people who have no economic incentive to buy energy-efficient appliances.

The no-appliance-standards decision was made by Energy Secretary Donald Hodel. Edwards and Davis are now gone from DOE. Both resigned of their own accord. Hodel and a former number-two man at Bonneville, Earl Jeldey, have replaced them. There is a certain irony in the fact that at this particular time in our history two former Bonneville executives, men who played such a key role in the WPPSS debacle, are now running DOE and formulating national energy policy.

Hodel is far more sophisticated than Edwards. He speaks of seeking "a balanced and mixed energy resource base from conventional resources such as oil, gas, coal, and nuclear, to renewables such as hydroelectricity, solar (both passive and active), wind, geothermal, ocean thermal conversion, biofuels, and so on, and through conservation as a resource." And perhaps he means it. But there is nothing "balanced" about how DOE is spending its research and development money. An ever increasing amount of it is being poured into one energy source: nuclear power.

THE NUCLEAR PORKBARREL

In President Carter's last budget, there was about $4 billion earmarked for energy technology research and development. Of that, 28 percent

---

*The Carrier Company was an exception. It builds some very efficient appliances and welcomed the standards.

went to nuclear fission. In President Reagan's first budget, nuclear power was the only major program outside of the Pentagon that was spared the knife. Its appropriation grew.

Funding for energy technology research and development in Reagan's three budgets has gone from $2.8 billion to $2.4 billion to $1.9 billion, but nuclear fission's share has risen to 38 percent, then 43 percent, and now 60 percent. Conservation's share has plummeted in both relative terms—from 19 percent in Carter's last budget to 4 percent in Reagan's 1984 budget—and in absolute terms—from $743 million under Carter to $74 million in fiscal 1984.

From the beginning, the federal government has succored the nuclear industry. The federal government financed the development of the industry's basic product—the light water reactor. The federal government enriches the fuel used in nuclear power plants. (Natural uranium contains only about 0.7 percent of the fissionable isotope Uranium-235, the rest is Uranium-238; for use in a light water reactor, the Uranium-235 content must be increased or "enriched" to about 3 percent. It is an expensive, electricity-intensive process.) The federal government limited nuclear power's liability, i.e., setting a lid on how much a citizen can collect for damages incurred to himself, his family, or his property by a nuclear accident, and helped to underwrite nuclear power plant insurance. The federal government has subsidized the nuclear industry's exports with low-interest loans.

The federal government has also helped soothe public uncertainty about nuclear power, no small task considering that images of Hiroshima and Nagasaki automatically spring to mind with the word "nuclear." A nuclear industry public relations man once put the problem thus: "It's like Edison had invented the electric chair and then tried to market lightbulbs." The federal government has promoted nuclear power through countless handouts, brochures, books, films, traveling exhibits, and gimmicks like "Atomic Energy Merit Badges" for Boy Scouts.

What has it all cost the taxpayers? Joe Bowring, an economist with DOE, looked into that question. His report, *Federal Subsidies to Nuclear Power Reactors,* concluded: "The total constant dollar value of these subsidies from 1950 to 1979 is just over $37 billion." But when DOE released his report, the word "subsidies" had been replaced by the more palatable "supports" and the $37 billion had been changed to $12 billion. He must have touched a sensitive nerve.

315

Federal government subsidies to the nuclear power industry now total about $40 billion. What has been the return?

In 1982 nuclear power plants supplied 4 percent of the nation's energy—about 3.1 quadrillion BTUs. That is nothing to sneeze at of course. But to put it in perspective, it is roughly the same amount of energy that we got from wood, and the wood energy did not cost us a nickel in federal subsidies.

Wood? Yes, wood. One of the myriad of ways Americans adjusted to the big energy price hikes of the 1970's was to return to an old standby —wood—as a supplemental heat source. Fuel wood use, after a long period of decline, has been growing since 1973 at five times the overall rate of growth in energy use (not without causing some air pollution problems, however). In addition, the lumber and pulp industries are now using mill wood wastes as a fuel to reduce their oil and gas costs.

So the returns from our $40 billion have been modest. A similar amount invested in conservation would have bought us a lot more energy and more jobs. According to a study done by the Council on Economic Priorities, an investment in energy conservation will create 2.5 more jobs than a comparable investment in a new nuclear power plant. The energy conservation investment has a multiplier effect. It saves households, businesses, and public institutions money that they can spend on other things, which creates jobs in addition to those created initially in the manufacture and installation of energy-efficient equipment or materials.

The Reagan Administration's answer to the nuclear industry's problems is to ask the taxpayers to subsidize the development of the next generation of nuclear reactors. The biggest single item in the Reagan energy budget is the breeder reactor. It is sometimes called "the Vietnam of energy technology" because we keep putting more and more money into it and never seem to get anything out of it. So far, the federal government has spent more than $10 billion on the breeder. And President Reagan wanted to spend more. Our money has financed the building of three breeder reactors already—the first in Idaho, the second near Detroit, and the third in Idaho. The first and second suffered malfunctions and partial meltdowns of their cores, but luckily no one was hurt. And the second produced electricity so expensive its owners never bothered to calculate the cost. The third has avoided meltdowns and has generated a little electricity, but it was designed only to test breeder fuels and does not breed fuel itself.

We have been financing a fourth breeder, a much bigger breeder.

316

It is called the Clinch River Breeder Reactor. Ground has been cleared along the Clinch River in Tennessee and construction has begun. It is a liquid metal fast breeder reactor, LMFBR for short. The idea for building it was hatched back in the heyday of nuclear power predictions —back when the Atomic Energy Commission (AEC) was predicting that there would be 850 to 1,400 nuclear power plants operating by the year 2000. Today there are 79 nuclear power plants operating and 57 more being built. There has not been a single new order for a nuclear reactor since 1977, and utilities have canceled plans for over 150 nuclear power plants. Tennessee Valley Authority Commissioner David Freeman explains: "The nuclear industry does not have a product that any utility in the United States can afford to buy." The Clinch River Breeder was hatched back when the AEC foresaw shortages of economical uranium supplies by the turn of the century, hence the breeder was necessary to stretch the uranium supply by converting Uranium-238 into fissionable plutonium. Today, there is a surplus of low-cost uranium. There is so much uranium available in fact that a secondary market has developed. Utilities saddled with surplus uranium they ordered several years ago under fixed contracts are unloading it to other utilities at discount prices.

DOE has asked for another $1.4 billion for a reactor that breeds fuel, while DOE is paying out penalties to the TVA for electricity it contracted to buy to operate a uranium enrichment plant which is no longer needed because there is a surplus of fuel. In 1984 these penalties will total more than $200 million, and by 1992 they will cumulatively amount to $1.23 billion, according to the General Accounting Office (GAO). And DOE recently refurbished the government's three existing uranium enrichment plants at a cost of $1.5 billion in order to increase their capacity, yet demand for enriched uranium is so depressed that the plants are operating at about 35 percent capacity. Meanwhile, DOE continues to build a mammoth new $10 billion enrichment plant at Portsmouth, Ohio. It is the biggest single construction project in the country, bigger even than the Clinch River Breeder. As Colin Norman reported in *Science*, DOE "grossly overestimated" the demand for enriched uranium. And as we learned with WPPSS, there is a high cost to being wrong about nuclear power.

On October 26, 1983, the United States Senate finally defied the Administration and Majority Leader Howard Baker and voted against funding for the Clinch River Breeder Reactor. Baker had successfully defended the project, which brought billions of dollars in federal funds into his state, despite House votes to kill it. In the end, according to Senator Dale Bumpers, who led the effort to kill the breeder, the Senate recognized "we put some money down a rathole, and decided not to spend any more."

The next day, Secretary Hodel, sensitive to the winds of politics if not the tides of change in the energy industry, ordered the elaborate Clinch River display removed from the DOE lobby. It was replaced by a display featuring solar energy.

Mark Hertsgaard points out that the 24 firms that dominate the nuclear industry "constitute what may be the single largest and most powerful business enterprise in history." They sold $400 billion worth of products in 1981. They have credit lines to eight of the nine biggest commercial banks in the nation, to the seven largest insurance companies, and to many of the top investment banks.

Why not sever the umbilical cord? Leave future decisions about the development and commercialization of nuclear power up to the market. If and when it makes economic sense, investors will put their money into it. And leave uranium enrichment and nuclear power plant insurance up to the market, too. Let the federal government focus on safety.

The battle over energy policy, even more than that over public lands or the control of pollution, is heavy with ideology on both sides. Opponents of nuclear power often seem to regard it as a moral, or at least a social, evil—the precursor of a kind of technological totalitarianism. But the proponents of nuclear power at times seem to love it beyond all rationality. They have been described as "the nuclear priesthood," and they show contempt and bitter anger toward those who challenge their views. Perhaps foreseeing that tendency, Albert Einstein said that "decisions about nuclear power should be made in the village square."

Of late, the Department of Energy seems profoundly uncomfortable with the village square and has sought to shape the debate. DOE is currently spending about $2.5 million per year on "nuclear information," including $250,000 on a half-hour film about nuclear power and $100,000 in support of a pro-nuclear group called Scientists and Engineers for Secure Energy. A congressional investigator reports: "The wastefulness of this public relations program seems to derive from the Department's notion that the debate over nuclear power is between pro-nuclear advocates who understand nuclear power and anti-nuclear advocates who have 'misconceptions.'"

318

The nuclear industry too has sought to add extra voices to its side of the debate. It is conducting a 26-million-dollar advertising campaign, under the aegis of something called the Committee for Energy Awareness, in an effort to regain the public opinion ground lost after the Three Mile Island accident. It is being funded by the major nuclear reactor manufacturers and the nuclear power plant construction/engineering firms as well as by some big private utilities who operate nuclear reactors. Electricity consumers are actually paying for about $21 million of this advertising campaign. Virginia Electric and Power Company, for instance, kicked in $600,000 and is charging it to its customers "as a legitimate business expense."

The occupants of the village square, however, seem somewhat skeptical. Public polls conducted before, during, and after the pro-nuclear TV and radio blitz in one city, Grand Rapids, Michigan, showed these results:

	Before	During	After
We should use the nuclear power plants we now have, and build more nuclear power plants.	28%	32%	28%
We should use the nuclear power plants we now have, but not build any more plants.	49%	52%	51%
We should shut down all existing nuclear power plants, and not build any more plants.	21%	14%	18%
Don't know.	1%	1%	4%

(The numbers have been rounded off, and so do not total 100.)

In an October 1981 policy statement, Ronald Reagan called for a major federal effort to revive the nuclear power industry, blaming the industry's problems on "a morass of regulations that do not enhance safety but that do cause extensive licensing delays and economic uncertainty." Despite the WPPSS default, reactor cancellations, and recurrent reactor safety problems identified by the Nuclear Regulatory Commission, the President has stuck to his view of reality, and federal energy policy continues to stumble down the path previously trodden by the Bonneville Power Administration and the Northwest utilities.

CONCLUSION: THWARTED BUT NOT CONVERTED

Now there has been a changing of the guard at the Department of the Interior and at the Environmental Protection Agency. James Watt and Anne Gorsuch Burford are gone, repudiated by the nation although not by the President whom they loyally served and whose rhetoric they tried to turn into reality.

With the departure of Mr. Watt and Mrs. Burford, some things have gotten better. There are no more tales of malfeasance, backroom deals, and political manipulation at EPA. There are no more hit lists of career civil servants to be fired for their commitment to the job assigned them by law. And from Judge Clark we should expect no outrageous and insulting statements about Americans, their beliefs, their race, their creed, their sex, or their physical abilities.

The rough exterior of this Administration's environmental policies has been changed, but have the policies been remodeled? There is not much evidence that they have or that they will be.

The President accepted James Watt's resignation as he had that of Anne Gorsuch, with regret. Each resigned because the political pressure to leave became irresistible, not because the President concluded that the policies that engendered that pressure were wrong. Reagan has conceded nothing to his environmental critics. He called Gorsuch's record at EPA "splendid" and said Watt had "done an outstanding job

. . . in his stewardship of the natural resources of the nation. He has initiated a careful balance between the needs of people and the importance of protecting the environment."

There has been no visible mitigation of consistently anti-environmental policies.

When the House of Representatives, after Gorsuch's departure, sought to restore the operating budget of the Environmental Protection Agency, which had been cut by over a third in real terms by President Reagan, OMB Director David Stockman threatened a Presidential veto if the increases were approved by the Congress. Six months later, when Ruckelshaus wanted more money for 1985, he took his case personally to the President, but he was rebuffed and got only one-third of what he asked for. As a result the EPA is now about the same size it was when William Ruckelshaus was last Administrator a decade ago, before EPA had responsibility to protect the nation from toxic substances and hazardous wastes. Malfeasance and maladministration are not the problem now. Too much work and too few people are the problem. With a tremendous backlog of work left to be done after two years of chaos, the Agency struggles from crisis to crisis, unable to meet its responsibilities under the law.

And OMB is still a problem. Ruckelshaus had promised action on acid rain after both the National Academy of Sciences and a scientific panel chosen by the White House reported that the only way to prevent ever-increasing acid rain damage was to control pollution. Ruckelshaus developed a modest proposal that would achieve pollution reduction sought by bills in the House and Senate. Six months later, Stockman has opposed even that measure. Too expensive, he says. Ruckelshaus took the issue to the President, and the President sided with Stockman. No pollution reduction, just more research.

In Chapter 2 we tell the story of EDB, a deadly pesticide that EPA and OSHA had long delayed regulating. In October 1983, prodded by information that food on supermarket shelves was contaminated by EDB, EPA finally took action, but OMB has blocked measures to protect workers proposed by OSHA. Too expensive, they say.

There has been no retreat from efforts to double the cut of timber in the National Forests or to lease massive quantities of federal coal (Congress put a temporary stop to the leasing). Sales of the public lands still go on, and purchases of parklands still do not.

The Administration has been thwarted but not converted.

The problem is perhaps most starkly illustrated in the Congress. Six major statutes enforced by EPA are now before the Congress for renewal: the Clean Air Act, the Clean Water Act, the Safe Drinking Water Act, the pesticide law, the hazardous waste law, and the Toxic Substances Act. Together they are the entire framework of pollution control in the United States.

Public opinion overwhelmingly favors strengthening these laws to deal with threats to our health and safety that have become ever more clear in recent years and to close the loopholes that allowed EPA to do so little during the first two years of this Administration. Yet, in each case, the best that can be said of the Administration is that they are no longer trying to dismantle statutory protections that are already in place.

After two years, during which Congress, spurred by public opinion, rebuffed Administration efforts to weaken each of those statutes, open still wider loopholes and undercut requirements for health protection, the Administration seems simply to have withdrawn from the fray.

Does President Reagan know that there is a problem with toxic wastes in this country? Does he think that his Administration has any obligation to try to resolve the problem? Does he have a position? Not that anyone on Capitol Hill can tell. Not that anyone in Washington knows.

Does President Reagan know that the underground sources of much of the drinking water in the United States is contaminated by toxic substances? Does he know that billions of pounds of suspected cancer-causing chemicals are released into the air every year because EPA has done nothing to regulate them? Not that anyone can tell. Congress is moving ahead on its own because there is no White House leadership.

Republicans and Democrats alike expressed dismay at the manner in which Secretary Watt squandered national resources, at his failure to consider any values but development when he looked at the lands and offshore resources owned by all the American people. Has President Reagan done anything to assure that the values of all the American public are considered when decisions are made about how to use their resources? He has not. Instead, in a gesture of contempt toward those concerned with the wise and thoughtful use of our resources, he named his friend William Clark to succeed, a man with absolutely no qualifications for the job except that he is conservative and the President likes him.

323

For the first time in a dozen years the White House has no one on the staff responsible for the environment. Norman Livermore, a Reagan associate from California days, traced the fate of the environment under Reagan to precisely this blind spot. Reagan "really hasn't had any environmental advisers. . . . So things are left up to Coors and people like that, who feel they've been strictured by environmental rules and regulations." Little has changed. When the President announced his appointment of William Ruckelshaus to replace Anne Gorsuch, a reporter asked whether his environmental policies would become more pro-environmental. He responded "they've always been pro-environmental." Would they change, he was asked. He replied, "I'm too old to change."

That is what is troubling, for if nothing has changed, the continued political stalemate over whether to weaken or strengthen environmental protection is the *best* we can hope for. One former aide to Mrs. Gorsuch said, "What really scares me, is who's gonna come in here if Reagan wins in '84. The regulatory relief guys will see it as their last best chance. They'll put in a nebbish, and then OMB will really go to work."

A
NOTE
ON OUR
METHODS

INTERVIEWS

In doing the research for this book, we have conducted interviews with more than 400 of the people who took part in the events we narrate. Many of them were government officials, current and past. They work, or worked, in the White House, the Interior Department, the Environmental Protection Agency, and other agencies. Many were civil servants. Some were political appointees. We have talked with lobbyists for industry and public interest groups, congressmen and their staffs, state and local government officials, journalists, and scientists or other independent researchers. Most important, we have talked to private citizens, people who learned about Ronald Reagan's environmental policies at home, where it counts.

Most of the people we interviewed spoke candidly with us. They also brought with them to our interviews points of view, prejudices, and interests. Sorting out their stories and the biases which inform them has been our extremely enjoyable job. It has led, however, to a set of editorial practices that require explanation.

1. We conducted interviews on a variety of bases. Some were taped, transcribed, and corrected by our subjects. Others were on-the-record, with the provision that quotations would be checked for accuracy. They

were. Others were off-the-record, when those we interviewed had reason to insist on confidentiality. While these people have not always been identified, all quotations were verified for accuracy. Other people we interviewed asked not to be quoted on any basis. In our text, as a rule, quotations from interviews we conducted for this book are marked by a narrative present tense (he or she "says," "recalls," etc.).

2. We have not talked to everyone we wanted to. About half a dozen officials of EPA, OMB, the Department of the Interior, and the Department of Energy declined to speak with us. While most of the senior officials at the Environmental Protection Agency agreed to be interviewed, for example, some did refuse. We asked, through their lawyers, to speak with Anne Gorsuch and Rita Lavelle, but were unable to do so.

In spite of this, we have often quoted these people, most notably Anne Gorsuch. Generally, their statements can be found in printed materials—speeches, affidavits, testimony, interviews. We have also relied on the recollections and notes of those who worked with them. As often as is stylistically feasible, we have noted the recollected nature of such quotations in the text. While it is impossible to be absolutely certain about these quotations, we have used no material which we have any reason—at all—to doubt.

PRINTED MATERIALS

In addition to our interviews, we have used a wide range of printed texts. Documents from the agencies and Congress have been made available to us, sometimes informally but more often in response to requests made under the Freedom of Information Act. Other documents were included in the records of congressional hearings held to oversee or inquire into events at the Interior Department and EPA or were released to interested parties at such hearings. The testimony and the questioning at those hearings was also important for the story we tell.

The press was often dogged in its investigation of these agencies, and contemporary newspaper and magazine articles have been a rich source of information for us. Books have also been useful, and we found William Greider's *The Education of David Stockman and Other Americans* (New York: E.P. Dutton, 1981), especially to the point.

BOOKS

Although he appears infrequently in this book, its real subject is Ronald Reagan. Without a doubt, the most revealing book about him is his own autobiography: Ronald Reagan and Richard C. Hubler, *Where's the Rest of Me?* (New York: Dell, 1981 [1965]). His statements as President can be found in *The Weekly Compilation of Presidential Documents*. The *Washington Post*'s Lou Cannon has written a helpful book called *Reagan* (New York: G.P. Putnam's Sons, 1982). Mark Green and Gail MacColl, in *There He Goes Again: Ronald Reagan's Reign of Error* (New York: Pantheon Books, 1983), investigate, often amusingly, many of his statements.

SOURCE NOTES

Notes at the end of this book catalogue exhaustively the sources on which we ultimately relied. Only the names of those we interviewed with a promise of anonymity have not been included. The authors will be pleased to answer questions addressed to them in care of the publisher.

SOURCE
NOTES

1. THE EDUCATION OF ANNE GORSUCH

Page 5

James Watt, 1977, quoted in Elizabeth Drew, "A Reporter At Large: Secretary Watt," *The New Yorker*, 4 May 1981, 104–138 at 108.

Dana Parsons, "Who *Are* Those Guys?," *Denver Post*, 9 January 1983, A1. Ron Wolf, "New Voice in the Wilderness," *Rocky Mountain Magazine*, March 1981, 29–34, esp. 33.

Interview with Rep. Timothy Wirth, Washington, D.C., 26 October 1983.

Page 6

Interview with Freda Poundstone, lobbyist, Denver, CO, 7 July 1983. Telephone interview with Betty Neal, State Representative, Denver, CO, 17 August 1983.

Anne M. Gorsuch in *Nominations of Anne M. Gorsuch and John W. Hernandez, Jr., Hearings before the Senate Environment and Public Works Committee*, No. 97–H26, 1 and 4 May 1981 (hereafter *Nominations*), at 48. She echoes James Sanderson as quoted in Lawrence Mosher, "Reagan's EPA Nominee Has Mixed Record," *National Journal*, 28 February 1981, 367, on "heavy-handedness" and MSLF suit.

Gorsuch speech to National Conference of State Legislators, 26 February 1982, quoted in Terry Brown, "Gorsuch Assails U.S.–Required Emission Tests," *Rocky Mountain News*, 27 February 1982, at 7.

Interview with Myrna Poticha, Colorado Water Quality Control Commission, Denver, CO, 6 August 1983.

Page 7

Interview with Paula Herzmark, businesswoman and former member of Gov. Richard Lamm's cabinet, Denver, CO, 7 July 1983.

329

Gorsuch's résumé can be found in *Nominations* at 277–280. See also Sharon Sherman and Kenneth T. Walsh, "Exit Is One More Chapter in a Stormy Career," *Denver Post*, 10 March 1983, A10. Todd Engdahl and Sharon Sherman, "Gorsuch Rose Fast in Colorado GOP," *Denver Post*, 22 February 1981, at G3.

Off-the-record interview with Colorado Republican legislator, Denver, CO, 6 August 1983. Interview with C. L. Harmon, lobbyist, Denver, CO, 6 August 1983.

Page 8

Gorsuch quoted in Joanne Omang, "Denver Lawyer Reagan's Choice to Head EPA," *Washington Post*, 21 February 1981, at A4.

Interview with Dr. Frank Traylor, former Republican legislator and now Colorado Commissioner of Health, Denver, CO, 7 August 1983.

Page 9

Recommendations for 1981, Committee on Hazardous Waste, Colorado Legislative Council, Research Publication No. 254, December 1980.

Interviews with Martha King, Colorado Legislative Council's office, Denver, CO, 7 July and 7 August 1983.

Page 10

Telephone interview with Maria Garcia, lobbyist, Denver, CO, 2 August 1983.

Off-the-record interview with former White House staff member, Washington, D.C., 10 August 1983. The following account is drawn from that interview as well as off-the-record interviews with a member of the EPA transition team, Washington, D.C., 3 and 8 August 1983, and interviews with individuals considered for the EPA Administrator job, Washington, D.C., 12 August and 26 September 1983.

Page 11

Nofziger quoted in Tom Gavin, "Burford-Gorsuch Tie OK—Nofziger," *Denver Post*, 13 March 1981, 2. See also Lou Cannon, *Reagan* (New York: G. P. Putnam's Sons, 1982) at 317.

Interview with John W. Hernandez, Jr., former EPA Deputy Administrator, Washington, D.C., 26 June 1983, and September 1983 telephone interview. Hernandez's vita may be found in *Nominations* at 306–315.

Page 13

Jack Nelson, "Pollution Curbed, Reagan Says, Attacks Air Cleanup," *Los Angeles Times*, 9 October 1980, I-1, I-20. Rachelle Patterson, "Reagan's Erratic Speeches," *Boston Globe*, 9 October 1980, 33. Lou Cannon, *Reagan*, at 287ff.

Page 14

Our figure for EPA's total employment is derived from: "Trimming the Federal Workforce," *Washington Post*, 15 December 1982, A25; and Warren Brookes, "Media Our 'Shadow Government,'" *Boston Herald*, 14 August 1983, 43. Confirmed in interview with Morgan Kinghorn, EPA Comptroller, Washington, D.C., 21 September 1983.

Page 15

The EPA is a unique experiment in a government in that, unlike the statutes administered by other regulatory agencies, the EPA statutes require the Agency to achieve specific goals by a specified date. See Alfred Marcus, "The Environmental Protection Agency," in James Q. Wilson, ed., *The Politics of Regulation* (New York: Basic Books, Inc., 1980) at 267–303.

In addition, her future husband, Robert Burford, was at the Department of the Interior, having been chosen by Watt to be Director of the Bureau of Land Management.

Frank O'Donnell, "Manager of the Year," *Washington Monthly*, December 1981, 36–38. See also Gavin, "Burford-Gorsuch," at 2.

Page 16

Watt, 9 March 1981 speech to Conference of National Park Concessioners, quoted in Drew, "A Reporter at Large," at 112.

Interview with Walter Barber, former EPA Acting Administrator, Washington, D.C., 5 July 1983.

Page 17

Interview with James Sanderson, attorney and former EPA Assistant Administrator-Designate for Policy and Resource Management, Denver, CO, 18 July 1983.

Off-the-record interview with EPA political appointee, Washington, D.C., 10 August 1983.

Page 18

Interview with Seth Hunt, EPA Region VIII, Denver, CO, 18 July 1983.

Interview with Joseph Foran, Special Assistant to the EPA Administrator and Deputy Chief of Staff, Washington, D.C., 9 August 1983.

Page 19

Remarks of Stafford and Domenici, in *Nominations* at 1, 27; Testimony of Gorsuch at 28.

Reagan, response to a question in Baton Rouge, LA, 1 April 1980, quoted in Bill Stall, "Reagan Would Ease Curbs on Oil Firms," *Los Angeles Times*, 2 April 1980, at 1-2.

Gorsuch, quoted in Brimberg and Engdahl, "Gorsuch Tapped for EPA Top Job," *Denver Post*, 22 February 1981, at 1; and in Pat McGraw, "EPA Nominee Gorsuch Backs Bid for Regulatory Reform," *Denver Post*, 23 February 1981, at 3.

"Avoiding a GOP Economic Dunkirk," reprinted in William Greider, *The Education of David Stockman and Other Americans* (New York: E. P. Dutton, 1982) at 139–159. See esp. 146, 156–158.

Page 20

Stockman, quoted in Lou Cannon, *Reagan*, at 309.

Page 21

Interview with Jim J. Tozzi, former OMB Deputy Administrator for Information and Regulatory Affairs, Washington, D.C., 29 July 1983.

"Former EPA Official Stork Gathers Industry Suggestions for Rule Changes," BNA *Environment Reporter*, 13 February 1981, 1951.

James Miller, quoted in Susan and Martin Tolchin, "The Rush to Deregulate," *New York Times Magazine*, 21 August 1983, 34ff. at 36.

"EPA Does Not Adequately Weigh Costs, Benefits of Rules, OMB Critique Says," BNA *Environment Reporter*, 8 May 1981, 62–64; plus excerpts from "Potential Regulatory Targets" section from OMB Draft Critique of EPA, at 78–83.

Interview with Foran. Asked about EPA's thinking on some current issues, at her confirmation hearing (1 May), Gorsuch told Senator Symms, "I frankly don't know what the discussions at EPA are, I have not been at the Agency." Earlier she had told Senator Stafford the same of the OMB hit lists: "I did not participate in the identification of any of the specific regulations." *Nominations* at 54 and 35. Timothy B. Clark, "Outgoing Carterites Rush to the Printer with a Flood of Rules," *National Journal*, 24 January 1981, at 127, 154.

Page 22

Remarks by the President, the White House, 22 January 1981, reprinted in *Role of OMB in Regulation, Hearing before the Subcommittee on Oversight and Investigations*, House Energy and Commerce Committee, No. 97–70, 18 June 1981 (hereafter *Role*) at 364. See also *Office of Management and Budget Control of OSHA Rulemaking, Hearing before the Subcommittee on Manpower and Housing*, House Government Operations Committee, 11 and 18–19 March 1982 (hereafter *OMB-OSHA*); and, Erik Olson, University of Virginia Law School, *Office of Management and Budget Review of Environmental Protection Agency Rulemaking Under Executive Order 12291*, draft article July 1983 (hereafter *OMB Review*).

Memorandum for Cabinet Officers and EPA Administrator on "Postponement of Pending Regulations," The White House, 29 January 1981; reprinted in *Role* at 365.

Notes on Regulatory Relief, Office of the Vice-President, 25 March 1981, 1, reprinted in *Role* at 417.

Miller quoted in Peter Behr and Joanne Omang, "Impact of Regulation Freeze Is Unclear," *Washington Post*, 30 January 1981, A4.

Page 23

Executive Order 12291 (signed 17 February 1981), "Federal Regulation," 46 *Fed. Reg.* 13193–13198, 19 February 1981; reprinted in *Role* at 371–6.

Interview with Gary Dietrich, President, Clement Associates, former Director, EPA Office of Solid Waste, Rosslyn, VA, 9 September 1983. See also testimony of Christopher DeMuth in *OMB-OSHA* at 301.

"Deregulation HQ, An Interview on the New Executive Order with Murray Weidenbaum and James C. Miller, III," *Regulation*, March–April 1981, 14–23 at 22. See also Miller at 22; Olson, *OMB Review* at 14, 18, 40.

Miller in "Deregulation HQ" at 19; testimony in *Role* at 132. Tozzi, quoted in Peter Behr, "If There's a New Rule, Jim Tozzi Has Read It," *Washington Post*, 10 July 1981, at A21.

Page 24

Testimony of Miller in *Role* at 122.

Transcription of Hall of Flags Reg. Reform Briefing, April 10, 1980 [sic: 1981], reprinted in *Role* at 88. See also testimony of DeMuth in *OMB-OSHA* at 347.

Page 25
Synar-Gray exchange in *Role* at 56.
Testimony of DeMuth in *OMB-OSHA* at 347.

Page 26
Tozzi quoted in Olson, *OMB Review*, at 61; see also senior OMB official quoted at 31.
Interview with Roy Gamse, former EPA Acting Associate Administrator for Policy, Washington, D.C., 27 June 1983.
Telephone interview with Michele B. Corash, former EPA General Counsel, San Francisco, CA, 6 September 1983.
Memorandum from Michele Beigel Corash, General Counsel, to C. Boyden Gray, Counsel to the Vice-President, 24 January 1981, concerning Regulations Freeze, at 3, 2.
"Confidential" memorandum from Walt Barber, EPA Acting Administrator, to Jim Miller, Administrator for Information and Regulatory Affairs, 11 February 1981, concerning "A Regulatory Reform Program for EPA," plus attachment, "Initial Reactions to Miller Proposals for Immediate EPA Regulatory Reforms." See also letter from Michele B. Corash, General Counsel, to James C. Miller, 12 March 1981, at 1 ("we have found it hard to deduce any consistent approach to EPA regulations from the items you selected").
"President Reagan's Initiatives to Reduce Regulatory Burdens," The White House, 18 February 1981, 1, 3; reprinted in *Role* at 383, 385.
Press release, Office of the Vice-President, 7 March 1981, at 1; reprinted in *Role* at 389 ("source" definition).
Transcript of Press Conference by Vice-President Bush, The White House, 25 March 1981, at 5. Statement by the Vice-President Regarding Actions Taken by the President's Task Force on Regulatory Relief, Office of the Vice-President, 25 March 1981, with attachments; reprinted in *Role* at 391–418.

Page 27
Summary of Reagan Administration's Regulatory Relief Actions, Report by OMB Staff to the Task Force, 13 June 1981 at 1; reprinted in *Role* at 229. See "Fact Sheet: President Reagan's Program for the U.S. Automobile Industry," The White House, 6 April 1981; reprinted in *Role* at 425–485.
Interview with Michael Walsh, former Director, EPA Office of Mobile Sources, Washington, D.C., 21 June 1983.
Testimony of George Eads in *Role* at 15.
Gray in *Transcription of Hall of Flags* at 20; reprinted in *Role* at 90.
Remarks of Vice-President George Bush at the Presidential Task Force on Regulatory Relief Briefing, Office of the Vice-President, 12 August 1981, and attachment.

Page 28
Gray, at 12 August press conference, quoted in "Environmental Regulations Dominate New Rules Review List Announced by Bush," BNA *Environment Reporter*, 14 August 1981, 483–484 at 483.
Statement by the Vice-President Regarding Progress Made in Achieving the President's

Goal of Regulatory Relief, Office of the Vice-President, 13 June 1981, at 1; reprinted in *Role* at 329.

Testimony of Miller in *Role* at 67.

Joseph R. Wright, Jr., Deputy Secretary of Commerce, Speech to U.S. Chamber of Commerce, in *Transcription of Hall of Flags* at 4; reprinted in *Role* at 74.

Miller quoted in "New EPA Regulators to Lead Agency, Not OMB or Task Force, Miller Says," BNA *Environment Reporter*, 24 April 1981, at 2244.

Interview with Robert Crandall, economist, Washington, D.C., 9 August 1983; telephone interview with Lawrence Ruff, economist, Washington, D.C., 26 September 1983; interview with Nolan Clark, attorney, Washington, D.C., 22 July 1983. Besides Crandall and Ruff, the group included Jim Miller and Marvin Kosters. Later, Gorsuch explained to the *Wall Street Journal* that the bottom line was simply that she was "certainly not encouraging any new regulations." Andy Pasztor, "Political Realities Slow Up EPA's Chief, But She Still Manages to Jolt the Agency," *Wall Street Journal*, 20 October 1981, at 56.

Page 29

Gorsuch statement to EPA employees, 21 May 1981, quoted in "Gorsuch Begins EPA Job with Pledge to Reform Rules, Decentralize Decisions," BNA *Environment Reporter*, 29 May 1981, at 152.

Health Standards for Air Pollutants, Hearings before Subcommittee on Health and the Environment, House Energy and Commerce Committee, No. 97, 14–15 October 1981, testimony of Harris at 263 and 286.

Page 30

Interview with Katherine (Kitty) Adams, former Special Assistant to the EPA Administrator, Alexandria, VA, 30 June 1983. See also Frank Greve, "Industry Partisans Now Run EPA," *Miami Herald*, 27 July 1981, at 1A, 8A.

Interview with David Menotti, former EPA Associate General Counsel for Air, Washington, D.C., 1 September 1983. In late 1981 Anne Gorsuch presented him the EPA's top award for meritorious service.

Off-the-record interview with a senior attorney, Office of the General Counsel for Air, Washington, D.C., 13 July 1983.

Page 31

Interview with Gordon Wood, a thoughtful and open-minded lobbyist for a large chemical company, Washington, D.C., 12 August 1983.

Off-the-record interview with environmental manager for a large oil company with a very good reputation on environmental issues, Washington, D.C., April 1983.

Page 32

Waxman, letter to President Reagan of 19 June 1981, cited in "EPA Draft Proposal for Clean Air Act Would Give States Far Greater Authority," BNA *Environment Reporter*, 26 June 1981, 275–276; interview with Kathleen Bennett, former Assistant Administrator for Air, Washington, D.C., 13 June 1983; "Draft Reagan Bill Retains NAAQS, Scraps Nonattainment, Softens PSD, NSPS," *Inside EPA* Special Report, 3 July 1981.

Vice-President Bush quoted in Pasztor, "Political Realities" at 56.

John W. Hernandez quoted in Frank Greve, "Hard-Line Activists Are Quitting a Softer EPA," *Detroit Free-Press*, 30 October 1981, at 4B.

Page 33

Interviews with Hernandez, Washington, D.C., 26 June 1983, and Las Cruces, NM, 6 July 1983, and a number of other officials and staff, including but not limited to, Paul Stolpman, Director, Office of Policy Analysis, Washington, D.C., 28 June 1983; Eric Eidsness, former Assistant Administrator for Water, Washington, D.C., 11 July 1983; Gene Lucero, Director, Waste Enforcement, Washington, D.C., 14 July 1983; Valdas K. Adamkus, Regional Administrator, EPA Region V, Washington, D.C., 21 July 1983; John Todhunter, former Assistant Administrator for Pesticides and Toxic Substances, Washington, D.C., 21 July 1983. See also Hernandez testimony in *Nominations*, e.g., at 288.

Page 34

Our account of the Dow dioxin episode is drawn from interviews with John Hernandez, Val Adamkus, and three congressional staff members; a package of documents provided by Hernandez entitled *Answers to Charges Relating to Changes in a 1981 EPA Region V Report on Dioxins in Great Lakes Waters*, 72-page statement with documentary attachments, March–April 1983; hundreds of pages of Region V documents obtained from EPA; testimony of Hernandez and Region V personnel before Investigations and Oversight Subcommittees of House Public Works Committee (16 March 1983) and House Energy and Commerce Committee (18 March 1983); letter from John A. Todhunter, AA for OPTS, to Rep. John Dingell, 23 March 1983, concerning Dow dioxin allegations; Howard Kurtz, "EPA Officials Testify About Pressure to Alter Report on Chemical," *Washington Post*, 19 March 1983, A2; Jeffrey Smith, "White House Names New EPA Chief," *Science*, 1 April 1983, 35–36; statement released by Hernandez (15 March) and quoted in Philip Shabecoff, "Scheuer Says EPA Aide Let Dow Delete Dioxin Tie in Draft Report," *New York Times*, 16 March 1983, A1; "Dow Chemical Urging Got EPA to Soften 1981 Dioxin Water Report, Officials Say," *Wall Street Journal*, 16 March 1983, A4; Howard Kurtz, "Dow Got to Suggest Dioxin Report Changes," *Washington Post*, 16 March 1983, at A1.

Page 36

Interview with W. Ernst Minor, member of EPA transition team and later Council on Environmental Quality and Special Assistant to Administrator Ruckelshaus, Washington, D.C., 3 August 1983.

Page 37

Letter from Hon. Gary Hart, U.S. Senate, to Hon. Robert Stafford, U.S. Senate, 1 March 1983, and enclosure. Hart reports that on the evening of 28 February his office received a package containing a list of EPA affiliated scientists, and later a telephone call identifying it as a small portion of a big package of materials supplied to "senior political appointees" after being "collated" by Cordia. The enclosure is a list, with commentary, of 89 scientists and technical experts, and six EPA program areas or work groups.

A second list, which Cordia called "pro and con assessments . . . the kind of work that's essential to any new Administration," rated political appointees and top Agency managers and was apparently transmitted by Cordia to Perry and Sullivan in July 1981 on Heritage Foundation stationery. Dale Russakoff and Howard Kurtz, "Compiler of EPA 'Hit Lists' Resigns," *Washington Post*, 16 March 1983, A1; Stuart Taylor, Jr., "Former Aide Says He Prepared EPA Lists," *New York Times*, 17 March 1983, at B14.

"Briefing: Someone Has Cracked the Crayola Code . . ." *New York Times*, 8 January 1982, at A12.

Sandy Graham, " 'Hit List' Just a Briefing Tool, EPA Aide Says," *Rocky Mountain News*, 13 May 1983, at 14.

Letter from Charles L. Dempsey, Acting Inspector General, EPA, to Richard Gordon, Senior Inspector, Merit Systems Protection Board, 22 April 1983, referring Miller hit list for investigation; Memorandum from Dempsey to Lee Verstandig, Acting EPA Administrator, transmitting Report of Investigation on Walter (Cliff) Miller, 9 May 1983, at 1.

Page 38

[Gregory Gordon, UPI], "Burford Gave 'Living Color' Billing to Top EPA Officials Marked for Firing," Newark *Star-Ledger*, 21 March 1983, 8; see also [Gordon, UPI], " 'Hit List' Targeted EPA Aides to be Fired," *Los Angeles Times*, 21 March 1983, at 4.

Interviews with Joseph A. Cannon, EPA Associate Administrator for Policy and Resource Management, Washington, D.C., 4 August 1983, and, Bennett and Stolpman.

Notes of John Daniel Consisting of A-P Parts, at M-1 (conversation with Craig Fuller, 3/2/83, ca. 12:15 P.M.), released at and entered into record of *The Administration of Superfund, The Withholding of Files, and the Role of OMB in EPA Rulemaking, Hearing before the Subcommittee on Investigations and Oversight,* House Energy and Commerce Committee, 27 September 1983 (hereafter *The Administration of Superfund*).

Testimony of Cannon, Hernandez, and others, before Subcommittee on Investigations and Oversight, House Public Works Committee, 16 March 1983, transcript at 140, 155ff., 179–185.

Quoted in "NAM Members Urged to Support Gorsuch, Expose Unsympathetic EPA Staffers," *Inside EPA*, 30 October 1981, at 7.

Page 39

Interview with Gamse; telephone interview with Nolan Clark, former EPA Associate Administrator for Policy and Resource Management, Washington, D.C., 8 September 1983. See also O'Donnell, "Manager of the Year," at 37. "Waxman Says OMB 'Distorted' Report by EPA on Energy Facilities Permitting," BNA *Environment Reporter*, 24 July 1981, at 409–410.

Page 41

Interviews with William Hedeman, Director, Office of Emergency and Remedial Response (Superfund), Washington, D.C., 29 July and 8 September 1983.

Interviews with Cannon, Foran, Hedeman, Lucero; see also Greve, "Industry Partisans," 27 July 1981, at 8A.

Interviews with Minor and Walsh.

On Perry: Interviews with eight present or former EPA lawyers; W. John Moore, "Perry Elbows His Way to the Top of EPA Legal Shop," *Legal Times of Washington*, 27 September 1982, 4; "EPA's 'Chief Cop' Is Cool in the Midst of a Shootout," *Chemical Week*, 23 February 1983, 27–28; *Report on the Investigation of Alleged Violations of Law by Present and Former Officials of the Environmental Protection Agency*, prepared by the Public Integrity Section, Criminal Division, U.S. Department of Justice, 11 August 1983 (hereafter *Justice EPA Report*), on Perry at 15–20. See also *U.S. EPA Investigations, Hearing before Subcommittee on Oversight and Investigations*, House Energy and Commerce Committee, 7 March 1983, transcript at 51–53.

Page 42
Interview with Foran.
Nominations of Frederic A. Eidsness, Jr., and Rita M. Lavelle, Hearings before the Senate Committee on Environment and Public Works, No. 97-H41, 15 and 23 March 1982, Lavelle curriculum vitae at 50–54.
Interviews with Hedeman, Lucero, Eidsness, Todhunter, Dietrich; Dale Russakoff and Mary Thornton, "Burford Fights to Save Job at EPA," *Washington Post*, 5 March 1983, at A1, A6; Stuart Taylor, Jr., "Meese Denies Asking for a Report on Toxic Dump," *New York Times*, 10 March 1983, B13; Stuart Taylor, Jr., "Jury Writes Postscript to a Stormy Career at EPA," *New York Times*, 24 July 1983, at E22; John Johnson and Ed Salzman, "Rita Lavelle Fights Back, Claims She Was Framed," *Sacramento Bee*, 28 August 1983, A1, A9. "I'd rather be playing tennis": among documents released by Oversight and Investigations Subcommittee, House Energy and Commerce Committee, 21 March 1983.

Page 43
Nominations of Matthew N. Novick and John A. Todhunter, Hearings before the Senate Committee on Environment and Public Works, No. 97-H27, 22 September and 16 October 1981, at 12–14, 21, 25; résumé at 20–21.
Interviews with Todhunter, Foran; interview with Andrew Jovanovich, Science Adviser to Todhunter and former Acting Assistant Administrator for Research and Development, Washington, D.C., 21 July 1983.

Page 44
Interviews with Eidsness and Bennett, as well as ten present or former EPA staff and officials who worked with or for them.
Nominations of Frederic A. Eidsness, at 20–25.
Nominations of John P. Horton and Kathleen M. Bennett, Hearing before the Senate Committee on Environment and Public Works, No. 97-H21, 17 July 1981, at 11ff.
Interviews with Hedeman, Foran, Cannon; see also Eleanor Randolph, "Feisty, Intense, EPA Chief at Open War With Staff," *Los Angeles Times*, 2 November 1981, at 1, 5–6.

Page 45
Telephone interview with Edward Kurent, former EPA Enforcement Counsel for Waste, Washington, D.C., 23 September 1983.
Hazardous Waste Enforcement, Report of the Subcommittee on Oversight and Investiga-

tions, House Energy and Commerce Committee, No. 97-NN, December 1982, at 29–36.

Page 46

Remarks of the Hon. Anne M. Gorsuch, Administrator, U.S. EPA, Environmental Industry Council, Washington, D.C., 21 September 1982, at 9.

Off-the-record interview with career staff member, Office of Water, Washington, D.C., 12 August 1983.

Interview with Michael A. Brown, Enforcement Counsel, Washington, D.C., 22 July 1983.

Page 47

Interviews with Adamkus and William Sullivan, former Enforcement Counsel, Washington, D.C., 21 July 1983. Sullivan says he meant only to emphasize the importance of seeking a fast, efficient, negotiated solution, not to discourage enforcement, but that was not how his comment was taken by others. See also Carolyn Phillips, "Morale, Enforcement in EPA Office Improve Since Burford Resignation," *Wall Street Journal,* 28 July 1983, at 21, 28.

Statistics: At different times, EPA has provided wildly varying statistics on enforcement activity. We quote those provided to Rep. Dingell's Oversight Subcommittee, which appear in *EPA Enforcement and Administration of Superfund, Hearings before the Subcommittee on Oversight and Investigations,* House Energy and Commerce Committee, No. 97–123, 16 and 18 November 1981 and 2 April 1982 (hereafter *EPA Enforcement and Administration*), at 289. Differing figures, dated 17–19 October 1983, were supplied to the Natural Resources Defense Council under Freedom of Information Act request RIN-6473-83. These figures, from EPA's computerized Enforcement Docket Retrieval System, were further complicated in: Courtney M. Price, Assistant Administrator Designate for Enforcement and Compliance Monitoring, Responses to Questions from Members of the Senate Committee on Environment and Public Works (response to Sen. Mitchell), 25 October 1983, submitted for inclusion in the record of Price's confirmation hearing. See also *Hazardous Waste Enforcement* at 29–31. In general, see Sen. Patrick Leahy, *Environmental Law Enforcement: A Case Study in Mismanagement,* 21 July 1982.

Interviews with Sullivan; Michael Cook, Deputy Director, EPA Office of Solid Waste, Washington, D.C., 14 September 1983; Colburn (Coke) Cherney, EPA Office of General Counsel, Washington, D.C., 13 September 1983.

EPA Enforcement and Administration of Superfund, 2 April 1982, testimony of MacMillan, Cherney, Field, and Sullivan at 322–324, 409–411; see also 466–473. Summary in: *Hazardous Waste Enforcement* at 36–37. Documents relating to the Inmont case are reproduced in: *Superfund Oversight, Hearing before the Senate Committee on Environment and Public Works,* S. Hrng. 98–41, Part 2, 8 April 1983, (hereafter *Superfund Oversight 2*), at 341–358.

Page 49

Telephone interview with Khristine Hall, Environmental Defense Fund, Washington, D.C., 19 September 1983; Lisa Friedman, EPA Associate General Counsel for OSWER, Washington, D.C., 13 September 1983; off-the-record interviews with two other EPA attorneys. W. John Moore, "EPA Shuts Door on DOJ, Works Out

RCRA Agreement," *Legal Times of Washington*, 31 August 1981, 2; "EPA Officials Criticized for Exclusion of Attorneys From Meeting On Work Rules," BNA *Environment Reporter*, 4 September 1981, at 556–557.

Interview with Frank Shepherd, former EPA Associate Administrator for Legal and Enforcement Councel, Washington, D.C., 16 September 1983; telephone interview with Mary Doyle, former EPA ethics officer, University of Arizona School of Law, 14 September 1983.

Page 50

Documents on the industry push to vacate the NRDC consent decree are reproduced in: *Environmental Protection Agency: Private Meetings and Water Protection Programs, Hearings before the Subcommittee on Environment,* House Government Operations Committee, 21 October and 4 November 1981 (hereafter *Private Meetings*), at 455–493.

Page 51

"Depression at EPA," letter to the editor from Steven Hoover, EPA enforcement attorney, *Washington Post*, 9 November 1981, A14. Attorney quoted in John Moore, "EPA Lawyers Fear Purge of Undesirables," *Legal Times of Washington*, 26 October 1981.

Interview with Geoff Grubbs, EPA enforcement attorney, Washington, D.C., 12 July 1983; interview with Kurent, Washington, D.C., 21 September 1983.

Interview with Thomas Gallagher, EPA National Enforcement Investigations Center, Washington, D.C., 1 September 1983.

Page 52

Gorsuch, Remarks to . . . Environment Industry Council, at 9.

Anne M. Gorsuch, EPA Enforcement Responsibilities, Remarks at the Regional Administrator's Meeting, Washington, D.C., 30 April 1982; interviews with Brown, Lucero, Adamkus, Cook; interview with James Thompson, EPA Region VI Counsel, Washington, D.C., 13 October 1983.

Page 54

Reagan, speech to steel and coal executives, Steubenville, OH, 7 October 1980; quoted in Lou Cannon, *Reagan*, at 287.

Anne Gorsuch quoted in "EPA in Disarray—Can It Do the Job Industry Expects?" *Chemical Week*, 21 October 1981, 82–85 at 82; see also transcript of interview with Gorsuch, "The McNeil-Lehrer Report," 14 October 1981, at 7.

In addition to sources named in text, our account of the FY 1983 budget battles is based on interviews with Cannon, Foran, seven other EPA officials who asked not to be named, and several thousand pages of budget documents obtained by the Natural Resources Defense Council, by Senator Patrick Leahy, and by William Drayton and the American Environmental Safety Council.

Page 55

Philip Shabecoff, "Funds and Staff for Protecting Environment May Be Halved," *New York Times*, 29 September 1981, 1. Joanne Omang, "Internal Rifts, Huge Staff Cut Hint EPA Retreat on Programs," *Washington Post*, 30 September 1981, A1. "Pre-

liminary Proposal for Fiscal 1983 Includes Major EPA Budget, Personnel Cuts,"
BNA *Environment Reporter*, 2 October 1981, 675–676. Documents reproduced at
697–703. Lawrence Mosher, "Move Over, Jim Watt, Anne Gorsuch Is the Latest
Target of Environmentalists," *National Journal*, 24 October 1981, 1899–1902.
Interview with William Drayton, American Environmental Safety Council, former EPA
Assistant Administrator for Policy, Washington, D.C., 21 September 1983.

Page 56

Gorsuch quoted in "EPA in Disarray," 21 October 1981, at 82.

*Environmental Protection Agency Oversight, Hearing before the Senate Committee on
Environment and Public Works*, No. 97-H29, 15 October 1981. Gorsuch testimony
at 12–13.

Gorsuch testimony in *Private Meetings* at 131ff.

Page 57

OMB 18 February 1981 budget and regulatory relief briefing package, quoted in: Caroline
E. Mayer, "Regulatory Agencies Feel Edge of Budgetary Knife," *Washington Star*,
19 February 1981, at A5.

Joanne Omang, "EPA's Cutbacks Are Overstated, Gorsuch Says," *Washington Post*, 19
November 1981, A6. Philip Shabecoff, "Ecology Unit Cut Reportedly Urged by
Budget Office," *New York Times*, 19 November 1981, 1. "OMB Reportedly Plans
to Halve EPA To $700 Million, 6,000 People by FY-84," *Inside EPA*, 27 November
1981, 1. "Gorsuch Blasts OMB FY-83 Cuts, Threatens to Take Case to President,"
Inside EPA Special Report, 27 November 1981 (reprints Gorsuch letter).

Page 59

See Omang, "Internal Rifts," A1, and Gorsuch's denials in Mosher, "Move Over Jim
Watt," 1900–1901. This account of the plans to cut back the EPA staff is based
on several hundred pages of internal documents (some obtained by the Natural
Resources Defense Council under Freedom of Information Act request RIN-6296-
83), interviews with most of the officials named in the text, and interviews with other
members of the staff closely involved in the process (17 June, 18 July, 9 August, 22
September, 29 September 1983).

Page 60

Attrition and RIF figures in: *Department of Housing and Urban Development—Independent Agencies Appropriations for 1983, Part 3, Hearing before the Subcommittee on
HUD-Independent Agencies*, House Appropriations Committee, 16 March 1982, at
89.

Page 61

Philip Shabecoff, "U.S. Environmental Agency Making Deep Staffing Cuts," *New York
Times*, 3 January 1982, at 20.

Memorandum from Joseph A. Cannon and C. Morgan Kinghorn to the Administrator,
undated but ca. 6 January 1982, concerning "To RIF or Not To RIF."

Action Memorandum from John Daniel, Chairman, Reorganization Review Committee,
to the Administrator, undated (January 1982), concerning Recommendations on

Reorganization Proposals, at 2, and related undated document headed Proposed
Reorganizations, at 1.

Russell E. Train, "The Destruction of EPA," *Washington Post,* 2 February 1982, at A15.
Gorsuch later met with Train for three hours trying to convince him that the reports
of problems at EPA "just weren't true" (interview with Train, New York, NY, 18
October 1983).

Page 62

Memorandum from [the Administrator] to Employees of the Environmental Protection
Agency, 5 February 1982, concerning reports and rumors of RIFs (Gorsuch aide Joe
Foran drafted this memo). Joanne Omang, "EPA's Gorsuch Promises No Firings
Through '83," *Washington Post,* 6 February 1982, at A7.

Page 63

Press release, The White House (Los Angeles, CA), 29 December 1981 ("The President
today announced his intention to nominate . . .").

Andy Pasztor, "White House Officials Asked EPA to Fire Burford's Chief Aide More
Than Year Ago," *Wall Street Journal,* 28 February 1983, 4. Robert Parry, Associated
Press wire service dispatch, "White House Alerted to EPA Allegations Last April,"
10 March 1983.

Letter from Rep. Patricia Schroeder to Matthew Novick, EPA Inspector General, 7
January 1982, attaching anonymous letter of 18 December 1981. Joanne Omang,
"Rep. Schroeder Requests Probe of EPA Nominee," *Washington Post,* 8 January
1982, at A2.

Memorandum from Mary Doyle, Deputy General Councel and ethics officer, EPA, to
Larry Harlow, Acting Director of Office of Legislation, EPA, regarding employment
of James Sanderson, 3 March 1981; Memorandum from Doyle to Sanderson regarding ethical obligations, 8 May 1981.

Page 64

EPA Office of the Inspector General, *Report of Investigations 1-82-017, Concerning
Allegations of Conflict of Interest Involving James W. Sanderson,* 13 April 1982.

Memorandum, Briefing Paper—James W. Sanderson, from Matthew Novick, Inspector
General, to Anne M. Gorsuch, Administrator, 20 April 1982, at 2–4.

Page 66

Justice EPA Report, 11 August 1983, section on Sanderson at 28–49.

Interview with Rep. John Dingell, Washington, D.C., 28 October 1983.

Page 67

[Frank O'Donnell], "EPA's Gorsuch Okays Lead-in-Gas Violations," *Synfuels Week,* 1
February 1982, 4. Joanne Omang, "EPA Acts to Force Dump Site Cleanup,"
Washington Post, 2 February 1982, at A16.

The Thriftway incident was investigated by the EPA Office of the Inspector General. Its
Report of Investigation 1-82-045, Thriftway Company, et al., 5 April 1982, is reprinted in *Lead in Gasoline: Public Health Dangers, Hearing before the Subcommittee on Environment,* House Government Operations Committee, 14 April 1982
(hereafter *Lead in Gasoline*), at 77–172.

Memorandum (EPA Action Item) from Anne M. Gorsuch to Ed Rollins, Assistant to the President for Political Affairs, 21 April 1982, on Thriftway Refinery. (One in a series of so-called "issue alerts" sent by Gorsuch to White House aides Rollins and Craig Fuller.)

Page 68

Fiscal Year 1983 Budget Review, Hearings before the Senate Committee on Environment and Public Works, No. 97-H37, 22-24, 26 February and 2 March 1982, at 152–154, 234–235.

"Memo Urges Prompt Superfund Action, But Provides 'No Action' RCRA Option," *Inside EPA,* 12 March 1982, 11–12 at 11.

Liquids in landfills ban lifted at 47 *Fed. Reg.* 8304 (25 February 1982) reimposed at 47, *Fed. Reg.* 12316 (22 March 1982). See Philip Shabecoff, "U.S. Agency Seeks Easing of Rules for Waste Dumps," *New York Times,* 1 March 1982, at A1.

Page 69

Eleanor Randolph, "Controversial EPA Director Reported on 'Short Leash,' " *Los Angeles Times,* 29 May 1982, at 20, 22. Philip Shabecoff, "White House Has EPA on Political 'Watch List,' " *New York Times,* 14 June 1982, at B11. Steven R. Weisman, "White House Links to EPA Studied," *New York Times,* 24 February 1983, at B8. Letter from James A. Baker III, White House Chief of Staff, to Rep. James Scheuer, 17 March 1983, concerning individuals receiving EPA Issue Alerts and providing copies of the alerts.

Livermore quoted in Cannon, *Reagan,* at 369.

Meese quoted in Peterson memo: "Through Their Looking Glass, Environmentalists See Malice in Reagan Land," *Inside EPA,* 12 February 1982, at 10–11; Philip Shabecoff, "Memo: Meese and the Environmentalists," *New York Times,* 5 February 1982, at A14. Council on Environmental Quality chairman Alan Hill, who attended the meeting, confirms the accuracy of Peterson's notes (telephone interview, Washington, D.C., 12 October 1983).

Page 70

"Our Perception Has Been Miscommunicated," interview with Gorsuch (21 October 1982), *National Journal,* 13 November 1982, at 1943.

"Gorsuch Moves to Shore Up Flagging EPA Image As Protector of Environment," *Inside EPA,* 14 May 1982, 1. Juanita Greene, "Official: EPA Cuts Not Alarming," *Miami Herald,* 21 May 1982, 2A. (Quotes John Hernandez on the road "to carry out EPA's new policy of 'trying to do a better job of talking with the folks.' ") Dale Russakoff and Sandra Sugawara, "Reagan EPA Aides Change Tone, Not Tune," *Washington Post,* 24 May 1982, at A1. "$221-a-Day Coach Hired to Brighten EPA's Image," *Baltimore Sun,* 6 July 1982, at A5.

Page 71

"Meese's Pieces" was formally titled *Setting EPA's Course for the Eighties: Directions of the U.S. Environmental Protection Agency During the Next Two Years,* Anne M. Gorsuch, Administrator, 18 October 1982. "Meese (AMG's office)" appears on Hernandez's calendar for 3:30, 18 October.

Based on a review by the Natural Resources Defense Council of 256 actions listed in the
EPA Regulatory Agency as published between January 1981 and October 1982.

Page 72
Presidential Task Force on Regulatory Relief, *Reagan Administration Regulatory Achieve-
ments*, Washington, D.C., 11 August 1983, Table 2 at 62.
Gore and Daniel in *The Administration of Superfund*, 27 September 1983, transcript at
68, 18 and 67.
"OMB Midterm Analysis Gives EPA Poor Marks on Reg. Reform, Other Programs,"
Inside EPA, 12 November 1982, 1, 4–5.

Page 73
Dingell in *EPA Enforcement and Administration*, 16 November 1982, at 3.
EPA *Withholding of Superfund Files, Hearings before the Subcommittee on Oversight and
Investigations*, House Energy and Commerce Committee, No. 97-192, 3 and 14
December 1982, Dingell statement at 2–3; subpoena at 297–298.

Page 74
Dingell, press statement to announce postponement of Gorsuch appearance, Washington,
D.C., 26 October 1982.
Off-the-record interview with former White House staff member, Washington, D.C., 10
August 1983.

Page 75
On Gorsuch's arguments against withholding and her lawyers' assurances, see the testimony of John Daniel and other aides in *The Administration of Superfund*, 27
September 1983, and her own testimony on the second day of these hearings, 28
September 1983. (All citations to both hearings refer to the transcripts, which had
not been printed at press time.) The notes taken by John Daniel during this period,
entered into the record of the 27 September hearing, chronicle the withholding
debacle in extraordinary detail: "Notes of John Daniel Consisting of A-P Parts"
(hereafter "Notes of Daniel"). Also helpful is a document prepared for this hearing
by subcommittee staff, "Working Chronology For Use At September 27, 1983,
Hearing Relating to the Withholding of EPA Documents and Claims of Executive
Privilege."
Memorandum for the Administrator, Environmental Protection Agency, from Ronald
Reagan, The White House, concerning Congressional Subpoenas for Executive
Branch Documents, 30 November 1982, reprinted in *Contempt of Congress, Report
of the House Committee on Public Works and Transportation*, Report No. 97-968,
15 December 1982, 42–43 at 43.
EPA *Withholding*, 3 and 14 December 1982; testimony of Gorsuch at 151–154, 156;
documents at 109–114; exchange between Tauzin and Gorsuch at 170ff.; statements
of Dingell at 1–3, 141–145; testimony of Steve Leifer at 60ff.; see also Robert L.
Jackson, "House Panel Votes to Cite EPA Chief for Contempt Over Files," *Los
Angeles Times*, 3 December 1982, at I-10.
Letter from Rep. Marc L. Marks to Robert A. McConnell, Assistant Attorney General,
8 December 1982, concerning "executive privilege."

Page 76

Off-the-record interview with senior EPA political appointee, Washington, D.C., 10 August 1983.

Proceedings against Anne M. Gorsuch, *Congressional Record*, No. 149, part 2, House of Representatives, 16 December 1982, at H10033–H10061. Motion of the House of Representatives to Dismiss and to Expedite Consideration, *United States of America v. The House of Representatives*, Civil Action No. 82-3583 (D.D.C., filed 30 December 1982) and attached Memorandum of Points and Authorities and exhibits (Exhibit 4 is the Justice Department statement concerning its 16 December 1982 action).

2 U.S.C. §194, quoted in letter from Speaker Thomas P. O'Neill, Jr., to Stanley S. Harris, U.S. Attorney, 4 January 1983.

Motion of the House of Representatives to Dismiss, at 2.

Page 77

"Lavelle's Firing: Reportedly At Odds With Gorsuch, Perry and Congress," *Inside EPA*, 11 February 1983, 6–7, reprints Ingold memo. The index to the computer file in which the memo was kept, which is not reprinted, titles it "62: Memo to WH on Bob Perry."

Page 78

Gorsuch response to question from Sen. Gary Hart, hearing before Senate Environment and Public Works Committee, 15 February 1983.

Gorsuch referrals of 2 February, 8 February, 10 February, reprinted in *Superfund Oversight 2* at 72–90.

"Notes of Daniel" at A-4, A-6.

The Administration of Superfund, 27 September 1983, testimony of Daniel, transcript at 50–51, 87–89, 96–97. See also "Notes of Daniel" at A-6, A-7.

"Notes of Daniel" from Gorsuch conversation with "Jim Baker—2/18/83, 11⁰⁰ AM," at H-1; See also at A-8, A-9.

"Notes of Daniel" from "Discussion w/Craig [Fuller] & Anne [Gorsuch] 2/24/83," at J-1ff, especially J-2 and J-6; testimony of Daniel, in *Administration of Superfund*, 27 September 1983, transcript at 103–110; see also "Notes of Daniel" at B-1.

"Notes of Daniel," "Events After Levitas Agreement," at B-2; testimony of Daniel, transcript at 121–130.

Off-the-record interviews with two high-level EPA officials, Washington, D.C., August 1983.

Letter from Rep. John Dingell, Oversight and Investigations Subcommittee, to President Ronald Reagan, 1 March 1983, detailing specific instances of criminal conduct and wrongdoing; see also "Notes of Daniel" at B-4, M-2, O-2. Stuart Taylor, "Dingell Reports He Has Evidence of 'Criminal Conduct' at EPA," *New York Times*, 2 March 1983, at A1. By this time, Gorsuch herself had referred evidence of political manipulation of Superfund to the Justice Department: letter from Anne M. Burford to Edward C. Schmults, Deputy Attorney General, 25 February 1983, enclosing notes of EPA enforcement attorneys (entered into record, *The Administration of Superfund*, 27 September 1983).

Page 80

"Notes of Daniel" on meeting of Schmults, Dinkins, Perry, Yamada, Modesitt, Gorsuch, and Daniel, 3 March 1983, at P-1ff; testimony of Daniel, transcript at 134–145; see also "Notes of Daniel" at B-6.

Memorandum from Richard A. Hauser, Deputy Counsel to the President, to John C. Keeney, Deputy Assistant Attorney General, 4 March 1983, concerning EPA Investigation. See also *Justice EPA Report*, section on Gorsuch, at 51–53.

Eleanor Randolph, "New Charges Made Against EPA Chief," *Los Angeles Times*, 4 March 1983, 1.

"Transcript of President's News Conference on Foreign and Domestic Matters," *New York Times*, 12 March 1983, A8.

2. RISKY BUSINESS

Page 82

Our Superfund statistics are derived from *Hazardous Waste Contamination of Water Resources, Hearing before the Subcommittee on Oversight and Investigations,* House Public Works Committee, 18 October 1983, testimony of Lee Thomas and Gene Lucero, transcript at 74. See also *Superfund Oversight* 2, at 26. Spending through Fiscal Year 1982, $88 million of $452 million: U.S. Congress, Office of Technology Assessment, *Technologies and Management Strategies for Hazardous Waste Control,* March 1983 (hereafter *OTA Report*), at 20.

EPA Mining Waste Policy for Superfund, Hearing before the Subcommittee on Oversight and Investigations, House Energy and Commerce Committee, 2 May 1983, transcript at 143–144 (hereafter *Globe;* exhibits released at the hearing cited by exhibit number).

Interviews with William Hedeman, Director of Superfund Office, EPA, 29 July 1983; 8 September 1983.

Page 83

On political manipulation of Superfund: Letter from Anne M. Gorsuch to Edward Schmults, Deputy Attorney General, 25 February 1983, attaching attorneys' notes on Stringfellow and Seymour; entered into hearing record in *The Administration of Superfund,* 28 September 1983, and documents released then: Memorandum from Subcommittee staff to Chairman John D. Dingell, 27 September 1983, concerning Withholding of Funds, and attachments. See also Memorandum from Rita M. Lavelle, AA, OSWER, to Michael Deaver, Deputy Chief of Staff, The White House, concerning Positive Environmental Action for President, 13 September 1982; and documents, primarily notes of Susan Baldyga, released at session of Subcommittee on Oversight and Investigations, House Energy and Commerce Committee, 21 March 1983; Gregory Gordon, "Questions Linger Over Chemical Cleanup Settlement," UPI dispatch, 20 April 1983.

Page 84

Our account of the Globe, Arizona, debacle is drawn from *Globe,* the exhibits released at that hearing, and off-the-record interviews with EPA staff members, Washington, D.C., August 1983.

Testimony in *Globe* of Sparks at 40–42.

Globe background: CH2M Hill, *Remedial Investigation/Feasibility Study: Mountain View Mobile Home Estates, Globe, Arizona,* prepared for EPA, 6 May 1983. *Community Asbestos Exposure in Globe, Arizona, Report to Director of Centers for Disease Control, from Chronic Diseases Division, Center for Environmental Health,* EPI-80-35-2, 19 August 1981, at 2 (Exhibit 7). Complaint, *United States of America v. Metate Asbestos Corporation, et al.* (D.Ariz., filed May 1983).

Page 85

William J. Nicholson, Ph.D., Mount Sinai School of Medicine, Environmental Protection Agency: Health Effects Update [on Asbestos], June 1983.

Community Asbestos at 1–2.

Page 86

Testimony of Luckie in *Globe* at 18–19.

Page 87

Letter from William H. Foege, M.D., Assistant Surgeon General, to Suzanne Dandoy, M.D., Director, Arizona Department of Health Services, 11 January 1980, at 1 (Exhibit 4).

Memorandum from Suzanne Dandoy, Director, Arizona Department of Health Services, to Governor Bruce Babbitt, concerning Asbestos in Globe—Permanent Solution, 18 January 1980, at 1–2 (Exhibit 5).

Page 88

Testimony in *Globe* of Luckie at 20–21; Scott at 25; Dingell at 5.

Interview with attorney in Superfund office who asked not to be identified, 3 August 1983.

Page 89

Memorandum from Russel H. Wyer, Hazardous Site Control Division, EPA, to H. D. Van Cleve, Emergency Response Division, EPA, concerning Potential Emergency at Globe, Arizona, 10 February 1982 (Exhibit 13).

Page 90

Testimony in *Globe* of Hedeman at 107–110, 120–126, 129–131.

Page 91

Exchange between Sen. Mitchell, Hedeman, Lucero, and Sen. Moynihan in *Superfund Oversight 2* at 17–18.

Document found in Mrs. Burford's EPA files labeled "December 1982: Environmental Protection Agency: Talking Points—FY 1984 Budget Passback Appeal," at II.E.c. Cover sheet is a roster of the Cabinet Council, with notations in Gorsuch's handwriting. This document was entered into the record in *The Administration of Superfund,* 28 September 1983, transcript at 134.

Page 92

OTA Report at 268, 314.

Exchange between Mitchell and Hedeman, *Superfund Oversight 2* at 30.

Page 93

Testimony in *Superfund Oversight 2* of Hedeman at 31; Lucero at 49, 31; Mitchell at 31, 49.

Off-the-record interview with EPA Superfund official, Washington, D.C. 14 September 1983. See also: Memorandum from Michael B. Cook, Director, OERR, to Christopher T. Capper, Acting AA, OSWER, concerning Santa Fe Springs, 18 August 1981.

Page 94

Testimony of Lucero in *Superfund Oversight 2* at 32.

Page 95

Irving T. Selikoff, et al., "Mortality Experience of Insulation Workers in the United States and Canada," *Annals NY Academy of Sciences*, 330, 1979, at 91–116.

Figures from Nicholson, Table 3-1 at 14.

Page 96

Testimony in *Globe* of Houk at 78.

Interview with Tom Anderson, *Arizona Silver Belt*, Globe, AZ, 16 July 1983.

Alvin Gerhardt and Mike Wood, *Chrysotile Asbestos and Health in Gila County, Arizona*, 25 September 1982, most recent update, 21 March 1983 (hereafter *Wood-Gerhardt Studies*), at 6, 5.

Interview with Alvin Gerhardt, Globe, AZ, 16 July 1983.

Transcription, "Horizon," Michael Grant interview of Dr. James Sarn, Arizona Department of Health Services, KAET-TV, 16 September 1982, included in *Wood-Gerhardt Studies*, 13–16 at 14.

Telephone interview with Dr. William Nicholson, Mt. Sinai Medical School, New York, July 1983.

Page 97

Interview with Catherine Scott, Globe, AZ, 15 July 1983.

Testimony of Luckie in *Globe* at 22.

Interview with John and Anna Insalaco, Globe, AZ, 15–16 July 1983.

Page 98

Memorandum from Ralph E. Yodaiken, M.D., Chairman, SAS, NIOSH, to Director, DSDTT, NIOSH, concerning Community Asbestos Exposure—Globe, Arizona, 8 January 1982 (Exhibit 11).

Interviews with two EPA attorneys in the Superfund office who asked not to be identified, 13 September 1983.

Page 99

Routing and Transmittal Slip, from Gene Lucero to Deborah Dalton, concerning Globe, AZ, 12 August 1982 (Exhibit 19).

Testimony of Lucero in *Globe* at 111–112, 177–181; Dingell at 5–6, 178; Sikorskiat 178.

Page 100

Testimony in *Globe* of Hedeman at 139ff., 144; confirmed in interview with Hedeman, 29 July 1983.

Memorandum from William N. Hedeman, Director, OERR, to the Administrator, through Rita M. Lavelle, Assistant Administrator, concerning National Priorities List, 8 December 1982, and notes of "12/13/82 meeting w/John Daniel" written on memo (Exhibit 22), at 4.

Page 101
Testimony in *Globe* of Hedeman at 132–133, 149–150, 192–194.

Page 102
James J. Westrick, J. Wayne Mello, and Robert F. Thomas, EPA Office of Drinking Water, *The Ground Water Supply Survey: Summary of Volatile Organic Contaminant Occurrence Data*, Cincinnati, Ohio, January 1983, at i–ii. The most commonly found chemical contaminant was trichlorethylene (TCE), a widely used solvent, found in almost one out of every ten wells tested (iii). TCE is a proven animal carcinogen and thus presumed to cause cancer in people as well.
OTA Report, Table 81 at 373.
EPA Office of Solid Waste, *Preliminary Highlights of Findings: National Survey of Hazardous Waste Generators and Treatment, Storage, and Disposal Facilities Regulated Under RCRA in 1981*, 30 August 1983 (hereafter *RIA Survey*), at Figure 7.
OTA Report at 116–125, 5, 268ff.

Page 103
Permit call-in: See 46 *Fed. Reg.* 38318, 24 July 1981. D.C. Circuit Court decision in *Environmental Defense Fund v. Gorsuch*, 26 July 1983, at 13 *Environmental Law Reporter* 20712 (September 1983).
Hazardous Waste Enforcement at 32.

Page 104
Off-the-record interviews with EPA Superfund officials and Solid Waste attorney, 13 September 1983.
Zero discharge: interviews with Gary Dietrich, 9 September 1983, and with Joe Cannon, Washington, D.C., 3 June 1983.

Page 105
Lavelle testimony at hearing before the Subcommittee on Natural Resources, House Science and Technology Committee, 16 December 1982, quoted in *OTA Report* at 16.
EPA, Hazardous Waste Management System, Permitting Requirements for Land Disposal Facilities, 47 *Fed. Reg.* 32274, 26 July 1982, at 32285. See also *OTA Report* at 178: "All liner materials are subject to breaches in their integrity."
Peter Montague, Princeton University, "Four Secure Landfills in New Jersey—A Study in the State of the Art in Shallow Burial Waste Disposal Technology," draft of 31 March 1982. See also: Peter Montague, "Hazardous Waste Landfills: Some Lessons from New Jersey," *Civil Engineering—ASCE*, September 1982, at 53–56.
North Carolina Academy of Science, *Managing Hazardous Wastes in North Carolina, Report to the Governor's Waste Management Board*, May 1983, at 1.

Page 106
See *OTA Report* at 372–374, 10, 133ff., 28–29, 12, 132, 15, 5–6.

Steven J. Marcus, "New Ways at Hand for Toxic Disposal," *New York Times*, 9 August 1983, C1. Ann Hughey, "Fearing New Love Canal, Chemical Firms Stress Safer Disposal of Hazardous Waste," *Wall Street Journal*, 30 June 1983, at 58.

Page 107
Off-the-record interview with EPA Solid Waste official, 14 September 1983.

Page 108
Telephone interview with Khristine Hall, Environmental Defense Fund, Washington, D.C., July 1983. Off-the-record interview with EPA Solid Waste attorney, 3 August 1983.

Page 109
EPA Office of the Inspector General, *Report of Investigations 1-82-017, concerning Allegations of Conflict of Interest Involving James W. Sanderson* (hereafter *IG Report*), 13 April 1982 (Exhibit 56); quoted in UPI, "Ex-EPA Official Disputes Claim by City Lawyer," *Rocky Mountain News*, 23 February 1983, at 35.
The *Post* article in question was Sandra Sugawara, "A 'Survivor' Weathers the Storm at EPA," *Washington Post*, 12 April 1982, A13.

Page 110
"No": Dietrich quoted in [UPI], "Ex-EPA Official," 35.
"Same day," e.g., 21 September 1981, Denver Water Board billed for 1.7 hours on "EPA Review in Washington;" see R. Jeffrey Smith, "Congress Investigates Malfeasance at EPA," *Science*, 25 March 1983, 1404–6 at 1405.
Nancy Shute, Linda Sarrio, and Frank O'Donnell (Network News), *Temik Investigations*, Washington, D.C., 1983; Gorsuch interview with Nancy Shute, 27 December 1982, at 20.

Page 111
Telephone interview with Clyde Wallace, Cheraw, SC, July 1983.
Cass Peterson, "Carolineans, Fighting Toxic Dump, Find No Ally in U.S. Rules," *Washington Post*, 31 March 1983, A8.

Page 113
See also: *Hazardous Waste Control and Enforcement Act of 1983, Hearings before the Subcommittee on Commerce*, House Committee on Energy and Commerce, No. 98–32, 22 and 24 March 1983 (hereafter *HWCEA*), testimony of Carol MacLennan, Citizens Against Lowry Landfill, at 15–16. Dale Russakoff, "Efforts of Terrified Neighbors Brought Belated End to Dump Site," *Washington Post*, 29 March 1983, at A4. Our discussion of the Lowry Landfill has benefited greatly from interviews with Bonnie Exner and Carol MacLennan, Denver, CO, 17 July 1983, and especially from our interview with Christopher Sutton, Colorado Department of Health, Denver, CO, 18 July 1983, and a number of subsequent telephone interviews with Sutton. We have also made extensive use of the records, primarily correspondence with Chemical Waste and Waste Management, of the Colorado Department of Health.
Hewlett-Packard official quoted in Russakoff, "Efforts," at A4.

Page 115
Waesche and Exner quoted in Russakoff, "Efforts," at A4.

Page 117
Letter from Albert J. Hazle, CDH, to Marianne Walls, Chemical Waste Management, Inc., 5 May 1981, concerning 29 April 1981 inspection. Letter from Kenneth L. Waesche, CHH, to Robert Peterson, Chemical Waste Management, Oak Brook, IL, 17 May 1983, concerning fluids in burial cell leachate collection sump, at 2.
Letter from Robert A. Arnott, CDH, to Marianne Walls, Chemical Waste Management, Inc., 5 January 1982, concerning commitment to install liquid waste fixation system.
From its opening day until 9 July 1982, the Lowry Landfill accepted 16,503 drums with liquids, including 9,588 of ignitable organics—50.97 percent of total drums in burial pit. Information Sheet on Denver-Arapahoe Chemical Waste Processing Facility Burial Cell, Colorado Department of Health, 23 September 1983, figure 4.

Page 120
Letter from Steven Durham, Regional Administrator, EPA Region VIII, to Donald Wallgren, Waste Management, Inc., Oak Brook, IL, 11 December 1981, concerning request to allow drummed liquids storage.
Chris Sutton, Colorado Department of Health, "Liquid Drums: 19 November 1981–22 February 1982" ("CWMI records of disposed drums obtained by C. Sutton in 1983. Drums received between Nov. 19, 1981, and Feb. 22, 1982. These drums were stored in the cell during the ban.")
Letter from Steven Durham, Regional Administrator, to Donald Wallgren, Waste Management, Inc., 15 January 1982, concerning storage of drummed liquid waste at Lowry.
DACWPF [Lowry] RCRA Inspection Report, inspection of 11 January 1982, prepared by Eric Finke, EPA inspector, reviewed by Toney Ott, EPA inspector, 20 and 28 January 1982; reprinted in *HWCEA* at 20.

Page 121
Chris Sutton, CDH, "Liquid Drums: 23 Feb. 1982–26 March 1982" ("Liquid in Drums received for disposal during 1 month lifting of ban. Total drummed liquids buried after Nov. 19, 1981.")
EPA Region VIII, In the Matter Of: Chemical Waste Management, Inc., DACWPF, Consent Agreement and Final Order, Docket No. RCRA (3008) VIII-82, 15 June 1982.
Letter from Kenneth Waesche, CDH, to Arend Lenderlink, CWMI, 21 May 1982, concerning inspections of 18, 19, 20 May 1982. Letter from Arend Lenderlink, CWMI, to Kenneth Waesche, CDH, 14 June 1982, concerning Action Plan responding to 21 May 1982 letter. Letter from Waesche to Lenderlink, 15 June 1982, concerning 14 June 1982 response and allowing resumption of burial of solid hazardous waste.
Woodward-Clyde Consultants, "Ground Water Conditions in the Vicinity of Phase A Drum Burial Cell at the Denver-Arapahoe Disposal Facilities," submitted to WMI, 3 June 1982.

Page 122

EPA Region VIII, In the Matter Of: CWMI, DACWPF, Complaint, Compliance Order and Notice of Opportunity for Hearing, Docket No. RCRA (3008) VIII-83-16, 25 May 1983.

Ponds: U.S. EPA Region VIII, In the Matter Of: CWMI, DACWPF, Complaint, Compliance Order and Notice of Opportunity for Hearing, Docket No. RCRA (3008) VIII-83-5, 21 January 1983.

Page 124

Chris Sutton, CDH, RCRA Inspection Report, 9 September 1982, DACWPF. Chris Sutton, CDH, RCRA Inspection Report (Supplemental), 16–17 September 1982, CWMI D-A Disposal Site, 18 October 1982, at 2, 3.

Interview with Hunt, 18 July 1983. Off-the-record interview with Region VIII staff member, Denver, CO, July 1983.

Letter from Lawrence Beck, Senior Vice-President, Waste Management, Inc., Oakbrook, IL, to Dr. Frank Traylor, Executive Director, CDH, 17 September 1982, concerning letter from Traylor and Durham of 14 September 1982 on Pond 2.

Page 125

Interview with Kenneth Waesche, Colorado Department of Health, Denver, CO, 18 July 1983. Off-the-record interviews with EPA and CDH participants. Telephone interview with Patrick Murphy, U.S. Attorney's Office, Denver, CO, 13 September 1983.

EPA Region VII press release, "EPA Files Complaint Against Chemical Waste Management, Inc.," Denver, CO, 21 January 1983, at 1.

Page 127

Larry Wapensky, EPA Region VIII, Hazardous Waste Facility Section Chief, Review of the Chemical Waste Management Ground Water Monitoring Plan, 21 June 1982.

Karaganis, Gail, and White, Ltd., *Report to the Board of Directors of Waste Management, Inc.*, submitted 22 September 1983, at 51, 53, 59.

Page 128

Telephone interview with Walter Barber, WMI Vice-President and former EPA Acting Administrator, Oakbrook, IL, October 1983.

Page 129

RIA Survey, Figure 17.

Staff Memorandum, Office of Technology Assessment, Industry, Technology, and Employment Program, "Use of Injection Wells for Hazardous Waste Disposal," 13 July 1983.

Off-the-record interview with EPA Solid Waste staff member, Washington, D.C., October 1983.

Page 131

Reagan, statement on EPA air pollution regulations, Youngstown, OH, 7 October 1980; quoted in "Reagan Rapped on EPA Stand," *Youngstown Daily Vindicator*, 10 October 1980, at 2.

Nominations at 33 and 289.

Eliot Marshall, "EPA's High-Risk Carcinogen Policy," *Science*, 3 December 1982, 975–978.

Devra Lee Davis, "Lead: Ancient Metal, New Concerns," *The Environmental Forum*, May 1982, 24–26, 35.

Testimony of Francis Phillips, Acting Regional Administrator, EPA Region VI, before Subcommittee on Investigations and Oversight, House Public Works Committee, 24 March 1983. This subcommittee, chaired by Rep. Elliot Levitas, also held a hearing on the Dallas lead case on 16 March 1983. At press time, neither hearing record had been printed, and the subcommittee refused to allow the authors of this book to cite the transcript. The quotations and factual material were verified by a reading of the transcript and are accurate.

Page 132

Needleman reported in: Michael Waldholz, "Lead Poisoning Takes a Big, Continuing Toll as Cures Prove Elusive," *Wall Street Journal*, 27 May 1982, 1, 18.

Houk quoted in Davis, "Lead" at 24.

Davis quoted in Waldholz, "Lead Poisoning" at 1.

Page 133

Letter from John A. DePaul, Vice-President, RSR Corporation, to Norman Myer, EPA Region VI, 21 April 1981, concerning meeting that day (RSR/EPA-VI) to discuss lead cleanup. *Protocol for Soil Clean-up and Biological and Soil Sampling Programs*, RSR Corporation, 10 June 1981.

EPA Region VI, *Status Report on the Lead/Cadmium Study Conducted in Dallas and a Scenario of Possible Actions*, 29 June 1981; and attached transmittal memo, 7 July 1981.

Stephen Engelberg, "EPA Understated Risk in Dallas, Official Says," *Dallas Morning News*, 25 March 1983, 1A. D. W. Nauss and Richard Fly, "Regional EPA Officials Opposed Lead Delay," *Dallas Times Herald*, 25 March 1983, 1.

Page 135

Exposure Evaluation Division, OTS, EPA, *Compilation of Blood Lead Data Collected by the City of Dallas*, March 1982.

Lead-Dallas, 5 April 1982, transmitted in letter from Vernon N. Houk, CEH, CDC, to Marilyn Bracken, EPA Toxics Integration, 5 April 1982 (conclusions at [3]). *Options Paper: Dallas, Texas, Lead Study*, 8 April 1982 (from Bracken to Hernandez). Memorandum from Norman Dyer, Environmental Toxicologist, to Lead Study Group and Liaison Members, 6 May 1982, concerning Lead Study Group Report on Dallas, Texas, Lead Study.

U.S. EPA, Lead Smelters Study Group, Toxics Integration, *Report of the Dallas Area Lead Assessment Group*, 1 February 1983. Attachment A is CDC report of 24 January 1983. EPA Environmental News, Region VI, for release 1 February 1983 ("no cases of lead poisoning"). Comments of Dick Whittington at Press Conference on Dallas lead study, 1 February 1983.

Page 136

D. W. Nauss, "EPA Official: Dallas Lead Study Misleading," *Dallas Times Herald*, 20

March 1983, 1. Bill Lodge, "EPA Official Faults Dallas Lead Testing," *Dallas Morning News*, 20 March 1983, at 1A.

D. W. Nauss, "Study Finds EPA Understated Lead Problem," *Dallas Times Herald*, 9 May 1983, 1, map at 10. David Pasztor, "Poisoned Path," *Dallas Times Herald*, 10 May 1983, at 1.

Debra Martine, "Girl Exposed to Lead Hospitalized," *Dallas Morning News*, 20 February 1982, 1A. Debra Martine, "Family Suffers Daily from Lead Toxicity," *Dallas Morning News*, 20 February 1982, at 25A.

Page 137
Interview with Alma Shaw, Dallas, TX, 14 April 1983.

Interview with Patricia Spears, Dallas, TX, 14 April 1983. See also Karel Holloway, "150 Urge Smelter Closure," *Dallas Morning News*, 27 April 1983, at 1A.

Page 138
Richard Dunham, "Lead Poisoning Victim Tells Legislators Her Story," *Dallas Times Herald*, 4 May 1983, at 1.

Page 139
Telephone interview with Dr. Philip Landrigan, NIOSH, Cincinnati, OH, September 1983.

Remarks of Anne M. Gorsuch, Administrator, before the National Environmental Development Association, 20 January 1982, at 19.

Page 140
Remarks of Vice-President George Bush at the Presidential Task Force on Regulatory Relief Briefing, Washington, D.C., 12 August 1981, at 1, and Attachments at 4.

Page 141
Lead in Gasoline, Thriftway IG Report at 77ff., esp. 92 and 108.

Interview with Joseph A. Cannon, EPA Associate Administrator for Policy and Resource Management, Washington, D.C., 3 June 1983.

Page 142
See testimony in *Lead in Gasoline* of Piomelli, at 15; M.R. Montgomery, "The Politics of Pollution," *Boston Globe Magazine*, 25 July 1982, at 26ff.

Page 143
Testimony in *Lead in Gasoline* of Needleman at 58; Moffett at 66–67; 54–56. See also: Olson, *OMB Review* at 77–81; testimony of John Daniel, *The Administration of Superfund*, 27 September 1983, transcript at 16, 66–67.

Page 144
Joanne Grozuczak, *Poisons on the Job* (Sierra Club: Natural Heritage Report No. 4, October 1982), (hereafter *Poisons*), at 3.

Page 145
Rabinowitz quoted in Jack Nelson, "Administration Hit for Health, Safety Cutbacks," *Los Angeles Times*, 8 May 1983, 1, 23–4, at 24; see also *Role* at 61.

Page 146
Telephone interview with Peg Seminario, AFL-CIO, Washington, D.C., July 1983.
OSHA "observer" quoted in Michael Wines, "Scandals at EPA May Have Done in Reagan's Move to Ease Cancer Controls," *National Journal*, 18 June 1983, 1264.
Auchter, 26 March 1981, quoted in *Poisons* at 23; see also *Poisons* at 7–8.

Page 147
Seth S. King, "Appeals Court Orders End to Delay on Ethylene Oxide Rules," *New York Times*, 16 March 1983, A21.

Page 148
PCB and Dioxin Cases, Hearing before the Oversight and Investigations Subcommittee, House Energy and Commerce Committee, No. 97-194, 19 November 1982, testimony of Houk at 138.
"Scientific Bases for Identification of Potential Carcinogens and Estimation of Risks." Report of the Interagency Regulatory Liaison Group, Work Group on Risk Assessment, *Journal of the National Cancer Institute* 63:1, July 1979, at 241–268.

Page 149
Gorsuch did keep the White House posted, in a memorandum titled "EPA Emergent Issues Report" from Anne M. Gorsuch to Craig Fuller, Secretary to the Cabinet, dated 29 April 1982. One of the emerging issues is EPA's decision to allow the use of permethrin on food crops. "Environmentalists," says the memo, "will be critical because this action would not have occurred under Carter Administration Cancer Policy—a policy this Administration is changing" (at 8). This memo was circulated through the White House and OMB, but not released publicly until requested by a congressional subcommittee after Gorsuch's resignation in March 1983.
Louis T. Cordia, "Environmental Protection Agency," in Charles L. Heatherly, ed., *Mandate for Leadership* (Washington, D.C., The Heritage Foundation, 1981) at 969–1038.
Elizabeth Whelan, "The Politics of Cancer," *Policy Review* 10, Fall 1979, 33–46, at 41. On Whelan, see: Peter Harnik, "Voodoo Science, Twisted Consumerism: The Golden Assurances of the American Council on Science and Health," Washington, D.C.: Center for Science in the Public Interest, January 1982, especially 26.

Page 151
Rall quoted in Frederica Perera and Catherine Petito, "Formaldehyde: A Question of Cancer Policy?" *Science*, 18 June 1982, 1285–1291 at 1288.
Formaldehyde: Review of Scientific Basis of EPA's Carcinogenic Risk Assessment, Hearings before the Investigations and Oversight Subcommittee, House Science and Technology Committee, No. 165, 20 May 1982 (hereafter *Formaldehyde*); *Review of the Scientific Basis of the Environmental Protection Agency's Carcinogenic Risk Assessment on Formaldehyde*, report prepared by Investigations and Oversight Subcommittee, House Science and Technology Committee, House Report 98-216, 24 May 1983. See also: *Control of Carcinogens in the Environment, Hearings before the Subcommittee on Commerce*, House Energy and Commerce Committee, No. 98-31, 17 March 1983 (hereafter *Control*).

Page 152

The term "science court," according to John Todhunter, was coined by Chemical Manufacturers Association lobbyist Geraldine Cox. Hundreds of pages of documentation of these unannounced meetings have been obtained by the Natural Resources Defense Council from EPA under Freedom of Information Act request No. RIN-6296-83.

"Staff Urges Formaldehyde Investigation Under Untested Section of TSCA," *Inside EPA*, 29 May 1981, 1, 7–8. "Details of EPA Staff Proposals for Formaldehyde Probe Under TSCA 4(f)," *Inside EPA* Special Report, 29 May 1981, 1–4. "Hernandez Moving to Balance Staff Science Views on Key Formaldehyde Issue," *Inside EPA*, 3 July 1981, 1, 6.

See *Formaldehyde* at 158–160 (Dailey), 532–542; see also *Private Meetings* at 54–65.

Hernandez testimony in *Private Meetings* at 16.

Hernandez quoted in: "Hernandez Says He Will Get Public Involved in 'Controversial' EPA Meetings," *Inside EPA*, 20 November 1981, 6–7.

Testimony of Dailey in *Formaldehyde* at 160, 200, 162.

Interviews with Edwin (Toby) Clark, Conservation Foundation, Washington, D.C., 23 May 1983, and Lisa Barrera, Special Assistant to the Deputy Administrator, Washington, D.C., 29 June 1983.

Page 153

Memorandum from Lester Brown, Subcommittee Staff, to Chairman Toby Moffett, 1 October 1981, concerning EPA's Regulation of Toxic Chemical: An Update, CMA/EPA Closed Meetings on DEHP, reprinted in *Private Meetings*, 31–48 at 34. Memorandum from John Galloway and Barry Hager, Subcommittee Staff, to Chairman Toby Moffett, 1 October 1981, concerning EPA Private Meetings with Industry, reprinted in *Private Meetings* at 51–3, at 52.

"Hernandez Meets 'Regularly' With Industry Groups, House Staffers Say," *Inside EPA*, 6 November 1981, 12.

Memorandum from John A. Todhunter, Ph.D., AA, OPTS, to Anne M. Gorsuch, Administrator, 10 February 1982, concerning Review of Data Available to the Administrator Concerning Formaldehyde and di(2-ethylhexyl) Phthalate (DEHP); reprinted in *Formaldehyde* at 248–271.

Page 154

Todhunter memo at 6–7, 11.

"Carcinogen Policy at EPA," letter to the editor from John A. Todhunter, *Science*, 18 February 1983, 794. This in spite of the fact that, according to Gorsuch's Deputy Chief of Staff Joe Foran, Todhunter had provided the draft information and wording for Gorsuch's memo of 29 April 1982 to Craig Fuller ("a policy this Administration is changing").

Telephone interview with Ellen Silbergeld, Environmental Defense Fund, September 1983.

Page 155

Testimony of Nelson and Albert in *Formaldehyde* at 29, 36; see also Nelson in *Control* at 71.

Albert quoted in Tracy Freedman and David Weir, "Polluting the Most Vulnerable," *Nation*, 14 May 1983, 600–604, at 600.

Memorandum from Don Clay, Director, Office of Toxic Substances, to John A. Todhunter, Assistant Administrator Designate, 11 September 1981, concerning Section 4(f) recommendation of formaldehyde, reprinted in "EPA Toxics Chief Rejects Formaldehyde Action; Offers Narrow TSCA Reading," *Inside EPA*, 25 September 1981, 3–5, at 5.

Page 156

Figures cited in Eliot Marshall, "EPA's High-Risk Carcinogen Policy," *Science*, 3 December 1982, 975–978 at 978. U.S. EPA, Additional U.S. EPA Guidance for the Health Assessment of Suspect Carcinogens With Specific Reference to Water Quality Criteria, draft of 21 June 1982. See also: testimony in *Control* of Perera, 99; Umberto Saffiotti at 419–421; Nelson at 78, 73; Weinstein at 91–92, 16, 4, 6; Weinstein letter to *Science*, 18 February 1983, 794, 796.

Page 157

Silbergeld quoted in Michael Wines, "Scandals at EPA," at 1269.

Memorandum from M. Adrian Gross, HED, to John Melone, HED, 7 May 1982, summary of Chronic and Oncogenic Effects of Permethrin. Permethrin, of course, was the insecticide referred to in the Gorsuch-Fuller memo of 29 April 1982.

Memorandum from Rita M. Lavelle, Assistant Administrator, to John W. Hernandez, Deputy Administrator, 5 October 1982, concerning NTP Study.

Page 158

Memorandum from Charles Benbrook, Staff Director, to Members and Staff, Department Operations Subcommittee, House Agriculture Committee, 22 February 1983, concerning Questions and Background Material for the February 22 and 23 Hearings on the Pesticide Report, Attachment at 2.

On benomyl, see: "The Odds on Cancer: EPA's Recent Bets," in Marshall, "EPA's High Risk," 976.

Page 159

Researcher quoted in Wines, "Scandals at EPA," at 1264.

Page 160

Whelan, "Politics of Cancer," at 46.

Richard Doll and Richard Peto, "The Causes of Cancer," *Journal of the National Cancer Institute* 66:6, June 1981, 1191–1308 at 1251.

Page 161

Alan McGowan, Nicholas Ashford, Terry Davies, Richard Dowd, Clifford Russell, and Terry Yosie, "Examining the Role of Science in the Regulatory Process," *Environment*, June 1983, 6–14, 33–41, at 7.

Testimony of Weinstein, Nelson, and Silbergeld in *Control* at 80, 73, 162.

Letter of John A. Todhunter, Assistant Administrator, to Rep. George E. Brown, 22 December 1982, concerning EPA Response to Report on "Understanding Regulatory Procedures and Public Health Issues in the EPA's Office of Pesticide Programs" (DORFA study), at 4.

Page 162

Telephone interview with Andrew Jovanovich, Science Adviser, OPTS, Arlington, VA 10 August 1983. Telephone interview with John Hernandez, Las Cruces, NM, 1 October 1983.

Memorandum from George A. Keyworth to the Vice-President, 19 January 1982, concerning Activities of the Regulatory Work Group on Science and Technology. Talking Points, Work Group Meeting, 5 January 1982. Discussion Paper, Regulatory Work Group on Science and Technology meeting of 5 January 1982. Agenda, Regulatory Work Group on Science and Technology meeting of 8 April 1982. John F. Morrall III [OIRA, OMB], "Federal Regulation of Carinogens" [sic], attached to Discussion Paper, at 5, 23, 26.

Testimony of George Keyworth in *Control* at 348–355.

Page 163

Testimony in *Control* of Dr. Henry Pitot at 81. Telephone interview with Roy Gamse, former EPA Deputy Associate Administrator for Policy, Washington, D.C., 12 September 1983.

Jim Sibbison, "Censorship at the New EPA," *The Nation*, 11 September 1982, 208–209 at 208. Hernandez quoted in Frank Greve, " 'Hazard?' It's Not a Word at the EPA," *The Detroit Free Press*, 30 August 1981, 1B.

Page 164

Testimony of Perera in *Control* at 99.

Letter from Michael Gough, Office of Technology Assessment to Denis Prager, White House Office of Science and Technology Policy, 7 December 1982.

Interview with Dr. Erik Svenkurud, Mercedes, TX, 10 April 1983. Riojas is not the family's real name.

Page 165

Data from the National Human Adipose Tissue Survey, reported in "PCBs in Humans Shows Decrease," *EPA Environmental News*, for release 9 May 1983, at 4.

Luther Shaw, National Agricultural Chemicals Association, quoted in Ward Sinclair, "America's Pesticide Use Raises New Safety Fears," *Washington Post*, 30 January 1982, A1, A8–A9, at A9.

Page 166

David Pimentel, et al., "Benefits and Costs of Pesticide Use in U.S. Food Production," *BioScience*, 28:12, December 1978, 777–784 at 778–779. See also comment of NACA in Sinclair, "America's Pesticide Use," at A9 ("about 30% annually").

Interview with George Mitchell, Texas cropduster, 1 April 1983.

Page 167

A good introduction to federal pesticide regulation with emphasis on the Reagan years is *Regulatory Procedures and Public Health Issues in the EPA's Office of Pesticide Programs*, staff report prepared for the Subcommittee on Department Operations, House Agriculture Committee, December 1982, reprinted in *EPA Pesticide Regulatory Program Study, Hearing before the Subcommittee on Department Operations,*

House Agriculture Committee, No. 97-NNNN, 17 December 1982, 77–291 (hereafter *DORFA Study*).

U.S. EPA Office of Pesticide Programs, *Status Report on Rebuttable Presumption Against Registration (RPAR) or Special Review Process, Registration Standards, and the Data Call In Program*, December 1982.

Page 168

Figures derived from *DORFA Study* at 183–187. Testimony of Jacqueline Warren on behalf of the Natural Resources Defense Council, et al., before Subcommittee on Agricultural Research, Senate Agriculture Committee, 24 May 1983, at 6–8. See also, Complaint for Injunctive and Declaratory Relief, *Natural Resources Defense Council, Inc., AFL-CIO, and Hector Chavez v. William D. Ruckelshaus and U.S. Environmental Protection Agency*, Civil Action No. 83-1509 (D.D.C., filed 26 May 1983) at 8.

Remarks of Vice-President George Bush at the Presidential Task Force on Regulatory Relief Briefing, Washington, D.C., Office of the Vice-President, 12 August 1981, at 1, and Attachment at 4.

On NACA consultation, see: John A. Todhunter, Assistant Administrator-Designate, Office of Pesticides and Toxic Substances, "Pesticides Registration in the 80's" Speech Outline, NACA Fall Regulatory Conference, Washington, D.C., 21 October 1981; National Agricultural Chemicals Association, *Proposals for the Improvement of Registration and Reregistration of Pesticides in the United States*, Washington, D.C., submitted to EPA, 6 November 1981.

Page 169

John A. Todhunter, Ph.D., Assistant Administrator, "Future Directions of the Office of Pesticides and Toxic Substances," Ohio Fertilizer and Pesticide Association convention, Columbus, OH, 1 March 1982, at 3 and 7.

Statement of John A. Todhunter, Ph.D., AA, OPTS, before the Nebraska Aviation Trades Association, Kearney, NE, 9 February 1983, at 7–8.

Testimony of Todhunter in *Nominations of Matthew N. Novick* at 11.

Page 170

EPA, OPP, *Ethylene Dibromide (EDB), Position Document 4*, 27 September 1983. The Agency's December 1980 *Position Document 2/3* is reprinted in PD4 at 117 ff. (Notes are to the PD 2/3 page number followed by its reprinted page in PD4.) EPA, Ethylene Dibromide—Notices of Decision and Emergency Order Suspending Registrations . . . , 48 *Fed. Reg.* 46228–46248, 11 October 1983. "EPA Acts to Ban EDB Pesticide," *EPA Environmental News*, for release 30 September 1983, plus attached Ethylene Dibromide Fact Sheet.

"Pesticide Inaction Prompts Inquiry," *New York Times*, 26 September 1983, B11. [UPI], "Action Delaying Ban on Chemical Laid to EPA Ex-Official," *New York Times*, 26 September 1983, B11. "Ex-EPA Official Says Pressure Didn't Delay Action on Pesticide," *New York Times*, 27 September 1983, A25.

David Brown, Sc.D., Northeastern University, *Quantitative Risk Assessment for EDB*, March 1983, Exhibit 11 in OSHA EDB Docket.

Harvey Lipman, "Letting America's Workers Die: OSHA's EDB Inaction: Not An Isolated Case," *City Paper* 3:38, 30 September–6 October 1983, 1, 6–7, at 1.

Page 171
PD 2/3 at 65/195, Table 25; summarized at 101/231. "Highest risks": PD 2/3 at 101/231. Fruit: PD 2/3 at 100–108/230–238. Soil: PD 2/3 at 112–116/242–246.

Page 172
Telephone interview with Ellen G. Widess, Attorney, Pesticide Unit, CalOSHA, 25 March 1983.

Page 173
EDB White House Meetings:
Testimony of Edwin Johnson and John Todhunter before Subcommittee on Environment, House Government Operations Committee, 26 September 1983, chaired by Rep. Mike Synar, and Exhibits 3, 4, 5, 15; *Environmental Protection Agency Research and Development Posture, Hearing before Subcommittee on Natural Resources*, House Science and Technology Committee, No. 123, 22 October 1981 (hereafter *Posture Hearing*), at 111–113; calendars of Deputy Administrator John W. Hernandez, August–November 1981; telephone interview with Hernandez, October 1983.
Handwritten letter from Bill [Wells] to John [Todhunter], 24 December 1981, concerning 28 December White House EDB meeting at 1 (Synar Exhibit 3).
Note to Correspondents, contact: Suzanne Weiss, EPA Press Office, 21 August 1981 (Exhibit 2).
The addendum is cited at length in "Todhunter Says Cancer Risk of EDB for Fruit Fly Equals 1–70 Cigarettes in Life," *Pesticide and Toxic Chemical News*, 2 September 1981, 14–15, at 15.
Discussion in *Posture Hearing* at 111–119; testimony of Anne Barton, OPP, at 118. Handwritten memo from John Todhunter to Joe Panetta, undated [August 1981], concerning "Points to include in briefing document + Q/A for Byron Nelson concerning 1 time use of EDB on citrus fruits." See discussion in *Posture Hearing* at 111–113. See also *Pesticide and Toxic Chemical News*, 26 August 1981, 19–20, at 20 ("about 100 times less than the risk of smoking one cigarette in a lifetime"). Statement of Edwin Johnson, from staff interview, cited in *Posture Hearing* at 119.

Page 174
Memorandum from M. Adrian Gross, HED, to Edwin L. Johnson, OPP, 5 September 1981, concerning risk analysis for the carcinogenicity of EDB, at 1–2, 7.
[UPI], "Action Delaying," at B11. Testimony of Johnson before Synar, 26 September 1983.
Wells letter to Todhunter, 24 December 1981, 1–2 (Exhibit 3).
Off-the-record telephone interview with OPP staff member, Washington, D.C., July 1983.

Page 175
Letter from Rep. Andy Ireland to Dr. John Todhunter, 15 July 1982, concerning meeting this afternoon (Exhibit 21). Memorandum from Edwin Johnson, Director, OPP (signed by James Conlon, Deputy), to John A. Todhunter, AA, OPTS, 21 June 1982, concerning EDB Final Decision—Coordination with OSHA (Exhibit 18).
Telephone interview with Dr. Keith Maddy, California Department of Food and Agriculture, 25 March 1983.

Page 176

Telephone interviews with James Emerson, Florida Citrus Packers, and Dr. John Attaway, Florida Department of Citrus, 4 May 1983.

"Japan May Ban EDB If EPA Phases Out Citrus Use, Consultant Tells Agency," *Pesticide and Toxic Chemical News,* 20 April 1983, 12–13. Letter from Jacek S. Sivinski, CH2M Hill Program Director, to Rick Johnson, OPP, 18 May 1983, on Wells and Lerch report on EDB/irradiation (Exhibit 10).

Telephone interview with Joseph Panetta, EPA, OPP, Arlington, VA May 1983.

Wade quoted in: "Arvin Firm Cited and Fined in Deaths of 2 Employees," *Bakersfield Californian,* 7 October 1982, A1, A6; and in Steve E. Swensen, "EDB Tragedy Story Developed Slowly," *Bakersfield Californian,* 10 October 1982, A4. See also discussion in David Brown, "Quantitative Risk," at 13–14.

Page 177

Water: PD 4 at 59–79; EPA, *Fed. Reg.* Notice, 11 October 1983 at 46230–46231, 46238. Testimony of Ed Johnson and Stuart Cohen before Rep. Synar, 26 September 1983.

Page 178

Testimony of Auchter and Bowman before Rep. Miller, 13 September 1983, quoted by Lipman "Letting America's Workers Die," at 6.

Memorandum for Roy Albert, Carcinogen Assessment Group, to Edwin Johnson, DAA Pesticide Programs, 30 September 1977, concerning Preliminary Risk Assessment for Ethylene Dibromide, at 2.

Page 179

EPA, OPP, Registration Division, *Audit of Emergency Exemption and Special Local Needs Programs As Authorized Under Section 18 and 24(c) of the Federal Insecticide, Fungicide, and Rodenticide Act, As Amended,* at 1, 12–17; Table 1, at 47. *DORFA Report,* 113–141, at 115; Eleanor Randolph and Robert L. Jackson, " 'Emergency Exemptions' by EPA Cited," *Los Angeles Times,* 20 March 1983, 1, 14. Frank O'Donnell, "EPA Exemptions Erasing 'Silent Spring' Legacy," *Portland Oregonian,* 14 November 1982 at 7.

Page 180

EPA, Dibromochloropropane: Withdrawal of Intent to Cancer Registrations for Use on Pineapples in Hawaii, 46 *Fed. Reg.* 19592–19596, 31 March 1981. Also see 19596–19599.

Ward Sinclair, "The Return of DBCP, a Classic Tale of Pesticide Regulation," *Washington Post,* 1 February 1983, A1, A4. Sue Bowman, "DBCP: Profits and Cancer Rates Up," *Harbinger: A Carolina Grassroots Journal,* No. 6 (Spring 1983), at 5–6, 9, 13, 30, 32.

Page 181

William K. Stevens, "Sterility Linked to Pesticide Spurs Fear on Chemical Use," *New York Times,* 11 September 1977, 1, 37. David Burnham, "Pesticide Work Suggested for Those Seeking Sterility," *New York Times,* 27 September 1977, 18.

"Dow Chemical Failed to Warn Adequately of Pesticide, Jury Says," *Wall Street Journal*, 11 April 1983, 20.

Interview with Russell Budd, attorney, Dallas, TX, 2 April 1983.

Page 182

Todhunter quoted in Sinclair, "Return of DBCP," at A4.

Telephone interview with Dr. Robert Jackson, South Carolina Commissioner of Health, 26 April 1983.

Figures, Wintemuth quoted, in Sinclair, "Return of DBCP," at A4.

Page 183

Telephone interview with Dr. O. J. Dickerson, Plant Pathology and Physiology, Clemson University, 26 April 1983.

Stuart Z. Cohen, HED, OPP, *Summary Report—DBCP in Ground Water in the Southeast*, 12 August 1981.

Telephone interview with Brett Bursey, GROW, 26 April 1983.

Page 184

The extraordinary 12 September 1977 letter from Phillips to Eula Bingham is cited in: Burnham, "Pesticide Work Suggested," 18.

Interview with Ralph Lightstone, Migrant Legal Action Program and California Rural Legal Assistance, Sacramento, CA, April 1983.

Crop information supplied by South Carolina Crop Reporting Service.

Page 185

Yonce quoted in Sinclair, "Return of DBCP," at A4.

Page 186

Letter from Eugene M. Wilson, Registration Division, OPP, to Dr. C. D. Ferrell, Thompson-Hayward Chemical Co., 5 August 1980, concerning establishment of tolerances for DuTer.

Stephen Barlas, "EPA Under Increasing Pressure to Grant Pesticide Exemptions," *Washington Post*, 14 August 1982, A2. Interview with Edwin Johnson, Director, EPA, OPP, Arlington, VA 16 May 1983.

Rominger, 12 February 1982 letter quoted at length in "California's Rominger Takes Another Swing at FIFRA Section 24 Amendments," *Pesticide and Toxic Chemical News*, 24 February 1982, 15–17. See also letter from G. C. Brayars, Crop Protection Division, T. H. Agriculture and Nutrition Company, to Rep. George E. Brown, Jr., 9 March 1982, concerning 12 February Rominger letter.

Memorandum from Cheng L. Liao, Staff Toxicologist, to Lori Johnston, Pest Management, via Keith T. Maddy, Chief Toxicologist, California Department of Food and Agriculture, 8 December 1982, concerning Completion of the Reevaluation of the Registration Status of Products Containing Triphenyltin Hydroxide, at 4, 3.

Page 187

Letter from John A. Todhunter, Ph.D., AA, OPTS (signed by Marilyn C. Bracken), to Rep. George E. Brown, Jr., 16 April 1982, concerning DuTer, at 2.

Page 188

Ward Sinclair, " 'Streamlining' at EPA Poses Questions About Safeguards," *Washington Post,* 31 January 1983, A1, A6–A7. *DORFA Study,* at 195–197. Memorandum from M. Adrian Gross, Benefits and Field Studies Division, to James G. Touhey, Director, BFSD, OPP, 19 October 1982, concerning Report on Laboratory Data Audit [Harvade "word-for-word regurgitation"].

Scientists quoted in *DORFA Study,* 189–211 at 193.

Page 189

Figures in *DORFA Study* at 272, 275.

Memorandum from Anne M. Gorsuch, Administrator, to OPP, 25 June 1981, concerning FY 83 budget guidance, at 15, quoted in testimony of Maureen K. Hinkle, National Audubon Society, before Department Operations Subcommittee, 6 April 1983, at 5.

Scientists quoted in DORFA Study at 273–74.

Page 190

John A. Todhunter, Ph.D., "Talking Points," NACA Spring Regulatory Conference, Washington, D.C., 21 April 1982, at 2. See also Ohio Fertilizer speech, 1 March 1982, at 7. Generally, on decision conferences, see Complaint, *NRDC v. EPA,* No. 83-1509 (D.D.C., filed 26 May 1983).

Letter from Maureen K. Hinkle, National Audubon Society, to Edwin L. Johnson, Director, OPP, 23 April 1982, commenting on the Bush Task Force initiatives on RPAR, at 1.

Page 191

Memorandum from Philip H. Gray, Exec. Secy., FIFRA SAP, to DAA, OPP, 15 July 1981, concerning Review of FIFRA Section 6(b)(1) Action on Pentachlorophenol, Inorganic Arsenicals, and Creosote (Wood Preservatives), at 1. Records of about thirty of the meetings and the Todhunter meeting, as well as other EPA documentation of the wood preservatives decision conferences were obtained by the Natural Resources Defense Council in July 1983 under EPA Freedom of Information Act request number RIN-5047-83. Two other meetings are noted in: OPP, Special Pesticide Review Division, Weekly Activity Report, 12–16 July 1982, at 3. John W. Hernandez's calendar shows a meeting with industry representatives for 10 June 1981, 2 P.M.

Statement of Dr. John A. Todhunter, AA, OPTS, at the University of Massachusetts, Amherst, MA, 20 October 1982, at 2.

Page 192

Keith Schneider, "Faking It: The Case Against Industrial Bio-Test Laboratories," *Amicus Journal* 4:14, Spring 1983, 14–26 at 14.

EPA, OPP, *The IBT Review Program* and attached *IBT Tracking System Report,* 10 May 1983. OPP, *Summary of the IBT Review Program,* July 1983. "EPA Releases Report on IBT Lab Studies; Warns of Suspension Action," *EPA Environmental News,* for release 11 July 1983. Keith Schneider, "Despite EPA's Assurance, Some Say Fake Lab Report Problems Remain," *St. Louis Post-Dispatch,* 20 September 1983, 1A, 14A. Testimony of Allen Spalt, RAF/NSF, and Albert H. Meyerhoff, Natural

Resources Defense Council, at Hearings on Improving the Quality of Pesticide Data Supporting EPA Regulatory Decisions, before Department Operations Subcommittee, House Agriculture Committee, 27 July 1983.

Page 193
W. John Moore, "EPA Aims to Halt Release of Pesticide Information," *Legal Times of Washington,* 22 February 1982, 1, 11.

Page 194
Todhunter, University of Massachusetts statement at 2.
Comments Concerning the Application of the Texas Department of Agriculture for a Pesticide Enforcement Grant, submitted by Texas Farm Workers Union, Southwest Region of the National Audubon Society, Frontera Chapter of the National Audubon Society, and Lone Star Chapter of the Sierra Club, to EPA, Region VI, 24 September 1981 (hereafter *Comments*), at 2.

Page 195
Aaron Blair, "Cancer Risks Associated with Agriculture: Epidemiologic Evidence," in Raymond A. Fleck and Alexander Hollaender, eds., *Genetic Toxicology* (Plenum Publishing, 1982), 93–111.
Owens study, cited in *Comments* at 2; verified in telephone interview with Dr. Emiel Owens, October 1983.
1980 study cited in *Comments* at 7. Tani Adams, "Regulating Pesticides in Texas: TDA's Chance—and Need—for a Fresh Start," *Texas Pesticide Watch,* Issue 4, May 1983, 5–7 at 7.
California Department of Food and Agriculture, *Summary Tables of Review of Physician's [sic] Reports of Possible Pesticide Exposure in California Received January 1– December 31, 1982,* HS-1098, 25 March 1983, Tabulation of Reports at 3.

Page 196
Telephone interview with Ephraim Kahn, M.D., CDHS consultant, June 1983; *Summary Tables,* Tabulation at 3.
1980 Study cited in *Comments* at 7.

Page 197
Affidavits attached to *Comments* as Exhibit 4, Exhibit 1.

Page 198
Interview with David Kibbe, M.D., McAllen, TX, 11 April 1983.
Interview with Jose Torres, Texas Rural Legal Aid, 11 April 1983.
Interview with Josefina Castillo, farmworker, *tk*, TX, 11 April 1983.

Page 199
Affidavit of Josefina Castillo, 21 September 1981, attached to *Comments* as Exhibit 4. 40 CFR §170.3(a), 170.3(b)(2), 170.5(a).
Interviews with Linda Billings, farmworker protection office, OPP, Washington, D.C., 29 March and 18 April 1983.
Comments; see also letter from Dick Whittington, Regional Administrator, EPA Region

VI, to Robin Alexander, Texas Rural Legal Aid, 11 December 1981, transmitting EPA's Responses to Allegations.

Page 200

Affidavit of Damacio Cano, sworn 27 October 1981, at 2; affidavit of Vicente Rodriguez, May 1982; provided by Texas Rural Legal Aid. David Hanners, "Temik Use Increases in Texas," *Dallas Morning News*, 8 August 1982, 1A, 14A at 14A. Telephone interview with Cervando Gonzalez, attorney, McAllen, TX, June 1983.

Temik Aldicarb Pesticide: *A Scientific Assessment*, Union Carbide Agricultural Products Company, Research Triangle Park, N.C., 1983, Toxicology of Aldicarb at 42–46; see also Specimen Label, Temik [Registered Trademark] 15% Granular Aldicarb Pesticide, Restricted Use Pesticide.

Interviews with Bruce Jaeger and Frank Sanders, OPP Temik team, Washington, D.C., April and May 1983. But see Carcinogenesis Testing Program, National Cancer Institute, *Bioassay of Aldicarb for Possible Carcinogenicity*, NIH Publication No. 79-1391, Summary at vii ("There was no indication . . . that maximum tolerated dose levels were used").

Page 201

Telephone interview with Bob Murphy, EPA Region VI, Dallas, TX, April 1983.

Interview with "Hector Sanchez" (pseudonym), farmworker, *tk*, TX, 11 April 1983.

Page 202

Interview with Carlos Ramirez, farmworker, *tk*, TX, 11 April 1983.

Telephone interview with Robin Alexander, Texas Rural Legal Aid, 18 April 1983.

Page 203

Interview with Dr. Tony Mollhagen, Texas Pesticides Laboratory, San Benito, TX, 12 April 1983.

Page 204

Interview with Cyndy Chapman, Frontera Audubon Society, April 1983.

David Hanners, "Texas Officials Ignored Pesticide Levels in Fish," *Dallas Morning News*, 24 October 1982, at 1AA, 8AA.

Interview with John Norman, Texas A&M/State of Texas Station, Weslaco, TX, 12 April 1983.

Page 206

Interviews with Norman; Hans Hansen, farmer, Weslaco, TX, 10 April 1983.

Page 207

Interview with Aaron Welch, DuPont Chemical Company, McAllen, TX, 11 April 1983.

Telephone interview with Prof. David Pimentel, Cornell University, Ithaca, NY, 4 April 1983.

Page 208

Telephone interview with Norma Adams, wage and hours inspector, Harlingen, TX, 12 April 1983. Abstract of testimony before Health Subcommittee, Harlingen, TX, 21 June 1982.

Interview with Ronald White, Deputy Commissioner of Agriculture, Austin, TX, 13 April 1983.

Page 210

Jeanette Foster, "The Poison from Pineapples," *In These Times*, 14–27 July 1982, at 16–18.

Page 211

Beverly Creamer, "An Expectant Mother's Anguish," *Honolulu Advertiser*, 21 April 1982, at A3. Telephone interview with Beverly Creamer, *Honolulu Advertiser*, May 1983.

Page 212

Toxicology Committee, National Research Council, National Academy of Sciences, *Chlordane in Military Housing*, August 1979. General Accounting Office, *Need For a Formal Risk/Benefit Review of the Pesticide Chlordane (CED-80-116)*, 5 August 1980.

Page 213

Mitchell Freedman, "House Razed in Pesticide Scare," *Newsday*, 31 March 1983, 3.

Testimony of Rep. Thomas Downey before Subcommittee on Department Operations, House Agriculture Committee, 6 April 1983, and questions to Edwin Johnson. See also, Letter from John W. Hernandez, Deputy Administrator, to R. M. Russell, Orkin Pest Control, 17 January 1983, concerning indoor residue levels for pesticides.

3. OUR LAND

Pages 215–220

Our account of the Salt Creek Wilderness trepass case is based on the following: Interview with Bob Burnett, Roswell, NM, 12 June 1983. Off-the-record interviews with federal officials at offices in New Mexico, 10 and 13 June 1983. Interviews with Bill Curtis and Michael Sherwood, Sierra Club Legal Defense Fund, Denver, CO, and San Francisco, CA, 10 and 16 June 1983; with Tim Mahoney, Sierra Club, Washington D.C., 9 June 1983; and with Peter Coppleman, Wilderness Society, Washington, D.C., 3 May 1983. We have also relied on *Additions to the National Wilderness Preservation System VIII, Oversight Hearings Before the Subcommittee on Public Lands*, House Interior Committee, No. 97-9, 10 November 1982 (hereafter *Additions VIII*), testimony of Burnett at 5–7, 70–73; Ed Burns at 11–12; written statement of Peyton Yates, Yates Petroleum Company, at 55–67; Good letter at 79.

Letter, quoted in Yates Statement, *Additions VIII* at 63, reproduced at 79; Yates Statement, *Additions VIII* at 62, 64.

Off-the-record interview with Interior Department attorney, Albuquerque, NM, 13 June 1983.

Page 221

Letter from John H. Harrington, Interior Department Counsel, Southwest Region, to A. J. Losee, Losee, Carson & Dickerson, 10 May 1983, concerning Settlement Agreement in *Re: Yates Petroleum Corporation*, IBLA 83-395.

Page 222

Additions VIII, Exchange between Rep. Hank Brown and Robert Gilmore at 40; remarks of Rep. Pat Williams at 50.

Page 223

Off-the-record interview with Interior Department official, Washington, D.C., June 1983.

Telephone interview with Harmon Kallman, Public Information Officer, U.S. Department of the Interior, 16 June 1983.

Page 224

U.S. Department of the Interior, Bureau of Land Management, *Public Land Statistics 1982,* April 1983, Table 8 at 12, Table 2 at 3.

Frederick Merk, *History of the Westward Movement* (New York: Knopf, 1978).

Charles A. and Mary R. Beard, *History of the United States,* revised edition, (New York: Macmillan., 1941 [1921]). Henry Nash Smith, *Virgin Land* (Cambridge: Harvard University Press, 1971 [1950]). Ray Allen Billington, *Westward Expansion: A History of the American Frontier,* 4th Ed. (New York: Macmillan, 1974 [1949]).

Page 229

Russell Lord, *Behold Our Land* (New York: Houghton Mifflin, 1938), at 214.

Vance Johnson, *Heaven's Tableland: A Dust Bowl Story* (New York: Farrar, Straus, 1947), at 158.

Page 230

Public Land Law Review Commission, *One-Third of the Nation,* Washington, D.C., 1970.

FLPMA: P.L. 94-579, 90 Stat. 2745, 43 U.S.C. 1701. Section 102(a)(8).

Page 232

Gary Bennethum and L. Courtland Lee, "Is Our Account Overdrawn," *Mining Congress Journal* 61:9, September 1975, at 48.

A. E. Paladino, Office of Technology Assessment, "The Availability of Federal Lands for Mineral Exploration and Development," 15 October 1976.

Page 233

E. M. Oakes and A. H. Voelker, Oak Ridge National Laboratory, *Wilderness Designation of Bureau of Land Management Lands and Impacts on the Availability of Energy Resources,* ORNL/TM-8310, February 1983, at 647.

The Wilderness Society, *Fact Sheet: Watt's Move to "Open Wilderness,"* March 1982.

Page 234

Geoffrey Norman, "The Taming of the Wild," *Esquire,* May 1983, at 133–134.

"Wilderness Endangered" (editorial), *Contra Costa Times,* 22 February 1983.

Interview with Rep. James Weaver, Washington, D.C., 15 June 1983.

Page 235

Interview with Dale D. Goble, University of Idaho College of Law, Moscow, ID, 23 May 1983.

Page 239
Interviews with Rep. Weaver; Jim Montieth, Eugene, OR, 16 May 1983; Andy Stahl, forester, National Wildlife Federation, Portland, OR, 19 May 1983.

Page 241
Sierra Club Public Lands Committee, *The Land Letter* 1:1, April 1983, at 3.
Interview with Peter Kirby, The Wilderness Society, Washington, D.C., 4 May 1983; Norm Brewer, Gannett News Service, *Selling Our Natural Resources* (compilation of newspaper articles), 1983, at 16–17.

Page 242
Ward Sinclair, "Reagan Orders An Extension of Logging Pacts," *Washington Post,* 29 July 1983, at A20.

Page 243
F. Kaid Benfield and Peyton M. Sturges, Natural Resources Defense Council, *Eliminate Hidden Timber Subsidies,* submitted to the Subcommittee on Interior, House Appropriations Committee, 16 February 1983. Letter from Benfield and Sturges, NRDC, to Craig Rupp, USDA Forest Service, Lakewood, CO, 17 February 1983, conveying Comments on DP and DEIS for Grand Mesa, Uncompahgre, and Gunnison National Forests.
V. Alaric Sample, Jr., "Review of the San Juan Forest Plan," *Forest Planning: The Citizens' Forestry Magazine* 3:9, December 1982–January 1983, at 22–28.
Interview with Darius Adams, Oregon State University, Corvallis, OR, 10 June 1983.
Darius M. Adams and Richard W. Haynes, "The Distributional Impacts of Departures: Groups and Regions," in Dennis Lemaster, et al., eds., *Sustained Yield:* Proceedings of a symposium, 27–28 April 1982, Spokane, WA (Pullman: Washington State University, 1982), 99–108.

Page 244
Interview with Randal O'Toole, economic consultant, Eugene, OR, 17 May 1983.

Page 245
National Forest Management Act of 1976, Section 13(a).
Memorandum from John B. Crowell, Jr., Assistant Secretary, Natural Resources and Environment, to R. Max Peterson, Chief, Forest Service, 19 January 1983, concerning National Forest Land Management Planning, at 1, 7.

Page 247
Terry F. Franklin, et al., *Ecological Characteristics of Old-Growth Douglas Fir Forests,* USDA Forest Service Pacific Northwest Station, General Technical Report PNW-18, February 1981, at 1, 3–4, 24–26, 31–39.

Page 249
Jay Heinrichs, "The Winged Snail Darter," *Journal of Forestry,* April 1983, 212–214, 262.

Page 250
Interview with James Hutchinson, Oregon Department of Fish and Wildlife, Springfield, OR, 18 May 1983.

Page 251
John Johnson, cited in Brewer, *Selling Our Natural Resources,* at 20.

Page 252
Opinion of Hon. E. P. Tuttle in *Reid Brothers Logging v. Ketchikan Pulp and Alaska Lumber and Pulp Co.,* Nos. 81-3444 and 81-3448, D.C. No. C75-165SR (9th Cir., opinion filed 1 March 1983), 699 F.2d 1292 (9th Cir.).
Testimony of F. Kaid Benfield and Peyton Sturges, Natural Resources Defense Council, before Subcommittee on Public Lands, House Interior Committee, 29 April 1982. Peter R. Mathers and F. Kaid Benfield, "The Tongass National Forest: Giveaway Under the Fifty-year Timber Contracts," unpublished, 10 October 1983. Ward Sinclair, "Probe Says Two Big Firms Buy U.S. Timber at Toothpick Prices," *Washington Post,* 12 June 1983, A6. Letter from Rep. Jim Weaver to R. Max Peterson, Chief, USDA Forest Service, 24 June 1982, concerning antitrust violations in Tongass logging.

Page 253
Judge Rothstein's decision quoted in Southeast Alaska Conservation Council, "Tongass Timber Problem," draft, summer 1983, at 15–16.

Page 255
Letter from Helmut F. Furth, Deputy Assistant Attorney General for Antitrust, to A. James Barnes, USDA General Counsel, 4 January 1983, concerning decisions not to prosecute antitrust violations.
Brizee quoted in Sinclair, "Probe Says," at A6.

Page 256
Memorandum to BLM State Director, Oregon, from Robert Burford, BLM Director, 14 July 1982, concerning Criteria for Application of O&C Forest Policy, plus attached Management Criteria to be Used in Developing Decision Record, with Respect to Forest Lands in Western Oregon, Attachment at 1. See also Memorandum from BLM State Director, Oregon, to District Managers, Western Oregon, 28 June 1982, concerning Transmittal of Criteria for O&C Forest Management.

Page 257
Reagan, in Klamath Falls, OR, quoted in Lou Cannon, "The President's Aides Are Losing their Boss in Translation," *Washington Post,* 7 March 1983, at A3.
Public Lands Statistics 1982, Table 8 at 11.

Page 258
See, for instance, BLM, *Your Fragile Legacy: Cultural and Fossil Resources on the Public Lands,* Washington, D.C., 1982.
Wallace Stegner, "If the Sagebrush Rebels Win, Everybody Loses," *The Living Wilderness* 45:153, Summer 1981, 30–35 at 35.

Page 259
Executive Order 12348, "Federal Real Property," dated 25 February 1982, at 47 *Fed. Reg.* 8547-8548, 1 March 1982. "Percy Hearings Promote Sale of Federal Public Lands," *PLI Newsletter* 5:4, April 1982, 1–2 (Stockman quoted at 2). U.S. Department of

the Interior, *Asset Management Program of the Department of the Interior: A Fact
Sheet*, plus attached *Preliminary Inventory of BLM Lands*, 14 June 1982. Statement
of Edwin L. Harper, Assistant to the President for Policy Development, Chairman,
Property Review Board, 2 July 1982. Philip Shabecoff, "U.S. Plans Biggest Land
Shift Since Frontier Times," *New York Times*, 3 July 1982, 1, 8. (Watt quoted at
8.) "Seiberling Panel to Continue Hearings on Land Sale Program," *PLI Newsletter*
5:9, September 1982, 1–2. See also Statement of Charles H. Callison, Public Lands
Institute, before Public Lands Subcommittee, House Interior Committee, 12 August
1982. "Legislation to be Sought for Sale of Some National Forest Lands," *USDA
News*, for release 10 August 1982. Property Review Board, *Fact Sheet*, Washington,
D.C., 17 August 1982 ("without adversely" at 2). Complaint, *Conservation Law
Foundation et al. v. Edwin Harper, et al.*, (D. Mass., filed 30 September 1982).

Page 260
Reagan, in Salt Lake City, UT, quoted in Howell Raines, "States' Rights Move in West
Influencing Reagan's Drive," *New York Times*, 5 July 1980, at 7.

Page 261
Stegner, "If the Sagebrush," at 31, 30.
*Arnett, Burford, Carruthers, Coldiron, and Johnson Nominations, Hearing before the
Senate Energy and Natural Resources Committee*, No. 97-17, 8 April 1981, at 19–31,
81–119. See also Burford's 1983 Financial Disclosure Report, SF 278, approved 26
May 1983.
L. Libecap, *Locking Up the Range*, Pacific Institute for Public Policy, 1982.
Overton quoted in Shabecoff, "U.S. Plans," at 8.

Page 262
Department of the Interior, *Asset Management Fact Sheet* at 4 and *Preliminary Inventory*.
Statement of Edwin Harper at 1.
Ward Sinclair, "Odd Alliance Emerges to Spare That Tree," *Washington Post*, 9 April
1983, A6.
Interviews with Brant Calkin, Deputy Secretary, New Mexico Department of Natural
Resources, 26 May 1983; (off-the-record) Interior Department official, Washington,
D.C., June 1983; and Earl Sandvig, retired U.S. Forest Service employee, Portland,
OR, 19 May 1983.
Earl D. Sandvig, "Federal Grazing Fees: An Economic Mockery," unpublished, 1982.
Oregon Wilderness Coalition, *Administration Allows Cattle Subsidies in the Form of
Land and Money*, 19 September 1982.

Page 263
30 August 1982 WESTPO resolution, quoted in "Western Political Leaders Denounce
Land Sale Plan," *PLI Newsletter* 5:10, October 1982, at 3.
Myron Stuck, "Surplus Western Lands Still May Be for Sale," *Washington Post*, 26
August 1983, at A17. "Legality of Land Sale Program Questioned at Hearing," *PLI
Newsletter* 6:7–8, July–August 1983, at 1–2. "Signs That 'Asset Management' Is
Going Down the Tubes," *PLI Newsletter* 6:9, September 1983, at 1–2.

Page 264

William E. Schmidt, "U.S. May Surrender Control of Public Rangeland," *New York Times*, 14 February 1983, at 22. Statement of Guy R. Martin, former Assistant Secretary of Interior, before Subcommittee on Interior, House Appropriations Committee, 5 May 1983.

U.S. Department of the Interior, *1982, A Year of Progress: Preparing for the 21st Century*, annual report, at 20–22.

Letter from Edward F. Strang, BLM State Director, Nevada, to Rose Strickland, Sierra Club, 24 February 1983.

"Solicitor's Opinion Further Narrows Federal Control of Water on BLM Land," Department of the Interior news release, for release 17 February 1983, plus attached opinion of 16 February 1983.

See, e.g., BLM Phoenix, AZ, District, Rangeland Management Program, Hualapai-Aquarius Planning Area, 10 March 1983, at 1.

Page 266

Affidavit of William R. Meiners, filed in *Natural Resources Defense Council, et al. v. James G. Watt, et al.*, Civil Action No. 1983-73 (D.D.C.), at 5–24.

Bureau of Land Management, "Briefing Paper: Cooperative Management Agreements," undated paper. Instruction Memorandum No. 83-330, from Director, Bureau of Land Management (signed by Assistant Director, Renewable Resources), to State Directors, concerning Review of Cooperative Management Agreement Guidance, plus attached draft Cooperative Management Agreement Program Guidance.

Page 267

Letter from William R. Meiners, Idaho Wildlife Federation, to Larry Woodard, BLM Associate State Director, Idaho, 30 May 1983, concerning Cooperative Management Agreements.

Letter from Russell W. Heughins to Clair Whitlock, BLM State Director, Idaho, 14 June 1983, concerning Cooperative Management Agreements.

Page 270

U.S. Navy, Western Division, Natural Resources Management Branch, *Soil and Water Conservation Plan for South Grazing Lease, Naval Weapons Systems Training Facility, Boardman, OR, Parcel 4A02*, June 1982.

Page 272

General Accounting Office, *Analysis of the Powder River Basin Federal Coal Lease Sale: Economic Valuation, Improvements and Legislative Changes Needed*, GAO/-RCED-83-119, 11 May 1983.

Surveys and Investigations Staff, "Coal Leasing Program of U.S. Department of Interior," report to the House Appropriations Committee, April 1983, manuscript.

Testimony of Rep. Yates and Assistant Secretary Carruthers, hearing before the Subcommittee on Interior, House Appropriations Committee, 27 April 1983.

Page 274

GAO, *Analysis*, at 8, 10.

Page 276
Dale Russakoff, "Single Bid in Coal Sale Followed Tract Division," *Washington Post*, 6 June 1983, A1, A8–A9, at A9.
Dale Russakoff, "Interior's Coal-Lease Sale Defies Hill Panel, but Draws Few Bids," *Washington Post*, 27 September 1983, A3.

Page 278
Bagge quoted in Helen Dewar and Dale Russakoff, "Senate, in Watt Victory, Rejects Coal-Leasing Ban," *Washington Post*, 15 June 1983, A6.

4. THE NATIONAL PARKS PUT AT RISK

Page 279
Robert Cahn, "New Urban Parks Face a Fight to Survive," *Christian Science Monitor*, 17 June 1982.
Interviews with John Reynolds, deputy superintendent, Santa Monica Mountains National Recreation Area, Los Angeles, CA, 21 September 1983, and Elsa Leviseur, Santa Monica, CA, 22 September 1983.
U.S. Department of the Interior, National Park Service, *Santa Monica Mountains National Recreation Area General Management Plan*, April 1982.

Page 280
Watt quoted in Robert Cahn, "The National Park System, The People, The Parks, The Politics," *Sierra*, May–June 1983, 52.

Page 281
"Wattville," cartoon, *Los Angeles Times*, 2 August 1981, v5.

Page 282
Telephone interview with Paul Rose, staff geologist, Santa Monica Mountains NRA, October 1983.

Page 283
The *Los Angeles Times* reported in mid-1982 that disaster relief loans for southern California amounted to more than $352 million from February 1978 through November 1980. Most of the relief loans were made after severe storms, mudslides, and flooding in January and February 1980.
Address by James Watt, Conference of National Park Concessioners, Washington, D.C., 9 March 1981. Quoted in: Philip Shabecoff, "Why Conservationists Are Growling at Watt," *Anchorage* [Alaska] *News*, 27 May 1981; other excerpts from this infamous speech, along with a great deal of interesting and valuable material on Watt, can be found in The Wilderness Society's *The Watt Book* (Washington, D.C., 1981). Associated Press, "Watt Would Shift Some Parks From U.S. System," *Seattle Post Intelligencer*, 16 April 1981 (*The Watt Book*); see also Watt speech, University of Vermont, April 1982, quoted in The Wilderness Society, *The Watt Record* (Washington, D.C., July 1983), at 18.

Page 285

Memorandum from Assistant Secretary Designate for Fish and Wildlife and Parks (G. Ray Arnett), to Acting Director, HCRS, and Director, National Park Service, undated but ca. April 1981, concerning History of Your Agencies' Opposition to Congressional Designation and Creation of New Areas within the National Park Service (reprinted in *The Watt Book*). See also statement by Russell Dickenson in Philip Shabecoff, "Administration Seeks Greater Role for Entrepreneurs at Federal Parks," *New York Times*, 29 March 1981, 1, 32, at 32.

For Watt denial of hit list and political reaction, see Robert D. McFadden, "Gateway Plan Surprises Officials in New York Area," *New York Times*, 29 March 1981; editorial, "Color Him Sickly Green," *Los Angeles Times*, 29 March 1981; Associated Press, "Two Area National Parks Periled in U.S. Order," *Chicago Sun-Times*, 29 April 1981; Seth D. King, "Watt Says There's No Hit List," *New York Times* (reprinted in *Anchorage News*, 27 April 1981; all collected in *The Watt Book*).

Seiderling quoted in Cahn, "New Urban Parks."

Nathaniel Pryor Reed, former Assistant Secretary of the Interior, address to the Sierra Club's 1981 Annual Meeting, San Francisco, CA, 2 May 1981 (reprinted in *The Watt Book*), at 9.

Page 286

Watt, address to Conference of National Parks Concessioners, 9 March 1981.

Page 287

U.S. Congress, House Committee on Interior and Insular Affairs (90th Cong., 2d Sess.), *Report: Amending Title I of the Land and Water Conservation Fund Act of 1965*, 24 April 1968, quoted in *The Watt Record*.

Watt quoted in *Bismarck Tribune*, 9 April 1982 (*The Watt Record*, 22).

Rep. Sidney Yates, on the House Floor, *Congressional Record*, 8 March 1983.

National Park Service, *State of the Parks* (U.S. Department of the Interior, 1980).

Page 289

Robert Cahn, "Chaco Canyon: Preserving a Cultural Treasure," *Christian Science Monitor*, 16 June 1982.

Page 290

Gordon Anderson, "Coal, Threat to the Canyonlands," *The Living Wilderness*, December 1980, 4–11.

Interview with Robert Benton, Superintendent, Bryce Canyon National Park, 23 September 1983.

Page 291

Robert Cahn, "Maintaining the Everglades' Delicate Balance," *Christian Science Monitor*, 15 June 1982. Our account of the situation in the Everglades is, unless otherwise noted, drawn from Interior Department documents and interviews with Destry Jarvis and William Leinisch, National Parks and Conservation Association, Washington, D.C., September–October 1983, and off-the-record interviews with National Park Service staff and officials.

Page 292
Interview with Rick Smith, Assistant Superintendent, Everglades Park, 25 September 1983.

5. REPEATING OUR MISTAKES

Page 298
Interview with Ralph Cavanagh, Natural Resources Defense Council, San Francisco, CA, 10 May 1983.
Letter from Donald Paul Hodel, Administrator, Bonneville Power Administration, to (e.g.) Hon. Douglas S. Mahoney, Mayor, City of Albion, ID (sent to all BPA preference customers), 24 June 1976, concerning Contract No. 14-02-38576 (Power Sales Contract)—"Notice of Insufficiency."

Page 299
"Restoring the Balance," remarks by Don Hodel, Bonneville Power Administrator, before the Edison Electric Institute, San Francisco, CA, 8 June 1976, at 9.

Page 302
Michael Blumstein, "The Lessons of a Bond Failure," *New York Times*, 14 August 1983, III-1, 24 (see "How It Works: Take Or Pay," at 24); Nancy L. Ross, "WPPSS Default is Declared, but Market Unmoved," *Washington Post*, 26 July 1983, at D8, 9; Jay Matthews, "Default of WPPSS Taints Development in Pacific Northwest," *Washington Post*, 27 July 1983, at F1, 5; Bartle Bull, "Keeping Track: Whoops," *Amicus Journal*, Spring 1983, 12–13.

Page 303
"$2.25 Billion Whoops" (editorial), *Washington Post*, 14 July 1983.

Page 304
James Barron, "Burden of Lilco Bills Could Slow Up Long Island's Economy," *New York Times*, 14 August 1983.
Eliot Marshall, "A Preliminary Report on Three Mile Island," *Science*, 20 April 1979, 280–281 at 280.

Page 305
Interviews with Nancy Culver and Sandy Silver, citizen activists, San Luis Obispo, CA, 14 August 1983.
Fact Sheet and Progress Report, Pacific Gas and Electric Company's Diablo Canyon Nuclear Project, June 1981.
Pacific Gas and Electric, *Nuclear Power From Diablo Canyon*, San Luis Obispo, CA, undated (ca. 1977).
Information provided by PG&E tour guide, Diablo Canyon, San Luis Obispo, 12 May 1983.
Tom Redburn, "How PG&E 'Shot Itself in the Foot,' " *Los Angeles Times*, 16 March 1982.

Tom Harris, "An Inside Look at Diablo Canyon Nuclear Plant," *San Jose Mercury*, 9 August 1983, 10B.

Page 307

Northwest Power Planning Council, *1983 Northwest Conservation and Electric Power Plan*, Volume 1, Portland, OR, 27 April 1983, at 1-1 through 1-4, 2-1 and 2-2, 3-1, 4-1 and 4-2, 5-8 and 5-13.

Mark Reis, "New Era of Energy Conservation Begins in Pacific Northwest," *Energy Conservation Bulletin* 2:6, May–June 1983, 7–9.

Page 308

"Experiment in Hood River, Oregon, Will Test Energy Savings from Maximum Weatherization Measures," *Energy Conservation Bulletin* 2:6, May–June 1983, 9.

Reagan quoted in "Reagan On Energy: Don't Laugh" (editorial), *Boston Globe*, 28 November 1980, at 18.

Reagan, speech to the Atomic Industrial Forum, 18 October 1979; see also: "Shortage of Sense: Reagan and Energy Policy," in Mark Green and Gail MacColl, *There He Goes Again: Ronald Reagan's Reign of Error* (New York: Pantheon Books, 1983), at 103–109.

See quotations from Reagan's 1977–1978 radio broadcasts in Mark Hertsgaard, *Nuclear, Inc.* (New York: Pantheon Books, 1983), 216–217.

Edwards-Yates exchange cited in "Budget Update," *Energy Conservation Bulletin* 1:2, August–September 1981, at 4.

Page 309

On Edwards and Davis, see Hertsgaard, *Nuclear, Inc.*, 212–213.

Edwards quoted in Joanne Omang, "Edwards Remark on 'Subversives' Stirs Controversy," *Washington Post*, 1 July 1981, A9.

DOE, Office of Policy, Planning and Analysis, *The Future of Electric Power in America: Economic Supply for Economic Growth, Report of the Electricity Policy Project*, DOE/PE-0045, June 1983.

Page 310

Marc H. Ross and Robert H. Williams, *Our Energy: Regaining Control* (New York: McGraw-Hill, 1981), at 136; interview with David Moulton, Energy Conservation Coalition, Washington, D.C., 21 April 1983.

Energy in Transition 1985–2010, Final Report of the Committee on Nuclear and Alternative Energy Systems, National Research Council, National Academy of Sciences, 1979, at 6–7.

Eric Hirst, "Effects of the National Energy Act on Energy Use and Economics in Residential and Commercial Buildings," *Energy Systems and Policy* 3:2, 1979; see also Eric Hirst, et al., Oak Ridge National Laboratory Energy Division, *Energy Use from 1973 to 1980: The Role of Improved Energy Efficiency*, ORNL/CON-79, December 1981.

Page 311

Telephone interview with Arthur Rosenfeld, Lawrence Berkeley Laboratory, Berkeley,

CA, 13 September 1983. See also Judith Goldhaber, "The Dollars and Sense of Conservation," *LBL Newsmagazine* 7:3–4, Fall–Winter 1982–83, 12–16 at 12.

Page 312

Interview with Maxine Savitz, former deputy director, DOE Conservation Office, Washington, D.C., 29 April 1983. Karlyn Baker, "Energy Department RIF Squabble Debated on Hill," *Washington Post*, 20 April 1983, C3. Maxine Savitz, *Energy Conservation Budget for FY84*, undated (ca. April 1983).

Page 313

Conservation Panel, DOE Energy Research Advisory Board, *Energy Conservation and the Federal Government: Research, Development, and Management*, DOE/S-0017, Washington, D.C., January 1983, at ix.

A New Prosperity: Building A Sustainable Future, prepared by the Solar Energy Research Institute (Andover, MA: Brick House Publishing, 1981).

"No Energy Standard for Six Major Appliances," *Washington Post*, 30 August 1983; Cass Peterson, "Wipeout of DOE Appliance Standards Blows the Fuses of State Regulators," *Washington Post*, 6 September 1983, A15.

Page 314

Telephone interview with David Goldstein, Natural Resources Defense Council, San Francisco, CA, 7 October 1983.

"Energy Policy," remarks by Secretary of Energy Donald Paul Hodel to the U.S. Delegates to the World Energy Conference, Washington, D.C., 7 September 1983, at 5.

Page 315

Edward Scherer, Combustion Engineering, Inc., quoted in Hertsgaard, *Nuclear, Inc.*, at 10.

Stephen Hilgartner, Richard C. Bell, and Rory O'Connor, *Nukespeak* (San Francisco: Sierra Club Books, 1982).

Hilgartner, et al., *Nukespeak* at 74, 192, 264; Hertsgaard, *Nuclear, Inc.*, at 221–223, 329.

Page 316

Council on Economic Priorities Study cited in "Seven Reasons," *Energy Conservation Bulletin* 1:1, June/July 1981, at 3.

William Lanouette, "Dream Machine," *The Atlantic*, April 1983, 35–52, 85–86.

Page 317

Eliot Marshall, "The Perils of Clinch River," *Science*, 8 October 1982, 137–138.

Project Management Corp., *Clinch River Breeder Reactor Plant Project, 1983 Progress Report*, April 1983.

Milton R. Benjamin, "Reactor That Won't Die Is on the Scaffold Again," *Washington Post*, 6 June 1983, A1, A4.

Freeman, May 1982 speech to industry and Administration officials, quoted in Hertsgaard, *Nuclear, Inc.*, at 272.

Colin Norman, "Uranium Enrichment: Heading for the Abyss," *Science*, 19 August 1983, 730–733.

Page 318

Martin Tolchin, "Senate Vote Virtually Kills Clinch River Atom Reactor," *New York Times*, 27 October 1983, A24.

Milton R. Benjamin, "Inside: The Energy Department—A Different Breed," *Washington Post*, 16 November 1983, A25.

Hertsgaard, *Nuclear, Inc.*, at 104.

Einstein, quoted by Rep. Edward J. Markey, in Fred Barbash and Milton R. Benjamin, "States Can Curb A-Plants," *Washington Post*, 21 April 1983, A1, A9, at A9.

Memorandum from David Schooler, Chief Counsel, Energy Conservation Subcommittee, to Rep. Richard L. Ottinger, Chairman, 2 May 1983, concerning DOE's Nuclear Propaganda Campaign—A Case of Government Waste, at 10.

David Burnham, "Industry and Government Efforts for Nuclear Power Draw Scrutiny," *New York Times*, 23 May 1983, A1, A17.

William J. Lanouette, "Industry Goliath, Environmental David Girding for Battle Over Nuclear Power," *National Journal*, 9 April 1983, 737–739.

Page 319

Committee for Energy Awareness, *Advertising Test Program in Grand Rapids, MI*, 3 March to 14 May 1982, at A2.

"Statement Announcing a Series of Policy Initiatives on Nuclear Energy," 8 October 1981, in *Public Papers of the Presidents, Ronald Reagan, 1981* (Washington, D.C.: Government Printing Office, 1982) at 903–905.

An extremely good analysis of the Reagan Administration's energy policies is the *Reagan Energy Plan: A Major Power Failure*, a report from fourteen environmental and scientific groups, Washington, D.C., 24 March 1982.

INDEX

acid rain, 33, 39, 322
Adamkus, Valdus, 34–36, 38, 53
Administrative Procedure Act, 24
AFL-CIO, 145–46, 193, 208
Agriculture Department, U.S., 167,
 172, 173, 255
air pollution, xi, 6, 29, 272
Alaska, lumbering in, 252–55
aldrin, 156, 210, 211, 213
Alexander, Robin, 194*n*, 197, 202, 203
Andrus, Cecil D., 238, 290
aquifers, pollution of, 89, 102, 104,
 105, 114–15, 116, 127, 177, 210
Arnett, G. Ray, 285, 291, 293–94,
 295–96
asbestos:
 dump sites for, 84–89, 90, 94, 95–96
 effects of exposure to, 85–86, 94–99
asbestos industry, 95, 97, 98–99
Auchter, Thorne, 145, 146, 172–73,
 178, 179

Babbit, Bruce, 87, 89
Baker, Howard, 11, 317–18
Baker, James, 58, 78, 91, 186, 259
Barber, Walter, 16, 17, 26, 28, 30, 31,
 36, 128
Bennett, Kathleen, 31–32, 38

Bonneville Power Administration,
 298–304, 307, 319
Brown, Michael, 46, 52, 53
Bureau of Land Management (BLM),
 238, 260
 citizen advisory councils of, 267–68
 Cooperative Management
 Agreements made with, 266–67,
 270, 271
 grazing policy of, 262–71
 O&C lands managed by, 256
 oil-gas leases and, 216–17, 218, 219,
 220–22
 public lands managed by, 256–71
 responsibilities of, 257–58
 WSAs catalogued by, 235, 236
Burford, Robert, 7, 9, 79, 256, 261,
 265, 267, 269
Burnett, Robert, 215–19, 221, 223,
 224
Bush, George, 21, 22, 26, 27, 79, 91,
 140
 hazardous wastes and, 102, 103
 pesticides and, 186

Cabinet Council on Natural Resources
 and the Environment, 31, 91–92,
 232

377

Lincoln National Forest, oil-gas leases in, 219
liquid metal fast breeder reactors (LMFBRs), 317–18
Los Angeles Times, 80, 282
Louisiana Pacific, 240, 242, 244, 252, 254
Love Canal, 42–43, 51, 82, 87, 106
Lowry Landfill, 63*n*, 109, 112–28
Lucero, Gene, 64, 65, 89–90, 91–93, 94, 99, 100, 157–58
Luckie, Sarah, 86–87, 88, 97

MacCleery, Douglas, 240–41, 245
McCloskey, Michael, 69
McClure, James A., 261, 262
McDonald, John C., 96–97
Maddy, Keith, 175, 176
Meese, Edwin, 58, 69, 78, 91, 259
  Lavelle and, 42
Menotti, Dave, 30, 32, 39–40
Metate Asbestos Corp., 84–85, 96, 99
Miller, Cliff, 37–38, 59, 60
Miller, James C., III, 21, 22–23, 25, 26, 28
mining industry:
  Lavelle's contacts with, 89–90
  political influence of, 100
mining waste sites:
  asbestos, 84–89
  Interior Department and, 100
  Superfund and, 88–89, 90, 100
  toxic metal, 89
Mitchell, George, 91, 92, 93
Moffett, Toby, 67
Monsanto, 105, 106, 129, 193
Mountain States Legal Foundation (MSLF), 5, 17, 37*n*, 231, 239, 261, 264
Moynihan, Daniel, 91
Multiple Use-Sustained Yield Act, 230

National Agricultural Chemicals Association, 166, 168–69, 190
National Audubon Society, 69, 199–200, 216, 239
National Cancer Institute, 151, 153, 179
National Enforcement Investigations Center, 51, 125

National Forest Management Act, 245, 255
National Forest System, 227, 228, 230, 240–57
National Institute of Occupational Safety and Health (NIOSH), 86, 87, 98, 139, 151, 171, 173, 178–79
National Parks, 4, 241, 257, 279–97
  coal mining and, 289, 297
  freeze on land purchases for, 280–82, 286, 288
  Land and Water Conservation Fund and, 287, 288, 297
  in urban areas, 279–86, 297
National Toxicology Program, 150–51, 155
National Wildlife Federation, 69, 216, 256
Natural Resources Defense Council, 22*n*, 26*n*, 50, 260, 301
Neal, Jack, 84, 97, 99
Needleman, Herbert, 132, 142
Nelson, Norton, 155, 156, 161
Niagara River Basin waste sites, 51–52
Nixon, Richard M., 4, 75
Novick, Matthew, 63, 64–66, 79
nuclear power, 299–307, 309–10, 314–19
Nuclear Regulatory Commission (NRC), 305

O&C Act, 256
O&C lands, 255–56
Occidental Chemical Corporation (Oxychem), 176–77, 181
occupational safety, 144–47, 148
  asbestos and, 85–86, 95
  lead and, 144–46
  pesticides and, 171, 172–73, 175, 176–77, 178–79, 194–203, 208
  in textiles industry, 146
Occupational Safety and Health Administration (OSHA), 152
  brown lung and, 146
  carcinogens regulated by, 85, 86, 95, 147
  lead levels regulated by, 144–46
  pesticides and, 173, 175, 178, 194, 203–4

382

Office of Management and Budget
(OMB), 19
Environment Branch of, 20
EPA budget and, 54, 55, 57–58,
59–60
EPA "issue alerts" sent to, 69
EPA regulations scrutinized by,
20–21, 22–26, 28, 72, 103, 141,
143
judicial review of decisions by, 24
Office of Information and
Regulatory Affairs in, 22
Reagan's strengthening of, 22–23, 24
Office of Technology Assessment, 92,
102, 105, 106, 129, 163, 208, 233
Overton, J. Allen, Jr., 261–62

Pallotta, Arthur, 98–99, 162
PCBs (polychlorinated biphenyls), 94
PCP (pentachloraphenol), 191
Pederson, William, 65
Pendley, William P., 274
Perera, Frederica, 154, 164
Perry, Robert, 41–42, 49, 51, 52, 65,
74, 77
pesticides, 15, 43, 147, 156, 158, 163,
164–214
alternatives to, 175–76, 185, 205–6
cancer and, 168, 169–70, 171–72,
180, 182, 186, 195
in drinking water, 177, 178
emergency suspension of, 179, 210
EPA exemptions for, 167–68,
179–80, 185–86
farmworkers' exposure to, 164–65,
195–203, 208
fetuses and, 212, 213
in milk, 210, 211
occupational safety and, 171,
172–73, 176–77, 178–79,
194–203, 208
poisoning from, 164–65, 170–71,
195–210, 213
reducing use of, 206, 207–8
registration of, 27, 167–68
in termite control, 212–14
testing of, 168, 188–90, 192–93, 204
wildlife and, 165, 204–5
poisons, poisoning:
lead, xi, 27, 131–39, 141–42

pesticide, 164–65, 170–71, 195–210,
213
Poticha, Myrna, 6, 8
Poundstone, Freda, 6, 7, 10, 12, 13, 54
Powder River Basin coal sale, 272–76
Preemption Act, 225, 226
Presidential Task Force on Regulatory
Relief, 22–28, 29
Clean Air Act reform sought by, 30
EPA cancer policy and, 162–63
hit list of, 26–27
lead regulation and, 139, 140, 144,
145
sensitivity to industry of, 24–25,
27–28, 188
Property Review Board, 258–59
Public Land Law Review Commission
(PLLRC), 230
public lands, 224–97
acquisition of, 224, 280
Constitutional provisions for, 224,
260
legislated protection of, 227–28
lumbering on, 240–57
oil and gas development on, xi,
215–24, 235
popular support for, 218, 233–35
ranchers' use of, 229–30, 260, 261,
262–63, 264–71
sale of, xi, 225–26, 258–63
water rights on, 264
Public Rangeland Improvement Act,
260

Rall, David, 150–51
Ramirez, Carlos, 201–2
Reagan, Ronald:
appointments of, 3, 10–13, 28,
62–63, 232, 268, 273
deregulation advocated by, xi–xiii,
13, 19, 56, 112, 130–31, 147
election of, 3
EPA budget cuts and, 54, 58–59
executive privilege asserted by,
75–80, 100–101
Gorsuch's allegiance to, xiv, 28, 81
on Gorsuch's resignation, 81
Lavelle fired by, 42, 77
OMB powers expanded by, 22–23
Stockman's mock debates with, 19,
20

ABOUT
THE
AUTHORS

Jonathan Lash, an attorney for the National Resources Defense Council, has done extensive work on the EPA scandal and toxic-waste issues. He is a former federal prosecutor and has written articles for various newspapers and magazines, including the *Washington Post*. He lives in Washington, D. C.

David Sheridan is a freelance writer whose articles have appeared in such journals as *Life*, *Saturday Review*, *New West*, *Smithsonian*, and *Gargoyle*. He has also published a volume of poems, *A Turtle's Progress*, and a book on the decline of the American West, *The Desertification of the United States*.

Katherine Gillman was a writer and an editor on the Ford Foundation's Energy Policy Project and has written a book on energy and the coastal environment for the President's Council on Environmental Quality. As the council's senior staff member for International Environmental Affairs, she worked on the *Global 2000 Report to the President*.